Shape Shifters

BORDERLANDS AND TRANSCULTURAL STUDIES

Series Editors:

Pekka Hämäläinen
Paul Spickard

EDITED BY LILY ANNE Y. WELTY TAMAI, INGRID
DINEEN-WIMBERLY, AND PAUL SPICKARD

Shape Shifters

Journeys across Terrains of Race and Identity

University of Nebraska Press | Lincoln

Library of Congress Cataloging-in-Publication Data
Names: Tamai, Lily Anne Y. Welty, editor. |
Dineen-Wimberly, Ingrid, editor. |
Spickard, Paul R., 1950– editor.
Title: Shape shifters: journeys across
terrains of race and identity / edited by
Lily Anne Y. Welty Tamai, Ingrid
Dineen-Wimberly, and Paul Spickard.
Description: Lincoln: University of
Nebraska Press, [2020] | Series:
Borderlands and transcultural studies |
Includes bibliographical references and index.
Identifiers: LCCN 2018050272
ISBN 9781496206633 (cloth: alk. paper)
ISBN 9781496216984 (epub)
ISBN 9781496216991 (mobi)
ISBN 9781496217004 (pdf)
Subjects: LCSH: Racially mixed people. |
Ethnicity. | Group identity.
Classification: LCC HT1523 .S465 2020 |
DDC 305.8—dc23
LC record available at
https://lccn.loc.gov/2018050272

Set in Sabon Next LT Pro by Laura Ebbeka.

IN MEMORY OF:

Amadou Diallo February 4, 1999

Malcolm Ferguson March 1, 2000

Prince Jones September 1, 2000

Kendra James May 5, 2003

Alberta Spruill May 16, 2003

Ousmane Zongo May 22, 2003

Timothy Stansbury January 24, 2004

Henry Glover September 2, 2005

Ronald Madison September 4, 2005

James Brisette September 4, 2005

Kathryn Johnston November 21, 2006

Sean Bell November 25, 2006

DeAunta Farrow July 22, 2007

Tarika Wilson January 4, 2008

Oscar Grant January 1, 2009

Shem Walker July 11, 2009

Victor Steen October 3, 2009

Kiwane Carrington October 9, 2009

Aaron Campbell January 29, 2010

Aiyana Jones May 16, 2010

Reginald Doucet January 14, 2011

Ashley Alonzo July 18, 2011

Ramarley Graham February 2, 2012

Manuel Loggins Jr. February 7, 2012

Trayvon Martin February 26, 2012

Dante Price March 1, 2012

Wendell Allen March 7, 2012

Shereese Francis March 15, 2012

Rekia Boyd March 21, 2012

Kendrec McDade March 24, 2012

Tamon Robinson April 18, 2012

Shantel Davis June 14, 2012

Chavis Carter July 29, 2012

Reynaldo Cuevas September 7, 2012

Malissa Williams November 29, 2012

Timothy Russell November 29, 2012

Kimani Gray March 9, 2013

Deion Fludd May 5, 2013

Larry Eugene Jackson July 26, 2013

Carlos Alcis August 15, 2013

Jonathan Ferrell September 14, 2013

Miriam Carey October 3, 2013

Andy Lopez October 22, 2013

Jamar Clark November 16, 2013

Ervin Edwards November 26, 2013

Jordan Baker January 16, 2014

McKenzie Cochran January 28, 2014

Yvette Smith February 16, 2014

Victor White III March 22, 2014

Dontre Hamilton April 30, 2014

Eric Garner July 17, 2014

Tyree Woodson August 2, 2014

John Crawford August 4, 2014

Michael Brown Jr. August 9, 2014

Ezell Ford August 11, 2014

Dante Parker August 12, 2014

Kajieme Powell August 19, 2014

Laquan McDonald October 20, 2014

Tanisha Anderson November 13, 2014

Akai Gurley November 20, 2014

Tamir Rice November 22, 2014

Rumain Brisbon December 2, 2014

Jermaine Reid December 30, 2014

Natasha McKenna February 3, 2015

Tony Robinson March 6, 2015

Philip White March 31, 2015

Eric Harris April 2, 2015

Walter Scott April 4, 2015

Thaddeus McCarroll April 17, 2015

Freddie Gray April 19, 2015

Brendon Glenn May 5, 2015

Samuel DuBose July 19, 2015

Christian Taylor August 7, 2015

Richard Perkins November 15, 2015

Jamar Clark November 15, 2015

Chandra Weaver November 17, 2015

Cornelius Brown November 18, 2015

Tiara Thomas November 18, 2015

Nathaniel Pickett November 19, 2015

Miguel Espinal December 8, 2015

Roy Nelson December 19, 2015

Leroy Browning December 20, 2015

Kevin Matthews December 23, 2015

Bettie Jones December 25, 2015

Keith Childress December 31, 2015

Gregory Gunn February 25, 2016

Akiel Denkins February 29, 2016

Alton Sterling July 5, 2016

Philando Castile July 6, 2016

Partial list, to be continued . . .

Contents

Illustrations

Acknowledgments

Many hands helped make this book. It began at a conference titled "Shape Shifters" at the University of California, Santa Barbara, in March 2016. Support for that conference came from Professor James Brooks; the History Department, led by Sharon Farmer; Executive Vice Chancellor David Marshall; the Mediterranean Borderlands Research Group, led by Beth DePalma Digeser; the Identity Research Focus Group, led by Adrienne Edgar and Cynthia Kaplan; Deans Melvin Oliver and John Majewski of the College of Letters and Science; Emily Zinn of the Interdisciplinary Humanities Center; Professor John Park of the Asian American Studies Department; the Black Studies Department, led by Jeffrey Stewart; the Center for Black Studies Research, led by Diane Fujino; and Chancellor Henry Yang. The editors are grateful to all these people and institutions for their encouragement and support not only of this project but also of several others over the years.

We are also grateful to Sarah Devoto, Lana Do, Ken Hough, Roxanne Houman, Jasmine Kelakay, Raymok Ketema, Bridget Kyeremateng, and Laura Moore for staff help. Several scholars helped us refine our thinking by chairing panels and moderating discussions: Debra Blumenthal, Marc Coronado, Adrienne Edgar, Karl Jacoby, Terence Keel, Luke Roberts, and Xiaowei Zheng. Several others contributed papers that spurred on our conversations, but their papers did not make it into this book: Grace Peña Delgado, Beth DePalma Digeser, Philip Deslippe, Greg Fisher, Mattie Harper, Kaily Heitz, Nam-lin Hur, Matt Kester, Sameer Pandya, John Park, Félix Racine, Dan Shao, and Kariann Yokota. We are grateful to them all for helping us find our way in this very new area of inquiry.

Finally, we owe thanks to Matt Bokovoy, Heather Stauffer, and their colleagues at the University of Nebraska Press for being model editors.

1

Shape Shifting

Reflections on Racial Plasticity

Paul Spickard

It has become a commonplace to note that racial identities are social constructions. Many scholars have rehearsed how Carolus Linnaeus, Johann Friedrich Blumenbach, Georges Cuvier, Arthur de Gobineau, Paul Broca, Madison Grant, and others made these constructions at the level of philosophy, scholarship, and public advocacy.[1] Very few scholars have traced how individuals, families, and small collectives have in fact gone about the work of constructing their identities. This book is about that process of racial identity formation, particularly racial identity *trans*formation.

There is a persistent trope that keeps popping up in the way people think about racial identities and interactions. They call it "passing." The editors of this volume, and the contributors by and large, think it's something else. In 1990 *Ebony* published a widely read article by Lynn Norment, a much-honored journalist, titled "Who's Black and Who's Not?" In it Norment accused a number of prominent people—many of them female entertainers—of trying to pretend they were not Black in order to reap social and financial benefits in a racist society that valued Whiteness over Blackness. Norment juxtaposed the people she regarded as self-deceiving wannabe Whites against the virtuous people who, despite also possessing multiracial ancestry and racial options, understood and embraced the *fact*, as it was in her view, that they were really and essentially Black. In the latter category, she featured prominently the American actor Jasmine Guy, whom she interviewed. Guy had one Black parent and one White parent. Then a star of the TV sitcom *A Different World*, Guy was quoted as saying: "I was never confused. . . . Mine was a normal, happy childhood. I always knew that I was—and am—Black."[2]

On the negative side of the ledger, Norment placed several people whom she regarded as racially self-deluded. Among them were actors Jennifer Beals and Rae Dawn Chong, figure skater Tai Babilonia, dancer Paula Abdul, and rock musician Lenny Kravitz, none of whom Norment seems to have interviewed. Norment charged them all with failing to own up to their true Black identities: "More and more individuals . . . who just a few years ago definitely would have been considered 'Black' are now calling themselves otherwise. People who grew up in Black or mixed neighborhoods, who socialized with Blacks and who reflected the Black experience and culture, are now, having achieved success and fame, calling themselves anything but Black. . . . The issue is the downplaying or denial of a Black parent or Black heritage for economic, social or career gain."[3] Norment did not make clear what specific economic, social, or career gain she supposed automatically would accrue to these people if they admitted to multiple ancestries. After singling out these various mixed race figures, Norment called on African American psychiatrist Alvin Poussaint and psychologist Halford Fairchild, who pronounced Beals, Babilonia, and the others to be psychologically confused and troubled.

For the record, there is no evidence that Beals, Kravitz, or any of the others Norment criticized ever said that they were not Black and proud. But they all did own up to having other ancestry as well and didn't want to leave it out. Beals's father, a Black South Side Chicago businessman, died when she was nine, and her White mother moved with Jennifer to an upper-middle-class neighborhood across town, where she grew up among White people. Tai Babilonia is half Filipino, one-quarter Hopi, and only one-quarter Black, but according to Norment, the Black ancestry must determine Babilonia's identity, and she must not connect with the other three-quarters. Rae Dawn Chong's father is the Chinese and White Canadian comedian, activist, and pot

entrepreneur Tommy Chong, her mother the Cherokee and AfroCa-
nadian Maxine Sneed. Unsurprisingly to anyone who is acquainted
with Chinese North Americans, Rae Dawn Chong showed considerable interest in the Chinese part of her ancestry, and there is racial
trauma on that side as well. She told *Asian Week* magazine that her
immigrant grandfather refused to teach Cantonese to his children
and grandchildren. "I think my grandfather had great racial shame,
which was hard on us growing up. We grew up desperate to know
anything about our Chinese culture." None of that made a dent in
Norment's consciousness; for her, Chong's necessary Blackness was
the only issue. Lenny Kravitz has presented himself as a Black Jewish musician from the beginning of his career; he has never hidden
either part of his ancestry. Even Paula Abdul did not say she wasn't
part Black, although in fact she is not part Black: her mother was a
Jew from Manitoba and her father a Jew from Syria. Unless he picked
up some Blackness when he spent his teenage years in Brazil, I cannot
imagine how Norment came to the conclusion that Abdul should be
required to identify as Black.[4]

Passing as Racial Imposture

Lynn Norment is a member of my generation. She and I are people
whose racial sensibilities were formed in the era of the Civil Rights and
Black Power movements. Ideas about race in that era were monoracially inflected, decisively shaped by the one-drop rule—the contention that anyone who has any known African ancestry, no matter how
small a trace, is simply and uncomplicatedly Black. This has not been
the rule everywhere or always. Brazil, South Africa, Colombia, and
other nations with large African-descended populations have long had
much more complicated ways of figuring racial identities. The same is
true for other polyglot territories in Asia and Africa, many of which
have few if any Whites or Blacks yet which have elaborate racial systems of their own.[5] The one-drop rule is in fact peculiar to the United
States, and it has not always operated here in the same way it did in
the middle decades of the twentieth century. The rule was created in
the early nineteenth-century South by slave-owning Whites. It was a

way to keep the part-White children of master-class men and enslaved women from creeping out of the race that was identified with enslaved people and into the race that was identified with enslaving people. It is not always recognized that, for a time after the formal end of slavery, some limited racial options opened up for people who were mixed. Those options disappeared again abruptly with the rise of Jim Crow segregation, political disenfranchisement, and spasms of lynching that ran from the last decades of the nineteenth century to the middle of the twentieth. From the early years of the century through the 1970s, Whites enforced the one-drop rule on Blacks, and people of African descent used the same rule to gather themselves in resistance.[6] That was the era when the rule held its greatest sway in American society, and it is the era in which Lynn Norment and I grew up. In the world where we both grew up, anyone with any measure of African ancestry was regarded by both White and Black Americans as simply Black. In those years, Blackness was a capacious identity, inclusive of many hues, ancestries, and mixtures; and for many it still is today. But by the time Norment wrote her screed against the identities of several mixed race celebrities, a mixed race movement was beginning to appear, yet she did not see it. The idea of racial complexity, or the possibility of racial multiplicity, was gaining ascendancy in American society at large, but it was nowhere on Norment's radar at that time.[7]

What Norment was doing in this article was accusing these public figures of trying to pass. We are all familiar with the trope of passing as racial imposture. It is one of the great, misbegotten themes of American literature.[8] The passing trope is about Black and White in America, although there are many other racial groups and kinds of encounters here and elsewhere (as we shall see in this book). According to this hoary trope, a person who is really Black but who has an ambiguous appearance passes for White and then suffers a miserable, lonely, tormented existence because of her choice. The idea of Black passing for White is the basis of the lurid fantasy cherished by many White Americans between the end of Reconstruction and the Black Power era, which had them wondering, "Am I going to wake up and find out that the person I'm sleeping next to is really Black and just pretending to be White? The sex has been great—does that mean that this person isn't really White? What does it mean for our kids? Will they start to look Black? Will I be tainted by my partner's Blackness? Will my friends and family shun me? That's kind of exciting, but it's also kind of scary." The passing phenomenon has also fascinated generations of African Americans: "What happened to that really Black person who used to live among us and who then passed out of our family and neighborhood and into the White world? She must have been miserable there. What a comfort it is to think that she is miserable and tormented there, while we remain safely here in our unquestioned Blackness."

Broadway shows and Hollywood movies have often embraced the passing theme, from Jerome Kern and Oscar Hammerstein's *Show Boat*—a hit Broadway musical in the 1920s, then three times a Hollywood movie—to *Imitation of Life* (told twice at the movies, in 1934 and 1959), to *Pinky*, starring Jeanne Crain as the daughter who passed as White and Ethel Waters as the Black mother who stayed in the South and suffered in virtue. *Ebony* and *Jet* obsessed over the thought of Black people passing for White from the 1940s through the 1960s. Some would even say that *The Matrix* movies and *Avatar* are sci-fi versions of racial passing stories.[9]

Despite massive attention to racial passing from novelists, moviemakers, journalists, historians, sociologists, memoirists, and others,[10] incredibly, there are still some people who think this is a new idea. I laughed out loud when I read the first line of Raymond Arsenault's *New York Times* review of Daniel Sharfstein's smart book, *The Invisible Line*: "Racial passing is one of America's deeply hidden traditions, a largely unacknowledged and unstudied aspect of national life."[11] Nonsense. Racial passing has been exorbitantly *over*studied, especially by literary critics. Moreover, the emphasis on the idea of passing—of a person who is really Black passing himself or herself off as White—is a fundamental misunderstanding of what is usually going on in the lives of people who move from one identity to another.

Nonetheless, a very smart scholar named Allyson Hobbs wrote a book about passing in 2015 that reenacts all these old tropes. The publisher's description says:

Between the eighteenth and mid-twentieth centuries, countless African Americans passed as white, leaving behind families and friends, roots and community. It was a chosen exile, . . . a separation from one racial identity and the leap into another. This revelatory history of passing explores the possibilities and challenges that racial indeterminacy presented to men and women living in a country obsessed with racial distinctions. It also tells a tale of loss. . . . African Americans came to regard passing as a form of betrayal, a selling of one's birthright. . . . Although black Americans who adopted white identities reaped benefits of expanded opportunity and mobility, Hobbs helps us to recognize and understand the grief, loneliness, and isolation that accompanied—and often outweighed—these rewards. By the dawning of the civil rights era, more and more racially mixed Americans felt [that] the loss of kin and community was too much to bear, that it was time to "pass out" and embrace a black identity. Although recent decades have witnessed an increasingly multiracial society and a growing acceptance of hybridity, the problem of race and identity remains at the center of public debate and emotionally fraught personal decisions.[12]

Hobbs is a fairly diligent historical researcher and a clear writer. The tales she tells are finely etched and told with sympathy. She has a warm regard for people. But I am not convinced that she fully understands the social and psychological dynamics at work in the lives she represents so stereotypically. Hobbs tells lots of stories of people from various times in American history who moved across racial lines. But they always move from Black to White, never any other way around. And every single time, when she wants to make her main point— that they were miserable in their imposture—she can't find any evidence in her historical records, so she resorts to fiction. She turns to characters in novels who were tragic mulattoes, who were found out, who died miserable and alone. All the novels she cites were printed by White publishers who demanded the passing narrative as a condition of publication. Compare the manuscript versions of the short story "Rena," which Charles Chesnutt turned into his 1900 novel *The House*

Behind the Cedars. There is no tragic mulatto in the short story or any of the other early versions, but Rena dies heartbroken and rejected in the novel that Houghton Mifflin finally accepted for publication.[13]

To be sure, there were people like this—people who grew up in a Black racial position and who chose to leave it and take on a White identity. Consider, for example, Anatole Broyard. He was born in 1920 in New Orleans to light-skinned Creole parents who were of the upper part but not the very top—that is, White—stratum of that city's complicated racial hierarchy. When they moved to Brooklyn, they lived in Black Bedford-Stuyvesant. Anatole's father, Paul Broyard, a construction worker, took the streetcar across Brooklyn each day, and each day he made the transition from Black to White because the carpenters union didn't take Blacks. He then made the transition back to Black on his return trip. His son Anatole, after serving in World War II as a White officer, came back to New York and quickly left his Black roots behind. He became a Greenwich Village bookseller, then a contributor to literary magazines, and finally the *New York Times*' daily book reviewer—one of the core arbiters of American intellectual affairs. He married a White woman who knew his racially complicated past and didn't much care. Most of his colleagues knew of his racially complicated past and didn't much care; others had heard rumors about his raciality and didn't much care. His children, apparently, he kept in the dark. But he was striving to become not a Black writer like Richard Wright or James Baldwin, with a political agenda trailing behind his writing, but simply an author. This ambition he shared with Ralph Ellison, though the two adopted different strategies toward their common goal. Broyard was for the next fifteen years one of the main influencers of American literary taste, with scarcely a hint of racial inflection. He successfully made the transit from Black to White.[14]

What are we to make of people like Broyard who initially lived in one racial box and then took themselves out of that box and put themselves into another?

Actor Halle Berry was raised by her White mother and had no relationship with her Black father past the age of four. Is she really Black? Or is she passing for Black when she identifies herself as a Black actress?

She didn't grow up in a Black family, and she only lived in a Black community for part of her childhood, but a lot of people would say she is Black now. (They deploy what Cynthia Nakashima calls the "claim-us-if-we're-famous" principle.)[15] Since adolescence Halle Berry has chosen to identify herself as a Black woman with a White mother. If she were to present herself as White, Allyson Hobbs and Lynn Norment would surely say that she was passing, abandoning her people, and so forth, but in fact Berry did grow up more or less as a tan-skinned White girl. This stuff is complicated.[16]

How about Vin Diesel (birth name: Mark Sinclair), another actor? He was born in New York City. His mother, Delora Sinclair Vincent, is White. Vin or Mark never knew his father nor what that man's race might have been; apparently, there were several possible candidates. Vin was raised by his White mother and his Black stepfather, and he has chosen to identify more or less with the stepfather. So Vin calls himself a person of color, although what color that might be he leaves unclear, and there is no evidence he has any African ancestry.[17]

That's the passing trope: denial of who you really are. Halle Berry and Vin Diesel would be viewed by Allyson Hobbs and Lynn Norment as people who didn't pass, who know who they really are: they are African Americans (although there is not much evidence that that is true either in their physiognomy or in their personal histories). I don't have a problem if Berry and Diesel choose to identify that way, but I do have a problem with people like Allyson Hobbs and Lynn Norment who insist that they must.

Shape Shifting

We are accustomed to thinking of identities—racial, ethnic, national, gendered, religious—as if they were permanent, essential, unalterable features of individuals and groups. A is Black, B is Jewish, C is Chinese, and so are all of the members of their respective families and kin groups. Theorists like Gloria Anzaldúa, Maria Root, G. Reginald Daniel, and Homi Bhabha in the 1980s and 1990s began to conceptualize a hybrid middle position, or "Third Space," occupied by racially and culturally mixed people.[18] Anzaldúa and Bhabha admitted of the possibility of movement among identities, but they concentrated on the betwixt-and-betweenness of hybrid identities. Root and Daniel had a little more room for actual identity change.[19]

Over the last couple of decades, since these theorists first sent us down the path to thinking about multiplicity as a Third Space of in-betweenness, some of us have begun to see identities not just as in-between but at least sometimes as fluid, ambiguous, contingent, multiple, and malleable.[20] As the eminent sociologist Rebecca King-O'Riain remarked in response to an earlier version of the paper that morphed into this chapter:

> There is movement, an undulation back and forth, up and down, within social contexts and with varying social agency granted to individual and collective identities. . . . In this sense, shape shifting moves us well beyond the mire of Homi Bhabha's rather static notion of hybridity as "neither one nor the other but something else besides, in-between." The third space, and its bipolar constraints of Bhabha's hybridity, are fundamentally shaped by a life view that is reactive—I am neither one, nor the other, but something else. I am rejected by one and the other, so therefore I must be something else. This is a largely negative view of social agency—that social actors can only respond to rejection and structural constraint.[21]

King-O'Riain is calling out Bhabha and his fellows for their static view of racial and cultural identities. She is putting them in the same box as Everett Stonequist, Edward Byron Reuter, and every novelist who ever wrote about the conscience of a tragic mulatto, imprisoned between Black and White. "Shape shifting, in contrast, is a positive and dynamic view of social agency and it gives us more conceptual leverage to better understand the dialectical relationships between social structures and social actors for not only shape shifters, but also shape shifting abilities and outcomes as well."[22]

The story of race has been written as if races were real, biologically discrete entities, not heuristic constructions of philosophers' minds. It has been written as if monoracially identified people—people who imagine they are racially pure—were the norm and multiracial people were anomalies. Even the study of multiraciality has focused mainly on the ways that mixed people have deviated from some presumed monoracial norm. The editors of this volume take another approach. We view racial mixture as normative. All populations, now and as far as we can reach into the past, are mixed populations. All individuals, no matter how pure they imagine their ancestry to be, are mixed. This book places mixedness and contingency at the center of attention. Mixture is the norm. Contingency is the norm.

We seek in this volume to disrupt the passing narrative, which says that a person who is really of X group is pretending to be a member of group Y, which says that racial authenticity is the main question in play. We are interested, rather, in the circumstances that drive racial change and the processes by which individuals, families, and communities remake their racial identities. The people whose lives are the subject of this book are not tragic mulattoes, caught in a static no-man's-land between two monoracial identities that reject them. They are shape shifters. At different times in their lives, or over generations in their families, as they have moved from one social context to another, or as new social contexts have been imposed on them, their identities have changed from one group to another. This is not necessarily racial, ethnic, or religious imposture. It is often simply the way that people's lives have unfolded in fluid social circumstances. Sometimes it is a matter of changes in the menu of available identities that causes the shift. Sometimes it is an individual's or a family's choice among existing categories. And sometimes changes in ethnic identity are imposed by governments, by institutions, or by society at large.

We owe the reader some explanation of our choice of the term "shape shifters" for people who change their race or other fundamental social identities. We might have chosen "race changers" or "identity morphers," but those terms clang on the tongue. "Shape shifters" is both memorable and mellifluous. How then, we thought, should we present the term: as one word, two words, or hyphenated?

Most commonly, "shapeshifters" appears as a single word and refers to Navajo skinwalkers, witches who sometimes assume animal and even alternate human forms. We did not wish to tread too closely to this usage, out of respect for that community and tradition. In other instances (primarily fantasy fiction and movies) "shapeshifters" has referred to Remus Lupin, Sirius Black, and other figures in the Harry Potter series; to Bram Stoker's Count Dracula; to Mystique from the X-Men; to Leah Clearwater in the Twilight series; to Simon Thorn from Aimee Carter's book series; to Maui in Disney's *Moana* movie; or to assorted ancient and medieval mythical figures like the Norse god Loki.

We did not want our concept to be associated with a sense of shape shifting as supernatural, mythical, outside the real. We also did not want to accept a sense of shape shifting as fictional or pretense, nor as trivial or ephemeral. What we are talking about is not some tricky person who—poof!—morphs from over here to over there. We are talking about the concrete social situations in which people change identity—not trivially, but practically, and for important reasons, with important results. That is a new way of thinking about racial identities, and it is deserving of a new term, but one that is recognizable.

Our grammarian friends encouraged us to hyphenate the term and use "shape-shifters." That seemed to us to be too close to the single word "shapeshifters." It might allow the impression to creep in that this was a trivial or temporary thing. We want to keep our analysis firmly located in the social. We don't want to convey the sense that the phenomenon we are examining is simply a matter of choice, without social pressures and constraints. We want to stress the relationship between this kind of change and social forces.

"Shape shifters"—two words—is declarative. It suggests that the processes that govern change of identity are natural, they are social, they are discernible, and they are significant. A person, family, or group starts out in this race, they go through social processes that we can describe and analyze, and they end up in that race. They shift their shape.

In this chapter I will offer several examples of shape shifting, some quite recent, and others reaching centuries into the past. For the purpose of thinking as clearly as possible about this, I have grouped the stories into three large categories, each with at least two subcategories, to help us try to figure out (1) what are the circumstances that lead to racial shape shifting and (2) what is happening when someone changes his or her or their identity. I will talk about the following categories in this chapter:

1. Categories Change
   a. A changing social context offers a different menu of identities, so one takes on the identity that seems best to fit in the new social setting.
   b. A close corollary to 1a involves another kind of identity overriding one's allegiance to one's ethnic or racial identity.
2. Choosing among Established Identity Categories
   a. Some people choose to gain a tangible benefit that we can perceive.
   b. Sometimes people move among established identity categories as a matter of choice but for reasons of which we cannot be sure.
   c. Sometimes people embrace a new identity as a matter of personal idealism or political purpose.
3. Change as Social Compulsion
   a. An entire society or ethnic group may decide to change its identity, and so individuals must comply.
   b. Sometimes a change of identity is forced upon an individual or a group by government decision or by social pressure.

Necessarily, these categories are not absolute and discrete. An individual's or a group's identity situation may contain elements from two or more of these categories. But articulating the categories helps us see the range of tasks that racial change is performing.

Context Changes, So Identity Changes

Most often, people change their identities in response to changes in the social systems around them.[23] In new social settings, there are different menus of identity options, and people must find new ways to locate themselves. We can see this on a large scale in human migrations. In the latter decades of the nineteenth century, thousands of

people who knew themselves ethnically and nationally to be Cal-
abrians, Sicilians, Genoese, and other peoples traveled abroad. When
they reached the United States, Argentina, or other destinations, they
were called, and soon they came to call themselves, Italians—an
identity they had not known previously, for Italy was just coming
together as a single nation in their lifetimes.[24] Earlier, Bambara and
Mandinka and Fon and Fulani and many other peoples left West
Africa in chains between the fifteenth century and the nineteenth.
They became Africans in the Middle Passage, then Negroes in the
New World.[25] These were broad, long-term processes of panethnic
or racial formation: bringing together smaller groups and remaking
them into larger collectivities. We can also see more specific racial
refashionings in the lives of individuals and families as their social
contexts change.

Karina's Story

My friend Karina (pseud.) was born in Kyrgyzstan.[26] She has a complicated ethnic background. She was born in the Kyrgyz Republic of the
Soviet Union. At that time she was simply a Soviet citizen, an amal-
gamated identity that was encouraged by the USSR at a time when
intermarriage was also encouraged. Then, when the Soviet Union
fell apart in 1991, for a brief period Karina was a Kyrgyz citizen. Soon,
however, she was able to immigrate to Germany because some of her
mother's distant ancestors had been Germans who migrated into the
Russian Empire in the time of Catherine the Great, two-plus centuries before.[27] Karina relates her identity wanderings: "My affiliation
to [German] ethnicity arises from a surname. My biological father is
half-Armenian and half-Tatar. My mother is [part] German (Swabian
and East Prussian). Her maiden name is Polish with a Russian ending. I had the Armenian name of my paternal biological heritage.
My grandmother, whose ethnic affiliation qualified us to go to Germany, her maiden name was full German [although she too had several other ancestries]."

So Karina was German for a while—long enough to get her into
Germany—but there her identity changed again.

In Germany, we, as the Russian-Germans, have been received like a wild horde of "fucking Russians" (sorry), who threatened in every way the German way of life. The people couldn't consider us as ethnic Germans, especially because we looked, behaved and talked like Russians. . . . I never felt so Russian before, just Soviet, and easily slipped over into a new glorious and awesome identity, unified with all the proletarians of all the ex-Soviet countries into a proud working-class German subculture named "The Russians." The teens like me (I was twelve when we moved to Germany) formed our own kind of behavior, speaking Russian and a kind of slang that distinguished us from the adults but emphasized our Russian origin, even though almost none of us had Russian genetic roots. . . . [S]tigma created . . . this defensive social identity.

So Karina had German citizenship, but in Germany she was treated as a Russian, and she joined with other former Soviet citizens to create a common Russian German youth culture. Then, during an extended period as a student in France, Karina became a German again.

I never have spoken and thought so much like a German as [when I lived for a year] in France . . . and learned to accept who I had become. If the French asked me "Where are you from?" I said that I'm living in Germany and was born in Kyrgyzstan. "So you are Kyrgyz?" they followed. "No, I'm Russian." It was frustrating for both sides . . . because it was obvious that the French hadn't any idea where Kyrgyzstan is and that Kyrgyz are Asians and that I didn't look like them. Further, there was an awareness of racial difference which I unknowingly sensed.

When I interviewed Karina a few years ago, she said that she increasingly felt not like a Russian or a German or a Kyrgyz but like a European. That is an identity that the leaders of the European Union were then trying hard to promote. In Karina's case, European is an easy identity to take on, since she has lived in several countries, and besides, her boyfriend is not German. Over the course of her young life, Karina has felt herself to be and has been treated by others, depending on the context of the moment, by turns as Soviet, Kyrgyz, perhaps a bit Armenian or Tatar, German, Russian, German again, and finally European.

The Bonga Family

Historian Mattie Harper explores the shifting grounds of identity and belonging in the western Great Lakes region from the late eighteenth century to the late nineteenth by telling the story of one large extended family, the progeny and relations of Jean and Marie Jeanne Bonga, over four generations.[28] Jean and Marie Jeanne were both French-speaking, African-descended slaves who were brought to the Upper Peninsula of Michigan in the 1780s by the British officer who owned them. They worked there alongside Native American workers, were manumitted, married, and became local entrepreneurs, proprietors of a hotel on Mackinac Island at the confluence of Lake Huron and Lake Michigan. They existed in the borderlands between three different servile labor systems: Native, French, and British.

Jean and Marie Jeanne had several children who went into the fur trade and related industries. Their children and grandchildren ultimately came to be counted among the elite in their part of the borderlands, which included Ojibwe, French, British, and American populations. This was Indian country, and no single nation defined social relationships locally. Several of the Bongas became members of Ojibwe Indian bands. Harper argues that in the eighteenth century and through much of the nineteenth, status was fluid and determined by occupation, family connections, and religion but not by race. As the United States gradually extended its influence and then control into the region, several racialized binaries began to emerge. Race became the issue in social placement. Meanwhile, individual family members and the Bonga family as a whole were classified variously in social relations as "white," "negro," "half-breed," "mixed-blood," "Indian," and several other categories. Grandson George Bonga, who was photographed late in life and whose features and skin tone speak distinctively of Africa, referred to himself and his brother as having been "the first white babies" to be born in Minnesota.

Fig. 1.1. George Bonga, from African to Indian to White. Photo by Charles A. Zimmerman, courtesy of the Minnesota Historical Society.

After the 1870s, as American control became more firm, lines began to be drawn on the basis of race, and some Bonga descendants declined in status for racial reasons; others maintained higher status by virtue of their religious associations and their embrace of emerging American middle-class dictates of domesticity. One great-granddaughter, Susan Bonga, became a stalwart of the Episcopal church, where she taught classes in how to perform Victorian-era White Christian womanly tasks. Although her Black ancestry was well known, she was courted by Charles Wright, an Ojibwe missionary, and eventually became his more or less White wife. Over three generations, then, the Bonga family moved from Black to Indian. Then in the fourth generation, as the system changed to a racialized set of definitions, they became Black in some cases and White in others, depending on how individuals behaved and were perceived. Black became Indian became White. In subsequent generations, there were Bonga descendants who were Indian, others who were Black, and some who were White.

Hanni's Story

Hanni was born in Colombia to a father who was the son of Lebanese immigrants and a mother who is one of those ethnically complicated people Colombia has so many of: a mix of Spanish, Indian, and probably some African descent.[29] When Hanni was a young girl, she came with her mother and sister to the United States, where they lived without papers for many years. As an adult, Hanni has acquired U.S. citizenship, an American PhD, a Colombian husband, and a daughter. Her career takes her back and forth between the United States and Colombia frequently. The two countries recognize a similar array of racial groups: Whites, Blacks, Indians, mestizos, and smaller numbers of other peoples, including Asians. But when Hanni is in Colombia she is viewed by others and sees herself as White. In the United States she is Brown. The two countries have the same racial categories, but they draw the line between White and Brown in different places. She wrote me: "I am glad you see racial/ethnic categories as flexible and importantly shaped by context. This is something that I . . . intuitively have known for a while, studying and learning from you have [given] me a language with which I can talk about this."[30]

Choosing Sides

Sometimes an individual has clear-cut ethnic options and simply chooses sides. Of the several modes of shape shifting that I have posited, this is the one that most nearly resembles the passing trope. But note that such choosers only sometimes do so for what seem to be purposes of personal benefit. Moreover, if there is a benefit, it does not necessarily come from eschewing a Black identity and taking on a White one. In the cases that I cite here, even though a choice was being made, it would be hard to prove that the shape shifter was acting cynically or pretending to be someone whom he or she did not feel himself or herself to be.[31]

P. B. S. Pinchback

Pinckney Benton Stewart Pinchback was one of the better-known political figures of the era of Reconstruction after the U.S. Civil War.[32] He was born in 1837 in Macon, Georgia, the son of Eliza Stewart, a free woman of mixed Black, White, and Cherokee ancestry, and William Pinchback, her former master, who kept a White family as well as a mixed race household. When Pinckney was a child his father bought a larger plantation in Mississippi and moved there with both his families. Pinckney Stewart (he did not take his father's name until after the Civil War) was sent to school in Cincinnati at age nine along with his older brother Napoleon. When his father died two years later, Eliza took the remaining children and fled to Ohio, in fear that her common-law husband's legal wife and relatives might try to enslave them. Pinckney soon left school to help support the family. In 1860 he married Nina Hawthorne, a light-skinned free woman of color.

Pinckney entered the Civil War as a White sergeant in the Union army. Then, changing his racial identity, as a Black captain he commanded a company of troops. After the war, as a Black politician, he became a Reconstruction-era Republican state senator, then lieutenant governor, and finally, briefly, governor of Louisiana. He was

Fig. 1.2. P. B. S. Pinchback, from White to Black. Photo by Matthew Brady, courtesy of the Library of Congress.

also elected to both the U.S. House of Representatives and the Senate (though both houses failed to seat him). He published a biweekly newspaper throughout the 1870s and invested in real estate and other ventures. Pinchback remained a powerful figure in African American politics throughout his life. He was highly successful in business, maintaining grand residences first in New Orleans and later in Washington DC.

Pinchback, in later conversations with his grandson Jean Toomer, did not fault his brothers for having chosen to pass for White nor apologize for his own choice to pass for Black: "They had every right to be white. I have every right to be colored. They saw it to their advantage to do what they did. I saw it to my advantage to do what I did. . . . I realized I could make more headway if I were known as black. . . . Besides . . . I was more attached to our mother."

Herb Jeffries, the Bronze Buckaroo

Umberto Alexandro Valentino (or Ballentino) was born in 1913 or 1914 to an Irish American mother and a Sicilian father.[33] He grew up in Detroit, hanging around clubs where jazz was played. He wanted more than anything to be a jazz singer. Sometime in his late teens he began to tell people that he was part Black. At various times in his life he attributed some small amount of Moorish, Ethiopian, or Louisiana Creole ancestry to his father, whom he never knew. He sang professionally for more than seventy years. At the suggestion of Louis Armstrong, Jeffries moved to Chicago and began singing with Erskine Tate's Vendome Orchestra, then with the Earl Hines Orchestra on tour and on national radio during the 1933 Chicago World's Fair. He sang later with Armstrong, Duke Ellington, and other giants of jazz. His last name was sometimes Jeffrey, sometimes Jeffries, Ball at one point.

When Gene Autrey and others made the singing cowboy a staple of B movies in the 1930s, Jeffries talked some producers of low-budget films for segregated Black audiences into following the craze. Tall, good-looking Herb Jeffries was a perfect fit for the job. He starred in several Black Western feature films, including *Harlem on the Prairie*

Fig. 1.3. Herb Jeffries, the Bronze Buckaroo, from Irish Italian to Black. Photo by John E. Reed, courtesy of LaBudde Special Collections, UMKC University Libraries.

(1937), *Two-Gun Man from Harlem* (1938), *The Bronze Buckaroo* (1939), and *Harlem Rides the Range* (1939).

Jeffries made a big point of refusing to "pass" as White in order to further his singing and acting career. He told *Ebony* in 1950: "I'd always heard if you had *any* Negro blood you were a Negro and that was that. . . . Then it can't be such inferior blood, can it? If you had a black paint that was so powerful that two drops of it would color a bucket of white, that'd be the most potent paint in the world, wouldn't it? So if Negro blood is as strong as all that it must be pretty good—maybe I'd better find out where I can get some more of it."[34]

But he *was* White, by ancestry if not by practice. If he could pass as Black, he could sing jazz with Ellington and Armstrong, and that was a powerful draw. He told jazz critic Gary Giddins, "I just knew that my life would be more interesting as a black guy. If I'd chosen to live my life passing as white, I'd have never been able to sing with Duke Ellington."[35] He told the *Los Angeles Times*: "This was a chance to make something good out of something bad. Little children of dark skin—not just Negroes, but Puerto Ricans, Mexicans, everybody of color—had no heroes in the movies. I was so glad to give them something to identify with."[36] Jeffries maintained a Black identity almost without interruption throughout the final eighty years of his long life.

Yamaguchi Yoshiko / Li Xianglan / Shirley Yamaguchi

Yamaguchi Yoshiko lived in the world where Japan and China intersected, and she inhabited both Chinese and Japanese identities—even a Japanese American one for a few years.[37] She was born in 1920 in Manchuria to ethnic Japanese parents as part of the wave of Japanese sent out to populate Japan's new colonial domain.[38] They were going to make a new, unified Asia, independent of Europe and America and led by Japan. Her father, a Sinophile and linguist who worked for the South Manchuria Railway, put his young daughter on a train to Beijing and told her, "From now on, you must start being a Chinese person."[39] She went to a Chinese school, took the name Pan Shuhua, learned to speak unaccented Chinese, and did her best to blend in at a time when anti-Japanese feeling was running high in China. At fourteen she was recruited to sing Chinese songs on the radio under the name Li Xianglan, which had been given her by Li Jichun, a friend of her father. That led to a series of radio and movie roles, all as a Chinese woman. In her private life she maintained the mannerisms of a young Chinese women, including wearing the *qipao* (Cantonese: *cheongsam*), a close-fitting, high-necked dress with side slits so the legs can move.

In the late 1930s and early 1940s Li made a series of increasingly popular films that were ambiguous in their sentiments about the relationship between China and Japan. They were all made by Japanese film companies and mainly employed Japanese actors. Li was often the only actor presented as Chinese. A frequent theme had her, as a beautiful young Chinese woman, initially resisting the aggression of a colonizing Japanese soldier but ultimately coming to love and appreciate him. Thus China was cast as feminine and passive and Japan as masculine and commanding. In the 1930s this came to be part of the Japanese government's policy of proclaiming the Greater East Asia Co-Prosperity Sphere, in which the peoples of Asia would unite under Japanese leadership and throw off the chains of European colonialism. But Chinese audiences actually liked these movies, despite the colonial overtones, and they loved Li Xianglan. As World War II progressed, the word went around that perhaps, then probably, then surely she was not born ethnic Chinese, but still her popularity soared with Chinese audiences. So Chinese audiences colluded in her Chinese identity.[40]

Li Xianglan / Yamaguchi Yoshiko here was enacting a kind of proto-panethnic Asianness, and Chinese audiences were going along with it.[41] She used "we" when talking about the Chinese people, although many years later, looking back, she felt some guilt and simplified her recollection to one of masquerade. Those who have studied her life most closely think that she saw herself in the 1940s as truly Chinese and that Chinese audiences saw her that way, too, despite her ancestry.

When World War II ended, Li was arrested and charged with treason for having betrayed China in her quisling performances in Japanese films. She might have been imprisoned or executed, but at the last minute a friend produced her Yamaguchi family register, which established that she was formally a Japanese and not a Chinese citizen. She was summarily "repatriated" to Japan, a place that had never been her home. She tried to work as a singer and actor in Tokyo but had little luck. In the 1950s she went to Hollywood and made a couple of movies under the name Shirley Yamaguchi, dated Yul Brynner, hung out with Charlie Chaplin and James Dean, and married the famous Japanese American sculptor Isamu Noguchi (himself a complex individual, the son of the bisexual Japanese poet Yone Noguchi and the White American writer Léonie Gilmour, although they never were a family).[42]

During the McCarthy years, Li/Yamaguchi was denied reentry to the United States on the grounds that she had been friends with suspected Communists in Hollywood. Later she made Chinese-language movies in Hong Kong as Li Xianglan again. In the fullness of time she made her way to Japan and reinvented herself as Otaka Yoshiko, taking the family name of a new husband. In 1969 she became host of the popular *Sanji no anata* (Three o'clock you) TV show in Japan. Five years later she was elected to the House of Councillors, the upper body of the Japanese parliament, where she served for eighteen years. She died in 2014.

Li Xianglan was born Japanese in the middle of that country's experiment in imperial pan-Asianism. She grew up a thoroughly Chinese woman and had a successful acting career that brought her fame and adulation as an emblem of a particular strain of Chinese womanhood. Life circumstances and the collapse of the Japanese Empire forced her to become Japanese, really for the first time, after the war. She floundered a bit before she was able to make the transition to a stable Japanese identity in middle age and go on to become a revered figure in Japan throughout the last several decades of her life.[43]

Sometimes it seems to be neither the dictates of social circumstance nor the appearance of opportunity that instigates a shift of identity. Sometimes it is a response of the heart to what one perceives to be a higher calling. Such was the case for many people who had racial options and who then chose to identify as Black Americans. Among them were such honored Black leaders as W. E. B. Du Bois, Walter White, Mary Church Terrell, T. Thomas Fortune, Azalia Hackley, Adella Hunt Logan, and Adam Clayton Powell.[44]

Du Bois, for example, grew up among White, small-town New Englanders and performed New England White culture perfectly. Only when he ventured out to attend college at Fisk (because White Harvard would not have dusky Burghardt Du Bois) did he make a decisive choice to see himself as unambiguously Black. Even then, all the rest of his long life, alongside a rock-solid commitment to being a member of and an advocate for African Americans, he acknowledged and maintained an acute interest in his White forebears. He often quarreled with his close friend and collaborator, Rayford Logan, about his racial identity. Logan asserted that Black identity was not an option and that Du Bois was Black by necessity. Du Bois, to the contrary, insisted that it was at Fisk that he learned to be Black and to cherish the connection to Black people. His commitment to Blackness was complete, but it was a learned identity, not a necessity of birth. He knew he was a man who had racial options—not wholly unfettered ones, to be sure, but options nonetheless—and he opted to be Black. He did not start out particularly Black, but there was no Blacker man in twentieth-century America.[45]

As Ingrid Dineen-Wimberly shows in *The Allure of Blackness among Mixed Race Americans, 1862–1916*, other African-descended but mixed people in Du Bois's era experienced racial options, and quite a number of them chose Blackness:

> If you follow the trajectory of the mixed race people, you may track the changes that occurred in the meaning of Blackness and Whiteness. As it turns out, during the latter nineteenth and early twentieth centuries many [African American] leaders were people of mixed race heritage who identified as Black in order to gain or maintain their leadership status. That was the allure of Blackness. These were people who had racial options and they chose to be Black. Choosing to be Black, when they might have chosen otherwise, was their way up, to social, political, and economic leadership positions. In

fact, some may have passed as Black in order to lead. Mixed race people who identified themselves as Black transformed the criteria for Black leadership. White authority had little impact on the matter. It was not a simple binary choice: Black or mixed race. The idea of multiraciality and Blackness coexisting in the same person was articulated by such luminaries as Charles W. Chesnutt and W. E. B. Du Bois. Many people in this era could see themselves as Black at the same time they articulated their mixedness.[46]

Dineen-Wimberly stresses the sort of opportunism that one might attribute to a Pinchback or a Jeffries. But I would argue that for other mixed race Black leaders like Du Bois and perhaps Yamaguchi Yoshiko, the choice was more idealistic.

The Identity Journey of Jean Toomer

What are we to make of Jean Toomer?[47] He chose a more complicated racial positioning. Toomer was an icon of Blackness who embodied racial multiplicity—indeed, who changed his race, and more than once. No more powerful or controversial figure exists in Black letters. Born Nathan Pinchback Toomer in 1894, he grew to adolescence in the Washington DC home and psychic shadow of his powerful grandfather P. B. S. Pinchback. Pinchback served as governor and was elected U.S. senator in Louisiana during Reconstruction. He won on the strength of Black votes and his constituents' understanding that Pinchback, though born the free son of a White planter, possessed slave ancestry.

The identity of his grandson Jean Toomer was a flexible item. Born Nathan, he became Eugene in childhood and later Jean. He lived through high school (at the segregated but elite M Street School) among Washington's light, bright, and almost White African American upper class in a neighborhood called the Gold Coast to this day. The young Jean Toomer identified as Black but traveled socially on the White side of the line nearly as much as on the Black. He then flitted through several colleges without telling anyone about his African ancestry. His life from beginning to end was personalist, a spiritual search for the center of himself and, through that center, for the universally human. Because of who his famous ancestor was and because of the racial angle of his own first coming to public notice, race was always part of that search, and he resented it.

For a brief time in the early 1920s Jean Toomer was a writer and a Black American. His spiritual search and the need for employment led him to live briefly in rural Georgia and to write about the experience. Out poured *Cane*, a jumble of prose, poetry, drawings, and a novella disguised in play form that ignited the imaginations of the makers of the Harlem Renaissance of the 1920s and, two generations later, the makers of the Black revolution of the 1960s. Toomer thought he was drawing from a dying well of Black peasant culture with which he had only the most tenuous personal connection. Readers, by contrast, from Langston Hughes to Alice Walker, found the well Toomer tapped to be deep, rich, and ever self-renewing.[48]

Within a year of the publication of *Cane*, Toomer was off on his spiritual quest, leaving behind both the New York intellectual world to which he had briefly aspired and the Black identity he had tried on. He became successively a disciple of the mystic Georges Gurdjieff, an itinerant teacher, a seldom-published philosopher, a Quaker leader, a recluse. Toomer died in 1967, just before his masterwork was republished and spoke transformatively to a new generation of monoracially identified African Americans.

Black critics saw and valued the powerful talent at work in the making of *Cane*, as well as the celebration of Black peasant life and the horrifying account of White racial oppression. But they tended to see Toomer the man as racially confused. Alice Walker confessed to "feelings of disappointment and loss. Disappointment because the man who wrote so piercingly of 'Negro' life in *Cane* chose to live his own life as a white man, while [Langston] Hughes, [Zora Neale] Hurston, [W. E. B.] Du Bois, and other black writers were celebrating the blackness in themselves as well as in their work. Loss because it appears this choice undermined Toomer's moral judgment: there were things [White racism] in American life and in his own that he simply refused to see."[49] Such an account suggests that, whatever Toomer's talent and contribution, he did not know who he really was: a Black man in a racist nation. Indeed, Walker's assessment might imply self-hatred on Toomer's part, the internalization of White America's contempt for Black people. It is clear that Walker thinks Du Bois and the others made a nobler choice in choosing to embrace an unambiguous Black identity.

Yet in addition to the remarkable sensitivity toward the Black folk to be found in *Cane*, Toomer's writings show that he saw things differently from the way Walker understood him. He thought he knew who he was: not simply a monoracial Black man but a man of multiple ancestries and identities in a nation that did not yet recognize multiplicity. Many decades before others took up the theme, Toomer asserted the constructed quality of race and proclaimed a vision of a society that went beyond race. He believed he was a universal man—not, as Walker would have it, a Black man who eschewed Blackness for Whiteness but a man who did not fit in racial boxes, whose very existence challenged monoracial categories and, behind them, the viciousness of racism. Thus, he could write in later years:

> I would liberate myself and ourselves from the entire machinery of verbal hypnotism. . . . I am simply of the human race. . . . I am of the human nation. . . . I am of Earth. . . . I am of sex, with male differentiations. . . . I eliminate the religions. I am religious. . . .
>
> What then am I?
>
> I am at once no one of the races and I am all of them.
>
> I belong to no one of them and I belong to all.
>
> I am, in a strict racial sense, a member of a new race. . . .
>
> I say to the colored group that, as a human being, I am one of them. . . . I say to the white group that, as a human being, I am one of them. As a white man, I am not one of them. . . . I am an American. As such, I invite them [both], not as [colored or] white people, but *as Americans*, to participate in whatever creative work I may be able to do.[50]

This was a personal vision, born out of mystical seeking, written into a vague program for humankind. It spoke in no concrete way to the needs of people in America who were marked off by color for domination and abuse. Rather, it was a psychological vision of a person who knew his mixedness and his wholeness and who believed them to be more important than group strivings. Ultimately, neither White nor Black America in the first half of the twentieth century had room for a racially multiple man like Jean Toomer, at least not for public recognition of his multiplicity. Perhaps now, in a new century, there is room for such recognition.

Compelled Identity Change

Sometimes it is not a change in one's context that causes a change in one's identity, nor is it that one chooses to make a change. Sometimes one is compelled by the state, by other institutions, or by the power of public opinion. Tatiana Seijas charts the complicated changes of social status that came upon enslaved people from the Manila slave markets (mostly ethnic Filipinos and Indians but also people from other parts of Asia) when they came to live and work in Mexico in the sixteenth century. Initially, their social status was as *chino* slaves. But some earned their freedom, whereupon they became viewed as ethnic Indians and members of the Republic of Indians, a distinct legal status. As Seijas says, "A man born in Goa could be categorized as a chino when he arrived in Mexico as a slave and then become an Indian once he was manumitted and lived as a free man."[51]

Compelled identities occurred under quite a variety of circumstances. In 1936 Korea had been part of the Japanese Empire for twenty-six years. Sohn Kee-chung was the best of a group of top Korean distance runners who were forced to run for the Japanese team in the Berlin Olympics and to appear there under Japanese versions of their names. Sohn (as Son Kitei) won the marathon; another Korean, Nam Sung-yong, took the bronze medal. At the medal ceremony, Sohn and Nam bowed their heads in anger and shame at being denied their Korean national identity at their moment of triumph. Sohn clutched a young oak tree to his chest, covering up the Japanese flag on his uniform. It was only more than half a century later that the Olympic bureaucracy corrected the records and named Sohn and Nam as Korean medal winners, not Japanese.[52]

On rare occasions, an entire people may abruptly change the nature of their common identity on order of the state. So it was with the Khazar Kingdom, which formed a rough triangle north of the Caucasus Mountains and the Black and Caspian Seas in western Asia. Long believers in a naturalistic faith and worshippers of the sky god Tengri, the people of the Khazar Kingdom in the eighth and ninth centuries came under pressure from their more powerful neighbors—Muslim Bulgarians and Orthodox Christian Byzantines—to adopt one of their faiths. In the end, it seems (there is some dispute about this), they chose Judaism as the new religious glue for their kingdom. First the royal house and nobles embraced the new faith, and then over a few generations the masses were converted as well.[53] In a similar move, the infant Russian state centered in Kiev took on Greek Orthodox Christianity as its official religion over a couple of generations' time in the tenth century, much to the dismay of the Old Believers.[54]

Becoming Mexican in China

Scores of thousands of Chinese men moved to Mexico in the latter decades of the nineteenth century and first decades of the twentieth.[55] They were part of a massive migration out of South China that went many places: the United States, Hawai'i, Cuba, Singapore, Thailand, Indochina, the Philippines, and many other places. Among them was Wong Fang, who left rural Guangdong Province and traveled to San Francisco with his brother shortly after 1900, then continued on alone to Sonora in northern Mexico. He learned Spanish and added a Mexican first name, becoming Alfonso Wong Fang. He made the transition from body work to keeping a small store. Like many Chinese Mexican men, he married a local woman: he and Dolores Campoy Rivera had a son, Alfonso Wong Campoy, in 1928, and two more children in subsequent years. All this was pretty typical of Chinese in Mexico in those decades.

But the Mexican Revolution of 1910 had aroused Mexican ethnonationalism. Anti-Chinese sentiment that had festered north of the border in the United States for a couple of generations manifested itself in Mexico as well, nowhere more than in Sonora. The *antichinista* movement came to a head in the early 1930s. Many hundreds of Chinese Mexican families were summarily deported, including Alfonso, Dolores, and their children. By Mexican law (copied from the United States), wives' citizenship necessarily followed that of their husbands. Some of the families were shipped directly to China; others, including the Wong Campoys, were dumped across the border in the United States. Since Chinese immigration to the United States was illegal, and since Dolores and the children were Chinese in the eyes of the law, the Americans shipped the family on to China.

In South China some women learned that they were the second or third wife of their husbands. Others chafed at Cantonese gender norms. Some families stayed together; others broke apart. Some mixed children stayed with their fathers, others—the majority probably—went with their mothers. The Wong Campoy family remained together. They lived first in a Cantonese village, but soon they moved, like many other Chinese Mexican families, to Macau. The colony's Catholic, Latin, and Iberian culture felt more like home. In Macau from the 1930s on there grew a vibrant international community, including mixed families of many kinds. Young Alfonso was already fluent in Spanish and Cantonese; now he learned Portuguese and Italian as well. The Mexican Chinese in Macau communicated and visited back and forth with other mixed families in Hong Kong and Canton and deeper inside China.

After World War II Ramón Lay Mazo and some other mixed Mexican Chinese led a repatriation movement. They petitioned the Mexican government to restore their citizenship. By the late 1950s they had attracted the attention of a Mexican consul in Macau, and repatriation became a real possibility. In 1960 Dolores Campoy Wong Fang and her three sons became Mexicans again, and they returned to their former hometown in Sonora after almost thirty years of being Chinese.

Our racial, ethnic, and religious identities are complicated things, and they don't always hold still. I believe that Lynn Norment, Allyson Hobbs, and many others who believe in the passing trope have become transfixed by a particular structure of racial categories. A is

Black, B is Jewish, C is Chinese, and so must be all of the members of their respective families and kin groups. And so must they remain throughout their lives, or they are being untrue. People must necessarily live according to the way we have set up the category structure. When we believe that, we grant those categories teleological power: the power to compel perception, belief, practice, history, even truth. We fail then to perceive the ways that individuals actually navigate their complex and contingent lives.

Karina was a pan-Soviet citizen, a German, a Russian, and now a European. The Bongas began the nineteenth century as Black people and ended it as Whites and Indians. Jean Toomer was a more or less raceless, privileged young man, then an African American, then not, and finally a person who sought (possibly unsuccessfully, depending on how one views these things) to transcend race. Otaka Yoshiko / Li Xianglan / Shirley Yamaguchi was the same person, whether she was at that moment Chinese or Japanese American or Japanese—and she was genuinely each of those by turns. The Khazars went shopping for a religion in the ninth century and ended up, after many historical twists and turns, becoming the ancestors of the Eastern European Jews. Mexican women became Chinese wives, and then some of them became Mexicans again. The core and consciousness of each of these people remained the same, but as their circumstances, ambitions, and options changed, their identities changed too. All of them, for their different reasons and in their different ways, were shape shifters.

The Shape of This Volume

The authors whose work appears in this book are exploring the phenomenon of shape shifting in several contexts and over many centuries. In this, together they are doing world history.

The chapters in part 1 reflect identities that change in response to changes in racial context. Ryan Abrecht takes us to ancient Rome and China in "Places of Possibility: Shape Shifting in the Roman and Chinese Borderlands." He posits that the borderlands of empires are places where shape shifting often occurs. In the Rhineland on the northeastern edge of the Roman Empire, early in the first century

CE, Arminius shifted from Cherusci to Roman and became a soldier and minor noble of some accomplishment, then moved his identity and loyalty back across the Rhine, rejoined his father's people, and drove the Romans out of his homeland. His reward in history was great: Germans remember him as Hermann, the progenitor of the German nation.[56] Other inhabitants of the Roman borderlands were able to make similar shifts in identity, but some, like Italicus, were stamped too deeply with the culture of Rome to repeat Arminius's feat. Abrecht compares such Roman/border people transformations to those that occurred between Chinese and Xiongnu in the northern borderlands during the Han dynasty.

Colleen C. Ho takes rather a different tack in chapter 3, "Rabban Ṣauma: A Medieval Eurasian Shape Shifter." Ṣauma and his friend Mark were thirteenth-century Ongut Turkish Christians who were born in Khanbalik (modern Beijing) and who made a pilgrimage to the Middle East. There Mark ultimately became patriarch of the Nestorian Christian Church and sent Ṣauma as his ambassador to the courts of Europe. Consider: these two Central Asian–descended Turks, born in the capital of the Chinese branch of the Mongol Empire, became religious and political leaders in the Persian branch of the Mongol Empire, and one of them met with the leaders of Europe. Were they Onguts? Chinese? Mongols? Persians? They spoke all those languages, lived in all those places, and inhabited all those identities in turn. But the identity—the ultimate loyalty—that screams out from their lives, according to Ho, is "Christian."

In chapter 4, "From *Fan Gui* to Friend: American Chinese, Social Identity, and the Quest for Subjectivity," David Torres-Rouff explores the shifting identities of immigrants from southeastern China to Los Angeles in the second half of the nineteenth century. He explores the various institutions through which these immigrants pursued group identity. He describes the transformation that occurred in Chinese racial sensibilities: In their country of origin, they were sharply divided between Sze Yup (Cantonese speakers) and Hakka, a despised and segregated minority people. In California, these two very different peoples made common cause in self-defense against discrimination from

White Americans, and gradually they all became Chinese (though not yet Chinese Americans).

In "Becoming Mixed Race: Northern California and the Production of Multiracial Identities," Alyssa Newman explores the multiracializing dynamic that operates in a subregion of Northern California that demographers have designated as the "multiracial belt." She finds that people who come to this subregion from other parts of the United States often find that their racial identity changes there. Because multiraciality is an oft-articulated option in this zone, people who saw themselves and were seen by others as monoracial in other parts of the country here identify themselves and are perceived as multiracial.

Angelica Pesarini tells the heart-wrenching stories of Bruna and Isabella in chapter 6, "'You Are the Shame of the Race': Dynamics of Pain, Shame, and Violence in Shape Shifting Processes." Both are mixed race women with East African mothers and Italian colonizer fathers. The simple version of the story is that such people were viewed as White in Somalia and Eritrea and therefore not eligible to be full, unencumbered members of the local society. When they went to Italy they were viewed as Black and therefore not eligible to be members of Italian society. Both women's stories are more complicated than that simple formulation, with many twists and difficulties and no small amounts of pain, shame, and rejection. Pesarini enunciates the idea of "color strategies" to highlight how these women negotiated places for themselves in hostile racial systems. As these women shift back and forth between societies and between identities, sometimes there is an element of choice in each woman's social placement, and sometimes the women are utterly forced to take a social place that they do not feel fits.

Part 2 describes people whose shape shifting was primarily a matter of personal choice among an established array of options.

William Leidesdorff is the subject of chapter 7, by Laura Moore. Born in St. Croix to a White father and part-Black mother, Leidesdorff became a ship captain and sailed to many ports in North America, the Caribbean, and South America. By the 1840s he had settled in Yerba Buena, the Spanish town that would soon become San Francisco. Now a White man, Leidesdorff became one of the new city's leading citizens. Moore analyzes the kinds of places and occupations that made his racial shape shifting possible. Saluted at his death as a White civic leader, Leidesdorff soon came under a hail of abuse as an imposter when the complexity of his racial ancestry was discovered. Many accounts in succeeding decades portrayed him as one of those tragic mulattoes that so fascinate Allyson Hobbs.

In chapter 8 Paul Barba examines the life of Peter Pitchlynn, a man who lived both as a Choctaw and as a White man, who defended his Indian nation against Whites who would degrade them, yet who thought other, more westerly Indians to be savages and was convinced of the inferiority of African Americans—indeed, who owned slaves himself. Together, chapters 7 and 8 tell us much about the evolving racial system of the United States in the nineteenth century and the gradual hardening of racial lines.

In chapter 9, "Half-Butterfly, Half-Caste," theater historian Rena Heinrich unfolds the life and identities of Sadakichi Hartmann through the plays he wrote and produced. Hartmann enunciated a more subtle Japanese Western love story—in his life and in his unpublished play "Osadda's Revenge"—than Puccini, John Luther Long, or David Belasco, before any of them brought Madame Butterfly to the page or the stage. Most important, he brought the voice of the mixed race child to the fore. Hartmann's parentage was Japanese and German; his upbringing and personal culture were unequivocally German; but the American public read his Germanness as Japaneseness. Over the course of his career, Hartmann took on many names and many identities and produced vast quantities of writing and art. Heinrich weaves together all these strands of a remarkable life as she, like Hartmann, fights the erasure of the hapa voice.

In "Shape Shifting in the Transpacific Borderlands," Maria Jose Plascencia and George J. Sánchez unpack the particular Japanese subpopulation that is fascinated by all things Chicano and that, indeed, identifies with Chicano culture so much that its members regard themselves as Chicanos. The Japanese who call themselves Chicanos occupy a similar social position vis-à-vis Japanese society at large as do Mexican

Americans vis-à-vis American society, and they adopt Chicano cultural styles in order to express their identification.

In chapter 11, "Betwixt and Between: A Personal Odyssey through the Twilight Zone," G. Reginald Daniel, one of our foremost racial theorists, takes us on a journey that is personal, sociological, and historical. He uses his own biography as a racially complicated person brought up in a binary, segregated society and struggling at first to find a racial identity that fit both his understanding of himself and the labels that others placed on him to show us the nuts and bolts of racial choosing. His essay takes us on a tour of the last two-thirds of a century of America's racial history from the point of view of a person who is betwixt and between monoracial categories and imperatives. He argues eloquently that monoraciality is the chief prop to White privilege. Moreover, he posits affirming not merely multiraciality as a reflection of the multiplicity of our ancestral backgrounds but also "metaraciality" grounded in a more inclusive, universal, or human self that transcends questions of racial, cultural, or any other specificity as a critical part of moving beyond the racial impasse of our troubled society.

Chapter 12, "Shape Shifting into Blackness in the Post–Civil Rights Era," takes up the notorious case of Rachel Dolezal, a woman of White parentage but Black sympathies who changed her identity from White to Black for many years, only to be exposed and called a fraud by many armchair observers. Here Margaret Hunter seeks not to judge Dolezal but to use her case and other material to posit an analytical framework for understanding political Blackness, intellectual Blackness, and cultural Blackness as three different expressions of Black American identity. Each may be expressed by Black people or by people who do not have Black ancestry, with different implications in each case.

Sometimes it is outside forces that compel a change of racial identity. In "Mudrooroo: Aboriginal No More?" (chapter 13) I examine the life and career of Colin Johnson / Mudrooroo, for decades the foremost literary figure in Aboriginal Australia and a leader in the Aboriginal movement of the 1970s to 1980s. After living for fifty-eight years as an Aboriginal man, he was at the height of his fame and influence when outside actors came to cast doubt upon his Aboriginality. In the scandal that ensued, Mudrooroo was compelled by others, some Aboriginal but most not, to give up his claim to an Aboriginal identity. In the end he disappeared from Australian public life. And then, decades later, he came back from exile to reclaim his Aboriginality.

It is our hope that these several stories of racial identity change in many time periods and in many geographical and social contexts may lead us toward an understanding of how it is that such identities are constructed and reconstructed as need be.

Notes

Thanks are due to a number of people. The students in my course Interracial Intimacy over the years at the University of California, Santa Barbara, and at International Christian University in Tokyo, where I taught in 2014 and where I first drafted this article, have been patient with me as I have tried to work through many of these ideas. I developed them further in presentations to the Mixed Heritage Students Conference at UCLA in April 2015; the Collegium for African American Research in Liverpool in June 2015; the New Challenges on Intermarriage and Mixedness in Europe and Beyond in Paris in November 2015; the Shape Shifters Conference at UC Santa Barbara in March 2016; the National Association for Ethnic Studies in San Francisco in March 2017; and public lectures at Australian National University in July 2016 and the University of Western Australia and Griffith University in August 2016. I am grateful to my hosts and fellow participants on all these occasions as they have helped me move my ideas along. Among the many people who have helped me think through these issues are (and I apologize to those whom I may have failed to name specifically here) Reg Daniel, Maria Root, Ingrid Dineen-Wimberly, Lily Anne Welty Tamai, Kip Fulbeck, Teresa Williams-León, Jeffrey Moniz, Matt Kester, Rudy Guevarra, Isaiah Walker, Becky King-O'Riain, Miri Song, Cindy Nakashima, Minelle Mahtani, Patrick Miller, Christine Su, Laurie Mengel, Stephen Murphy-Shigematsu, Bill Wetherall, Beth DePalma Digeser, Fanshen Cox DiGiovanni, Julia Maria Schiavone Camacho, Mattie Harper, Circe Sturm, Evelyn Alsultany, Luke Roberts, Adrienne Edgar, Sameer Pandya, Andrés Reséndez, and Roxanne Houmann. At ICU I received encouragement, leads, and intellectual stimulation from my colleagues, including especially Peter Nosco, Bill Steele, John Maher, Shaun Malarney, Chris Bondy, Kimie Takahashi, Mayumi Uno, and Bev Curran. Among the people who contributed to my thinking in

Australia are Ann McGrath (my generous host), Malcolm Allbrook, Cressida Fforde, Bill Fogarty, Karen Fox, Maria Haenga-Collins, Barry Higman, Geoff Hunt, Juliette Milner-Thornton, Carroll Pursell, Peter Read, Carolyn Strange, and Angela Woollacott. Anna Lucky Louise Spickard, Daniel Spickard, Naomi Kelly, and Elsa Martinez have endured more hours of hearing about this stuff than any family should have to, and for that I am very grateful. My other debts will be clear from the notes.

1. Places to begin on the history of racial ideas are Stephen Jay Gould, *The Mismeasure of Man*, rev. ed. (New York: Norton, 1996); Jonathan Marks, *Human Biodiversity: Genes, Race, and History* (New York: Aldine DeGruyter, 1995); Robert Wald Sussman, *The Myth of Race: The Troubling History of an Unscientific Idea* (Cambridge MA: Harvard University Press, 2014); William H. Tucker, *The Science and Politics of Racial Research* (Urbana: University of Illinois Press, 1996).

2. Lynn Norment, "Who's Black and Who's Not? New Ethnicity Raises Provocative Questions about Racial Identity," *Ebony* 45, no. 5 (March 1990): 134–39. The interested reader can find out more about these actors on their websites, IMDb, and Wikipedia pages. Jasmine Guy: http://iamjasmineguy.com/; http://www.imdb.com/name/nm0004982/?ref_=fn_al_nm_1; http://en.wikipedia.org/wiki/Jasmine_Guy.

3. Norment, "Who's Black," 134.

4. Jennifer Beals: http://www.jennifer-beals.com/; http://www.imdb.com/name/nm0000884/; http://en.wikipedia.org/wiki/Jennifer_Beals. Tai Babilonia: http://priscillagilman.com/2014/01/the-experience-of-the-butterfly-a-conversation-with-tai-babilonia/; http://en.wikipedia.org/wiki/Tai_Babilonia. Rae Dawn Chong: http://www.imdb.com/name/nm0001044/; n.wikipedia.org/wiki/Rae_Dawn_Chong; Paul E. Pratt, "Growing Up a Chong," *Asian Week*, November 18, 2005. Lenny Kravitz: http://www.lennykravitz.com/; http://www.imdb.com/name/nm0005107/; http://en.wikipedia.org/wiki/Lenny_Kravitz. Paula Abdul: http://www.paulaabdul.com/; http://www.paula-abdul.net/; http://en.wikipedia.org/wiki/Paula_Abdul. All retrieved October 18, 2014.

5. See, for example, G. Reginald Daniel, *Race and Multiraciality in Brazil and the United States: Converging Paths?* (University Park: Pennsylvania State University Press, 2006); Frank Dikötter, *The Discourse of Race in Modern China* (Stanford CA: Stanford University Press, 1992); Adrienne Edgar, *Tribal Nation: The Making of Soviet Turkmenistan* (Princeton NJ: Princeton University Press, 2004); Camilla Fojas, Rudy P. Guevarra Jr., and Nitasha Sharma, eds., *Beyond Ethnicity: New Politics of Race in Hawaiʻi* (Honolulu: University of Hawaiʻi Press, 2017); George M. Fredrickson, *White Supremacy: A Comparative Study*

of American and South African History (New York: Oxford University Press, 1981); Basak Ince, *Citizenship and Identity in Turkey: From Atatürk's Republic to the Present Day* (London: Tauris, 2012); Rebecca Chiyoko King-O'Riain et al., eds., *Global Mixed Race* (New York: New York University Press, 2014); Jeffrey Lesser, *Negotiating National Identity: Immigrants, Minorities, and the Struggle for Ethnicity in Brazil* (Durham NC: Duke University Press, 1999); Anthony W. Marx, *Making Race and Nation: A Comparison of the United States, South Africa, and Brazil* (Cambridge: Cambridge University Press, 1998); Juliette Milner-Thornton, *The Long Shadow of the British Empire: The Ongoing Legacies of Race and Class in Zambia* (London: Palgrave Macmillan, 2012); T. Dunbar Moodie, *The Rise of Afrikanerdom: Power, Apartheid, and the Afrikaner Civil Religion* (Berkeley: University of California Press, 1980); Zarine Rocha and Farida Fozdar, eds., *Mixed Race in Asia* (New York: Routledge, 2017); Paul Spickard, "Ethnicity," in *Oxford Bibliographies in Sociology*, ed. Jeff Manza (New York: Oxford University Press, 2013), 1–31; Paul Spickard, ed., *Race and Nation: Ethnic Systems in the Modern World* (New York: Routledge, 2005); L. Ayu Saraswati, *Seeing Beauty, Sensing Race in Transnational Indonesia* (Honolulu: University of Hawai'i Press, 2013); Yasuko Takezawa, ed., *Racial Representations in Asia* (Balwyn North, Victoria, Australia: Trans Pacific Press, 2011); Edward E. Telles, *Pigmentocracies: Ethnicity, Race, and Color in Latin America* (Chapel Hill: University of North Carolina Press, 2014); Edward E. Telles, *Race in Another America: The Significance of Skin Color in Brazil* (Princeton NJ: Princeton University Press, 2004); Peter Wade, *Race and Ethnicity in Latin America*, 2nd ed. (London: Pluto Press, 2010).

6. Winthrop D. Jordan, "Historical Origins of the One-Drop Racial Rule in the United States," ed. Paul Spickard, *Journal of Critical Mixed Race Studies* 1, no. 1 (2014): 98–132; Ingrid Dineen-Wimberly, *The Allure of Blackness among Mixed Race Americans, 1862–1916* (Lincoln: University of Nebraska Press, 2019); Paul Spickard, "The Power of Blackness: Mixed Race Leaders and the Monoracial Ideal," in *Racial Thinking in the United States: Uncompleted Independence*, ed. Paul Spickard and G. Reginald Daniel (Notre Dame IN: University of Notre Dame Press, 2004), 103–23; Joel Williamson, *New People: Miscegenation and Mulattoes in the United States*, rev. ed. (Baton Rouge: Louisiana State University Press, 1995); F. James Davis, *Who Is Black? One Nation's Definition* (University Park: Pennsylvania State University Press, 1992).

7. On the mixed race movement, see Maria P. P. Root, ed., *Racially Mixed People in America* (Newbury Park CA: Sage, 1992); Maria P. P. Root, ed., *The Multiracial Experience: Racial Borders as the New Frontier* (Thousand Oaks CA: Sage, 1995); G. Reginald Daniel, *More Than Black? Multiracial Identity and the New*

Racial Order (Philadelphia: Temple University Press, 2001); Teresa Williams-León and Cynthia Nakashima, eds., *The Sum of Our Parts: Mixed-Heritage Asian Americans* (Philadelphia: Temple University Press, 2001); Jayne O. Ifekwunigwe, ed., *"Mixed Race" Studies: A Reader* (New York: Routledge, 2004); David L. Brunsma, ed., *Mixed Messages: Multiracial Identities in the "Color-Blind" Era* (Denver: Lynne Rienner, 2005); Kim M. Williams, *Check One or More: Civil Rights in Multiracial America* (Ann Arbor: University of Michigan Press, 2006); Kimberly McClain DaCosta, *Making Multiracials: State, Family, and Market in the Redrawing of the Color Line* (Stanford CA: Stanford University Press, 2007); Stephen Murphy-Shigematsu, *When Half Is Whole: Multiethnic Asian American Identities* (Stanford CA: Stanford University Press, 2012); Greg Carter, *The United States of the United Races: A Utopian History of Racial Mixing* (New York: New York University Press, 2013); Joanne L. Rondilla, Rudy P. Guevarra, and Paul Spickard, eds., *Red and Yellow, Black and Brown: Decentering Whiteness in Mixed Race Studies* (New Brunswick NJ: Rutgers University Press, 2015); G. Reginald Daniel, Laura Kina, Wei-Ming Dariotis, and Camilla Fojas, "Emerging Paradigms in Critical Mixed Race Studies," *Journal of Critical Mixed Race Studies* 1, no. 1 (2014).

8. See, for example, William Wells Brown, *Clotel, or, The President's Daughter: A Narrative of Slave Life in the United States* (1853; repr., Boston: Bedford / St. Martin's, 2000); Frank J. Webb, *The Garies and Their Friends* (1857; repr., Baltimore MD: Johns Hopkins University Press, 1997); William Dean Howells, *An Imperative Duty* (New York: Harper, 1891); Frances E. W. Harper, *Iola LeRoy or, Shadows Uplifted* (Philadelphia: Garrigues Brothers, 1893); Mark Twain, *Pudd'nhead Wilson* (London: Chatto and Windus, 1894); Charles W. Chesnutt, *The House Behind the Cedars* (Boston: Houghton Mifflin, 1900); Pauline Hopkins, *Hagar's Daughter, a Story of Southern Caste Prejudice*, in *The Magazine Novels of Pauline Hopkins* (1901–2; repr., New York: Oxford University Press, 1988), 1–284; Sutton E. Griggs, *The Hindered Hand: or, The Reign of the Repressionist* (Nashville: Orion, 1905); James Weldon Johnson, *The Autobiography of an Ex-Colored Man* (Boston: Shearman, French, 1912); Walter White, *Flight* (New York: Knopf, 1926); Nella Larsen, *Quicksand* (New York: Knopf, 1928); Jessie Fauset, *Plum Bun* (New York: Stokes, 1929); Nella Larsen, *Passing* (New York: Knopf, 1929); George S. Schuyler, *Black No More* (New York: Macauley, 1931); Dorothy Lee Dickens, *Black on the Rainbow* (New York: Pageant, 1952); Reba Lee [pseud.], *I Passed for White* (New York: Longmans, Green, 1955); John Howard Griffin, *Black Like Me* (Boston: Houghton Mifflin, 1961); Grace Halsell, *Soul Sister* (New York: World, 1969); Walter Mosley, *Devil in a Blue Dress* (New York: Norton, 1990); Dorothy West, *The*

Wedding (New York: Doubleday, 1995); Danzy Senna, *Caucasia* (New York: Riverhead, 1998); Philip Roth, *The Human Stain* (Boston: Houghton Mifflin, 2000); Anita Reynolds, *American Cocktail: A "Colored Girl" in the World*, ed. George Hutchinson (Cambridge MA: Harvard University Press, 2014). For literary analysis, see, for example, Elaine K. Ginsburg, *Passing and the Fictions of Identity* (Durham NC: Duke University Press, 1995); Werner Sollors, *Neither Black nor White Yet Both: Thematic Explorations of Interracial Literature* (New York: Oxford University Press, 1997); Juda Bennett, *The Passing Figure: Racial Confusion in Modern Literature* (New York: Peter Lang, 1998); Gayle Wald, *Crossing the Line: Racial Passing in Twentieth-Century U.S. Literature and Culture* (Durham NC: Duke University Press, 2000); M. Giulia Fabi, *Passing and the Rise of the African American Novel* (Urbana: University of Illinois Press, 2003); Mar Gallego, ed., *Passing Novels in the Harlem Renaissance: Identity Politics and Textual Strategies* (Münster, Germany: LIT Verlag, 2003); Steven J. Belluscio, *To Be Suddenly White: Literary Realism and Racial Passing* (Columbia: University of Missouri Press, 2006); Baz Dreisinger, *Near Black: White-to-Black Passing in American Culture* (Amherst: University of Massachusetts Press, 2008); Susan Prothro Wright and Ernestine Pickens Glass, eds., *Passing in the Works of Charles W. Chesnutt* (Jackson: University Press of Mississippi, 2010); Kathleen Pfeiffer, *Race Passing and American Individualism* (Amherst: University of Massachusetts Press, 2010); Teresa C. Zackodnick, *The Mulatta and the Politics of Race* (Jackson: University Press of Mississippi, 2010); Sinéad Moynihan, *Passing into the Present: Contemporary American Fiction of Racial and Gender Passing* (Manchester, UK: Manchester University Press, 2011); Michele Elam, *The Souls of Mixed Folks: Race, Politics, and Aesthetics in the New Millennium* (Stanford CA: Stanford University Press, 2011), 96–124; Sika A. Dagbovic-Mullins, *Crossing B(l)ack: Mixed-Race Identity in Modern American Fiction and Culture* (Knoxville: University of Tennessee Press, 2013); Julie Cary Nerad, ed., *Passing Interest: Racial Passing in U.S. Novels, Memoirs, Television, and Film, 1990–2010* (Albany: SUNY Press, 2014).

9. Edna Ferber, *Show Boat* (1926; repr., New York: Random House, 2014); *Show Boat* (Warner Bros., 1936), dir. James Whale, written by Edna Ferber and Oscar Hammerstein II, starring Irene Dunne, Allan Jones, Charles Winninger, and Paul Robeson; *Show Boat* (Metro-Goldwyn-Mayer, 1951), dir. George Sidney, written by Edna Ferber, Oscar Hammerstein II, Jerome Kern, and John Lee Mahin, starring Kathryn Grayson, Ava Gardner, Howard Keel, Marge Champion, and Gower Champion; Fannie Hurst, *Imitation of Life* (New York: Harper, 1933); *Imitation of Life* (Universal Pictures, 1934), dir. John M. Stahl, written by Fannie Hurst and William Hurlburt, starring Claudette

Colbert, Louise Beavers, and Fredi Washington; *Imitation of Life* (Universal Pictures, 1959), dir. Douglas Sirk, written by Fannie Hurst, Eleanore Griffin, and Alan Scott, starring Lana Turner, John Gavin, Sandra Dee, and Juanita Moore; *Pinky* (20th Century Fox, 1949), dir. Elia Kazan, written by Cid Ricketts Sumner, Philip Dunne, and Dudley Nichols, starring Jeanne Craine, Ethel Barrymore, and Ethel Waters; Leilani Nishime, "*The Matrix* Trilogy, Keanu Reeves, and Multiraciality at the End of Time," in *Mixed Race Hollywood*, ed. Mary Beltrán and Camilla Fojas (New York: New York University Press, 2008), 290–310; Leilani Nishime, *Undercover Asian: Multiracial Asian Americans in Visual Culture* (Urbana: University of Illinois Press, 2014); Jane Park, "Virtual Race: The Racially Ambiguous Action Hero in *The Matrix* and *Pitch Black*," in Beltrán and Fojas, *Mixed Race Hollywood*, 182–202; Analee Newitz, "When Will White People Stop Making Movies Like *Avatar*?," http://io9.com/, retrieved October 22, 2014; Mikhail Lyubansky, "The Racial Politics of *Avatar*," *Psychology Today*, December 28, 2009; David Brooks, "The Messiah Complex," *New York Times*, January 7, 2010.

10. See, for example, E. B. Reuter, *Race Mixture* (1931; repr., New York: Negro University Press, 1969), 129–216; Everett V. Stonequist, *The Marginal Man: A Study in Personality and Culture Conflict* (1937; repr., New York: Russell and Russell, 1965), esp. 184–209; Lee, *I Passed for White*; James E. Conyers, "Selected Aspects of the Phenomenon of Negro Passing" (PhD diss., Washington State University, 1962); Erving Goffman, *Stigma: Notes on the Management of Spoiled Identity* (Englewood Cliffs NJ: Prentice-Hall, 1963); John G. Mencke, "Mulattoes and Race Mixture: American Attitudes and Images, 1865–1918" (PhD diss., University of North Carolina, 1976); Judith R. Berzon, *Neither Black nor White: The Mulatto Character in American Fiction* (New York: New York University Press, 1978); Paul Spickard, *Mixed Blood: Intermarriage and Ethnic Identity in Twentieth-Century America* (Madison: University of Wisconsin Press, 1989), 329–39; F. James Davis, *Who Is Black? One Nation's Definition* (University Park: Pennsylvania State University Press, 1991); Shirlee Taylor Haizlip, *The Sweeter the Juice: A Family Memoir in Black and White* (New York: Free Press, 1995); Teresa Kay Williams, "Raceing and Being Raced: The Critical Interrogation of 'Passing,'" *Amerasia Journal* 23, no. 1 (1997): 61–65; Gregory Howard Williams, *Life on the Color Line: The True Story of a White Boy Who Discovered He Was Black* (New York: Dutton, 1995); Edward Ball, *Slaves in the Family* (New York: Ballantine, 1999); Henry Wiencek, *The Hairstons: An American Family in Black and White* (New York: St. Martin's, 1999); Lawrence Otis Graham, *Our Kind of People: Inside America's Black Upper Class* (New York: Harper, 1999), 376–94; Maria C. Sanchez, *Passing: Identity and*

Interpretation in Sexuality, Race, and Religion (New York: New York University Press, 2001); Heidi Ardizzone and Earl Lewis, *Love on Trial: An American Scandal in Black and White* (New York: Norton, 2001); James M. O'Toole, *Passing for White: Race, Religion, and the Healy Family, 1820–1920* (Amherst: University of Massachusetts Press, 2002); Brooke Kroeger, *Passing: When People Can't Be Who They Are* (New York: Public Affairs, 2003); Beltrán and Fojas, *Mixed Race Hollywood*; Dreisinger, *Near Black*; Gerald Horne, *The Color of Fascism: Lawrence Dennis, Racial Passing, and the Rise of Right-Wing Extremism in the United States* (New York: New York University Press, 2006); Bliss Broyard, *One Drop: My Father's Hidden Life—a Story of Race and Family Secrets* (New York: Back Bay Books, 2007); Heidi Ardizzone, *An Illuminated Life: Bella da Costa Greene's Journey from Prejudice to Privilege* (New York: Norton, 2007); Martha A. Sandweiss, *Passing Strange: A Gilded Age Tale of Love and Deception across the Color Line* (New York: Penguin, 2009); Elizabeth M. Smith-Pryor, *Property Rites: The Rhinelander Trial, Passing, and the Protection of Whiteness* (Chapel Hill: University of North Carolina Press, 2009); Daniel Sharfstein, *The Invisible Line: Three American Families and the Secret History of Race in America* (New York: Penguin, 2011); Nadine Ehlers, *Racial Imperatives: Discipline, Performativity, and Struggles against Subjection* (Bloomington: Indiana University Press, 2012); Marcia Alesan Dawkins, *Clearly Invisible: Racial Passing and the Color of Cultural Diversity* (Waco TX: Baylor University Press, 2012); Angela Onwuachi-Willig, *According to Our Hearts: "Rhinelander v. Rhinelander" and the Law of the Multiracial Family* (New Haven CT: Yale University Press, 2013); Mika E. Thornburg, "Passing, Covering, and Disclosing in Multiracial Asian America" (BA honors thesis, University of California, Santa Barbara, 2013); Matthew Pratt Guterl, *Seeing Race in Modern America* (Chapel Hill: University of North Carolina Press, 2013), 166–81; Penelope Bullock, "The Mulatto in American Fiction," *Phylon* 6 (1945): 78–82; James E. Conyers, "Negro Passing: To Pass or Not to Pass," *Phylon* 24 (1963): 215–23; Sterling A. Brown, "Negro Characters as Seen by White Authors," in *Dark Symphony: The Negro in American Literature*, ed. James A. Emanuel and Theodore L. Gross (New York: Free Press, 1968), 157–63; "The Vanishing Mulatto," *Opportunity* 3 (1925): 291; Herbert Asbury, "Who Is a Negro?," *Negro Digest*, October 1946, 3–11; John Hewlett, "Four Who Are Passing," *Negro Digest*, April 1949, 8–13; Nanette Kutner, "Women Who Pass for White," *Negro Digest*, August 1949, 43–46; "White by Day . . . Negro by Night," *Ebony*, April 1952, 31–36; Cotye Murdock, "What Happened to the 'Lost Boundaries' Family," *Ebony*, August 1952, 52–66; Gladys Stevens, "My Father Passed for White," *Ebony*, April 1957, 41–46; "I Lived Two Lives for

Thirty Years," *Ebony*, December 1958, 156–62; "Why I Never Want to Pass," *Negro Digest*, June 1959, 49–54.

11. Raymond Arsenault, "Shades of White," review of *The Invisible Line*, by Daniel Sharfstein, *New York Times*, February 25, 2011, Sunday Book Review.

12. Hobbs's book is a pretty good one. She tells a good story, she has done some archival research, and she has a sympathetic spirit, even if she does not think all that clearly about her subject. Allyson Hobbs, *A Chosen Exile: A History of Racial Passing in American Life* (Cambridge MA: Harvard University Press, 2014). Another recent book that purports to explain passing but that is, frankly, incomprehensible is Dawkins, *Clearly Invisible*.

13. William L. Andrews, "Charles W. Chesnutt," in *African American Writers*, ed. Valerie Smith, 2nd ed. (New York: Scribner's, 2001), 1:111–22; Robert P. Sedlack, "The Evolution of Charles Chesnutt's *The House Behind the Cedars*," *CLA Journal* 19, no. 2 (1975): 125–35.

14. Anatole Broyard, *Kafka Was the Rage: A Greenwich Village Memoir* (New York: Vintage, 1997); Henry Louis Gates Jr., "The Passing of Anatole Broyard," in *Thirteen Ways of Looking at a Black Man* (New York: Random House, 1997), 180–214; Broyard, *One Drop*; "Broyard, Anatole," *American National Biography Online*, http://www.anb.org/articles/16/16-03544.html, retrieved October 22, 2014. Gates's assertion that the reason Broyard never wrote the novel he hoped to write was because he was crippled by his racial imposture is scurrilous.

15. Cynthia Nakashima, "An Invisible Monster: The Creation and Denial of Mixed-Race People in America," in Root, *Racially Mixed People*, 162–78.

16. France Winddance Twine, "Brown Skinned White Girls: Class, Culture, and the Construction of White Identity in Suburban Communities," *Gender, Place, and Culture* 3, no. 2 (1996): 205–24; Christopher John Farley, *Introducing Halle Berry* (New York: Pocket Books, 2002); http://www.halleberryfan.com/; http://www.imdb.com/name/nm0000932/; http://en.wikipedia.org/wiki/Halle_Berry, retrieved October 19, 2014; Susan Donaldson James, "Halle Berry Cites 'One-Drop' Rule in Battle Over Whether Her Daughter Is Black or White," *ABC News—Good Morning America*, February 9, 2011; Sonia Poulton, "I Feel Proud to Call My Daughter Mixed-Race—So Should Halle Berry!," *Daily Mail* (UK), February 10, 2011.

17. http://www.vindiesel.com/; http://www.imdb.com/name/nm0004874/; http://en.wikipedia.org/wiki/Vin_Diesel. Retrieved October 19, 2014.

18. In cultural studies quarters, Bhabha often gets credit for thinking this stuff up, but in fact Anzaldúa, Root, and Daniel preceded him in time and thought the issue through much more clearly. See Homi K. Bhabha, *The Location of*

Culture (London: Routledge, 1994), 36–39 and passim; Gloria Anzaldúa, *Borderlands / La Frontera: The New Mestiza Consciousness* (San Francisco: Aunt Lute Books, 1987); Maria P. P. Root, "Within, Between, and Beyond Race," in Root, *Racially Mixed People*, 3–11; G. Reginald Daniel, "Beyond Black and White: The New Multiracial Consciousness," in Root, *Racially Mixed People*, 333–41. Jayne O. Ifekwunigwe understood this when she included Root, Daniel, and forty-one other theorists but not Bhabha in her canonical *"Mixed Race" Studies: A Reader* (London: Routledge, 2004). Others who followed (and sometimes contested) Bhabha's cultural studies line on hybridity include Robert J. C. Young, *Colonial Desire: Hybridity in Theory, Culture and Race* (London: Routledge, 1995); Pnina Werbner and Tariq Modood, eds., *Debating Cultural Hybridity: Multi-cultural Identities and the Politics of Antiracism* (London: Zed, 1997); Anthony Easthope, "Homi Bhabha, Hybridity and Identity, or Derrida versus Lacan," *Hungarian Journal of English and American Studies* 4, no. 1–2 (1998): 145–51; Ien Ang, *On Not Speaking Chinese: Living between Asia and the West* (London: Routledge, 2001); Jan Nederveen Pieterse, *Globalization and Culture: Global Mélange* (Lanham MD: Rowman and Littlefield, 2003); Haj Yazdiha, "Conceptualizing Hybridity: Deconstructing Boundaries through the Hybrid," *Foundations* 1, no. 1 (2010): 31–38; among many others. Root's and Daniel's line of thinking on racial and identity complexity is analytically much sharper and conceptually richer and includes most of the books and articles that appear in the notes to this chapter.

19. G. Reginald Daniel, "Passers and Pluralists: Subverting the Racial Divide," in Root, *Racially Mixed People*, 91–107; and Maria P. P. Root, "A Bill of Rights for Racially Mixed People," in Root, *The Multiracial Experience*, 3–14.

20. Jeffrey Moniz does this with the fluid concept of the "midaltern" in Moniz and Paul Spickard, "Carving Out a Middle Ground: Making Race in Hawai'i," in Spickard, *Race in Mind* (Notre Dame IN: University of Notre Dame Press, 2015), 261–90.

21. Rebecca Chiyoko King-O'Riain, "Plastic Paddies, Citizenship Tourists, and Migrants in Ireland: Will the 'Real' Irish Please Stand Up?," paper presented to the Collegium for African American Research, Liverpool, June 25, 2015.

22. King-O'Riain, "Plastic Paddies"; Everett V. Stonequist, *The Marginal Man: A Study in Personality and Culture Conflict* (New York: Charles Scribner's Sons, 1937); Edward Byron Reuter, *The Mulatto in the United States* (1918; repr., New York: Negro Universities Press, 1969).

23. Wendy D. Roth does an admirable job of laying out the theoretical issues involved in changes of individuals' racial perceptions and identities as they

change contexts in *Race Migrations: Latinos and the Cultural Transformation of Race* (Stanford CA: Stanford University Press, 2012). See also Spickard, *Race and Nation*; King-O'Riain et al., *Global Mixed Race*.

24. Richard D. Alba, *Italian Americans* (Englewood Cliffs NJ: Prentice-Hall, 1985); John W. Briggs, *An Italian Passage: Immigrants to Three American Cities, 1890–1930* (New Haven CT: Yale University Press, 1978); Dino Cinel, *From Italy to San Francisco* (Stanford CA: Stanford University Press, 1982); Francesco Cordasco and Eugene Bucchioni, eds., *The Italians: Social Backgrounds of an American Group* (Clifton NJ: Augustus M. Kelley, 1974); Alexander DeConde, *Half Bitter, Half Sweet: An Excursion into Italian-American History* (New York: Scribner's, 1971); Donna R. Gabaccia, *Italy's Many Diasporas* (New York: Routledge, 2003); Donna R. Gabaccia, *From Sicily to Elizabeth Street: Housing and Social Change Among Italian Immigrants, 1880–1930* (Albany: SUNY Press, 1984); Thomas A. Guglielmo, *White on Arrival: Italians, Race, Color, and Power in Chicago, 1890–1945* (New York: Oxford University Press, 2003); Humbert S. Nelli, *From Immigrants to Ethnics: The Italian Americans* (New York: Oxford University Press, 1983); Virginia Yans-McLaughlin, *Family and Community: Italian Immigrants in Buffalo, 1880–1920* (Ithaca NY: Cornell University Press, 1978).

25. Michael A. Gomez, *Exchanging Our Country Marks: The Transformation of African Identities in the Colonial and Antebellum South* (Chapel Hill: University of North Carolina Press, 1998); Douglas B. Chambers, "'My Own Nation': Igbo Exiles in the Diaspora," in *Routes to Slavery: Direction, Ethnicity and Mortality in the Transatlantic Slave Trade*, ed. David Eltis and David Richardson (London: Frank Cass, 1997), 72–97; Peter Caron, "'Of a Nation Which Others Do Not Understand': Bambara Slaves and African Ethnicity in Colonial Louisiana, 1718–60," in Eltis and Richardson, *Routes to Slavery*, 98–121; "The Cultural Implications of the Atlantic Slave Trade: African Regional Origins, American Destinations and New World Developments," in Eltis and Richardson, *Routes to Slavery*, 122–45; Ira Berlin, "From Creole to African: Atlantic Creoles and the Origins of African-American Society in Mainland North America," *William and Mary Quarterly*, 3rd ser., 53, no. 2 (1996): 251–88; David Northrup, "Igbo Myth and Myth Igbo: Culture and Ethnicity in the Atlantic World, 1600–1850," *Slavery and Abolition* 21, no. 3 (December 2000): 1–20; Allan Kulikoff, "The Origins of Afro-American Society in Tidewater Maryland and Virginia, 1700–1790," *William and Mary Quarterly*, 3rd ser., 35, no. 2 (1978): 226–59; Gwendolyn Midlo Hall, *Slavery and African Ethnicities in the Americas* (Chapel Hill: University of North Carolina Press, 2006); Yen Le Espiritu, *Asian American*

Panethnicity (Philadelphia: Temple University Press, 1992); Michael Omi and Howard Winant, *Racial Formation in the United States*, 3rd ed. (New York: Routledge, 2014).

26. I have told Karina's story before in an essay I wrote with Miriam Nandi, "The Curious Career of the One-Drop Rule: Multiraciality and Membership in Germany Today," in King-O'Riain et al., *Global Mixed Race*, 188–212. I interviewed Karina in Münster, Germany, and we exchanged several emails. A version of her story appeared on the website of the Brooklyn Historical Society's Crossing Borders, Bridging Generations Project, http://cbbg .brooklynhistory.org/.

27. Fred C. Koch, *The Volga Germans: In Russia and the Americas* (College Park: Pennsylvania State University Press, 1977); James W. Long, *The Volga Germans: From Privileged to Oppressed* (Lincoln: University of Nebraska Press, 1988).

28. Mattie Marie Harper, "French Africans in Ojibwe Country: Negotiating Marriage, Identity and Race, 1780–1890" (PhD diss., University of California, Berkeley, 2012).

29. Peter Wade, *Blackness and Race Mixture: The Dynamics of Racial Identity in Colombia* (Baltimore MD: Johns Hopkins University Press, 1993); Telles, *Pigmentocracies*.

30. Hanni, email to the author, July 31, 2015. Hanni and I have had many conversations about this.

31. There are several other figures who might appear in this section, for example:
    William Ellis / Guillermo Eliseo, sometimes Black American and sometimes White Mexican; see Karl Jacoby, *The Strange Career of William Ellis: The Texas Slave Who Became a Mexican Millionaire* (New York: Norton, 2016). I am grateful to Professor Jacoby for the gift of a prepublication copy.
    Emilio Kosterlitzky, by turns Russian, German, Mexican, Apache, and American; see Samuel Truett, "Transnational Warrior: Emilio Kosterlitzky and the Transformation of the U.S.-Mexico Borderlands," in *Transnational Crossroads: Remapping U.S.-Mexico Borderlands History*, ed. Samuel Truett and Elliott Young (Durham NC: Duke University Press, 2004), 241–70.
    Archduke Wilhelm von Habsburg, born an Austrian noble, took on the task of becoming the first king of Ukraine as the Habsburg Empire fell apart. During World War II, when Nazi Germany took over Ukraine, he might have stood on his Germanic heritage and avoided imprisonment, but he chose to stand with Ukraine; ultimately, he died in a Soviet prison after the war. Wilhelm's older brother Karl Albrecht von Habsburg aspired to be king of Poland and died in a Nazi prison for his adopted allegiance.

See Timothy Snyder, *The Red Prince: The Secret Lives of a Habsburg Archduke* (New York: Basic Books, 2008).

32. Pinchback's historian is Ingrid Dineen-Wimberly, who has taught me much about him and about race in American history. This analysis is based on her book *The Allure of Blackness in Mixed-Race America*, as well as some research of my own. Some of the language in these paragraphs derives from an essay Ingrid and I wrote together, "It's Not That Simple: Multiraciality, Models, and Social Hierarchy," in *Multiracial Americans and Social Class*, ed. Kathleen Korgen (New York: Routledge, 2010), 205–21. The quotation is from Jean Toomer, draft autobiography, p. 30, JWJ MSS series 1, box 18, folder 493, Beinecke Library, Yale University. See also James Haskins, *Pinckney Benton Stewart Pinchback* (New York: Macmillan, 1973); James Haskins, *The First Black Governor: Pinckney Benton Stewart Pinchback* (Trenton NJ: Africa World Press, 1996); A. J. Languth, *After Lincoln: How the North Won the Civil War and Lost the Peace* (New York: Simon and Schuster, 2014), 65–80.

33. Sources for this section include John R. Tumpak, *When Swing Was the Thing: Personality Profiles of the Big Band Era* (Milwaukee WI: Marquette University Press, 2008), 176–80; "He Wouldn't Cross the Line," *Life*, September 3, 1951; Herb Jeffries and Cork Proctor, "An Interview with Herb Jeffries," All That Jazz Oral History Project, Oral History Research Center, Library Special Collections Department, University of Nevada, Las Vegas (2009, 55 pp.); Michael K. Johnson, *Hoo-Doo Cowboys and Bronze Buckaroos: Conceptions of the African American West* (Jackson: University Press of Mississippi, 2014); Dennis McLellan, "Herb Jeffrues Dies at 100: Hollywood's First Black Singing Cowboy," *Los Angeles Times*, May 25, 2014.

34. "He's Too Light to Be Negro and Too Known to Be White," *Ebony*, March 1950, 22–26.

35. William Yardley, "Herb Jeffries, 'Bronze Buckaroo' of Song and Screen, Dies at 100 (or So)," *New York Times*, May 26, 2014.

36. Bill Kohlhaase, "Back from the Saddle Again," *Los Angeles Times*, October 2, 1998.

37. Sources for this section include Shelley Stephenson, "'Her Traces Are Found Everywhere': Shanghai, Li Xianglan, and the 'Greater East Asia Film Sphere,'" in *Cinema and Urban Culture in Shanghai, 1922–1943*, ed. Yingjin Zhang (Stanford CA: Stanford University Press, 1999), 225–45; Shelley Stephenson, "A Star by Any Other Name: The (After) Lives of Li Xianglan," *Quarterly Review of Film and Video*, January 1, 2002, 1–13; Masayo Duus, *The Life of Isamu Noguchi: Journey without Borders*, trans. Peter Duus (Princeton NJ: Princeton University Press, 2004); Yiman Wang, "Affective Politics and the

Legend of Yamaguchi Yoshiko / Li Xianglan," in *Sino-Japanese Transcultur-ation: Late Nineteenth Century to the End of the Pacific War*, ed. Richard King, Cody Poulton, and Katsuhiko Endo (Lanham MD: Lexington Books, 2011), 143–66; Faye Yuan Kleeman, *In Transit: The Formation of the Colonial East Asian Cultural Sphere* (Honolulu: University of Hawaiʻi Press, 2014); Yama-guchi Yoshiko and Fujiwara Sakuya, *Fragrant Orchid: The Story of My Early Life*, trans. Chia-ning Chang (Honolulu: University of Hawaiʻi Press, 2015); Michael Baskett, *The Attractive Empire: Transnational Film Culture in Impe-rial Japan* (Honolulu: University of Hawaiʻi Press, 2008). Otaka/Li/Yamagu-chi's life is explored in a novel by Ian Buruma, *The China Lover* (New York: Penguin, 2008).

38. The interested reader can learn about those who went to Japan's then newly acquired island territories in Mark Peattie, *Nan'yo: The Rise and Fall of the Japanese in Micronesia, 1885–1945* (Honolulu: University of Hawaiʻi Press, 1988); and about how Japanese imagined their empire in Michele Mason and Helen Lee, eds., *Reading Colonial Japan: Text, Context, and Critique* (Stan-ford CA: Stanford University Press, 2012). For the particular Chinese con-text, see three volumes edited by Peter Duus, Ramon H. Myers, and Mark R. Peattie, *The Japanese Colonial Empire, 1895–1945* (Princeton NJ: Prince-ton University Press, 1983); *The Japanese Informal Empire, 1895–1937* (Prince-ton NJ: Princeton University Press, 1988); and *The Japanese Wartime Empire, 1931–1945* (Princeton NJ: Princeton University Press, 2010). For insight into the Japanese occupation of Manchuria around the same time as Yamagu-chi Yoshiko, see Kazuko Kuramoto, *Manchurian Legacy: Memoirs of a Japa-nese Colonist* (East Lansing: Michigan State University Press, 2004); Yosano Akiko and Joshua A. Fogel, *Travels in Manchuria and Mongolia* (New York: Columbia University Press, 2001); Katsuei Yuasa, *Kannani and Document in Flames: Two Colonial Japanese Novels*, trans. Mark Driscoll (Durham NC: Duke University Press, 2005).

39. Stephenson, "Star by Any Other Name," 3.

40. Some even claimed other identities for her: Korean, half Russian, Taiwan-ese. She was indeed a shape shifter. Shelley Stephenson is particularly acute on this matter in "Star by Any Other Name": "Li Xianglan was, it seems, many things to many people, and more often than not she was somehow 'theirs'" (7).

41. Japanese audiences learned her name as Ri Koran.

42. On the elder Noguchi, see Amy Sueyoshi's marvelous book, *Queer Compul-sions: Race, Nation, and Sexuality in the Affairs of Yone Noguchi* (Honolulu: University of Hawaiʻi Press, 2012).

43. Two stories from the same era, one of an ethnic Taiwanese and one of an ethnic Manchu, but each exhibiting similar tricultural issues to those of Yamaguchi/Li, are told in Dan Shao, "Princess, Traitor, Soldier, Spy: Aisin Gioro Xianyu and the Dilemma of Manchu Identity," in *The Crossed Histories: A New Approach to Manchuria in the Age of Empire*, ed. Mariko Asano Tamanoi (Honolulu: University of Hawai'i Press, 2005), 83–118; and Zhuoliu Wu, *Orphan of Asia*, trans. Ioannis Mentzas (New York: Columbia University Press, 2008).

44. Ingrid Dineen-Wimberly wrote about many such people in *Allure of Blackness*, as did I in "The Power of Blackness." Some would include President Barack Obama among such leaders who had racial options and who chose Black identities; see my essay "Obama, Race, and the 2012 Election," in *Race and the Obama Phenomenon: The Vision of a More Perfect Multiracial Union*, ed. G. Reginald Daniel and Hettie V. Williams (Jackson: University Press of Mississippi, 2014), 329–38.

45. See W. E. B. Du Bois, "The Concept of Race," in *Dusk of Dawn* (New York: Harcourt, Brace and Company, 1940; repr., New Brunswick NJ: Transaction Publishers, 1984), 97–133; W. E. B. Du Bois, *The Autobiography of W. E. B. Du Bois: A Soliloquy on Viewing My Life from the Last Decade of Its First Century* (New York: International Publishers, 1968), esp. 61–131. For Logan interaction, see David Levering Lewis, *W. E. B. Du Bois: Biography of a Race* (New York: Holt, 1993), 72–73, 597.

46. Dineen-Wimberly, *Allure of Blackness*, introduction.

47. Sources for this section include Cynthia Earl Kerman and Richard Eldridge, *The Lives of Jean Toomer: A Hunger for Wholeness* (Baton Rouge: Louisiana State University Press, 1987); Charles R. Larson, *Invisible Darkness: Jean Toomer and Nella Larsen* (Iowa City: University of Iowa Press, 1993); Charles Scruggs and Lee Vandemarr, *Jean Toomer and the Terrors of American History* (Philadelphia: University of Pennsylvania Press, 1998); Jon Woodson, *To Make a New Race: Gurdjieff, Toomer, and the Harlem Renaissance* (Jackson: University Press of Mississippi, 1999); H. William Rice, "Searching for Jean Toomer," *American Legacy* 3, no. 3 (Fall 1997): 16–22; Frederik L. Rusch, ed., *A Jean Toomer Reader: Selected Unpublished Writings* (New York: Oxford University Press, 1993); Jean Toomer, *The Wayward and the Seeking* (Washington DC: Howard University Press, 1983). Much of the language in this section derives from Spickard, "Power of Blackness." The language here echoes the language in that earlier essay partly because, after that essay was published in 2004, I received a letter from Toomer's stepdaughters (with whom he lived for many years) in which they said how much they appreciated that I got his story right.

48. Jean Toomer, *Cane*, introduction by Darwin T. Turner (1923; repr., New York: Liveright, 1975).

49. Alice Walker, "The Divided Life of Jean Toomer," *New York Times*, July 13, 1980, reprinted in Walker, *In Search of Our Mothers' Gardens* (New York: Harcourt Brace Jovanovich, 1983). It is worth noting that Langston Hughes owned his multiplicity even as he chose a mainly Black identity; see Hughes, *The Big Sea* (New York: Hill and Wang, 1940), esp. 50–51. It is important to understand that Toomer was emphatically not attacking African Americans after the fashion of the racially mixed Negrophobe William Hannibal Thomas; John David Smith, *Black Judas: William Hannibal Thomas and the American Negro* (Athens: University of Georgia Press, 2000).

50. Kerman and Eldridge, *Lives of Jean Toomer*, 341–42.

51. Tatiana Seijas, *Asian Slaves in Colonial Mexico: From Chinos to Indians* (Cambridge: Cambridge University Press, 2014), 173.

52. Andy Bull, "The Forgotten Story of Sohn Kee-chung, Korea's Olympic Hero," *Guardian*, August 27, 2011. Some would argue that transracial international adoptions are instances of compelled racial identity change. See, for example, Mia Tuan and Jiannbin Shiao, *Choosing Ethnicity, Negotiating Race: Korean Adoptees in America* (New York: Russell Sage, 2011); Dianne Marre and Laura Briggs, eds., *International Adoption: Global Inequalities and the Circulation of Children* (New York: New York University Press, 2009); Laura Briggs, *Somebody's Children: The Politics of Transracial and Transnational Adoption* (Durham NC: Duke University Press, 2012); Eleana J. Kim, *Adopted Territory: Transnational Korean Adoptees and the Politics of Belonging* (Durham NC: Duke University Press, 2010); Kim Park Nelson, *Invisible Asians: Korean American Adoptees, Asian American Experiences, and Racial Exceptionalism* (New Brunswick NJ: Rutgers University Press, 2016).

53. Sources on the Khazar conversion include Kevin Alan Brook, *The Jews of Khazaria*, 2nd ed. (Lanham MD: Rowman and Littlefield, 2006); Schlomo Sand, *The Invention of the Jewish People*, trans. Yael Yotan (London: Verso, 2010); Arthur Koestler, *The Thirteenth Tribe: The Khazar Empire and Its Heritage* (New York: Fawcett, 1978); D. M. Dunlop, *The History of the Jewish Khazars* (New York: Schocken, 1967); René Grousset, *The Empire of the Steppes: A History of Central Asia*, trans. Naomi Walford (New Brunswick NJ: Rutgers University Press, 1970), 179–82; Peter B. Golden, Haggai Ben-Shammai, and András Róna-Tas, eds., *The World of the Khazars* (Leiden: Brill, 2007); Peter B. Golden, *Nomads and Their Neighbours in the Russian Steppe: Turks, Khazars, and Qipchaqs* (Aldershot, UK: Variorum, 2003); Peter B. Golden, *Turks and Khazars: Origins, Institutions, and Interactions in Pre-Mongol Eurasia*

(Aldershot, UK: Ashgate, 2010); Michael Chabon, *Gentlemen of the Road* (New York: Random House, 2007).

54. On the embrace of Greek Orthodoxy by the Kievan Rus, see Daniel H. Shubin, *A History of Russian Christianity, Volume 1: From the Earliest Years through Tsar Ivan IV* (New York: Algora, 2004), 9–36; John L. Fennell, *A History of the Russian Church to 1488* (London: Longman, 1995; repr., New York: Routledge, 2013), 20–44. In the second half of the sixteenth century Catholic missionaries brought their religion to Japan. Several daimyo (feudal lords) adopted Christianity. The nature of the social structure was such that the thousands of people in each of their domains were compelled to convert as well. Lest one think that this was superficial conversion, when the Tokugawa government banned Christianity several decades later, thousands of Japanese Christians endured persecution, torture, and death rather than renounce their new faith. See Charles R. Boxer, *The Christian Century in Japan*, 3rd ed. (Manchester, UK: Carcanet, 1993); Neil Fujita, *Japan's Encounter with Christianity: The Catholic Mission in Pre-modern Japan* (New York: Paulist Press, 1991); Ikuo Higashibaba, *Christianity in Early Modern Japan: Kirishitan Belief and Practice* (Leiden: Brill, 2001); Stephen Turnbull, *The Kakure Kirishitan of Japan: A Study of Their Development, Beliefs and Rituals to the Present Day* (London: RoutledgeCurzon, 1998); Shusaku Endo, *Silence*, trans. William Johnston (Rutland VT: Tuttle, 1969).

55. The historian of this movement is Julia Maria Schiavone Camacho, "Crossing Boundaries, Claiming a Homeland: The Mexican Chinese Transpacific Journey to Becoming Mexican, 1930s–1960s," *Pacific Historical Review* 78, no. 4 (2009): 545–77; and Julia Maria Schiavone Camacho, *Chinese Mexicans: Transpacific Migration and the Search for a Homeland, 1910–1960* (Chapel Hill: University of North Carolina Press, 2012). See also Grace Peña Delgado, *Making the Chinese Mexican: Global Migration, Localism, and Exclusion in the U.S.-Mexico Borderlands* (Stanford CA: Stanford University Press, 2012).

56. Tacitus, *The Annals of Imperial Rome*, trans. Michael Grant, rev. ed. (New York: Penguin, 1971), 61–89; Peter S. Wells, *The Battle That Stopped Rome: Emperor Augustus, Arminius, and the Slaughter of the Legions in the Teutoburg Forest* (New York: Norton, 2004); Andreas Dörner, *Politischer Mythos und symbolische Politik: Der Hermannmythos; Zur Entstehung des Nationalbewußtseins der Deutschen* (Reinbeck: Rowohlt, 1996); Richard Kuehnemund, *Arminius or the Rise of a National Symbol in Literature: From Hutten to Grabbe* (New York: AMS Press, 1966); W. Bradford Smith, "German Pagan Antiquity in Lutheran Historical Thought," *Journal of the Historical Society* 4, no. 3 (2004):

351–74; Herbert W. Benario, "Arminius into Hermann: History into Legend," *Greece and Rome* 51, no. 1 (April 2004): 83–94; Richard Ernest Walker, *Ulrich von Hutten's Arminius, an English Translation with Analysis and Commentary* (Bern: Peter Lang, 2008); Malcolm Todd, *The Early Germans*, 2nd ed. (Malden MA: Wiley-Blackwell, 2004).

PART 1

Different Context, Different Identity

2

Places of Possibility

Shape Shifting in the Roman and Chinese Borderlands

Ryan R. Abrecht

A shape shifter exchanges an old life for a new one, leaves a familiar community to find fellowship elsewhere, departs one world to enter another. People make these journeys for a variety of reasons. As Paul Spickard notes in his introduction to this volume, over the centuries untold millions have been pushed out of one life and into another by conquest, captivity, climate change, or other disasters natural or manmade over which they had no control. Other individuals choose to change, adopting different personas and joining new communities of their own volition for reasons that might range from ambition to desire for wealth to strong emotions like love and spite. While the motives behind it can vary, it is clear that shape shifting is inextricably tied to questions of power and privilege. It is also often a spatial as well as a social journey as people find new ways to locate themselves in new settings with, as Spickard puts it, "different menus of identity options." This process, however, is often only possible in certain key places or at certain opportune times. In this chapter, I will examine the careers of some individuals from the distant past who chose to reinvent themselves and join new communities. My goal is to better understand how these people managed to construct different identities and move between social worlds. Their lives help illustrate two important facts about shape shifting: (1) shape shifting is not equally possible for *everyone*, and (2) shape shifting is not equally possible *everywhere*.

While it is reasonable to assert that some people are able to move between social worlds more easily because of their unique backgrounds or personalities—they might be mixed race, multilingual, better connected, or simply more adept at embodying and performing a new identity than others around them—it is also safe to say that there are contextual limits to any individual's powers of reinvention. As Alyssa Newman, Laura Moore, Paul Barba, and several other contributors to this volume have observed in their case studies, location matters even for the most charismatic chameleons. This is because to remake themselves, people need access to different possibilities, models, and ways of life. Reinvention cannot take place in the absence of diversity, just as shape shifting cannot be considered complete until the shifter has been accepted by the new group he or she seeks to join. It's for this reason that people have moved to big cities to find themselves since time immemorial—such places provide access to paths and possibilities that cannot be found at home.[1]

This chapter will focus not on cities, however, but on frontiers and borderlands as special places that facilitate shape shifting and tend to generate shape shifters because of their uniquely heterogeneous natures. Specifically, I will focus on the northern borders of the Roman Empire in the first century CE, with a comparative look at Han China roughly two centuries earlier.[2] Places where two or more societies meet and overlap, borderlands are diverse in ways that can mirror the heterogeneity of the urban landscape. Their residents live poised between different political, ethnic, linguistic, or social worlds and are exposed to diverse customs and traditions. Over time, this can lead to the evolution of a uniquely blended or entangled local culture.[3] It's for precisely this reason that borderlands, more than other environments, function as *places of possibility* that facilitate shape shifting and produce individuals who are both more inclined and better equipped to successfully reinvent themselves. Simply put, liminal places produce liminal lives. Comparing the careers of a few individuals from the northern fringes of the Roman and Han Empires will, I hope, illuminate the relationship between shape shifting and borderland spaces that helped shape the histories not only of ancient Rome and China but also of many modern communities around the world today.

First, to Rome. More specifically, to the Rhine River, which formed the focal point of a contested frontier zone between the Roman Empire and "free Germany" (Germania) from the first century BCE to the fifth century CE.[4] In some ways, the Rhine acted as a fortified border, protecting the Roman provinces on its western and southern banks from the indigenous Germanic tribes and encompassing forts, watchtowers, a military highway, and a fleet of patrol boats. At the same time, the river never marked a crisp dividing line separating the Roman and German worlds. Rather, the area between the Rhine and the Weser and Elbe Rivers was a mixed zone where Roman control overlapped with Germanic culture before gradually tapering off in the forests of north-central Europe. The tribes living in this borderland could be alternatingly hostile or friendly to Rome depending on which way the winds of imperial and tribal politics were blowing. In times of peace, communication, cooperation, and commerce among the Romans and the various Germanic tribes living near the river were normal, even common.[5] These interactions helped shape the Rhine borderlands into a unique point of contact between Romans and Germans and a flash point for shape shifting.

The career of the Germanic chieftain Arminius, famous for inflicting a shocking and costly defeat on the Roman army in the Battle of the Teutoburg Forest in 9 CE, illustrates this relationship between place and possibility. Although he was later immortalized as a hero of the modern German nation, information about Arminius's early life is scarce. He was born in the late first century BCE among the Cherusci, one of the tribes that resided between the Rhine and Weser Rivers, the son of a chieftain named Sigimer.[6] The Roman historian Velleius Paterculus, a military man who served in the region and knew Arminius personally, described him as "a young man of noble birth, brave in action and alert in mind, possessing an intelligence well beyond that of a normal barbarian."[7] Despite the backhandedness of this last comment—a typical display of ethnocentrism that says more about the bias of our sources than it does about German intelligence—the Roman authors who wrote about Arminius all agreed that he possessed cleverness and charisma to match his courage and skill on the battlefield.[8]

Arminius grew up at a time when Rome was establishing its military and commercial presence in the Rhine region. Roman traders had been active in the area for decades, bringing both new goods for sale and new avenues for tribal leaders to increase their influence through connection to the imperial economy to the south.[9] At the same time, Roman commanders were also establishing relationships with Germanic chiefs, in keeping with Rome's policy of securing the loyalty of local elites to help pacify newly acquired lands.[10] While the speed, intensity, and precise nature of "Romanization" in the frontier zone at the start of the Common Era is debated, it is clear that the region offered talented individuals like Arminius multiple outlets for their ambition because of the interactions taking place there.[11] The Cheruscan prince had access to resources and relationships not available to Germans who lived farther north, outside the interaction zone.

Arminius took advantage of these options by choosing to cross the Rhine and enlist in the Roman army as an auxiliary soldier sometime in his late teens.[12] This service in the Roman army was his first act of shape shifting. Working with the Romans meant becoming fluent in Latin. Fighting alongside them required an adherence to Roman military discipline, in a departure from the traditional Germanic fighting style.[13] Rising in the ranks meant earning the respect and trust of men like Quinctilius Varus, commander of the Rhine armies, by displaying both military ability and a high level of cultural competency. Arminius excelled at these tasks. He moved with ease between Latin and the Germanic language of his people.[14] He fought with the Romans on a number of campaigns, earning Roman citizenship, the respectable rank of equestrian prefect (a minor but not insignificant title), and the command of one or more units of Cheruscan auxiliary troops in the process.[15] Most significantly, he earned the admiration of officers such as Varus and the historian Paterculus, who served with him in the Roman army.[16] Rather than a Germanic chieftain, in these years (6–9 CE), Arminius lived as an acculturated Roman soldier, well regarded by his superiors.[17]

This situation drastically changed when Arminius organized a mutiny of Germanic auxiliaries that led to a mass uprising, the death of Varus, and the annihilation of three legions in the Teutoburg Forest in 9 CE. This was his second act of shape shifting. The imperial biographer Suetonius, writing in the early second century, famously described these events as the "disaster" that ended Roman expansion beyond the Rhine and inspired the emperor Augustus to cry, "Quinctilius Varus, give me back my legions!"[18] The historian Tacitus went a step further, describing Arminius as the "undoubted liberator of Germany."[19] In time, this Tacitean epithet helped mythologize the Cheruscan chieftain into a hero of medieval folklore, earning him a more appropriately German-sounding name (Hermann) in the sixteenth century, a "nom de Teuton" that may have been coined by none other than Martin Luther.[20] By the eighteenth and nineteenth centuries, Arminius/Hermann was being hailed by thinkers like Johann Gottfried Herder and Johann Gottlieb Fichte as the founding father of the German nation.[21] This transformation is a fascinating story in and of itself, but it leads away from a crucial question about the man behind the myth: *Why did he do it?* Here we again chafe against the biases and limitations of the ancient surviving sources. As is so often the case, we have nothing written by Arminius himself to shed light on his motives, and the Roman historians who wrote about him operated under historiographical conventions that differ significantly from our own.[22] Ancient authors seldom concerned themselves, for example, with the questions of identity that capture our attention today.

An episode in Tacitus's *Annals*, written in the early second century CE, may provide some insight into Arminius's decision to shape shift from Roman soldier back to Germanic chieftain. It concerns a meeting between Arminius and his brother Flavus at the River Weser in the aftermath Arminius's victory in the Teutoburg Forest. In Tacitus's telling, Arminius stood on the far bank and spoke across the river with his brother, who had come to treat with him as a representative of the Roman army. This juxtaposition is significant. Flavus, like Arminius, came from a noble family of the Cherusci. Like Arminius, he had chosen to fight for Rome as an auxiliary soldier, taking a Latin name and losing an eye while serving under the future emperor Tiberius.[23] Unlike Arminius, however, Flavus chose to remain loyal to Rome. In their meeting at the Weser, Flavus reportedly tried to convince his brother to stand down by stressing the benefits of Roman civilization and the honor of remaining loyal to the empire. The encounter did not go well. According to Tacitus, Arminius rebuffed his brother, shouting across the river that Flavus had forgotten "the sacred call of their country, their ancestral liberty, the gods of their German hearths, and their mother . . . who prayed that he would not choose the title of traitor to his kindred."[24] The brothers were reportedly at the point of wading into the river to come to blows until one of his Roman comrades pulled Flavus away.

Tacitus almost certainly invented this scene, following conventions of ancient historiography that date back to Thucydides.[25] Nevertheless, the episode reveals something about the process of *choosing* that lies at the heart of shape shifting and its relationship to physical movement in a borderland space. In Tacitus's set piece, Flavus functions as a mirror image of his brother that emphasizes the similar choices they had made up until Arminius's rebellion, when their paths diverged.[26] Like Arminius, Flavus chose to "become" Roman; the key difference is that he also chose to remain that way. Thus he remained on the Roman bank. The brothers' confrontation across the Weser, which functions in Tacitus's telling as both a symbolic and a physical barrier separating two different worlds, shows, on the one hand, that shape shifting is a matter of individual choice. On the other, the confrontation also serves as a reminder that certain choices are only available to individuals living along a fault line of empire and that the decision to change also involves a physical as well as a social relocation.[27] In the case of these two brothers, a line had to be crossed, literally and figuratively.

In reality, of course, rivers are never impassable boundaries; indeed, this is precisely the point. It was both the presence and the permeability of the riverine border (whether the Weser or the Rhine) that enabled Flavus and Arminius to reinvent themselves in the ways that they did. One can easily imagine the tables turned, with Flavus choosing to lead a Germanic mutiny and Arminius choosing to remain loyal to Rome. For his part, Arminius was able to "become German" again because, even while serving in the Roman army, he remained in the Rhine borderlands. Doing so allowed him to keep a foot in both worlds, maintaining key ties to his family and tribal history (the Cherusci had fought the Romans in the recent past, and Arminius came from a prominent family connected to this tradition of resistance).[28] He understood how to command the respect of his people and other neighboring tribes and knew how to charismatically appeal to them in terms they understood.[29] He may also have bolstered support for his rebellion by appealing to Germanic religious traditions, if Roman reports of the sacrifice of captive soldiers in sacred groves after the Teutoburg can be believed.[30]

Arminius's laurels didn't carry him too far; he was assassinated in 21 CE by disaffected partisans who believed he was plotting to make himself king over the "free" Germans.[31] A series of events that took place not long after his death sheds further light on the relationship between shape shifting and borderlands that lies at the heart of this chapter. Twenty-six years after Arminius's death, the Cherusci sent a delegation to Rome asking the emperor Claudius to appoint them a new leader. The irony of this is hard to miss, but such a request is in fact in keeping with the ever-shifting political landscape of the frontier zone.[32] Claudius chose to send a young man named Italicus, Arminius's nephew and the son of the very same brother, Flavus, who had remained loyal to Rome. Italicus thus came from good Cheruscan stock (indeed, he was the last surviving member of the royal house). Trained to fight in both the Roman and the German manners, he was noted for his energy and many admirers and was initially warmly received by the Cherusci as their king.[33]

The situation quickly soured, however, as rivals emerged to question Italicus's Germanic bona fides. As his name indicates, he came from a world different from that of his father and uncle: he was born and raised in Rome, which proved to be a hindrance when he returned to his ancestral homeland. In addition to declaring him "infected by foreign upbringing, refinement, and servitude," the young king's enemies argued that a man not born on German soil was unfit to rule even over his own people.[34] Ultimately expelled, Italicus spent the rest of his life fighting against the people he had hoped to join; all in all, the incident was a net negative for Roman-Cheruscan relations.[35] Why was this young man, nephew of Arminius himself, unable to pull off the transformation from Roman hostage to Germanic king? Simply put, he came from the wrong place. Unlike his uncle and father, who were native to the Rhine borderlands and spent their lives on the threshold of the Roman and German worlds, Italicus was, in essence, an Italian. Despite his royal lineage and the fact that he had been educated in the language, customs, and fighting style of his people, he could not move between the two cultures because in the eyes of at least some of his countrymen he was an outsider: a city-bred Roman and thus one of Caesar's slaves.[36] Being raised in Rome meant that he could never effectively maintain a foot in both worlds. His inability to shape shift is a reminder that location matters.

Twenty-two years after Italicus's failed attempt at transformation, the Rhine borderlands produced another shape shifter who moved with ease between Roman and Germanic identities. Though not as well known as Arminius, this individual, Julius Civilis, resembled him in several key ways and was arguably a more successful shifter than the "liberator of Germany" had been. Civilis came from a royal family of the Batavians, a tribe found along the Lower Rhine in what is today the Netherlands. Closer to the Roman orbit than the Cherusci, the Batavians had maintained a decades-long alliance with the empire that obliged them to provide men for the Roman army.[37] In compliance with this treaty, Civilis served twenty-five years as an auxiliary commander of Batavian cohorts, far longer than Arminius's brief career.[38] He was thus more fluent in Latin and familiar with Roman tactics and social mores than Arminius had been. His Latin name indicates that he, too, was a Roman citizen. Unlike Arminius, Civilis moved at ease in rarefied social circles and was well connected enough to claim friendship with the future emperor Vespasian while Vespasian was still a private citizen.[39] Civilis's career indicates that he had a sophisticated understanding of Roman politics and diplomacy, which he used to his advantage on several occasions.[40] Civilis was, in short, a shape shifting German who had more successfully adopted the mantle of Romanitas than had Arminius sixty years earlier.

Yet Civilis, too, chose to abandon his Roman life to lead his countrymen in a revolt against the empire. This second shift happened in 69 CE, the Year of Four Emperors, during a brief period of civil war following the death of the emperor Nero. Backed by eight Batavian cohorts and a coalition of allied tribes, Civilis drew upon his knowledge of Roman tactics and his familiarity with Batavian traditions to lead a rebellion that, in Tacitus's estimation at least, aimed at creating a breakaway Gallic empire.[41] As with Arminius, we don't have Civilis's own words to verify his intentions or illuminate his worldview. It is clear, though, that his motivations for shifting from well-connected Roman officer to Batavian rebel chieftain were related to the confused events that followed Nero's untimely end. Civilis had been arrested after Nero's death along with his brother, another Batavian nobleman–cum–Roman citizen named Claudius Paulus, on charges of treason and narrowly escaped execution through a pardon by the emperor Galba, Nero's successor.[42] His brother, unfortunately, was not so fortunate. It's reasonable to imagine that a desire for revenge, coupled with continued fears for his safety amid the uncertain politics of civil war, contributed to Civilis's decision to defect.[43] The fact that he chose a moment of internal political instability to make his move is another indication of his sophisticated grasp of Roman politics.

To make the shift back to Germanic society, Civilis emphasized his royal bloodline and high standing in Batavian society.[44] He also drew upon his familiarity with the customs and expectations of the Batavian people, pairing them with leadership skills honed in Roman service. To initiate his revolt, for example, Civilis held a traditional feast in a sacred grove and exacted both Germanic- and Roman-style oaths of allegiance from his followers.[45] These troops also carried native-style military standards into battle.[46] In an appeal to native religious customs, Civilis associated himself with a woman named Veleda, a respected prophetess from the neighboring tribe of the Bructeri who previously had successfully foretold the destruction of a Roman legion at Vetera.[47] Civilis was conscious, too, that he had to look the part, dyeing his hair red and growing it long in the Batavian style to more fully embody his transformation from Roman soldier to fierce Germanic warlord.[48] All of this amounts to a carefully executed plan for reinvention. Conscious of the need to frame his rebellion in as strong a native context as possible, Civilis aligned his goals with those of his countrymen, offering them rich spoils and freedom from Rome while at the same time taking pains to emphasize as many aspects of his Batavian background as possible.[49]

The Batavian Revolt proved to be short-lived, collapsing in 70 CE after Civilis's coalition suffered a decisive defeat. Frustratingly, Tacitus's narrative also breaks off at this point due to a gap in the manuscript. However, the surviving sections suggest that, in the end, Civilis may have been able to pull off one last feat of shape shifting, from Germanic warlord back to respectable Roman citizen. According to Tacitus, toward the end of the revolt Civilis entered into negotiations with the Roman commander Cerealis, a military envoy speaking on behalf of Civilis's old friend, the now-emperor Vespasian. In the end, it seems that Civilis was offered a full pardon; his lands and houses were also to be spared and returned to him upon cessation of hostilities.[50] Although Tacitus's narrative breaks off in the middle of a speech in which Civilis justifies his choice to the rest of the Batavian commanders, he seems to have accepted Vespasian's offer.[51]

If so, Civilis displayed an ability to shape shift far beyond that of Arminius, managing to go full circle. Born Batavian, he became Roman as a young man and remained so for over twenty years of military service. Putting aside his Roman life, Civilis became Batavian again, playing the part of a traditional king leading his people in a freedom fight against Rome. Then, mutatis mutandis, he managed to make his way back into the Roman fold, relying, it seems, on key social connections with Roman elites he made during his army career. All in all, it's an impressive record that speaks to his charisma, cleverness, and audacity. The key thing to remember, though, is that such a career would not have been possible if Civilis had not been a product of the Rhine borderlands. A native son who maintained ties to his people even after crossing the river to work in Rome's service, he consistently found ways to further his ambition by exploiting the unique possibilities that the frontier region had to offer. As the story of Italicus suggests, it's hard to imagine an outsider pulling this off, no matter how thoroughly he was schooled in Batavian fighting styles or religious traditions. Because he was a local, Civilis's Roman connections worked to his advantage but did not inhibit his ability to return to his people when the circumstances around him changed. Being from the borderland gave him the skills and the knowledge necessary to successfully shape shift. Staying in the borderland allowed him to use them.

The careers of Arminius and Civilis demonstrate how, to certain talented and ambitious individuals, being from the fringe of empire helped facilitate shape shifting. Yet this phenomenon was not limited to the Roman Empire's border with Germany. The northern borderlands of China's Han dynasty (206 BCE–220 CE) were also home to a number of shape shifters who took advantage of the unique opportunities that the fringes of empire have to offer. Obviously, the history and topography of northern China differed from the Roman frontier in several significant ways. Here there was no convenient river to function as a boundary line; instead, there was a shifting series of rammed-earth walls, watchtowers, and garrison towns laboriously constructed over centuries.[52] China's northern neighbors hailed from the Eurasian steppe rather than the forests of Europe and had customs and institutions that differed from those of the ancient Germans. The peoples of the steppe were nomadic pastoralists, whose economic and social institutions revolved primarily around herding, especially of horses. Many were also masters of fighting from horseback, famous for their swiftness, ferocity, and skill with the bow. Particularly in the Han dynasty's early centuries, these tribes represented a greater threat to China's security than the Germans did to Rome. Nomads who approached the Han frontier seeking access to goods typically had three options: become vassals of the Han, attempt to trade as equals, or take what they wanted by force.[53] Aware of their strength and met with Chinese chauvinism, they often chose the latter.

There were political differences too. While the German tribes remained disunited throughout much of Roman history, China's northern neighbors were forged into a powerful steppe empire—the Xiongnu Confederacy—mere decades after the Han dynasty's foundation under Emperor Gaozu (r. 202–195 BCE). Under the control of a supreme leader (*shanyu*), the Xiongnu developed into a fighting force that could match or surpass Chinese armies, particularly when exploiting the terrain and tactics of the steppe to the disadvantage of the largely infantry-based Han forces.[54] With this in mind, it is unsurprising that the three standard histories of the Han regime—Sima Qian's *Shiji* (Records of the grand historian, first century BCE), Ban Gu's *Hanshu* (History of the former Han, third century CE), and Fan Ye's *Hou Hanshu* (History of the later Han, fifth century CE)—devote considerable time to Han-Xiongnu relations and the history of the northern frontier. These historians relate how, after suffering a nearly disastrous defeat at the hands of the *shanyu* Maodun (r. 209–174 BCE) in 200 BCE, Emperor Gaozu developed a policy of "peace and kinship" (*he qin*) toward the Xiongnu. In return for annual gifts of gold, silk, grain, and an occasional Han princess to join the *shanyu*'s harem, the Xiongnu agreed not to attack China. In essence, this was a policy of appeasement through the paying of tribute. Yet Gaozu and his successors also hoped that in time the *he qin* system would corrupt the Xiongnu by making them dependent on Chinese luxuries.[55] As one Han statesman put it: "When the Xiongnu have developed a craving for our rice, stew, barbeques, and wine, this will have become their fatal weakness."[56]

In spite of these clear differences between the Roman and Han frontiers, clear parallels nevertheless present themselves. Commerce at frontier markets, for example, was a major component of China's peace and kinship system. In addition to "softening" the Xiongnu by exposing large numbers of nomads to Chinese goods, frontier markets were a way for the Han government to funnel revenue into the imperial treasury through taxation and to gather intelligence on the activities of nomads beyond the frontier.[57] Still, it was difficult for Han officials to exert complete control over the frontier zone. Many frontier markets were located in a "debatable margin" between a true steppe environment of herding and horsemanship and the fully agricultural economy to the south, where cultivation of a crop such as wheat, millet, or barley was the norm.[58] Residents of this marginal environment were often governed by their own interests. Economically, this meant that residents of the borderland blended Chinese-style agriculture with steppe-style herding to adapt to local environmental conditions and crossed the border regularly in pursuit of profit.[59] The story of a frontier merchant named Lo, who became very rich selling cattle and horses both to a king of the Jung barbarians and to Emperor Qin Shi Huang (r. 221–206 BCE), eventually receiving honorific titles from both rulers for his troubles, is one example of this cross-border commerce.[60] The works of Han historians and archaeological data also make it clear that, in addition to livestock and foodstuffs, goods such as clothing, brocade, combs, and ornaments were regularly exchanged at frontier markets.[61]

Intermarriage formed another important part of China's frontier policy. As early as the reign of Gaozu, Han emperors sent Chinese princesses to the Xiongnu court as brides for the *shanyu*. Many of these young women suffered badly, cut off from their homelands and unable or unwilling to adopt Xiongnu culture ("the lamenting exiled princess" in fact became a later trope in Han poetry).[62] These ladies were as much diplomats as wives, strangers in a strange land who served, in a sense, as living proof of the *shanyu*'s clout at the Han court.[63] Yet their children could have a very different experience. The son of a Xiongnu chief and a Han princess, like a Roman soldier with German blood, could entertain options that others could not. Evidence for this shows in literature from the Han dynasty and later periods of Chinese history. In the fragmentary text *Handling the Lute*, widely attributed to the writer Cai Yong (133–92 CE), a Chinese palace lady named Wang Zhaojun, given in marriage to the *shanyu* Huhanye (r. 58–31 BCE), asked her half-Xiongnu son Shiwei whether he intended to live as a Chinese man or as a Xiongnu upon her husband's death. When Shiwei replied that he wished to live as a Xiongnu, Wang Zhaojun committed suicide by swallowing poison.[64] Here again we find the connection between shape shifting and the borderlands. Shiwei had the ability to choose between two very different paths because he was a product of a mixed marriage and spent his youth in and beyond the frontier. The fact that he chose to be counted among "the barbarians" was so beyond the comprehension of his mother—herself still an outsider in spite of her presumably long residence in China's northlands—that she killed herself rather than accept his decision. The story clearly represents the Chinese perspective on this choice; it is intended to teach a lesson about filial piety through the "bad example" of the son's decision to go against his mother's wishes and his acceptance of "barbarian" over Chinese mores.[65] Nevertheless, it also points to important truths about the ambiguity of mixed heritage and the uncertainties (or opportunities) that are at the heart of shape shifting and of life in the borderlands.

Thus it is possible to observe some parallels between Roman and Chinese borderlands. Like the Rhine borderlands, northern China had a mixed population that engaged in regular trade at border markets and garrisons.[66] These commercial exchanges helped foster symbiotic relationships among locals who shared economic interests despite coming from a different linguistic, ethnic, or cultural background.[67] Along with economic factors, social and kinship ties also played a part in shaping the culture of China's northern frontier in a way that ensured that local populations were influenced by—and open to— *both* Chinese culture *and* that of the steppe. In other words, "there was as much barbarization of the frontier Chinese as there was Sinicization of the nomad."[68] Though often troubling to residents of the imperial center, this "barbarization" offered unique possibilities to those who dwelt in the periphery.

Another similarity is the often precarious relationship between imperial governments and their northern neighbors. As they did for the Romans, political alliances with tribal leaders sometimes amounted to "a dangerous game of knife-juggling" for the Chinese.[69] Xiongnu leaders remained embroiled in a complex web of tribal politics even after signing peace treaties and exchanging gifts with Han emperors. The system was fragile; between 198 and 135 BCE the Han government was compelled to renegotiate the peace and kinship system with the Xiongnu no fewer than ten times.[70] Eventually, it broke down completely in the face of Xiongnu raiding and the criticisms of Han officials who saw it as making China submissive to nomadic demands. In 134 BCE Emperor Wudi (r. 141–87 BCE) went on the offensive, attempting to annihilate a Xiongnu army and capture the *shanyu* by luring them into a trap at the frontier town of Mayi. Wudi's plan revolved around a ruse—facilitated, we are told, by a local merchant who was known and trusted on the nomadic side of the border—in which the *shanyu* was led to believe that the residents of Mayi had killed their Han governor out of a desire to join with the Xiongnu. Though the plan did not ultimately succeed (the *shanyu* saw through the deception before the Han armies could deliver the fatal blow), the episode points again to the uncertain allegiances of frontier populations and the ability of figures like the merchant spy to move easily between the Chinese and nomad worlds.[71]

Full-scale war broke out between the Han Empire and the Xiongnu Confederacy after the events at Mayi; unfortunately, my remaining space does not permit a detailed investigation of this conflict and its resolution here.[72] However, against the bloody backdrop of the Han-Xiongnu Wars, a few more examples of shape shifting on the Han frontiers come into sharp relief. The Chinese borderlands, like their Roman counterparts, had a tendency to produce military men who pledged themselves to imperial service, only to renounce it later and reassert their native allegiances. Sima Qian, court historian to Emperor Wudi, related several stories of such "traitors" in his monumental work *Shiji* (Records of the grand historian), completed around 90 BCE. In Sima Qian's analysis, men from the frontier repeatedly proved themselves unreliable to the Han and displayed an unsettling tendency to switch sides when necessity dictated or opportunity arose. His history includes stories of men like Zhao Xin, a Xiongnu chief who pledged himself to Han service, was granted a Chinese title as marquis of Xi, and fought for the Han army as a general in 123 BCE, only to later return to the Xiongnu, become a trusted advisor to the *shanyu*, marry his sister, and become commander of a Xiongnu stronghold at Mount Tianyan.[73] Though his description of this episode is fairly brief, Sima Qian noted that the time Zhao Xin spent fighting for the Chinese helped him earn his high position at the Xiongnu court, since he could draw upon his understanding of Han politics to advise the *shanyu* on how to deal with Han envoys. In Sima Qian's telling, Zhao Xin knew how to fight, but he also understood "when to use soft words and request a peace alliance" that would prove most advantageous to Xiongnu interests.[74]

"Traitorous" military men show up repeatedly in Sima Qian's history and occasionally in wooden documents discovered at garrison towns like Dunhuang, on the Han Empire's northwest frontier.[75] This should perhaps not be surprising, since the Han government relied heavily upon frontier populations to supply generals and soldiers for the war effort. Men from the margins of the steppe who had been around horses from boyhood, knew how to shoot an arrow from horseback, and perhaps knew the Xiongnu language were of great use to the Han: they understood the terrain, knew how to fight the Xiongnu, and were familiar with the hazards of leading troops out into the steppe.[76] Zhao Xin was one of several Han commanders of Xiongnu origin, just as a significant number of officers in the Roman army were born among the Germanic tribes. Some Han strategists even started out as merchants, such as the man who helped plan the ambush at Mayi. It is natural that such men proved to be "political amphibians" who were willing to fight either for the Han or for the Xiongnu depending on the political situation in the borderland at a given time.[77]

Nevertheless, the Han continued to rely upon individuals of mixed background whose cross-cultural knowledge could provide insight into the tribal politics of the Xiongnu Confederacy. Sima Qian also mentions the case of a diplomat in the service of the Han emperor by the name of Wang Wu, "who had been born in the north and was familiar with barbarian customs."[78] To gain access to the *shanyu*'s court, we are told, Wang Wu allowed his face to be tattooed in black as a sign of his acquiescence to nomadic customs. Tattooing, a practice associated with foreign peoples, carried strong connotations of primitivism and barbarism within the Han Empire. Considered unfilial (because the body is a "gift" from one's parents that should not be defaced or damaged), tattooing was typically used within China as a form of corporal punishment; certainly, Wang Wu's facial tattooing would not have registered as a marker of dignity and high status at the Han court.[79] It is possible, however, that he was already familiar with this practice due to his northern origins. His willingness to submit to the procedure suggests at the very least that this was an individual comfortable moving between social worlds. We might think of such an act as "high stakes shape shifting"—Wang Wu's facial tattooing certainly ups the ante on Julius Civilis's red hair dye!

One final episode will have to serve as my conclusion and perhaps a look toward future inquiries that might arise from further analysis of the shape shifting/borderland connection. Sima Qian's *Shiji* includes an extended anecdote about Zhonghang Yue, a eunuch at the Han court who worked as a tutor to a Chinese princess during the reign of Emperor Wen (r. 180–157 BCE).[80] Zhonghang Yue was not a native of the Han capital of Chang'an; instead, he was born in the state of Yan, a formerly independent kingdom in the northeast frontier zone whose leaders had formed alliances with the Xiongnu in the past.[81] Like some other disaffected Han officials from the northern borderlands, Zhonghang Yue performed an act of shape shifting that proved damaging to the Han government when the princess he tutored was promised to the *shanyu* as part of a diplomatic marriage and he was ordered by Emperor Wen to accompany his young charge to the north. Very reluctant to undertake this mission, Zhonghang ominously warned that his going "would bring nothing but trouble to the Han."[82] Nevertheless, he and his charge were sent north.

Once among the Xiongnu, Zhonghang Yue promptly switched sides and spent the rest of his life as a favored advisor to two successive Xiongnu leaders. The former courtier's advice was considered especially valuable because he understood the Han protocol and diplomatic strategy so well. Zhonghang Yue informed the *shanyu* that Han gifts of silk and other delicacies were simply tools intended to make the Xiongnu soft and dependent on Chinese handouts. He taught the nomads how to keep careful records of the number of people and animals in their territory and thus to know the full extent of their strength at the negotiating table. He advised the *shanyu* to diplomatically put the Han emperor in his place by embellishing Xiongnu correspondence with elaborate titles and official seals finer than the ones that the Chinese used. The tutor turned advisor also publicly shamed a group of Han envoys that arrived at the Xiongnu court, pointing out the superiority of Xiongnu customs over their Confucian ethics and using the same terminology to describe Han customs that the Han themselves used to describe the behavior of "barbarians."[83]

In some ways, this episode recalls the "set piece" speeches that feature prominently in the works of Roman historians like Tacitus. Sima Qian has not given us Zhonghang Yue's actual words but a literary invention created for his own historiographical purposes. As several scholars have observed, the story of the renegade eunuch functions as a mirror that turns the Han ethnographer's gaze back on himself, echoing a classical trope in which the perspective of a foreigner is used to indirectly critique the self.[84] Still, it is interesting to note that the "foreigner" in this case is so thoroughly a creature of the Chinese court that he can easily dispel any argument about the superiority of Chinese over Xiongnu culture. Despite this thorough Sinicization, the courtier found a way to fit in and thrive among the Xiongnu when circumstances forced him to return to the borderlands of his birth. If we accept that the episode has a core of historical truth and that the man Zhonghang Yue did exist, his ability to jump cultures in this way serves as a reminder that, to a shape shifter, knowledge is power. It is also a reminder that the extent of that power also depends on where one happens to be standing.

To stand on the margins of a great empire is to have access to a range of possibilities that cannot be found elsewhere. This is why the Roman and Chinese borderlands each played host to a number of shape shifters who moved between identities and allegiances with relative ease. To men like Arminius of the Cherusci, Julius Civilis, Shiwei, and Zhonghang Yue, these places held out the possibility of advancement, reinvention, refuge, or revenge. For the Roman and Han governments, on the other hand, the borderlands might be more accurately described as places of *peril*, where people's loyalties were unreliable and "traitors" tended to crop up with troubling frequency. The difference, of course, lies in one's point of view.

Notes

1. As the sociologist Richard Sennett put it, city dwellers are people "always in the presence of otherness." See Richard Sennett, *The Conscience of the Eye: The Design and Social Life of Cities* (New York: W. W. Norton & Company, 1992), 123.

2. Most historians of ancient Rome and China tend to use the term "frontier," a word still sometimes associated with processes of acculturation and images of "empty" lands waiting to be tamed. In recent decades, the terms "borderland" and "borderlands" have become common in an effort to highlight the connective functions of borders, the everyday actions among people who live near them, and the social complexity of their surrounding regions. I will use both terms in this chapter, but I draw inspiration from the work of borderlands scholars who stress the creative and integrative aspects of border regions. For examples, see Linda T. Darling, "The Mediterranean as a Borderland," *Review of Middle East Studies* 46, no. 1 (2012): 56; Oscar Martinez, *Border People: Life and Society in the U.S.-Mexico Borderlands* (Tucson: University of Arizona Press, 1994), xvii; Bradley Parker, "Toward an Understanding of Borderland Processes," *American Antiquity* 71, no. 1 (2006): 79.

3. Michiel Baud and Willem Van Schendel, "Toward a Comparative History of Borderlands," *Journal of World History* 8, no. 2 (1997): 234; James G. Cusick, "Creolization and the Borderlands," *Historical Archaeology* 43, no. 3 (2000): 48; Michael Dietler, *Archaeologies of Colonialism: Consumption, Entanglement, and Violence in Ancient Mediterranean France* (Berkeley: University of California Press, 2010), 55–75; Stuart Tyson Smith and Michele R. Buzon, "Colonial Entanglements: 'Egyptianization' in Egypt's Nubian Empire and the Nubian Dynasty," in *Proceedings of the 12th International Conference for Nubian Studies*, ed. Derek Welsby and Julie Anderson (London: British Museum Publications on Egypt and Sudan, 2010), 431–42; Martinez, *Border People*, xvii, 306.

4. A detailed retelling of Rome's expansion into the Rhine region is not possible here. Suffice it to say that the Romans first established a presence on the Rhine in the first century BCE, during and after Julius Caesar's conquest of Gaul (58–50 BCE), and consolidated their hold in the following century. By the end of the Julio-Claudian dynasty (27 BCE–68 CE), an elaborate infrastructure of roads, forts, and watchtowers was taking shape along this riverine border, as well as along the Danube. See Caesar, *Gallic War* 4; Suetonius, *Augustus* 21.

5. Tacitus, *Histories* 4.15; Tacitus, *Germania* 41; Ammianus Marcellinus, *History* 21.4.3; Hugh Elton, *Frontiers of the Roman Empire* (Bloomington: Indiana University Press, 1996), 77, 81; C. R. Whittaker, *Frontiers of the Roman Empire: A Social and Economic Study* (Baltimore MD: Johns Hopkins University Press, 1994), 122–24; Steven K. Drummond and Lynn H. Nelson, *Western Frontiers of Imperial Rome* (Armonk NY: M. E. Sharpe, 1994), 107; Olwen Brogan, "Trade between the Roman Empire and the Free Germans," *Journal of Roman Studies* 26, no. 2 (1936): 195.

6. Velleius Paterculus, *Compendium of Roman History* 2.118.2: "principis gentis eius filius."

7. Velleius Paterculus, *Compendium of Roman History* 2.118.2: "iuvenis genere nobilis, manu fortis, sensu celer, ultra barbarum promptus ingenio." See also Dieter Timpe, *Arminius-Studien* (Heidelberg: C. Winter, 1970), 128.

8. Velleius Paterculus, *Compendium of Roman History* 2.118.2; Tacitus, *Annals* 1.60.

9. Tacitus, *Histories* 4.15; Stephen L. Dyson, "Native Revolts in the Roman Empire," *Histzeitalte Historia: Zeitschrift für alte Geschichte* 20, no. 2/3 (1971): 253–54; Thompson, *Early Germans*, 20–28.

10. Dyson, "Native Revolts," 254; Alain M. Gowing, "Tacitus and the Client Kings," *Transactions of the American Philological Association (1974–)* 120 (1990): 316.

11. Paterculus and Cassius Dio indicate that Arminius's revolt drew strength from local resentment brought on by Roman efforts to compel the Germans to adopt Roman ways. See Velleius Paterculus, *Compendium of Roman History* 2.117.2; Cassius Dio, *Roman History* 56.16.4; Florus, *Epitome of Roman History* 2.30; Dyson, "Native Revolts," 254.

12. In doing so, he took advantage of an opportunity available to any ablebodied local fighting man from the region. Just as the Romans stabilized their empire by establishing alliances with local elites, they added to their manpower reserves by enlisting locals to serve as auxiliary soldiers. Tacitus, *Annals* 2.17, 4.73; Tacitus, *Histories* 4.15; Suetonius, *Gaius* 45; Elton, *Frontiers*, 50; G. R. Watson, *The Roman Soldier* (Ithaca NY: Cornell University Press, 1969), 15–16, 24–25; Graham Webster, *The Roman Imperial Army of the First and Second Centuries A.D.* (London: Black, 1969), 141–56.

13. Tacitus, *Germania* 608; Tacitus, *Agricola* 36; Caesar, *Gallic War* 1.48.

14. Tacitus, *Annals* 2.10.3; Elizabeth Tylawski, "What's in a Name, a Face, and a Place: Significant Juxtaposition in Tacitus' *Annales*," *Historia: Zeitschrift für alte Geschichte* 51, no. 4 (2002): 256. Indeed, although we know the Germanic names of Arminius's wife, Thusnelda, infant son, Thumelicus, father,

Segimerus, father-in-law, Segestes, and cousin Segimerus, we have only the Latin Arminius for the man himself.

15. Velleius Paterculus, *Compendium of Roman History* 2.118.2; Tacitus, *Annals* 2.45; Martin M. Winkler, *Arminius the Liberator: Myth and Ideology* (New York: Oxford University Press, 2016), 2, 25–26; Dieter Timpe, *Römisch-germanische Begegnung in der späten Republik und frühen Kaiserzeit Voraussetzungen-Konfrontationen-Wirkungen; gesammelte Studien* (Munich: Saur, 2006), 216–41; Dieter Timpe, *Arminius-Studien* (Heidelberg: C. Winter, 1970), 50–80.

16. Velleius Paterculus, *Compendium of Roman History* 2.118.4.

17. As such, he would have resembled a number of other local recruits in Roman service in the Rhine borderlands at that time. See Dyson, "Native Revolts," 255; Timpe, *Arminius-Studien*, 304; Erich Sander, "Zur Arminius-Biographie," *Gymnasium* 62 (1955): 83–98. See also the works cited in note 12 above.

18. Suetonius, *Augustus* 23.

19. Tacitus, *Annals* 2.88.2: "liberator haud dubie Germaniae."

20. Martin M. Winkler, *Arminius the Liberator: Myth and Ideology* (New York: Oxford University Press, 2016), 56–58.

21. Winkler, *Arminius the Liberator*, 59–63; Patrick J. Geary, *The Myth of Nations: The Medieval Origins of Europe* (Princeton NJ: Princeton University Press, 2002), 24–25.

22. Writers such as Velleius Paterculus (*Compendium of Roman History* 2.117–20), Florus (*Epitome of Roman History* 2.30), and Cassius Dio (*Roman History* 56.19–22.2) often emphasized emotional set pieces over precise facts, stressing the gory details of battle or the moral failings of the men involved. Another popular theme was the pathological decline of world empire caused by the mutability of Fortune (Greek, Tyche) and the vices of human actors. None of these explanations tells us much about the man Arminius or the thought process behind his decision to abandon the Roman army and rejoin his people. See Winkler, *Arminius the Liberator*, 26–29.

23. Tacitus, *Annals* 2.9.

24. Tacitus, *Annals* 2.10: "ille fas patriae, libertatem avitam, penetralis Germaniae deos, matrem ... denique gentis suae desertor et proditor quam imperator esse mallet."

25. He wasn't there to record it, although he did have access to Pliny the Elder's lost work on the German Wars to consult as a reference. Tacitus, *Annals* 1.69; Tylawsky, "What's in a Name?," 256.

26. Tylawsky, "What's in a Name?," 257.

27. Tylawsky, "What's in a Name?," 255, 258.

28. Velleius Paterculus, *Compendium of Roman History* 2.105.1; Dyson, "Native Revolts," 255; E. A. Thompson, *The Early Germans* (Oxford: Clarendon Press, 1965), 34, 72, 79–80.

29. Tacitus, *Annals* 1.60.

30. Tacitus, *Annals* 1.61.5–6; Velleius Paterculus, *Compendium of Roman History* 1.120.5; cf. Tacitus, *Germania* 9.1–2; Dyson, "Native Revolts," 257.

31. Tacitus, *Annals* 2.88.

32. Tacitus, *Annals* 11.16.1; Gowing, "Tacitus and the Client Kings," 321. The request stemmed from the fact that the nobility had been decimated by infighting in the decades since Arminius's assassination. Putting in a request to Rome for an appointed king was common in such circumstances and accorded well with standard Roman foreign policy, since, as stated above, the Romans preferred whenever possible to rule through alliances with local elites.

33. Tacitus, *Annals* 11.16.2.

34. Tacitus, *Annals* 11.16.3: "infectum alimonio servitio cultu, omnibus externis . . . adeo neminem isdem in terris ortum qui principem locum impleat."

35. Tacitus, *Annals* 11.17.

36. Gowing, "Tacitus and the Client Kings," 322.

37. Tacitus, *Annals* 2.8.3.

38. Tacitus, *Histories* 4.32.

39. Tacitus, *Histories* 5.26; Dyson, "Native Revolts," 264.

40. Tacitus, *Histories* 4.13, 5.23–26; Dyson, "Native Revolts," 264.

41. Tacitus, *Histories* 4.54.2; P. A. Brunt, "Tacitus on the Batavian Revolt," *Latomus* 19, no. 3 (1960): 496.

42. Tacitus, *Histories* 4.13; Dyson, "Native Revolts," 264.

43. The fact that he chose this moment of internal political instability to make his move is another indication of his strong grasp of Rome's internal politics.

44. Tacitus, *Histories* 1.59, 4.13.

45. Tacitus, *Histories* 4.14–15.

46. Tacitus, *Histories* 4.22; Tacitus, *Germania* 7.

47. Tacitus, *Histories* 4.61; Tacitus, *Germania* 8.

48. Tacitus, *Histories* 4.61.

49. Dyson, "Native Revolts," 264–65; Brunt, "Tacitus on the Batavian Revolt," 498.

50. Tacitus, *Histories* 5.23–24.

51. Tacitus, *Histories* 5.25. Tacitus, *Germania* 29 also suggests that the Batavians received favorable peace terms.

52. The "Great Wall of China" as it appears today is the product of the much later Ming dynasty (1368–1644 CE), but its origins lie in the Han (206 BCE–220

CE) and immediately preceding Qin (221–206 BCE) periods. See Arthur N. Waldron, "The Problem of the Great Wall of China," *Harvard Journal of Asiatic Studies* 43, no. 2 (1983): 650–52.

53. Sechin Jagchid and Van Jay Symons, *Peace, War, and Trade along the Great Wall: Nomadic-Chinese Interaction through Two Millennia* (Bloomington: Indiana University Press, 1989), 13.

54. There has been considerable scholarly debate about the origins of the Xiongnu. The current consensus is that, despite the frequent use of the name in the Chinese sources to refer to the Han's main antagonists, the Xiongnu were likely not a single people bound together by material, linguistic, or ethnic affinities. Rather, the term more precisely refers to a frequently shifting political and military alliance, possibly with a territorial component, that united an array of steppe peoples under the leadership of the *shanyu*. Indications of this appear in the sources as well, such as the assertion that the Xiongnu had "a hundred tribes" following them at the height of their power. See Nicola Di Cosmo, "Han Frontiers: Toward an Integrated View," *Journal of the American Oriental Society* 129, no. 2 (2009): 207; Jagchid and Symons, *Peace, War, and Trade*, 32.

55. Mark Lewis, *The Early Chinese Empires: Qin and Han* (Cambridge MA: Harvard University Press, 2007), 132.

56. Quoted in Ying-shih Yu, "The Hsiung-nu," in *The Cambridge History of Early Inner Asia*, ed. Denis Sinor (Cambridge: Cambridge University Press, 1990), 124.

57. Jagchid and Symons, *Peace, War, and Trade*, 16.

58. Owen Lattimore, *Inner Asian Frontiers of China* (Boston: Beacon Press, 1962), 470.

59. Lattimore, *Inner Asian Frontiers*, 481–82.

60. Jagchid and Symons, *Peace, War, and Trade*, 166; Sima Qian, *Shiji* 129.69, in *Records of the Grand Historian: Han Dynasty*, trans. Burton Watson, 2 vols. (New York: Columbia University Press, 1993).

61. Jagchid and Symons, *Peace, War, and Trade*, 27; Sima Qian, *Shiji* 110.50.

62. Daphne Pi-Wei Lei, "Wang Zhaojun on the Border: Gender and Intercultural Conflicts in Premodern Chinese Drama," *Asian Theater Journal* 13, no. 2 (Autumn 1996): 230–31.

63. Jagchid and Symons, *Peace, War, and Trade*, 27; Sima Qian, *Shiji* 110.50.

64. Story quoted in Paul R. Goldin, "Steppe Nomads as a Philosophical Problem in Classical China," in *Mapping Mongolia: Situating Mongolia in the World from Geologic Time to the Present*, ed. Paula L. W. Sabloff (Philadelphia: University of Pennsylvania Press, 2011), 230.

65. The decision affected her directly as well, since it was Xiongnu custom for the son of a dead *shanyu* to marry his father's wives, in this case, his own mother. See Pi-Wei Lei, "Wang Zhaojun on the Border," 231.

66. Sunny Y. Auyang, *The Dragon and the Eagle: The Rise and Fall of the Chinese and Roman Empires* (Armonk NY: M. E. Sharpe, 2014), 229; Nicola Di Cosmo, "Inner Asian Nomads: Their Economic Basis and Its Significance in Chinese History," *Journal of Asian Studies* 54, no. 4 (1994): 1101–3, 1114–15; Anatoly M. Khazanov, *Nomads and the Outside World* (Cambridge: Cambridge University Press, 1984), 202–6, 320–21.

67. Auyang, *The Dragon and the Eagle*, 261; Di Cosmo, "Han Frontiers," 204, 207, 213.

68. Jagchid and Symons, *Peace, War, and Trade*, 4.

69. Auyang, *The Dragon and the Eagle*, 258; Di Cosmo, "Han Frontiers," 205.

70. Yu, "The Hsiung-nu," 125.

71. Jagchid and Symons, *Peace, War, and Trade*, 28; Yu, "The Hsiung-nu," 129; Sima Qian, *Shiji* 110.50; Ban Gu, *Hanshu* 52.22, in *The History of the Former Han Dynasty*, trans. Homer H. Dubs, 3 vols. (Baltimore MD: Waverley Press, 1938).

72. It is worth noting, however, that in the decades of warfare that followed, Han commanders typically chose to attack the Xiongnu in border markets, where the Xiongnu could reliably be found. Wudi and his successors also ordered the construction of new sections of the "great wall" and the establishment of new commanderies along the northern border as part of an expansionist strategy intended to gain firmer control over the frontier. In 51 BCE the tide turned significantly in Chinese favor when internal conflict among the nomads led to a permanent rift between the northern and southern Xiongnu; in time, the leader of the southern Xiongnu surrendered and became a vassal of the Han emperor. By the late first century CE, an estimated two hundred thousand southern Xiongnu had been resettled on the Han side of the border within the frontier provinces, where they provided manpower for the Han armies against their northern cousins. The later Han government also forced thousands of Chinese to migrate to these frontier provinces to prevent them from becoming too heavily "nomadized." By the second century CE, mixed Xiongnu-Chinese settlements had become common across the frontier zone. See Di Cosmo, "Han Frontiers," 205; Jagchid and Symons, *Peace, War, and Trade*, 118; Yu, "The Hsiung-nu," 129, 144–48.

73. Nomads who pledged themselves to Chinese service were typically granted the rank of marquis. Lewis, *Early Chinese Empires*, 146; Sima Qian, *Shiji* 110.

74. Sima Qian, *Shiji* 110.

75. For example, an edict of Wang Mang (r. 9–23 CE) written with brush and ink on wood and dated to 10 CE refers to frontier soldiers who "committed the crime of betrayal" and "those who are especially wicked among the officers and people [whose crimes are high treason and] perversion." For a description of this text with a complete translation, see Enno Giele, "Evidence for the Xiongnu in Chinese Wooden Documents from the Han Period," in *Xiongnu Archaeology: Multidisciplinary Perspectives of the First Steppe Empire in Inner Asia*, ed. Ursula Brosseder and Brian K. Miller. Vor- und Frühgeschichtliche Archäologie (Freiberg: Freiburger Graphische Betriebe, 2011), 55–58.

76. Lattimore, *Inner Asian Frontiers*, 484.

77. Yu, "The Hsiung-Nu," 122; Lattimore, *Inner Asian Frontiers*, 485.

78. Yu, "The Hsiung-Nu," 122; Lattimore, *Inner Asian Frontiers*, 485.

79. Daphne P. Lei, "The Blood-Stained Text in Translation: Tattooing, Bodily Writing, and Performance of Chinese Virtue," *Anthropological Quarterly* 81, no. 1 (Winter 2009): 102–3. A thief, for example, might have the character for "robbery" tattooed on his cheeks or forehead.

80. Ancient information on Zhonghang Yue comes from Sima Qian, *Shiji* 110, and Ban Gu, *Hanshu* 48. See also Jagchid and Symons, *Peace, War, and Trade*, 25; Nicola Di Cosmo, *Ancient China and Its Enemies: The Rise of Nomadic Power in East Asian History* (Cambridge: Cambridge University Press, 2002), 269.

81. Tamara Chin, "Defamiliarizing the Foreigner: Sima Qian's Ethnography and Han-Xiongnu Marriage Diplomacy," *Harvard Journal of Asiatic Studies* 70, no. 2 (2010): 336, 345; Auyang, *The Eagle and the Dragon*, 81. Modern Beijing is located in what used to be Yan territory.

82. All information about Zhonghang Yue comes from Sima Qian, *Shiji* 110.

83. Chin, "Defamiliarizing the Foreigner," 327.

84. Chin, "Defamiliarizing the Foreigner," 329.

3

Rabban Ṣauma

A Medieval Eurasian Shape Shifter

Colleen C. Ho

Early in the summer of 1287, Rabban Ṣauma, an Önggüd Turk from China, spoke to an audience of curious cardinals in Rome: "I have come from remote countries neither to discuss, nor to instruct [men] in the matter of the Faith, but I came that I might receive a blessing from Mar Papa, and from the shrines of the saints, and to make known the words of King [Arghun] and the Catholicus."[1] Why and how he traveled from Qubilai Khan's Yuan dynasty to the political and spiritual home of Latin Christianity are the subjects of this chapter.

Rabban Ṣauma (ca. 1220–94) was a shape shifter par excellence, a polyglot whose many identities and talents enabled him to function in complex social settings. Born into the Turkic Önggüd tribe in modern-day Beijing, Ṣauma witnessed the rapid expansion of the Mongol Empire across much of the Asian continent.[2] The Önggüd, who were primarily Christians of the Church of the East, more commonly known as Nestorians, were early allies of Chinggis Khan.[3] Partially as a result of this wise political decision but mostly because of Chinggis's policy of religious tolerance, Nestorian Christians held important positions in Mongol courts across the empire.[4]

Rabban Ṣauma would become a significant figure in the Ilkhanate, the Mongol regime in the Middle East, several decades after he took monastic vows at the age of twenty-five. He gained a reputation for living a saintly life and being a wise teacher, and he attracted a student named Mark, who proposed that they should embark on a pilgrimage to visit Jesus's tomb in Jerusalem and obtain remission of their sins. Given supplies and letters of introduction by Qubilai Khan (r. 1260–94) and several Mongol princes, the pair spent months on the road but due to unrest in western Asia never reached Jerusalem. They settled in the Ilkhanate at a monastery near Arbil (Erbil, now in Iraq), where there was a historic and prominent Nestorian community. Upon the death of the Nestorian catholicos (patriarch) Mar Denha in 1281, Mark, now known as Mar Yahballaha III, was elected head of the Church of the East because of his knowledge of Mongol customs and language. When Ilkhan Arghun (r. 1284–91) asked him to suggest a candidate to be a diplomat to Europe, Mar Yahballaha recommended his old friend and traveling companion, Rabban Ṣauma. Arghun commissioned Ṣauma to visit European kings and the pope to propose military cooperation against their mutual enemy, the Mamluk Sultanate (1250–1517); the goal was to shore up the Mongol presence in Syria and relieve beleaguered Outremer cities. It is in these conversations that Rabban Ṣauma demonstrated a remarkable ability to shape shift.

This chapter examines shape shifting as the process by which an individual presents their collective self-identities—that is, their identities based on group memberships and social roles—for particular purposes. Ṣauma spoke and performed a Christian language in order to accomplish his political goal of delivering Ilkhan Arghun's proposal and personal religious goal of visiting Christian holy sites and meeting the pope. Given the nature of the sources, Ṣauma's private self-identities, such as his feelings and attitudes toward his group memberships and social roles, are seldom explicit.[5] As a result, I look at Ṣauma's identities as the product of strategic self-presentation through which we are occasionally able to catch glimpses of the specific meanings he had for his identities.

My Approach

Scholars tend to focus on Rabban Ṣauma's diplomatic goals and evaluate their successes and failures.[6] After all, Ilkhans and European kings never did join in a military alliance against the Mamluks, and the last Latin Outremer city of Acre fell in 1291, just a few years after Rabban Ṣauma's overtures. Rather than judge Ṣauma's political accomplishments, I focus on the cognitive flexibility behind his social aptitude and shape shifting.

In a volume that contains numerous examples of the dynamic processes behind the shifting of racial, ethnic, gender, and national identities, it is not easy to study the identity fluidity of Rabban Ṣauma as he traveled through three Mongol khanates and twelve modern countries and visited the courts of eight regimes.[7] Ṣauma also traversed a complex religious landscape generated by the Mongol Empire. An interdisciplinary methodology is necessary to analyze the nature of Ṣauma's shape shifting in varied environments.

An Emphasis on Time and Place

Rabban Ṣauma saw the rapid growth of the dynamic Mongol Empire in his youth. Though he traveled across Eurasia after the Mongol Empire had split into four khanates, Mongol khans continued to rule over dozens of people groups who spoke numerous languages, had widely diverse cultures, and professed many faiths. As a result of the migration of conquered peoples, along with the Mongol practice of employing foreigners in government administration, Mongol Eurasia was a unique place that generated multi-identitied persons and rewarded linguistically talented individuals like Rabban Ṣauma who easily shape shifted between communities.

Race and Ethnicity

Some of this volume's chapters focus on shape shifting across categories like race and ethnicity, whose definitions vary widely. For some, race "suggests a distinction based on an inherited biological feature" such as skin color, while ethnicity "points to cultural differences between groups."[8] Arguing that this perspective is too vague, Stephen Cornell and Douglas Hartmann specify that an ethnic group's identity is primarily constructed by the group itself and is based on, among other things, a putative common descent and claims of shared history. A racial group's identity, in contrast, is initially constructed by others based on perceived physical differences, reflects power relations, and implies inherent differences in worth. Cornell and Hartmann conclude that some groups may be ethnic groups, others may be races, and some may be both.[9] While I cannot discount the possibility that Rabban Ṣauma's Önggüd ethnicity impacted how and why he shape shifted, most important to Ṣauma was his identity as a Nestorian Christian.

Group Membership

This chapter shows how Rabban Ṣauma's Christian identity framed his social interactions. I turn to social psychology theories to think about how his membership in this religious community impacted his identities and underpinned the cognitive processes that begot his shape shifting. Ṣauma presented himself primarily as a Christian pilgrim, which informed his language choices, guided his diplomatic conversations, and was an identity familiar to his audiences, especially when, for example, he visited saints' shrines and performed rituals like the Mass. I argue that the concurrent activation of Rabban Ṣauma's identities of pilgrim and diplomat, a fascinating illustration of sophisticated shape shifting, facilitated his conversations with kings, cardinals, and the pope.

Secondary to Ṣauma's religious identity was his status as a subject of Mongol rule. When Ṣauma and Mark embarked on their journey, the empire had separated into four khanates, making transcontinental travel at times quite challenging. Ṣauma and Mark always presented themselves to local authorities to explain their intentions and obtain letters of introduction to ensure safe passage. This keen understanding of Mongol expectations and attention to courtly protocol benefited Ṣauma and Mark in all Mongol lands and, for the former, in Europe as well.

Religious Identity, Diplomacy, Language, and Performance

When Ilkhan Arghun turned to Catholicos Mar Yahballaha to suggest someone for a diplomatic position, Ṣauma's old friend "saw that there was no man who knew the language except" Ṣauma. The language in question could refer to Mongolian, Persian, or, as I will suggest, perhaps an ecumenical Christian language, because Arghun selected Ṣauma as diplomat "so that his word would be believed" by Latin Christians.[10] Rabban Ṣauma's overarching Christian identity and subsumed social and ethnic identities of Ilkhanid diplomat, Yuan dynasty subject, and ethnic Önggüd facilitated his shape shifting and linguistic skills.

I argue that Rabban Ṣauma's religious shape shifting and linguistic abilities enabled him to codeswitch in ever-changing social situations in order to gain access to audiences.[11] Crucially, Ṣauma spoke a Christian lingua franca based on a rhetoric of piety and pilgrimage that diminished sectarian differences between Latin and Nestorian Christianity and enabled cross-confessional communication. Furthermore, Ṣauma's knowledge of the performative aspects of Christian liturgy, most evident in his participation in Eucharist rituals, demonstrated his consecrational power and Christianness. In essence, Ṣauma shape shifted his Nestorian Christian identity to one of ecumenical, that is, universal, Christian.[12]

Sources

The most important source for my study is a Syriac abridgment and translation of Rabban Ṣauma's original Persian-language travel narrative, which unfortunately does not survive.[13] As a result, analysis of the document produces a limited understanding of Rabban Ṣauma's identities because we only know the edited person presented in the narrative. In any case, the Syriac author remains anonymous, but Pier Giorgio Borbone is certain he was a Nestorian cleric who knew the two men personally.[14] Anonymous must have outlived Mar Yahballaha, because he writes about the catholicos's violent death in 1317. Regrettably, the Syriac translator abridged the Persian source rather severely.[15] Heleen Murre–van den Berg hypothesizes that Anonymous may have been the metropolitan (bishop) of Arbil and successor to Mar Yahballaha III, Catholicos Timothy II (r. 1318–32).[16] Whoever he was, Murre–van den Berg recognizes that the translator edited the document to highlight the history and achievements of the Church of the East, an important self-preserving task, as the Ilkhanate faced increasing internal and external challenges in the 1320s.[17]

Relevant documents contemporary to Rabban Ṣauma's travel narrative include the Syriac-language *Ecclesiastical Chronicle* of Bar Hebraeus (1226–86), a Jewish convert to Syrian Orthodox Christianity who resided in Ilkhanid Maragheh.[18] This is supplemented by diplomatic correspondence mainly from the Latin Western perspective. Sadly, the letters that Rabban Ṣauma presented to European kings and the pope and the official diplomatic report he submitted to Arghun upon his return to the Ilkhanid capital of Tabrīz do not survive.[19]

The chapter has two sections. The first outlines Rabban Ṣauma's journey from China to Europe and explores Ṣauma's shape shifting identities during his audiences with Ilkhan Arghun, cardinals, and the pope. The second highlights Ṣauma's language skills in speaking and performing the Eucharist to a Christian audience. The chapter is theoretically inspired by studies in social psychology, linguistics, and ritual and performance studies.

Rabban Ṣauma's Travels: From China to Iran

Rabban Ṣauma was born in Daidu (Mongolian, Khanbaligh) in modern-day Beijing.[20] Displaying an early commitment to his Christian faith, he rejected his parents' desire for him to marry his betrothed, took monastic vows at the age of twenty-five, and withdrew into isolation. His reputation for piety and wisdom attracted the attention of a young Önggüd man of about fifteen named Mark, who joined Ṣauma and took monastic orders at the age of eighteen (1263). In about 1275 Mark convinced his elder to embark on a pilgrimage to visit Jerusalem and other holy sites.

The duo encountered resistance from the Nestorian community in Daidu/Khanbaligh, who stressed the dangers of the trip. To this the monks reiterated their commitment to the pilgrimage and replied: "We have renounced the world; we consider ourselves to be dead men in respect of it. Toil doth not terrify us, neither doth fear disturb us."[21] Their trip was funded primarily by Nestorians with presumably some assistance from Qubilai Khan's court, though the narrative says little about finances or Qubilai.[22] A fourteenth-century Arabic-language account on the patriarchs of the Church of the East asserts that Qubilai asked Ṣauma and Mark to soak clothes he had given them "in the Jordan and to put [them] in contact with the tomb of the Lord Christ."[23] As Morris Rossabi points out, if Qubilai indeed requested this, he would have subsidized their journey.[24] Moreover, the khan may have invested in it because his mother, Sorqaqtani Beki, was a Nestorian Christian and more generally because he presented himself as the protector of major religions in his realm. Khanal patronage of multireligious holy men was one manner in which Mongol rulers integrated faith communities and ethnic groups into the Mongol polity. Rossabi and E. A. Wallis Budge are certain that Ṣauma and Mark sought and received letters of introduction or letters patent as well as supplies from Qubilai to ensure safe passage.

Indeed, the pair always sought khanal support in Mongol-ruled realms, illustrating their astute understanding of Mongol political demands. Furthermore, Rabban Ṣauma and Mark were also knowledgeable of complex interkhanate conflicts. When they met with Qaidu, head of the Chaghatay Khanate (r. 1271–1301), in the trade city of Talas (today in Kyrgyzstan), they took care to omit any talk of politics, because Qaidu was at war with his uncle Qubilai. Instead, they prayed blessings and a long life for Qaidu, who gave them letters of protection.[25] Ṣauma and Mark were always mindful of their duties as Mongol subjects.

Sometime in early 1280, Rabban Ṣauma and Mark entered the Ilkhanate in Khorasan. They soon met the catholicos (patriarch) of the Church of the East, Mar Denḥâ, in the former Ilkhanid capital of Maragheh. He blessed Ṣauma and Mark, wrote them a letter of introduction "so that they might be honourably entreated whithersoever they went," and provided them with a guide. The travelers then visited a number of saints' shrines in and around Baghdad, the seat of the catholicos.[26] Ṣauma and Mark marveled at the monasteries and churches in the Armenian city of Ani but were turned back from the Georgian Black Sea coast due to unsafe passage.

The duo's dream of visiting the holy city dashed, Rabban Ṣauma and Mark settled temporarily at a monastery near Arbil in northern Iraq. Catholicos Mar Denḥâ ordained Mark the metropolitan (bishop) of Cathay (northern China) with the name Mar Yahballaha III and appointed Rabban Ṣauma as visitor-general, assistant to his friend. Ṣauma was probably forty-five to fifty years old, his companion around thirty-five.[27] The catholicos sent the newly promoted friends to China to undertake their diocesal duties, but civil war in the Chaghatay Khanate halted their progress, and they returned to the monastery near Arbil.

Upon Mar Denḥâ's death in 1281, Mar Yahballaha was elected catholicos of the Church of the East, despite his protests that he did not know the liturgical language of Syriac: "I am wholly ignorant of your language, Syriac, which it is absolutely necessary for the Patriarchy to know."[28] The council of elders reasoned that "there was no man except Mar Yahballaha who was acquainted with their [Mongols'] manners and customs, and their policy of government, and their language."[29] As Christian clergy, they understood that their tax-exempt status and position among the Ilkhanate's majority-Muslim subjects were dependent on good relations with the Ilkhan.[30] The new catholicos and his old friend went to confirm their appointments with Ilkhan Abagha (r. 1265–82) at his summer palace Takht-i-Sulayman. The Ilkhan approved the positions and provided money for Mark's enthronement celebration, which took place in Baghdad in November 1280.[31]

When Ilkhan Arghun (r. 1284–91) sought to subjugate the countries of Palestine and Syria and needed a wise man suitable for and "capable of undertaking an embassy" to increase communication with Western kings, he asked Catholicos Mar Yahballaha for a recommendation. This was not surprising, as the founder of the Ilkhanate and Arghun's grandfather, Ilkhan Hülegü (r. 1256–81), had married a Nestorian Christian named Toghus (Doquz) Khatun, initiating decades of Ilkhanid patronage of and positive relations with the Church of the East; indeed, the Mongols counted numerous Nestorians among their royal women.[32] It was Mar Yahballaha who suggested his former teacher and travel companion Rabban Ṣauma to serve as the Ilkhan's

ambassador.[33] Instructed to propose an alliance to the pope and European kings to assist beleaguered Latin crusader states, the seasoned
traveler Ṣauma was the perfect candidate to convey such an important message. Ilkhan Arghun's selection of Rabban Ṣauma added diplomat to his menu of identities, one dependent on the religious identity
enabled by his Önggüd tribe's conversion to Nestorian Christianity in
the twelfth century and his experience as a subject of Mongol rule.[34]

Journey through Europe

Rabban Ṣauma did not endure his mission alone. Among his companions was an Italian interpreter named Ughetto (Ugeto?), a Genoese merchant and interpreter named Thomas of Anfossi, a *nobilis
vir* (noble man) named Sabadinus, and "a number of excellent men
from among the priests and deacons of the Cell of the Catholicus."[35]
Thomas knew Persian, which was the language Ṣauma probably used
to communicate with the Ilkhan.[36] The diplomat and his international
entourage show how the Mongol Empire promoted transcontinental
travel and rewarded multilingual individuals.

Departing from Baghdad, Rabban Ṣauma's first stop in early 1287
was Constantinople, where he had an audience with Byzantine emperor
Andronikos II Palaiologos (r. 1282–1328). Ṣauma's visit was a reaffir-
mation of the positive Byzantine-Ilkhanid relations that had begun
with Arghun's father. Ilkhan Abagha (r. 1265–82) had married Maria,
daughter of Byzantine emperor Michael VIII Palaiologos, in 1265 or
1266.[37] Thereafter, Abagha's overtures of an alliance with Western
powers against the Mamluks were predicated on Western-Byzantine-
Ilkhanid teamwork, with the first two armies approaching from the
west and the third army marching from the east.[38] Like his father,
Michael VIII, Emperor Andronikos II had personal connections to
Mongol khans, having married an illegitimate daughter also named
Maria to Toqto'a, the khan of the Golden Horde. Rabban Ṣauma likely
confirmed with the emperor that the Byzantines were still willing to
provide auxiliaries for Ilkhanid campaigns. Ṣauma also happily saw
the city's numerous churches, like the marvelous Hagia Sophia, and
saints' tombs.[39]

Setting sail for Italy, "after two months of toil, and weariness, and exhaustion, Rabban Ṣauma . . . landed at . . . Napoli. . . . [T]he king [probably Charles II] welcomed him and paid him honor."[40] While there, Ṣauma likely witnessed the eruption of Mount Etna on June 18 and a terrific naval battle in the Bay of Sorrento between Charles II and King James II of Aragon on June 24, 1287.[41]

When Rabban Ṣauma arrived in Rome at the end of June 1287, the Holy See was vacant, as Pope Honorius IV had died on April 3, 1287. Twelve cardinals welcomed the diplomat warmly, and one of them, the future pope Nicholas IV, asked about the reason for his journey. Ṣauma replied, "'The Mongols and the Catholicus of the East have sent me to Mar Papa concerning the matter of Jerusalem; and they have sent letters with me.'" At their next meeting, the cardinals asked him numerous questions about the catholicos and the "king of the Mongols." Rabban Ṣauma also explained that "many Mongols . . . are Christians . . . and pay honor to the Christians." The cardinals were pleased to hear that Ilkhan Arghun was a friend to the catholi-cos, had "the desire to take Palestine, and the countries of Syria," and demanded help in order to take Jerusalem.[42] They stressed, however, that Ṣauma would have to wait for the election of a pope to discuss any military plans.

Instead, the cardinals questioned Ṣauma's "confession of faith" and "way." Ṣauma described the Trinity thusly: "'I believe in One God, hidden, everlasting, without beginning and without end, Father, and Son, and Holy Spirit: Three Persons, coequal and indivisible; among Whom there is none who is first, or last, or young, or old: in Nature they are One, in Persons they are three: the Father is the Begetter, the Son is the Begotten, and the Spirit proceedeth.'" Ṣauma continued that Jesus Christ was born of "Mary the holy virgin." The cardinals tried to test Ṣauma's understanding of the Trinity by claiming that "'the Father is the cause of the Son, and the Son is the cause of the Spirit,'" but Ṣauma refuted the statement and declared that "'the Father is the cause of the Son and the Spirit, and that both the Son and the Spirit are causations of His.'"[43] The cardinals did not challenge the sugges-tion that the three natures were not coequal, which Rossabi sees as an attempt to avoid any controversy but may have been the result of confusing interpreting.[44]

Though it is unclear how much the cardinals knew about the Church of the East, its theology, and its status in the Ilkhanate, they tried to discern the diplomat's Christian orthodoxy and stated so: "'[The cardinals] confess that the Spirit proceedeth from the Father and the Son, but not as we said, for we were only putting thy modesty [or religious belief?] to the test.'"[45] The cardinals' suspicion derived from the controversy surrounding Nestorius of Antioch, fifth-century patriarch of Constantinople (r. 428–31). He was accused of heresy for the belief that there existed in Jesus two separate natures, human and divine, which were loosely joined in a moral union. His argument stemmed from his dislike of the title "Mother of God / God Bearer" (Theotokos) for the Virgin Mary because he felt the title denied Christ's full humanity; he proposed "Mother of Christ" as a more suitable title.[46] Nestorius accused his critics of misconstruing his teachings but was excommunicated at the Council of Ephesus in 431 CE. His followers fled east and found safety in Mesopotamia, from where Nestorian missionaries spread across Asia; they obtained many converts in Central Asia and reached China as early as 638 CE.

In her important book *The Invention of Race in the European Middle Ages*, Geraldine Heng argues that Latin Christians in a sense racialized heretical Christians like the Nestorians and set them apart by emphasizing their fundamental doctrinal differences.[47] While the cardinals probably knew the story of Nestorius, it is uncertain that they understood if and how their visitor's beliefs were connected to the fifth-century figure (they were not). Rabban Ṣauma, however, seems to have been aware of the conversation's pitfalls. In the end, as his account portrays it, Ṣauma's "power of argument" commanded the cardinals' respect: "Now though the Cardinals restrained his speech by means of very many demonstrations, they held him in high esteem because of his power of argument."[48] Sounding frustrated, Rabban Ṣauma asked to "set aside discussion" so that he might meet the pope, deliver Arghun's message, and visit saints' shrines. The cardinals obliged, and thus the diplomat became a Christian pilgrim in Rome. The detailed descriptions of the sites visited and saints' relics seen, nearly twice as long as the declaration of faith before the cardinals, reveals how meaningful personal piety and pilgrimage were to Rabban Ṣauma and his abridger.

Since there was no pope with whom to discuss Ilkhan Arghun's plan, the embassy continued through Tuscany to Genoa, where they were welcomed "honorably," likely because Ṣauma's translator, Thomas, was a member of the Genoese Anfossi banking family.[49] The next stop was Paris. King Philip IV (r. 1285–1314) greeted Rabban Ṣauma with "great honor and ceremony." The diplomat proposed a campaign against the Mamluks for the recovery of Jerusalem.[50]

The plans Rabban Ṣauma presented, of which we have few concrete details, had already been offered to Western powers in various forms many times, the earliest to King Louis IX of France in 1262. In that year, Ilkhan Hülegü, calling himself "Destroyer of the power of the Muslims and friend of Christianity," sent a letter to Louis in which the Mongol khan proclaimed his intention of destroying the Mamluks and returning Jerusalem to the pope.[51] Hülegü proposed that Louis IX send his fleet to blockade Egypt by sea. Louis forwarded the letter to Pope Urban IV, whose response to the Ilkhan was positive but noncommittal.[52]

Hülegü's son Abagha continued Ilkhanid communication with the Latin West. In a letter dated 1267, Ilkhan Abagha proposed that Western armies meet up with the forces of his father-in-law, Byzantine emperor Michael VIII Palaiologos, to trap the Mamluks between themselves and the Mongols.[53] Thereafter, most Ilkhanid overtures of an alliance with the West included Byzantine involvement.[54]

Abagha's son Arghun was in regular contact with the West during his reign, and Rabban Ṣauma was his most famous envoy. According to Ṣauma's account, Philip IV said that if the pagan Mongols were so concerned about the recapture of Jerusalem, then it was incumbent upon Western Christians to join in the struggle to regain the Holy Land.[55] We have no reason to doubt his affirmative response, though he did not give plans for concrete assistance.[56] With the French king's reply in hand, Ṣauma asked to be escorted through the most renowned

shrines and churches in Paris, to which Philip responded enthusiasti-
cally and obligingly. Ṣauma spent a month as a pilgrim touring saints'
shrines and Parisian churches such as Saint-Denis. Philip also showed
him the crown of thorns and a piece of the holy cross.[57]

Next, Rabban Ṣauma arrived in Bordeaux in mid-October 1287
to see King Edward I of England (r. 1272–1307), perhaps the monarch
most open to cooperation due to previous contacts with the Ilkhanate. When Lord Edward (the future Edward I) was in Acre in the
late spring of 1271, he sent an embassy to Ilkhan Abagha (the letter
does not survive). The prince conducted some petty raids, and after
receiving Abagha's response asking Edward to coordinate with Mongol actions against the Mamluks, Edward attacked Qaqun (Caco) in
November 1271. Nothing resulted from this action, and Edward left
Palestine soon after.[58] In any case, Rabban Ṣauma's proposal to recapture Jerusalem and the Holy Land excited Edward, who had vowed to
take the cross and go on crusade earlier that spring.[59] In a gesture that
Rossabi interprets as indicating his commitment to Arghun's plans,
Edward asked Rabban Ṣauma to "celebrate the Eucharist . . . and the
king partook of the Sacrament, and made a great feast that day."[60] As
usual, Ṣauma asked for permission to tour the churches and shrines
in English domains on the Continent, though they are not outlined
in any detail.

Activities with the Pope in Rome

At this point, Rabban Ṣauma's mission had been on the road in Europe
for between nine and ten months. While wintering in Genoa, he
expressed frustration at the papal interregnum to a papal legate ("Visitor of Mar Papa"), who assured Ṣauma that he would urge the cardinals to come to a consensus; they had been delayed due to illness.[61]
A pope was finally elected on February 22, 1288, and the first Franciscan pope, Nicholas IV, who had spoken to Ṣauma in Rome previously as Bishop Girolamo, immediately invited the weary diplomat to
Rome (he was roughly sixty-eight years old). Rabban Ṣauma greeted
the pope excitedly, declaring, "'May thy throne stand for ever, O our
Father! And may it be blessed above all kings and nations! And may it

make peace to reign in thy days throughout the Church to the utter-most ends of the earth! Now that I have seen thy face mine eyes are illumined, and I shall not go away brokenhearted to the countries [of the East]. I give thanks to the goodness of God who hath held me to be worthy to see thy face.'"[62] Rabban Ṣauma presented Pope Nich-olas with gifts and letters from Ilkhan Arghun and Catholicos Mar Yahballaha; unfortunately, none of them have survived. It is assumed that, as he did in Paris and Bordeaux, Ṣauma proposed a joint cam-paign in the Holy Land.[63]

Rabban Ṣauma's subsequent time in Rome was primarily devoted to church events. He asked the pope "'to celebrate the Eucharist so that ye may see our use.'" When "a very large number of people gath-ered . . . to see how the ambassador of the Mongols celebrated the Eucharist," "they rejoiced and said, 'The language is different, but the use is the same.'" While the text does not specify what language Rab-ban Ṣauma spoke during the Mass, it was likely Syriac, the liturgical language of the Church of the East. After that the pope blessed Ṣauma thusly: "'May God receive thy offering, and bless thee, and pardon thy transgressions and sins.'"[64]

Pope Nicholas IV's Response to Ilkhan Arghun

Soon after the Easter festivities, Ṣauma asked to depart. The pope stalled and invited the diplomat to remain in Rome, but Ṣauma prom-ised Nicholas that he would tell the Ilkhan and the Eastern Church that he had been treated exceptionally well.[65] After asking for a gift of relics, Rabban Ṣauma returned to Persia by late September 1288.[66]

While we do not have surviving copies of Ilkhan Arghun's and Mar Yahballaha's letters from 1287, we have Nicholas's responses to Arghun and the catholicos and his letters to *reginam Tartarorum* and the "Franciscans amongst the Tartars."[67] The pope praises Arghun for his respect for Christians but reveals his minimal understanding of Mongol attitudes toward religion when he calls for the Ilkhan to be baptized before any military campaign for Jerusalem.[68] Pope Nicho-las was not the first pope to propose baptism to a Mongol khan; Pope Innocent IV did so to the Great Khan Güyüg in the 1240s. In urging the

Ilkhan and Nestorians to accept papal authority, the pope was attempting to impose his vision of a papal monarchy in which the pope, as the Vicar of Christ, reigned supreme over earthly sovereigns.[69] Even though Arghun was friendly to Christians in his realm, he had no concept of this idea of religious supremacy. He had inherited a worldview that proclaimed that Mongol sovereigns ruled with the strength of their good fortune and by virtue of a mandate from heaven, which had first blessed Arghun's great-grandfather Chinggis Khan. While the Mongol Yuan dynasty retained suzerainty over the Ilkhans (literally, "obedient khans"), practically speaking, Arghun operated independently from his great-uncle Qubilai in Daidu/Khanbaligh.[70] There was no room in Arghun's perspective for the pope's demands.

In a move perhaps intended to reassure the pope that he was serious in his affection toward Christians, Arghun baptized his son Kharbanda, the future Ilkhan Oljeitü (r. 1304–16), Nicholas in the pope's honor. Ignoring Pope Nicholas's request for Mongol submission, two years later, Arghun confirmed his commitment to the plan Rabban Ṣauma proposed in 1287–88 and promised to send troops to aid King Philip IV of France in a forthcoming campaign against the Mamluks; they planned to depart in January 1291.[71] Nothing came of it. In addition to the logistical difficulties in planning a joint military campaign and troubles Philip faced at home, Peter Jackson postulates that despite positive communication, Western monarchs still viewed the Mongols with suspicion.[72] The last crusader city of Acre fell in May 1291. Arghun had died six weeks earlier, in March.

Shape Shifting Identities

Rabban Ṣauma's journey to Europe is important for many reasons. It indicated that Ilkhan Arghun had a concrete approach to foreign policy and a keen understanding of complicated European-Crusader-Byzantine-Mamluk relations. The Ilkhan also exhibited the particularly Mongol aptitude for recognizing useful talent, selecting Rabban Ṣauma for his Christian affiliation, his language skills, and his impressive endurance for travel.[73] Finally, even though Acre was lost soon after Ṣauma's visit, his mission and further Ilkhanid campaigns against the Mamluks inspired hope in the West for the retaking of Jerusalem for years to come.

Despite the fact that his mission did not result in joint Latin-Mongol military action, an outcome far outside of Rabban Ṣauma's influence, it is remarkable how he made his audiences amenable to his message. After their initial meeting, Ṣauma's skillful shape shifting between his social identity as a Christian and his role identities as a diplomat and pilgrim, as well as his subtle obscuring of the theological differences between Nestorian and Latin Christianity, granted him fruitful meetings with Pope Nicholas IV in Rome. In order to elucidate the shape shifting process, I examine how Ṣauma interacted with people he encountered, since the text provides little information on Ṣauma's person. Despite the translator's abridgment, there is no doubt that Rabban Ṣauma had an impressive ability to perform different identities. He was an Önggüd, a subject of the Mongol Empire, a monk, a diplomat, and a Christian pilgrim. It is this last identity that I contend was most important to Rabban Ṣauma's social identity, that is, how he defined himself as a member of a social group and how he valued that group membership.[74]

In a modern context, groups often are defined by broad traits such as race, ethnicity, gender, sexual orientation, national origin, and religion, but a group can be marked by an almost infinite number of characteristics. In Rabban Ṣauma's case, consistent requests to visit holy sites and see saints' relics show that the category of social identity most important to him during his travels in Europe was that of Christian pilgrim.[75] Indeed, Rabban Ṣauma's original motivation to leave Daidu/Khanbaligh was to go on pilgrimage to Jerusalem. Ṣauma's detailed descriptions of the churches and saints' shrines reflect his belief in the power of saints and their capacity for intercession, the healing power of their relics housed in sacralized spaces, and the conviction that pilgrimage to holy places merited the remission of sins.[76]

I further argue that Rabban Ṣauma strategically deployed his identity of Christian pilgrim in order to establish strong diplomatic relations and acquire European allies. For example, when in Rome for the first time Rabban Ṣauma politely but firmly ended the cardinals' interrogation by emphasizing that he had traveled to Rome to deliver Arghun's message to the pope and visit saints' shrines.[77] This action falls in line with a concept social psychologists call the common in-group identity model. Changing categorical representations from "us" (Nestorian Christian) and "them" (Latin Christians) to a more inclusive "we" (ecumenical Christians) can help reduce intergroup conflict.[78] In other words, Rabban Ṣauma *recategorized*, or *shape shifted*, those present into the superordinate category of Christians without theological differences by reminding the cardinals that he was a humble Christian pilgrim.[79] In creating a new, more inclusive group, he reduced the cardinals' uncertainty about his intentions and possibly heterodox Christianity.[80] This act enabled Rabban Ṣauma to deliver Arghun's message and ensured a positive reception in Rome by the future pope. Fortunately, the identity most meaningful to Ṣauma, that of Christian pilgrim, also happened to be most conducive to making his audiences congenial to his diplomatic message.

Shape Shifting Languages: Rabban Ṣauma the Codeswitcher

Thus far I have discussed how Rabban Ṣauma skillfully shape shifted from diplomat to Christian pilgrim to encourage a positive reception. He could not have done so, however, without knowledge of each identity's language. I contend that Ṣauma, clearly comfortable in politicoreligious settings such as courts, demonstrated communication competence by speaking a nondenominational, ecumenical Christian language to help him achieve his diplomatic and religious goals.[81] In essence, as Ṣauma shape shifted, he also codeswitched.[82]

Codeswitching (hereafter cs) is the use of two or more languages in one speech exchange by bi- or multilingual speakers.[83] Until recently, cs has been viewed by some linguists as a unidirectional step in the acculturation process whereby the ultimate goal is monolingualism in the dominant language and by the general public as an indication of language degeneration.[84] This is a flawed assumption. The sociolinguistic approach to cs helps elucidate the social factors and historical and cultural contexts that promoted Ṣauma's cs.[85] I argue that Ṣauma codeswitched between spoken languages, written languages, and a performative language of Christian religiosity to gain access to material resources, such as allies and saints' relics, and symbolic resources, like the spiritual reward of visiting pilgrimage sites.[86]

Although Ṣauma's narrative says that Arghun chose the seasoned traveler for his Christianness, the Ilkhan also recognized Ṣauma's linguistic talent: "And when the Catholicus saw that there was no man who knew the language except Rabban Ṣauma, and knowing that he was fully capable of this, he commanded him to go [on the embassy]."[87] While it is not clear which language the passage refers to—it is possible Arghun was referring to a Christian language—Rabban Ṣauma certainly knew several languages. His native language was Önggüd, a Turkic language. Rossabi is also confident that Ṣauma knew Chinese well.[88] Given that Ṣauma's original travel account was written in Persian, he was at least trilingual. I am certain that Ṣauma had some knowledge of spoken and written Syriac, because his family's position in Daidu/Khanbaligh provided him with "a praiseworthy system of education" and a "worthy teacher" who "trained him diligently in ecclesiastical learning" so that he became a priest by the age of twenty.[89]

As impressive as Ṣauma's language knowledge was, he would not have been unusual in the Mongol Empire. Chinggis Khan's order that his native tongue be written in the Uyghur alphabet meant that from the beginning, imperial administrators were multiethnic and multilingual, often drawn from Uyghurs, as well as Nestorian Christian communities, whose liturgical language, Syriac, was written in an alphabet ancestral to Uyghur-Mongolian.[90] Chinggis's grandson Qubilai, looking for a solution to the Uyghur-Mongolian script's drawbacks, found it in a new alphabet created by Phags-pa (1235–80), a Tibetan lama. The script was used to write Mongolian, Sanskrit, Tibetan, Turkic, and Chinese.[91] As a result of these decisions and the empire's multicultural makeup, knowledge of scripts and languages commanded respect, often conferred status and power, and was a means of career advancement.[92]

While Rabban Ṣauma's languages helped him communicate with Nestorian Christian communities across Central Asia and members of Ilkhan Arghun's court, it was Ṣauma's knowledge of a Christian language that proved most important to his religious and diplomatic activities in Europe. This is not to claim that varied Christian groups spoke a Christian language that followed the same rules of syntax, morphology, and grammar. Rather, Ṣauma was well-versed in a system of communication based on Christian rituals.

Rabban Ṣauma spoke the language of Christian theology and pilgrimage to the cardinals to accomplish three things: diminish or eliminate the theological differences between Nestorian and Latin Christianity by presenting himself as an ecumenical Christian; acquire valuable material goods such as saints' relics; and perhaps most importantly, facilitate access to the to-be-determined pope. At Edward's court in Bordeaux, Ṣauma's emphasis on the Mongols' desire to reclaim Jerusalem and the Holy Land stirred in the English king a crusading spirit. Ṣauma may have also reminded Edward of his ongoing relationship with the Ilkhanate and his past activities in the Holy Land.[93] In these instances, Ṣauma's dexterous employment of a Christian language that was grounded in his personal pilgrimage goals reflects his accommodation to the language abilities of his audiences.[94]

The multicultural Mongol Empire, whose religious, cultural, and linguistic diversity continued as the empire fragmented into khanates, created opportunities for men like Rabban Ṣauma, as well as his European interpreters and translators. Ṣauma's translators included Thomas of Anfossi, a Genoese merchant who was fluent in Persian, and Ughetto, who was repeatedly referred to in letters as an interpreter.[95] The distinction between the two positions is important, because as Denis Sinor emphasizes, they require different skills. An interpreter "provides a simultaneous or near simultaneous oral translation of an oral communication" and negotiates the way messages are understood by others.[96] A translator transfers a written text from one language to another.[97] All too often, regrettably, we have few or no details of interpreted events and have to rely on faulty texts to reconstruct conversations.

In any case, the Önggüd Christian's communications with his Italian translator and interpreter were conducted in no one's native language.

It cannot be overstated how important interpreters were; their language knowledge, ability to solve problems of interpretation, and comprehension of situated interactions mediated communication between Ṣauma and his audiences.[98] To be clear, we are not certain what languages Thomas, Ughetto, and the even more mysterious Sabadinus knew. The first two likely knew some Persian, which scholars have generally assumed was the lingua franca across the Mongol khanates.[99] Stephen G. Haw recently disputed this and claims that Turkic was in more common usage than Persian.[100] Rossabi thinks that while both Persian and Turkic were used in conversation, Persian was still the primary language of texts.[101] In any case, Luciano Petech's conclusion that Thomas and Ughetto were Italian merchants who had traveled from Yuan China to the Ilkhanate introduces the possibility that they knew some Turkic or Chinese.[102] Taking into consideration that Ṣauma's speech was interpreted into Greek in Constantinople, vernacular Italian in Rome (Pope Nicholas IV was from central Italy), and Parisian and/or Anglo-Norman French in France, as well as translated into Latin, it is important to think about how these interpreter- and translator-guided interactions shaped Ṣauma's conversations with kings, cardinals, and Pope Nicholas.[103]

There are several ways to bring together Ṣauma's shape shifting and codeswitching abilities. In a simple interpretation, I might argue that as Ṣauma shape shifted between his diplomat and Christian identities, he codeswitched between their respective languages. While this was true in some cases, it does not account for the language(s) Ṣauma spoke when his identities were concurrently activated. In many situations, Ṣauma's Christian language was adequate for both his diplomatic and his personal religious purposes, which makes understanding the cognitive processes behind codeswitching more difficult. Finally, codeswitching is not always a political act; some bilinguals codeswitch simply because they can and oftentimes may not be aware that they have done so.[104] In Ṣauma's case, I assert that his fluency in the discourse of Christian ritual helped him reshape how his audiences perceived his Christianness. To see this process in action most clearly, I turn to Ṣauma's participation in Eucharist rituals.

The Eucharist as Unifier: Rabban Ṣauma
as Consecrator of the Eucharist

Thus far I have argued that Rabban Ṣauma's Christian identity and familiarity with an ecumenical Christian language aided reception of his diplomacy and, as Heng notes, elicited "from his Latin Christian hosts their best behavior."[105] In this section, I discuss how this language included ritual action and performance.[106] I show how Ṣauma's participation in rituals such as the Eucharist eliminated doubts about his Christian identity and encouraged a positive reception to Arghun's proposal. By performing in these rituals, Ṣauma displayed his Christian knowledge and piety and fulfilled a personal goal by celebrating Mass with Pope Nicholas IV.

Rabban Ṣauma's travels in Europe are noteworthy for a number of reasons, not the least because he performed East Syrian Eucharistic rites in a Roman setting. By the Middle Ages, the Eucharist, a sacrament that commemorated and reenacted the words and actions of Jesus at the Last Supper the night before he died, had developed into a complex ritual full of symbolism with a salvific function.[107] While theologians and laity agreed that the Eucharist was foundational to Christian practice and, indeed, necessary for salvation, it did not occur without controversy and much spilled ink. Debates regarding the meaning, preparation, and administration of the Eucharist raged across Christendom.[108]

Despite denominational liturgical variety, the Mass, the church service in which a priest consecrates the Eucharist, generally followed the same format: introductory rites included an opening blessing; a confession of sin; readings from the Bible; the offertory, during which the priest arranged the bread and wine; the priest's consecration of the bread and wine, by which they became the sacrificial body and blood of Christ; Communion, when those present received the Eucharist; and concluding rites.[109] Variations in Western and Eastern Christian rites involve different preparation of the bread and wine and varying liturgies, processions, and reading selections.[110] One might say that religious differences were performed, witnessed, and entrenched in rituals like the Eucharist.

In Ṣauma's case, however, it is not important to outline the technical differences between Pope Nicholas IV's Roman Rite and Rabban Ṣauma's East Syrian Rite because, as Miri Rubin establishes, Mass was not usually celebrated as described in normative liturgical texts.[111] A more useful approach is Catherine Bell's distinction between religious orthodoxy, the correct belief in theological doctrines, and orthopraxy, the correct performance of behavioral responsibilities (*praxis* = correct action).[112] As noted earlier, after Ṣauma administered the Eucharist a large crowd "rejoiced and said, 'The language is different, but the use is the same.'"[113] By requesting to celebrate the Eucharist publicly with the pope, Ṣauma astutely understood the power of ritual performance and used the sacrament to exhibit his Christian orthopraxy.[114]

Scholars have long recognized that the medieval Eucharist, a sacrament in the Latin and East Christian Churches, was an event that brought together text, history, ritual, and performance on a sacred altar stage.[115] Richard D. McCall emphasizes that Jesus's command at the Last Supper, "Do this in remembrance of me," is a call to action and performance.[116] Gary Macy calls it a "multimedia event," "a drama, a pageant, a liturgy."[117] The performative aspects of the Eucharist include but are not limited to the priest (someone) making God flesh (action) by reciting scripture and prayers (script) and moving his body (behavior) at a church's altar (place) in order to join the audience with the mystical body of Christ and reaffirm their membership in the church of the saved (end).[118] Bell calls the entire service "a grand allegorical drama of the whole process of human redemption."[119] The Eucharist was (is) a ritual that encoded into action the memory of Jesus's words and actions at the Last Supper.[120]

Given the spiritual implications of the Eucharist, it is no wonder that the person with the power to accomplish the *transubstantio*—an ordained priest whose words and actions transformed the bread and wine into the body and blood of Jesus—became legally and spiritually set apart from the laity in the twelfth and thirteenth centuries. This elevated status meant that the Eucharist was not only a moment of divine presence but a statement of clerical power.[121] Without knowing

Syriac or the details of the East Syrian Rite, a number of factors would have helped the audience feel the full impact of the Eucharist. The physical space of the church and the decoration of its altar, along with sensory stimuli provided by chiming bells, lit candles, songs, and murmured prayers, clearly communicated the Eucharist's significance.[122] As Ṣauma elevated the Host so it could be seen by the audience, his words demonstrated his power to consecrate Christ's presence in the bread, created a critical moment in which the audience achieved a momentary physical oneness with God, and confirmed his priestly and orthopraxic Christianness.[123] In this spiritually charged environment, I believe Ṣauma saw himself and his audience as one ecumenical Christian community without theological and ritual differences.

The fact that Ṣauma was present in Rome for Easter celebrations made the sacrament all the more significant. The Fourth Lateran Council of 1215 decreed that all laity should receive the Eucharist once a year at Easter from their parish priest. The self-preparation process was a rigorous one and followed a period of intensified Lenten preaching, stringent fasting and abstinence, the confessing of sins, and the completing of penance. Those in Ṣauma's audience who had properly conducted themselves benefited most from the Eucharist.[124]

Presenting the Eucharist not only served to elevate Ṣauma's standing but also benefited his host. As the newly elected first Franciscan pope, Nicholas faced challenges such as the rapidly deteriorating Latin crusader states in Outremer and his order's internal struggle over the issue of poverty.[125] He also had an international legacy of mission to uphold, as Franciscans had spearheaded Western diplomatic communication with the Mongols.[126] Generously hosting Ilkhanid representatives validated Pope Nicholas's status as the leader of Christendom and worthiness as an ally, and it confirmed the order's importance in worldly diplomatic matters. To that end he assigned to Ṣauma "a mansion in which to dwell, and he appointed servants to give him everything that he might require."[127] Pope Nicholas IV continued using Franciscans as diplomats when in 1289 he commissioned the Franciscan Giovanni of Montecorvino to meet with Ilkhan Arghun and Qubilai.[128] Including the important visitor and compelling Christian performer in Nicholas's entourage during Easter week festivities elevated the pope's prestige.

Rabban Ṣauma as Receiver of the Eucharist

After his grand Eucharistic performance, Rabban Ṣauma requested to receive the Eucharist from Nicholas's hands, which was clearly one of the personal high points of Ṣauma's journey. The following week, on Palm Sunday, "countless thousands and tens of thousands of people gathered together before the papal throne. . . . And he [Pope Nicholas IV] consecrated the Mysteries and gave the Eucharistic Mystery to Rabban Sawma first of all—he having confessed his sins—and the Pope pardoned his transgressions and his sins and those of his fathers. And Rabban Sawma rejoiced greatly in receiving the Eucharistic Mystery from the hand of Mar Papa. And he received it with tears and sobs, giving thanks to God and meditating upon the mercies which had been poured out upon him."[129] Traveling with an entourage of cardinals and bishops, Ṣauma received the Eucharist from the pope three more times at three churches to celebrate Passover, the Passion, and the Resurrection.[130]

In contrast to the frequency with which most contemporary Christian groups partake in Communion, in the Middle Ages the sacrament was taught as an annual duty, most often taken on the major feasts of Christmas, Easter, and Pentecost. As a result of the laity's often sporadic participation, the occasion for the reception of Christ's body became more important. Preachers stressed that the faithful must be in a worthy state to attend Mass, which one might achieve by confessing sins, paying tithes, or abstaining from sexual intercourse, among other things.[131] As Gary Macy establishes, medieval theologians were fixated on one's state of reception, especially because of concerns about infidels or animals purposefully or accidentally ingesting Jesus's body. Ṣauma was certainly in the correct state to receive the full blessing of Christ's body; he confessed his sins, gazed upon the Host, and took the bread from the hand of Christ's Vicar on Earth with humility and joy.[132]

To sum up, Ṣauma's administration and reception of the Eucharist was the culmination of his travels in Europe. The audience's warm response to his consecration of the Host reflected Ṣauma's successful shape shifting from a potentially heterodox Christian to a powerfully ordained priest. Ṣauma's social and performative reception of Christ's body and blood from Pope Nicholas's hands signified Ṣauma's orthopraxic faith and his unity with the church and the community of the saved.[133] There is little evidence that Rabban Ṣauma was distressed at having to downplay his Nestorianness. Rather, he seems joyful that his diplomatic standing and Christian piety gained him access to cathedrals and saints' relics.

Conclusion

What happened to our intrepid protagonist? Ilkhan Arghun, who was supposedly delighted with what he saw as the success of the mission, welcomed Rabban Ṣauma back with an elaborate feast and bestowed upon him many gifts. Ṣauma lived out the rest of his days as a devout Christian and faithful subject of the Ilkhan. Arghun's successor, Ilkhan Geikhatu (r. 1291–95), fulfilled Ṣauma's request for funds to build a permanent church in Maragheh. Ṣauma's old companion Mar Yahballaha assisted in constructing the church, which was completed in October 1293, and raised funds to maintain it. After traveling to Baghdad to participate in a feast that the future Ilkhan Baidu hosted in honor of the catholicos, Rabban Ṣauma became ill. He died on January 10, 1294, departing from "this world of nothingness and tribulations to the world of holiness and to the City of the Saints, Jerusalem which is in the Heavens."[134]

Mongol Eurasia was a time and place when shape shifters like Rabban Ṣauma were valued and rewarded. This chapter has shown that the identity of ecumenical Christian pilgrim was the most useful to Rabban Ṣauma's diplomacy and personal religious goals. This religious identity was the most stable aspect of Ṣauma's life as he traveled far from his Önggüd homeland; wherever he went he communed with coreligionists. Similarly, Ṣauma spent his whole life as a subject of or in service to Mongol khans. Recognizing this identity's demands facilitated Ṣauma's travel through Asia, presented him the opportunity to serve the Ilkhan, and helped him see pilgrimage destinations like Rome. All of Ṣauma's identities—Önggüd, Mongol subject in China and Persia, and Ilkhanid diplomat—served his primary and most important identity as a Christian of the Church of the East.

While Ṣauma's actions cannot be analyzed without historically contextualizing the geopolitical and religious complexity of late thirteenth-century Europe, Asia, and North Africa, I demonstrate how social science theories may help historians understand how historical figures navigated unfamiliar social settings and interactions. Social identity theories from psychology highlight Ṣauma's ability to shape shift and recategorize himself, a Nestorian Christian, and Latin Christians into a superordinate group of ecumenical Christians to facilitate his diplomatic and religious objectives. Linguistic and social psychology methodologies converge to show that the diplomat spoke a Christian lingua franca centered on piety and pilgrimage to further minimize sectarian differences between him and his audience. Performance theory and liturgical studies underscore the power in Ṣauma's Eucharistic actions: as the consecrator of the Host, Ṣauma proved himself worthy to perform *transubstantio* of bread and wine into the body and blood of Christ; as receiver of the Host, Ṣauma publicly affirmed his salvation and orthopraxic Christianness. Rabban Ṣauma was an extraordinary figure with a remarkable ability to communicate across geographical, political, and religious boundaries.

Notes

1. E. A. Wallis Budge, trans., *The Monks of Kûblâi Khân Emperor of China* (London: Religious Tract Society, 1928; repr., New York: AMS, 1973), 177. Unless otherwise noted, page references are to the reprint edition.

2. There is some disagreement over Rabban Ṣauma's tribal affiliation. The following scholars argue that Rabban Ṣauma was from the Önggüd tribe: Morris Rossabi, *Voyager from Xanadu: Rabban Sauma and the First Journey from China to the West* (Tokyo: Kodansha International, 1992; repr., Berkeley: University of California Press, 2010), 23; Pier Giorgio Borbone, *Storia di Mar Yahballaha e di Rabban Sauma: Un orientale in Occidente ai tempi di Marco Polo* (Turin: Silvio Zamorani, 2000), 149; A. C. Moule, *Christians in China before 1550* (London: SPCK, 1930; repr., 1977), 94, 103; Paul Pelliot, "Chrétiens d'Asie

Centrale et d'Extrême-Orient," *T'oung-pao* 15 (1914): 623–44 (here 630–36). Rossabi notes that by this time the Uyghurs had become primarily Buddhists, and the Önggüd were the principal Nestorians among Turko-Mongol groups. Rossabi, email message to the author, February 26, 2016. Based on thirteenth-century writer Bar Hebraeus, the following scholars claim that Rabban Ṣauma was Uyghur: Budge, *Monks of Kûblâi Khân*, 7, 15; James A. Montgomery, trans., *The History of Yaballaha III Nestorian Patriarch and of His Vicar Bar Sauma: Mongol Ambassador to the Frankish Courts at the End of the Thirteenth Century* (New York: Columbia University Press, 1927), 8.

3. Scholars of the Church of the East point out that its opponents erroneously and derogatorily referred to it as Nestorian after Nestorius, a monk who was condemned at the Council of Ephesus in 431 CE. I take after Tjalling H. F. Halbertsma, who begrudgingly uses Nestorian "for lack of a better adjective or term" (*Early Christian Remains of Inner Mongolia: Discovery, Reconstruction and Appropriation*, 2nd ed. [Leiden: Brill, 2015], 12). On the term "Nestorian," also see Sebastian P. Brock, "The 'Nestorian' Church: A Lamentable Misnomer," *Bulletin of John Rylands Library* 3 (1996): 23–35; reprinted in *Fire from Heaven: Studies in Syriac Theology and Liturgy* (Burlington VT: Ashgate, 2006), 1–14. Also useful are Wilhelm Baum and Dietmar W. Winkler, *The Church of the East: A Concise History* (London: RoutledgeCurzon, 2003); Igor Doffman-Lazarev, "Beyond Empire I: Eastern Christianities from the Persian to the Turkish Conquests, 604–1071," in *The Cambridge History of Christianity*, vol. 3, *Early Medieval Christianities, c. 600–c. 1100*, ed. Thomas F. X. Noble and Julia M. H. Smith (Cambridge: Cambridge University Press, 2008), 65–85; Françoise Micheau, "Eastern Christianities (Eleventh to Fourteenth Century): Copts, Melkites, Nestorians and Jacobites," in *The Cambridge History of Christianity*, vol. 5, *Eastern Christianity*, ed. Michael Angold (Cambridge: Cambridge University Press, 2008), 373–403. Today the church is known as the Assyrian Church of the East, with the addition of Assyrian made in the twentieth century. See *The Blackwell Dictionary of Eastern Christianity*, ed. Ken Parry et al. (Oxford: Blackwell Publishers, 1999), 468.

4. See the following on Nestorian Christians in the Mongol Empire: Ian Gillman and Hans-Joachim Klimkeit, *Christians in Asia before 1500* (Ann Arbor: University of Michigan Press, 1999); Li Tang, *East Syriac Christianity in Mongol-Yuan China* (Wiesbaden: Harrassowitz Verlag, 2011); Roman Malek, ed., *Jingjiao: The Church of the East in China and Central Asia* (Sankt Augustin: Institut Monumenta Serica, 2006); Moule, *Christians in China*; Paul Pelliot, *Recherches sur les chrétiens d'Asie centrale et d'Extrême-Orient* (Paris: Imprimerie nationale, 1973); Igor de Rachewiltz et al., eds., *In the Service of the Khan:*

Eminent Personalities of the Early Mongol-Yüan Period (Wiesbaden: Harrassowitz Verlag, 1993); P. Y. Saeki, *The Nestorian Documents and Relics in China*, 2nd ed. (Tokyo: Toho Bunkwa Gakuin, 1951); Dietmar W. Winkler and Li Tang, eds., *Hidden Treasures and Intercultural Encounters: Studies on East Syriac Christianity in China and Central Asia* (Vienna: LIT Verlag, 2009); Dietmar W. Winkler and Li Tang, eds., *From the Oxus River to the Chinese Shores: Studies on East Syriac Christianity in China and Central Asia* (Berlin: LIT, 2013).

5. Dominic Abrams and Michael A. Hogg, "Collective Identity: Group Membership and Self-Conception," in *Self and Social Identity*, ed. Marilynn B. Brewer and Miles Hewstone (Malden MA: Blackwell Publishing Ltd., 2004), 147–81 (here 154).

6. John A. Boyle, "The Ilkhans of Persia and the Princes of Europe," *Central Asiatic Journal* 20 (1976): 25–40 (here 30–31). Also see Peter Jackson, *The Mongols and the West, 1221–1410* (New York: Pearson Longman, 2005), 177; Jean Richard, *The Crusades, c. 1071–c. 1291*, trans. Jean Birrell (Cambridge: Cambridge University Press, 1999), 456.

7. Rabban Ṣauma traveled through the Yuan dynasty, the Chaghatay Khanate, and the Ilkhanate. He journeyed through the countries of China, Kyrgyzstan, Uzbekistan, Turkmenistan, Iran, Iraq, Turkey, Armenia, Georgia, Greece, Italy, and France.

8. Robert Bartlett, "Medieval and Modern Concepts of Race and Ethnicity," *Journal of Medieval and Early Modern Studies* 31, no. 1 (2001): 39–56 (here 39).

9. Stephen Cornell and Douglas Hartmann, *Ethnicity and Race: Making Identities in a Changing World*, 2nd ed. (Thousand Oaks CA: Pine Forge Press, 2007), 35–36.

10. Budge, *Monks of Kûblâi Khân*, 165–66, 174.

11. Monica Heller, "The Politics of Codeswitching and Language Choice," *Journal of Multilingual and Multicultural Development* 13, no. 1–2 (1992): 123–42.

12. On Christianness, see Éric Rebillard, *Christians and Their Many Identities in Late Antiquity, North Africa, 200–450 CE* (Ithaca NY: Cornell University Press, 2012), 3n3.

13. In addition to Budge, *Monks of Kûblâi Khân*, Pier Giorgio Borbone has a critical Italian translation (*Storia*). J. B. Chabot's annotated French translation is still very good (*Histoire de Mar Jabalaha III et du moine Rabban Cauma* [Paris: Ernest Leroux, 1895]). The Syriac abridgment was edited by Paul Bedjan (*Histoire de Mar-Jabalaha*, 2nd ed. [Leipzig: Otto Harrassowitz, 1898]). Also see Richard Gottheil for details on Bedjan's sources ("Review: Bedjan's *Histoire de Mar Jabalaha*," *American Journal of Semitic Languages and Literatures* 13, no. 3 [1897]: 222–27).

14. Borbone, *Storia*, 21.

15. Montgomery, *History of Yaballaha III*, 80. Budge's translation is less clear. "Now without making over long [our] narrative, and making [our] History, which has a definite object, become somewhat different . . ." (*Monks of Kûblâi Khân*, 209).

16. Heleen Murre-van den Berg, "The Church of the East in Mesopotamia in the Mongol Period," in *Jingjiao: The Church of the East in China and Central Asia*, ed. Roman Malek (Sankt Augustin: Institut Monumenta Serica, 2006), 377–94 (here 393). Borbone finds this proposal convincing ("L'autore della 'Storia di Mar Yahballaha e di Rabban Sauma," *Loquentes linguis: Studi linguistici e orientali in onore di Fabrizio A. Pennacchietti*, ed. Pier Giorgio Borbone et al. [Wiesbaden: Harrassowitz, 2006], 103–8 [here 105]). Jean-Maurice Fiey argues that the text stops after the events of 1312 and that the death of the patriarch was added by a hand different from Anonymous's "Le Grand Catholicos Turco-Mongol Yahwalaha III (1281–1317)," *Proche-Orient Chrétien* 38 (1988): 209–20 (here 210). This does not necessarily detract from Murre-van den Berg's candidate.

17. In addition to Murre-van den Berg, see Halbertsma, *Early Christian Remains*, 25.

18. Bar Hebraeus has been most recently translated by David Wilmshurst, *The Ecclesiastical Chronicle* (Piscataway NJ: Gorgias Press, 2016). Also translated by E. A. Wallis Budge, *The Chronography of Gregory Ab'ûl Faraj, the Son of Aaron, the Hebrew Physician Commonly Known as Bar Hebraeus*, 2 vols. (London: Oxford University Press, 1932).

19. Rossabi, *Voyager from Xanadu*, 101.

20. *Rabban* was an honorific title meaning "master," which he would acquire later in life.

21. Budge, *Monks of Kûblâi Khân*, 134.

22. Though the account does not mention Qubilai's financial contribution, it does say that two Önggüd Christian princes, Ai Buqa (son-in-law of Qubilai) and Kun Buqa (son-in-law of the deceased Great Khan Güyüg, Qubilai's cousin), gave them "beasts on which to ride, and gold, and silver, and wearing apparel [and rugs]" (Budge, *Monks of Kûblâi Khân*, 137). Also see Rossabi, *Voyager from Xanadu*, 50–51.

23. English translation of the Latin translation of the fourteenth-century Arabic treatise *Kitāb al-majdal li-l-istibṣār wa-l-jadal* (*The Book of the Tower*) by 'Amr bin Mattā from Montgomery, *History of Yaballaha III*, 21: "Advenerat et sua terra munere perfuncturus sibi Ḥano [khan] magno commisso: huc autem adventandi causa et fuit invisitio Hierosolymorum. Ḥanus quippe

vestes miserat cum ipso quas in Jordane flumine intingeret, obduceretque super sepulcrum Christi Domini." See also Henry Gismondi, *Amri et Slibae de patriarchis Nestorianium commentaria*, 4 parts in 2 vols. (Rome: 1896, 1899; repr., Gorgias Press, 2011), 3–4:71.

24. Rossabi, *Voyager from Xanadu*, 43.

25. Budge, *Monks of Kûblâi Khân*, 139.

26. Budge, *Monks of Kûblâi Khân*, 142–43.

27. *Mar* is a title of respect in Syriac meaning "my lord."

28. Mark also said, "'I am deficient in education and in ecclesiastical doctrine, and the member of my tongue halteth. How can I possibly become your Patriarch?'" (Budge, *Monks of Kûblâi Khân*, 153).

29. Budge, *Monks of Kûblâi Khân*, 152–53.

30. Under Arghun, the religious leaders of Buddhism, Christianity, Islam, and Judaism had tax-exempt status and received limited subsidies in return for their prayers for the Ilkhan. Christopher Atwood, *Encyclopedia of Mongolia and the Mongol Empire* (New York: Facts on File, Inc., 2004), 235, 107.

31. Budge, *Monks of Kûblâi Khân*, 155.

32. The most notable Christian Mongol woman was Sorqaqtani Beki, wife of Chinggis's youngest son, Tolui, and mother of Möngke Khan (r. 1251–59), Qubilai (r. 1260–94), Hülegü (r. 1256–81), and Ariq-Böke. Her youngest son may have converted to Nestorian Christianity. Generally positive, Ilkhanid-Nestorian relations saw some tense moments, most notably under Ilkhan Geikhatu (r. 1291–95). In fact, Catholicos Mar Yahballaha was imprisoned in 1295. See Baum and Winkler, *The Church of the East*, 85–86, 97. Also see Bruno de Nicola, *Women in Mongol Iran: The Khātūns, 1206–1335* (Edinburgh: Edinburgh University Press, 2017), chap. 5.

33. Budge, *Monks of Kûblâi Khân*, 165.

34. On the Önggüd, see Atwood, *Encyclopedia*, 424.

35. Budge, *Monks of Kûblâi Khân*, 167. Rossabi takes after Luciano Petech and says Sabadinus was a Nestorian (*Voyager from Xanadu*, 102–4). Luciano Petech, "Les marchands italiens dans l'Empire Mongol," in *Selected Papers on Asian History*, Serie Orientale 60 (Rome: Istituto Italiano per il Medio ed Estremo Oriente, 1988), 161–86 (here 175).

36. Rossabi, *Voyager from Xanadu*, 102.

37. Byzantine emperor Michael VIII Palaiologos married other daughters to Mongol generals and princes as well, such as Euphrosyne to Golden Horde general and prince Noghai.

38. John A. Boyle, "Ilkhans of Persia and the Christian West," *History Today* 23, no. 8 (1973): 554–63 (here 556).

39. Noteworthy sights also included the stone bowl in which Jesus changed water into wine at Cana and the tomb of Emperor Constantine. Budge, *Monks of Kûblâi Khân*, 168–69.

40. Budge, *Monks of Kûblâi Khân*, 170–71.

41. The battle was another episode in the struggle between the Angevins and the Aragonese that had originated in the Sicilian Vespers' revolt against Charles of Anjou. Rossabi, *Voyager from Xanadu*, 118; Budge, *Monks of Kûblâi Khân*, 171.

42. Budge, *Monks of Kûblâi Khân*, 172, 173, 174.

43. Budge, *Monks of Kûblâi Khân*, 174, 175, 177.

44. Rossabi, *Voyager from Xanadu*, 125.

45. Budge, *Monks of Kûblâi Khân*, 177.

46. Nestorius did not contest the use of Theotokos by the "simple believer," but he insisted for homiletic purposes and in the liturgy on designating and venerating Mary only as the Mother of Christ: "Mary did not give birth to a god. I cannot worship a god who was born, died and was buried" (Karl-Heinz Uthemann, "History of Christology to the Seventh Century," in *The Cambridge History of Christianity*, vol. 2, *From Constantine to c. 600*, ed. Augustine Casiday and Frederick W. Norris [Cambridge: Cambridge University Press, 2008], 460–500 [here 474]).

47. Geraldine Heng, *The Invention of Race in the European Middle Ages* (Cambridge: Cambridge University Press, 2018), 317.

48. Budge, *Monks of Kûblâi Khân*, 177.

49. We have little information on Thomas's activities in the Ilkhanate. Petech, "Les marchands italiens," 174–75.

50. Budge, *Monks of Kûblâi Khân*, 182.

51. Richard, *The Crusades*, 421. Hülegü was not lying about his friendship with Christians; his mother, Sorqaqtani Beki, and his wife, Toghus Khatun, were both Nestorian Christians, and as a result of their influence, the Ilkhan gave special favor to Armenian and Georgian nobles and clergy. Atwood, *Encyclopedia*, 226.

52. Boyle, "Ilkhans of Persia," 556.

53. Boyle, "Ilkhans of Persia," 556.

54. Ilkhan Abagha sent at least four more diplomatic missions to the West. See Boyle, "Ilkhans of Persia."

55. Budge, *Monks of Kûblâi Khân*, 183–85; Rossabi, *Voyager from Xanadu*, 140–42, 153.

56. Jackson, *The Mongols*, 169.

57. Budge, *Monks of Kûblâi Khân*, 185.

58. Jackson, *The Mongols*, 167; Reuven Amitai, *Mongols and Mamluks: The Mamluk-Îlkhânid War, 1260–1281* (Cambridge: Cambridge University Press, 1995), 99; Amitai, "Edward of England and Abagha Ilkhan: A Reexamination of a Failed Attempt at Mongol-Frankish Cooperation," in *Tolerance and Intolerance: Social Conflict in the Age of the Crusades*, ed. Michael Gervers and James M. Powell (Syracuse NY: Syracuse University Press, 2001), 75–82 (here 77).

59. Rossabi, *Voyager from Xanadu*, 153.

60. Budge, *Monks of Kûblâi Khân*, 186.

61. Chabot identifies the visitor as John of Tusculum, Italy (*Histoire de Mar Jabalaha III*, 83). Rossabi agrees with Chabot (*Voyager from Xanadu*, 157). Pier Giorgio Borbone thinks the visitor was German ("A 13th-Century Journey from China to Europe: The Story of Mar Yahballaha and Rabban Sauma," *Egitto e Vicino Oriente* 31 [2008]: 221–42 [here 234]).

62. Budge, *Monks of Kûblâi Khân*, 189–90.

63. Rossabi, *Voyager from Xanadu*, 159.

64. Budge, *Monks of Kûblâi Khân*, 190, 191.

65. Rossabi, *Voyager from Xanadu*, 163.

66. The relics included a scrap of Jesus's clothing, a piece of the Virgin Mary's handkerchief, and miscellaneous relics of various saints. Rossabi, *Voyager from Xanadu*, 164.

67. The most recent edition of Pope Nicholas's Latin letters is in Karl-Ernst Lupprian, ed., *Die Beziehungen der Päpste zu islamischen und mongolischen Herrschern im 13. Jahrhundert anhand ihres Briefwechsels* (Vatican City: Biblioteca Apostolica Vaticana, 1981), 247–53. The former three letters are also in Luke Wadding, ed., *Annales minorum seu trium ordinum a San Francisco institutorum Tomus V, 1276–1300* (Florence: Quaracchi ad claras aquas, 1931), 170–73. Nicholas's letter to Franciscans *inter Tartaros* is in Giovanni Sbaraglia, ed., *Bullarium Franciscanum Romanorum Pontificum* (Rome: Typis Sacrae Congregationis de Propaganda Fide, 1768; repr., Assisi: Edizioni Porziuncola, 1983), 4:6–11. Lupprian identifies *reginam Tartarorum* as Nuqdan Khatun (*Die Beziehungen*, 251). Chabot does so as well (*Histoire de Mar Jabalaha III*, 203). The "queen of the Tartars," Nuqdan, was a Kereyid princess and Christian of the Church of the East, like her aunt Toghus Khatun. Atwood identifies Nuqdan as Tuqtani (*Encyclopedia*, 542).

68. Rossabi, *Voyager from Xanadu*, 166.

69. See Felicitas Schmieder, "Cum hora undecima: The Incorporation of Asia into the *orbis Christianus*," in *Christianizing Peoples and Converting Individuals*, ed. Guyda Armstrong and Ian N. Woods (Turnout: Brepols, 2000), 259–65.

70. Atwood, *Encyclopedia*, 233.

71. John A. Boyle, "Dynastic and Political History of the Ilkhans," in *The Cambridge History of Iran*, vol. 5, *The Saljuq and Mongol Periods*, ed. John A. Boyle (Cambridge: Cambridge University Press, 1968), 303–421 (here 371). The message was carried by a Genoese man named Buscarello di Ghisolfi, and the letter is preserved in the French National Archives. See Antoine Mostaert and Francis Woodman Cleaves, *Les lettres de 1289 et 1305 des ilkhan Aryun et Oljeitu à Phillipe le Bel* (Cambridge MA: Harvard University Press, 1962).

72. Jackson, *The Mongols*, 183.

73. Budge, *Monks of Kûblâi Khân*, 174.

74. Henri Tajfel, *Human Groups and Social Categories: Studies in Social Psychology* (Cambridge: Cambridge University Press, 1981), 255. Also see Katharina Schmid, Miles Hewstone, and Ananthi Al Ramiah, "Self-Categorization and Social Identification: Making Sense of Us and Them," in *Theories in Social Psychology*, ed. Derek Chadee (Malden MA: Wiley-Blackwell, 2001), 211–31 (here 214).

75. Self-categorization theory does not address how the categorization processes change over time; thus, I cannot prove that the category of Christian pilgrim was always the most salient to Rabban Ṣauma. Abrams and Hogg, "Collective Identity," 160.

76. André Vauchez, "Saints and Pilgrimages: New and Old," in *The Cambridge History of Christianity*, vol. 4, *Christianity in Western Europe, c. 1100–c. 1500*, ed. Miri Rubin and Walter Simons (Cambridge: Cambridge University Press, 2009), 324–39 (here 326). While scholarship on pilgrimage to saints' shrines in Latin Christianity is abundant, there is much less written on the subject for the Church of the East, though stories of East Christian pilgrimages to holy sites such as Jerusalem are numerous. See Baum and Winkler, *The Church of the East*, 13, 45; Micheau, "Eastern Christianities," 399.

77. Budge, *Monks of Kûblâi Khân*, 177.

78. Richard J. Crisp and Miles Hewstone, "Multiple Social Categorization," in *Advances in Experimental Social Psychology*, ed. M. Zanna (San Diego: Academic Press, 2007), 39:163–254 (here 180). Also see Samuel L. Gaertner and John F. Dovidio, *Reducing Intergroup Bias: The Common Ingroup Identity Model* (Philadelphia: Psychology Press / Taylor & Francis, 2000), 33–52.

79. Abrams and Hogg, "Collective Identity," 167–68.

80. Crisp and Hewstone, "Multiple Social Categorization," 17. Also see Marilynn B. Brewer et al., "Social Identity and Social Distance among Hong Kong School Children," *Personality and Social Psychology Bulletin* 13 (1987): 156–65; Peter J. Burke, "Relationships among Multiple Identities," in *Advances*

in *Identity Theory and Research*, ed. Peter J. Burke et al. (New York: Kluwer Academic / Plenum Publishers, 2003), 195–214; Samuel L. Gaertner et al., "Reducing Intergroup Bias: The Benefits of Recategorization," *Journal of Personality and Social Psychology* 57, no. 2 (1989): 239–49; Natalie R. Hall and Richard J. Crisp, "Considering Multiple Criteria for Social Categorization Can Reduce Intergroup Bias," *Personality and Social Psychology Bulletin* 31, no. 10 (2005): 1435–44; C. Neil Macrae, Galen V. Bodenhausen, and Alan B. Milne, "The Dissection of Selection in Person Perception: Inhibitory Processes in Social Stereotyping," *Journal of Personality and Social Psychology* 69 (1995): 397–407.

81. Cynthia B. Roy, *Interpreting as a Discourse Process* (New York: Oxford University Press, 2000), 24.

82. Barbara E. Bullock and Almeida Jacqueline Toribio, "Themes in the Study of Code-Switching," in *The Cambridge Handbook of Linguistic Code-Switching*, ed. Barbara E. Bullock and Almeida Jacqueline Toribio (Cambridge: Cambridge University Press, 2009), 1–17 (here 6).

83. Benjamin Bailey, "Switching," *Journal of Linguistic Anthropology* 9 (1999): 241–43 (here 241). See Erica J. Benson for a bibliography and history of cs research until 2000: "The Neglected Early History of Codeswitching Research in the United States," *Language & Communication* 21 (2001): 23–36. See also Alexandra Jaffe, "Codeswitching and Stance: Issues in Interpretation," *Journal of Language, Identity, and Education* 6, no. 1 (2007): 53–77.

84. Bullock and Toribio, "Themes," 1.

85. Penelope Gardner-Chloros, "Sociolinguistic Factors in Code-Switching," in Bullock and Toribio, *The Cambridge Handbook*, 97–113 (here 97). The other two major approaches to codeswitching are psycholinguistic and structural. The psycholinguistic approach investigates codeswitching "to better understand the cognitive mechanisms that underlie bilingual production, perception, and acquisition" (Bullock and Toribio, "Themes," 14). I am less interested in the structural approach to cs, which examines "what cs can reveal about language structure at all levels," for example, lexicon, morphology, and syntax.

86. Helpful for my analysis is Monica Heller's Bourdieu-informed perspective that codeswitching is a means of drawing on symbolic resources and deploying them in order to gain or deny access to other resources, symbolic or material ("Politics of Codeswitching," 124).

87. Budge, *Monks of Kûblâi Khân*, 165–66. Chabot also translates "language" as singular: "Le Catholique, voyant que personne ne savait la langue, excepté Rabban Çauma . . . lui ordonna de partir. Rabban Çaume dit: 'Je desire

moi-même et souhaite cela'" (*Histoire de Mar Jabalaha III*, 53). Montgomery translates "language" as plural: "And when the Catholicus saw that there was none acquainted with the languages except Rabban Sawma, since he was competent for this, he commissioned him to go. Then Rabban Sawma said: 'I am desirous of this and eager for it'" (*History of Yaballaha III*, 51).

88. Rossabi, email message to the author, March 1, 2016.

89. Budge, *Monks of Kûblâi Khân*, 125. Ṣauma's father, Shîbân was rich and a nobleman, and he "belonged to a famous family and a well-known tribe" (Budge, *Monks of Kûblâi Khân*, 124). He held the rank of visitor in the Nestorian Church, which was a role in between priest and bishop. As for Mark's ignorance of Syriac, though he "was trained in ecclesiastical learning more than all his brethren" (he had three brothers), I can only guess that his more humble beginnings in Koshang, Shanxi Province, about fifteen days' journey from Daidu, gave him a less exemplary religious education than Ṣauma. See Budge, *Monks of Kûblâi Khân*, 130.

90. Thomas T. Allsen, "The *Rasûlid Hexaglot* in Its Eurasian Cultural Context," in *The King's Dictionary: The Rasûlid Hexaglot; Fourteenth Century Vocabularies in Arabic, Persian, Turkic, Greek, Armenian and Mongol*, ed. Peter B. Golden, trans. Tibor Halasi-Kun et al. (Leiden: Brill, 2000), 25–49 (here 25).

91. Allsen, "The *Rasûlid Hexaglot*," 26.

92. Allsen, "The *Rasûlid Hexaglot*," 29, 33.

93. See note 58. In 1274 King Edward also received Mongol envoys from Arghun's father, Ilkhan Abagha. See Thomas Madden, *Concise History of the Crusades*, 3rd ed. (Oxford: Rowman & Littlefield Publishers, 2005), 171–72.

94. Jaffe, "Codeswitching," 72.

95. Rossabi assumes that Ughetto was Italian (*Voyager from Xanadu*, 102). Denis Sinor argues that Ughetto may have been a personal name or nickname, as well as a descriptor. In classical Mongolian, *ügetü* means "he who has (the gift) or tongues/words," or "interpreter" ("Interpreters in Medieval Asia," *Asian and African Studies* 16, no. 3 [1982]: 293–320 [here 295]). Ughetto is mentioned in four letters: in a Latin translation of a letter Ilkhan Arghun sent to the pope dated May 18, 1285 (*Ugeto terciman*); in two Latin letters dated April 2, 1288, by Pope Nicholas IV to Arghun (*Uguetus interpres* and *Uguetto interprete*, respectively); and in a letter dated April 7, 1288, by Nicholas IV to Mar Yahballaha. Letters in Lupprian, *Die Beziehungen*, 246, 248, 254. Also see Allsen, "The *Rasûlid Hexaglot*," 30–33.

96. Quote from Sinor, "Interpreters," 305. Also see Philipp Sebastian Angermeyer, "Interpreter-Mediated Interaction as Bilingual Speech: Bridging Macro- and Micro-Sociolinguistics in Codeswitching Research," *International*

Journal of Bilingualism 14, no. 4 (2010): 466–89; Susan Berk-Seligson, *The Bilingual Courtroom: Court Interpreters in the Judicial Process* (Chicago: University of Chicago Press, 1990); Basil Hatim and Ian Mason, *The Translator as Communicator* (London: Routledge, 1997); Monica Heller, "Negotiations of Language Choice in Montreal," in *Language and Social Identity*, ed. J. J. Gumperz (Cambridge: Cambridge University Press, 1982), 108–18; Roy, *Interpreting*, 27; Cecilia Wadensjö, *Interpreting as Interaction* (London: Longman, 1998).

97. Sinor, "Interpreters," 305.

98. Roy, *Interpreting*, 30.

99. This was first argued by David Morgan in *The Mongols* (Oxford: Basil Blackwell, 1986; 2nd ed., Oxford: Wiley-Blackwell, 2007). Morgan repeats his argument in many publications: "Persian as a Lingua Franca in the Mongol Empire," in *Literacy in the Persiate World: Writing and the Social Order*, ed. Brian Spooner and William L. Hanaway (Philadelphia: University of Pennsylvania Press, 2012), 160–70; *Medieval Persia, 1040–1797*, 2nd ed. (Oxon: Routledge, 2016), 6.

100. Stephen G. Haw, "The Persian Language in Yuan-Dynasty China: A Reappraisal," *East Asian History* 39 (2014): 5–32.

101. Rossabi, email message to the author, November 25, 2015.

102. Petech, "Les marchands italiens," 174.

103. Roy, *Interpreting*, 6, 100. Also see Philipp Sebastian Angermeyer, "Translation Style and Participant Roles in Court Interpreting," *Journal of Sociolinguistics* 13, no. 1 (2009): 3–28.

104. Bullock and Toribio, "Themes," 11.

105. Heng, *The Invention of Race*, 375.

106. For an overview of the performance studies scholarship, see Catherine Bell, *Ritual: Perspectives and Dimensions* (Oxford: Oxford University Press, 1997; repr., 2009), 72–83 (page references are to the reprint edition). Also see Mary Suydam, "Background: An Introduction to Performance Studies," in *Performance and Transformation: New Approaches to Late Medieval Spirituality*, ed. Mary A. Suydam and Joanna E. Ziegler (New York: St. Martin's Press, 1999), 1–25.

107. The Bible passages upon which the Eucharist is based are Matthew 26:20–29, Mark 14:17–25, Luke 22:14–20, and 1 Corinthians 11:23–26. Scholarship on the Eucharist in the Roman tradition dominates the field. The following are important for my study: John Bossy, "The Mass as a Social Institution, 1200–1700," *Past & Present* 100 (1983): 29–61; Paul F. Bradshaw and Maxwell E. Johnson, *The Eucharistic Liturgies: Their Evolution and Interpretation*

(Collegeville MN: Liturgical Press, 2012); Gary Macy, *The Theologies of the Eucharist in the Early Scholastic Period: A Study of the Salvific Function of the Sacrament According to the Theologians, c. 1080–c. 1220* (Oxford: Oxford University Press, 1984); Miri Rubin, *Corpus Christi: The Eucharist in Late Medieval Culture* (Cambridge: Cambridge University Press, 1991).

108. Topics of contention included whether to use leavened or unleavened bread; the process by which Christ became present in the Host, referred to as transubstantiation; and the theological impact of an animal's accidental ingestion of the Host. On the second subject, see Macy, *Theologies*, 140. On the last subject, see Rubin, *Corpus Christi*, 67; and Gary Macy, "Theology of the Eucharist in the High Middle Ages," in *A Companion to the Eucharist in the Middle Ages*, ed. Ian Christopher Levy, Gary Macy, and Kristen Van Ausdall (Leiden: Brill, 2012), 365–98 (here 379). For more on the concept of transubstantiation, see Macy, "Theology," 375.

109. Bossy, "Mass," 32.

110. Perhaps the most significant difference in the East Syrian Rite is the inclusion of the baking of the bread, into which Holy Leaven, or Malka, is added. It is seen as having been made from the bread used at the Last Supper (Bradshaw and Johnson, *The Eucharistic Liturgies*, 140, 143). Also see Bryan Spinks, "The Mystery of the Holy Leaven (*Malka*) in the East Syrian Tradition," in *Issues in Eucharistic Praying in East and West: Essays in Liturgical and Theological Analysis*, ed. Maxwell E. Johnson (Collegeville MN: Liturgical Press, 2010), 63–70.

111. Rubin, *Corpus Christi*, 2. Carol Symes demonstrates that liturgical texts were the points of origin for the performance of liturgies, but medieval liturgies often came into being after a social and performative process. See "Liturgical Texts and Performance Practices," in *Understanding the Medieval Liturgy: Essays in Interpretation*, ed. Helen Gittos and Sarah Hamilton (Burlington VT: Ashgate, 2015), 239–67 (here 241). For scholarship on the East Syrian liturgy, see the following: Paul F. Bradshaw and Maxwell E. Johnson, *The Eucharistic Liturgies: Their Evolution and Interpretation* (Collegeville MN: Liturgical Press, 2012); Brock, *Fire from Heaven*; Peter D. Day, *The Liturgical Dictionary of Eastern Christianity* (Collegeville MN: Liturgical Press, 1993); Johnson, *Issues*; Heleen Murre–van den Berg, "Syriac Christianity," in Parry, *The Blackwell Companion*, 249–68; Ronald Roberson, *The Eastern Christian Churches: A Brief Survey*, 7th ed. (Rome: Pontifical Oriental Institute, 2010). Also see Gerd Althoff, "The Variability of Rituals in the Middle Ages," in *Medieval Concepts of the Past: Ritual, Memory, Historiography*, ed. Gerd Althoff, Johannes Fried, and Patrick Geary (Washington

DC: German Historical Institute; Cambridge: Cambridge University Press, 2002), 71–88; Edward Foley, "A Tale of Two Sanctuaries: Late Medieval Eucharist and the Analogous," in Levy, Macy, and Van Ausdall, *A Companion*, 327–63.

112. Bell, *Ritual*, 191.

113. Budge, *Monks of Kûblâi Khân*, 190.

114. Rubin, *Corpus Christi*, 9.

115. For example, Mark Allman, "Eucharist, Ritual and Narrative: Formation of Individual and Communal Moral Character," *Journal of Ritual Studies* 14, no. 1 (2000): 60–68; C. Clifford Flanigan, Kathleen Ashley, and Pamela Sheingorn, "Liturgy as Social Performance: Expanding the Definitions," in *The Liturgy of the Medieval Church*, ed. T. J. Heffernan and E. A. Matter, 2nd ed. (Kalamazoo MI: Medieval Institute Publications, 2005), 695–714; O. B. Hardison Jr., *Christian Rite and Christian Drama in the Middle Ages: Essays in the Origin and Early History of Modern Drama* (Baltimore MD: Johns Hopkins Press, 1965); Richard D. McCall, *Do This: Liturgy as Performance* (Notre Dame IN: University of Notre Dame Press, 2007); Symes, "Liturgical Texts."

116. McCall, *Do This*, 2. See Luke 22:19 and 1 Corinthians 11:24.

117. Gary Macy, introduction to Levy, Macy, and Van Ausdall, *A Companion*, 1–9 (here 1).

118. Regarding categories of performance, see McCall, *Do This*, 79.

119. Bell, *Ritual*, 217.

120. Richard Schechner, *Performance Studies: An Introduction*, 2nd ed. (New York: Routledge, 2006), 52.

121. Macy, "Theology," 370.

122. Rubin, *Corpus Christi*, 58. Regarding the physical space in which the Eucharist is consecrated, frame analysis is helpful. Jan Blommaert, James Collins, and Stef Slembrouch, "Spaces of Multilingualism," *Language & Communication* 25 (2005): 197–216 (here 207).

123. Rubin, *Corpus Christi*, 26, 55; Schechner, *Performance Studies*, 46; Bell, *Ritual*, 112. Macy also discusses the biological imagery surrounding the consumption of the risen Lord in the Eucharist (*Theologies*, 70).

124. Miri Rubin, "Popular Attitudes to the Eucharist," in Levy, Macy, and Van Ausdall, *A Companion*, 447–68 (here 448, 459).

125. After Rabban Ṣauma left Rome, Pope Nicholas embarked on an ambitious and expensive plan to decorate and expand the Basilica of St. Francis in Assisi, which caused further discomfort in the order, given St. Francis's insistence on evangelical poverty. On the subject of Franciscan poverty,

see David Burr, *The Spiritual Franciscans: From Protest to Persecution in the Century after Saint Francis* (University Park: Pennsylvania State University Press, 2001).

126. In 1245 Pope Innocent IV sent Franciscan friar Giovanni of Plano Carpini to establish diplomatic relations with the Great Khan Güyüg. Giovanni of Plano Carpini's Latin narrative "Historia Mongalorum" was most recently edited by Enrico Menestò, *Giovanni di Pian di Carpine: Storia dei Mongoli* (Spoleto: Centro Italiano di Studi sull'alto Medioevo, 1989). It is also in *Sinica Franciscana I: Itinera et relations Fratrum Minorum saeculi XIII et XIV*, ed. Anastasius van den Wyngaert (Florence: Quaracchi, 1929), 27–130.

127. Budge, *Monks of Kûblâi Khân*, 190.

128. Jean Richard dates Giovanni's arrival in Khanbaligh to 1293. See *La papauté et les missions d'Orient au moyen âge (XIIIe–XVe siècles)* (Rome: École Français de Rome, 1977), 146. Peter Jackson dates Giovanni's arrival to shortly after Qubilai's death in 1294 (*The Mongols and the West*, 258). In 1307 Pope Clement V appointed Giovanni the archbishop of Khanbaligh, with ecclesiastical jurisdiction over China.

129. Budge, *Monks of Kûblâi Khân*, 191–92.

130. Budge, *Monks of Kûblâi Khân*, 192–94.

131. Rubin, *Corpus Christi*, 148–49; Macy, *Theologies*, 120.

132. Rubin, "Popular Attitudes," 448.

133. Macy, *Theologies*, 120–21.

134. Budge, *Monks of Kûblâi Khân*, 206; Rossabi, *Voyager from Xanadu*, 177–78.

4

From *Fan Gui* to Friend

American Chinese, Social Identity, and the Quest for Subjectivity

David Torres-Rouff

Sometime in the mid-1890s, a person toting a newfangled Kodak Bulls-Eye camera wandered the streets of central Los Angeles. On a bright, sunny winter day, he or she captured images common to Los Angeles's visual tourist lexicon: the main plaza and a church, a street railway car, and the courthouse. The photographer—possibly a relative of Andrew McNally, who together with William Rand formed the Rand-McNally publishing company in Chicago before moving west to Pasadena in 1880 and later Altadena—took several other typical California tourist photos (San Diego's famed Hotel del Coronado, Pasadena's Raymond Hotel) and several shots of the McNally estate. While in central Los Angeles, he or she also took two pictures in the Chinese district: one a street scene and the other a rather striking portrait of three Chinese men (fig. 4.1).[1]

The photographer was not alone in considering living Chinese people as part of Los Angeles's tourist landscape in the late nineteenth century, nor was making three Chinese men into objects of curiosity unique. However, our enduring inability to do more than make objects of these three men, even a century later, serves as the point of departure for this essay. The Chinese men photographed on that sunny day *remain* objects in the hands of scholars. We still stare *at* them. We have

Fig. 4.1. Three Chinese men, Los Angeles Chinatown, late 1890s. Courtesy of the Henry E. Huntington Library, photo LC 403 2b.

no way of inverting the frame and thus no way of inverting the power dynamics implicit in our historical gaze. We cannot see out through their eyes at the photographer or at the surrounding street scene because we know little of how ordinary Chinese immigrants understood themselves, other Angelenos, and the city in which they lived. We know even less about their thinking along the lines of race and social identity. This essay offers a starting point from which to shift the shape of this power relationship across time, to bend the terms on which we study Chinese immigrants to the Pacific coast during the nineteenth century, and to ask new questions about the experience of Chinese migrants.

   Los Angeles's Chinese community grew from just 29 to more than
1,200 between 1861 and 1890. Like American Chinese in cities along
the Pacific coast, Chinese Angelenos participated in vigorous contests
regarding space, society, the economy, and the law with their neighbors.[2] In Los Angeles they did so within an already polyglot society that included Indigenous, Mexican, European, African, biethnic,
and multiethnic residents. Los Angeles's Chinese made their homes
in a de facto segregated and densely populated district just east of the
main plaza, where they and their landlords subdivided once sprawling Spanish- and Mexican-era adobe townhomes. Despite an anti-
Chinese massacre perpetrated by European and Mexican Americans
in 1871, the city's Chinese population grew rapidly. Indeed, Chinese
Angelenos played critical roles in Los Angeles's social and spatial history during the second half of the nineteenth century—as merchants,
cooks, launderers, domestics, sex workers, farmers, parents, and community builders. However, no research has yet fully captured the ways
Chinese Angelenos understood themselves as agents in this history.[3]

   Scholars have chronicled the racialization of American Chinese
and the trailing consequences for local racial hierarchies and national
immigration policy. The paucity of Chinese voices in the archive means
that such works, with few exceptions, retain Chinese as objects rather
than subjects. Consequently, recovering American Chinese subjectivity is an essential if difficult objective. Expanding our sense of the
American Chinese past requires working against both the silence of
the archive and the veil of silence that the archival limitations have
subsequently cast over scholarly practice. The dearth of documents,
diaries, letters, and other items researchers value as fonts of knowledge has, however unwittingly, led too many academics to replicate in
their scholarship the very Orientalisms that were propagated in mid-
and late nineteenth-century public discourse. As Lisa Lowe argues, the
loss of migrant Chinese subjectivity is an act of "violence [that] continues to be reproduced in liberal humanist institutions, discourses,
and practices."[4] The Orientalist veil has in part resisted the sea change
in work on racial formation. Whereas scholarship has shifted to con-
structivism, too much work on nineteenth-century American Chinese

remains mired in an earlier mode of thinking about identities, as Paul Spickard writes in the introduction to this volume, "as if they were permanent, essential, unalterable features of individuals and groups." Consequently, this essay addresses the questions of shape shifting and plasticity simultaneously in the American Chinese past and in scholarly practice. Drawing on a variety of published and archival sources, I make two arguments: first, that American Chinese arrived in the United States with considerable experience as makers and inhabitants of a racialized society; second, that Chinese immigrants shifted the shape of their racial worldview when they migrated to the other side of the Pacific Ocean.[5] In doing so, I take up Madeline Hsu's call to "place migration and migrants—with their complicated sets of negotiations, multilayered realities, and multidirectional orientations—at the center" of the scholarly agenda.[6]

Within the context of this volume, those negotiations and multilayered realities require a few clarifications as to the nature, possibilities, and limits of American Chinese shape shifting. As Paul Spickard writes elegantly in his introduction, migrants who find themselves "in new social settings" confront "different menus of identity options, and people must find new ways to locate themselves." I suggest here that American Chinese found considerable opportunities to both retain and modify their individual and collective racial selves in Los Angeles. While Chinese migrants could alter their sense of themselves and the world around them, complete personal racial plasticity would have been impossible. An intensifying cycle of political animus, sensationalism, and racialization rendered immigrant Chinese bodies hyperracialized and hypervisible.

Second, I aim to impart some plasticity to scholarly practice regarding American Chinese and to begin to cut a pathway to Chinese subjectivity. In part, this requires a shift in perspective regarding the intrinsic nature of historical archives. As Lisa Lowe, Helen Siu, Liu Zhiwei, and others have suggested, approaching the archive as a contested site of knowledge production rather than a font of factual information leads to more malleable approaches to narrating and interpreting the past.[7] This approach is especially useful in the case of American Chinese between 1850 and 1890, as there are few places in which to locate Chinese voices. When Chinese voices come forth they almost always manifest in translation, translations all too often mediated in ways that strip away the very nuances that would facilitate an analysis of Chinese racial worldviews. Specifically, my hope here is to build toward a platform from which we can recover the ability to look out on the North American Pacific coast in the nineteenth century through the eyes of immigrant Chinese. All these considerations lead back to the image with which this essay begins and the desire to reverse the photo's perspective.

This bull's-eye image, a genre of street-scene photography popular in the late 1800s, intentionally foregrounds three Chinese men in sharp focus with only a small amount of the city behind them. Based on my earlier work in Los Angeles, I can roughly locate them in space, guess the year the photo was taken, and so on.[8] The photo also demonstrates a certain amount of plasticity. Despite living in the midst of a city that openly reviled most Chinese, these three men are comfortable in their culturally specific (yet not entirely traditional) clothes and, seemingly, their skins. They look confidently into the camera lens and stand proudly, if not defiantly. They appear entirely at home in Los Angeles's Chinese district. Their poses exude a certain masculine toughness and a more general confidence that suggests they have both remade something of China for themselves in Los Angeles and made themselves at home on foreign shores. While I glean something of their sense of self, as well as their sense of place and how they fit into it, I can only speculate as to the specifics. Fully inverting the perspective remains impossible. I want—to the extent possible—to see *out from* this narrow hole punch into Los Angeles's Chinese district and assess the city's broader, complicated social landscape through the eyes of these men and the eyes of the larger American Chinese community of which they were a part.

In an effort to make some progress, this essay tacks back and forth between several bodies of published scholarship and archival research focused on Chinese legal activism and testimony in Los Angeles during the 1870s and 1880s. Wanting for ample prima facie evidence of American

Chinese subjectivity, I begin with a review of scholarship on race in late imperial China. Since an overwhelming majority of American Chinese hailed from seven counties within the Pearl River delta region of Guangdong, I zero in on that region's social topography during a tumultuous time of economic crises, civil war, and European imperialism. Although Chinese migrants to the Pacific coast did not directly export complete community structures to North America, the techniques upon which they relied for crafting social identity and defining its boundaries traveled with them and influenced the communities migrants made on the farther shore. After triangulating the meaning of race and identity in nineteenth-century Guangdong, I turn to the swiftly expanding body of Chinese diaspora studies to tease out the contours of institutions and communities, particularly the *jinshan-zhuang* (transnational businesses) and *huiguan* (native place associations), that stretched across the Pacific Ocean from China and took root everywhere Chinese migrants settled. In nineteenth-century Guangdong, as I will suggest, racial formation turned in part on ties to place. *Huiguan* membership while abroad, therefore, allowed migrants to remain entwined with their racial identities, reciprocal obligations, global networks of capital and labor, and more sentimental bonds of home. The remainder of the essay works with those Chinese voices that emerge in the Los Angeles Area Court Records, a sprawling collection of all civil and legal proceedings in the municipal and county courts. This evidence, situated in a transnational, diasporic context, offers a window, albeit a narrow one, through which to view the ways American Chinese understood themselves and others in terms of race and identity in Los Angeles from the 1870s to the 1890s.

The arguments in the published scholarship are clear. Immigrants from the Pearl River delta left a place where boundaries among local groups had become racialized even as all locals had developed similar, categorically negative, racialized views of European-descended people. With equal clarity, extant scholarship indicates that American Chinese, like others in the broad Pacific Chinese diaspora, carried with them to North America specific institutions that nurtured the maintenance of this variegated racial landscape. Perhaps more tantalizingly than conclusively, I argue here that American Chinese in Los Angeles remained connected to these racial identities on multiple levels. Their legal activism alone constitutes a discursive claim to a standing before the law equal to that of U.S. citizens. Evidence from the legal records also suggests that some Chinese carried racialized views of Europeans with them across the ocean. Nevertheless, American Chinese in Los Angeles built economic and social relationships across this racial divide. As residents, workers, and litigators, Chinese Angelenos negotiated racial boundaries between themselves and others, imprinting their own mark on the city and drawing it socially and spatially into the broader Pacific world. Recovering Chinese racial subjectivity opens new ways forward for studying polyethnic communities, particularly on the Pacific coast.

Lineage, Place, and Administrative Legibility: Social Identity in the Pearl River Delta

Although histories of Chinese immigrants and their encounters with a frequently hostile U.S. society are legion, few have considered how American Chinese understood themselves and others through the prism of race. Doing so requires careful consideration of the extended kinship relationships, practices, and institutions that stretched across the Pacific for multiple generations, tracing and creating migration circuits.[9] According to Him Mark Lai, somewhere between 90 and 95 percent of immigrants from China to North America's Pacific coast before 1965 "could trace their roots to the Pearl River Delta and Wuyi in Guangdong Province."[10] Among this group, an overwhelming majority of American Chinese in Los Angeles hailed from the ethnically Cantonese Four Counties (Sze Yup in Cantonese, Siyi in Mandarin) within Guangdong Province. Most of the rest came from the Sam Yup (Sanyi in Mandarin), or Three Counties, including the city of Guangzhou (Canton), which are geographically just northwest of Sze Yup. Migrants from Sam Yup constituted a larger percentage of the merchant, skilled, and educated classes of migrants to North America than their Sze Yup neighbors, who most often had experience as farmers or small-scale merchants. Scholarship on social identity in China, especially the areas encompassing Gaungdong, Guangzhou (Canton), and the Pearl River delta, thus offers a starting point from which to consider the locally specific racial landscape from which most Chinese came to the Pacific coast.

These seven counties in Guangdong Province, like much of the region encompassed by the broader Pearl River delta, had become an ethnically diverse place and fertile ground for racial formation by the mid-nineteenth century. Historian Frank Dikötter argues that the development of race in China was not "a 'derivative discourse' of a more 'authentic' form of 'white racism'" but instead possessed "an internal cohesion which was based on the active reconfiguration of indigenous modes of representation." Across all groups, discourses of ancestry had special power in race-making projects, and the "cult of patrilineal descent" became ever more popular and hegemonic during the Qing dynasty, especially in southeast China.[11] The conquest of China by ethnic Manchus, which ushered in the Qing Empire, created friction between Manchus and Han Chinese, those people who considered themselves "pure" ethnic Chinese with geographic origins in the great central plains and historical ties to the glorious Han Empire (206 BC–AD 220). During the Qing dynasty (1644–1912), Han Cantonese had to adapt to being officially ruled by non-Han Manchus, a tension that lasted beyond the empire's fall. At the beginning of the nineteenth century, a surge in the frequency and duration of European forays into Guangdong—to trade, proselytize, and sow the seeds of colonialism—added a new layer to the milieu in which people negotiated social identity.

Cantonese speakers in Guangdong's Sze Yup and Sam Yup had, by the mid-nineteenth century, developed a distinct and complex racial worldview. They tethered their history to the Tang dynasty (618–907) and identified themselves as Tangren (literally, people of the Tang culture). At the same time, they claimed to be descendants of migrants from Zhongyuan, the great Central Plain and the cradle of Chinese civilization, which amounted to a claim of Han ethnoracial purity. Tangren in the Sze Yup and Sam Yup controlled land, politics, and culture. In formal terms, Tangren bonded location in space, relationships to work, and the development of households to forge their identity claims. According to Sow-Theng Leong, "a (male) Chinese was identified by his native place, institutionally expressed by household registration, which endowed him and his family with rights and obligations." Within this framework, "territorial identity was powerfully reinforced by the ideology of kinship and localism," and outsiders without "legitimate business, such as officeholding or trade, remained" outsiders, "sometimes for generations." Imperial regulations enforced popular notions and considered outsiders "no different from a criminal evading taxes or plotting revolt."[12] Thus both law and culture bound together place, ancestry, official administrative standing, and identity.

In addition to these ties to people and place, Sze Yup residents tethered their identity to claims of ancient Han descent, proper Han gender relationships, regional dress, location in the economic order, and a commitment to Confucian education. Despite this claim to purity, Cantonese had certainly mixed with both the lowland Zhuang and highland Yao whom they displaced, and they certainly did not all descend from the landed aristocracy of the Zhongyuan. Indeed, more recent scholarship suggests that a considerably multiethnic populace competed for political, social, and economic advantage by linking themselves to Ming and Qing imperial structures. Indeed, Siu and Zhiwei argue that "from the Ming to the early twentieth century, the delta could be seen as a constantly reconfigured social ecology."[13] Examining this claim through the prism of gender, Zhiwei uncovered evidence that in the Pearl River delta important lineages remain tied not to the central plains but to indigenous customs, especially regarding the reverence of female (rather than male) ancestors who lived either alone or with their parents (rather than with their husbands' parents). Women who rejected marriage or married and remained with their own families would have been completely at odds with Han gender norms and Confucian dictates. Only later, Zhiwei argues, did literati and Qing administrators rewrite local family histories to be more compatible with Confucian family and gender norms in order to incorporate such lineages into the empire as Han.[14] Historical and ethnographic work on the Dan minority identity—applied to those people who lived principally on boats in the same region—similarly suggests that attachment to the empire was an active contest. The same people, Siu and Zhiwei found, had been labeled pirates and Dan (boat-dwellers who lived honestly). The same families also competed with farmers to be counted as Tangren by having their lineages officially registered in place, being given the opportunity to send representatives for civil service exams, and gaining formal legal standing. From this perspective, they argue, "ethnic labels are the end products of a complicated historical process involving shrewd maneuvering of cultural resources and power play. Out of this process arose reified categories for identifying and differentiating local populations" such as Han, Dan, and Hakka.[15] Nevertheless, by the mid-nineteenth century, those claiming to be Tangren had as much as five hundred years of administrative history on their side, and few challenged their claims.

Asserting Han ancestry and the privileges that derived from it anchored Cantonese speakers' identities, as did practicing Han gender relationships. Adult males and heads of households worked, married women avoided labor and remained generally secluded from public life, and Han children received a Confucian education to the extent allowable by the family's economic situation. Attachment to place, Han heritage, and Han gender practices stood together as the core of Cantonese personhood within the Sze Yup and Sam Yup.[16] As they invoked and conformed to the language of imperial homogeneity, Sze Yup's Tangren also defined themselves in opposition to others with whom they had frequent contact. From the sixteenth to the nineteenth century, the Pearl River delta's economic and human diversity expanded rapidly, creating a dynamic and frequently contested social landscape. Since the 1500s, a growing and economically active community of "foreign" Hakka immigrants had settled and made their homes in the region. They faced social, political, and legal marginalization. Accustomed to episodic mass migration after centuries of movement, Hakka tried to avoid prohibitions on landholding and social hostility. They settled in mostly unoccupied valleys and hilly regions farther from the river and worked at forestry, mining, and nonrice farming. Their success drew a chain migration, and the Hakka community accounted for one-third of the Pearl River delta's total population at the end of the seventeenth century. In addition to their choice of economic activity, Hakka family and gender practices distinguished them from their Cantonese neighbors. Hakka emphasized family labor over education, eschewed footbinding, and imposed less stringent boundaries between public and private life. Hakka children and women worked on farms and in mines, and Hakka women went to market with Hakka men.[17]

Sze Yup's and Sam Yup's Cantonese drew lines of racial difference between themselves and their Hakka neighbors along axes of ancestry, economic mode, gender norms, and family practices. Hakka spoke their own dialect, and Hakka women donned black cloth hats with wide brims as they worked in the fields and peddled in the marketplace.[18] Cantonese speakers found themselves overwhelmed by the scale and pace of the Hakka migration and observed that Hakka congregated "like ants and bees." To counter the impact of this migration, Tangren in the Sze Yup and Sam Yup prevented Hakka from owning land and limited Hakka access to formal administrative recognition, legal standing, and public political participation. Despite these concerns, Tangren necessarily engaged in commerce of multiple kinds with Hakka, and such interactions became another node of racial formation. Most Cantonese deemed Hakka labor "to be of no benefit to the local community," since most Hakka worked land owned by absentee landlords. Tangren complained about Hakka cultural failings and economic habits. As one scholar notes, to local Cantonese, "Hakka immigrants were clearly intruders, alien in speech and outlandish in social and cultural practices." Moreover, "the sight of Hakka women laboring alongside their menfolk in the fields" and mingling with males in the region's marketplaces—all the while flaunting their unbound feet—challenged Tangren social norms. Proper Cantonese strictly separated the sexes and viewed the presence of Hakka women in the workforce and the public square as a corruption of "the moral tenor of native society."[19] Hakka/Cantonese asymmetries thus reinforced the power of attachment to place, legal recognition, gender practices, and economic production as markers of racial difference in the Sze Yup.

National and international developments added further undulation to this already uneven local topography. The local articulation of Cantonese and Hakka racial formations took place within the broader national context of the Qing dynasty. The Qing ruling class was Manchu rather than Han, foreign warriors who had conquered China from the north and east (north of what we know today as the Korean peninsula) in the seventeenth century. Throughout the Qing dynasty, the ethnic discourse of Han/non-Han lurked just below the surface. According to Mark Elliott, neither Manchus nor Han could afford to invoke the ethnic boundary "too overtly or self-consciously without inviting serious consequences: exile or capital punishment (for the Han), delegitimation and rebellion (for the Manchus)." By the early 1800s, this tension "was more politically charged" than ever.[20] When Sze Yup residents asserted their Han origins as Tangren, they were asserting their ethnic difference from the Qing rulers even as they manipulated imperial proclivities favoring those with long-term claims to land and lineage. The swift and dramatic increase in contact with Europeans—either directly through trade and missionary efforts or indirectly through stories, print culture, and conflict—created another layer of racialization in the Pearl River delta.

By the mid-nineteenth century, Tangren in the Sze Yup and Sam Yup had developed strong negative stereotypes of Europeans and established rigid racialized boundaries between themselves and Europeans. Dikötter argues that Chinese enmity toward foreigners developed from the sixteenth to nineteenth century, whereas Lydia He Liu points to the tense interactions created by British colonial aspirations during and after the Opium Wars as the source of anti-European racial formation.[21] While Liu's argument that colonial encounters provoked definition and racialization is more appealing than Dikötter's basic contact model, they agree that intense racial antagonism characterized nineteenth-century Sino-European relations, especially at midcentury, when migration from China across the Pacific began in earnest. Chinese responded to Europeans with both "repulsion and pity," dismissing them as uneducated brutes, criticizing their religion, and characterizing their foodways as savage. Moreover, Chinese took exception to European phenotypes, saying that "their complexion was not merely white, it was 'ash-white' (*huibai*), the exteriorization of the demonological forces that drove the foreign devils to undertake their expansion overseas."[22] As Liu recounts, the British in particular took exception to racial name calling, especially the word *yi*, which originally meant "foreigner" but later took on (according to the British) the connotation of "barbarian." British colonial authorities banned the use of *yi* in the press and in official documents in 1858, following the first Opium War. Although the British were successful in suppressing the printed word, *yi* remained spoken and was, by the 1860s, supplanted by *fan gui*, or "foreign devil," about which there could be no semantic quibble.[23] Dikötter notes that Han Chinese by the 1850s described British troops as "white devils" (*fan gui*) who were "cold and dull as the ashes of frogs," the "teratological products of death."[24] Liu argues compellingly that it was the violence British and other Europeans perpetrated "rather than the exotic appearance of Westerners, that contributed to the rise of epithets *fan gui* and *gui zi* [a dialectical variation of the same] among the Cantonese and their spread to the rest of the country after the first Opium War."[25] Along these many axes, Tangren, Hakka, Manchus, and Europeans differentiated themselves, creating a variegated racial landscape by the turn of the nineteenth century.

International developments, bad weather, and overpopulation plunged Guangdong into an intense economic depression during the nineteenth century that served as the backdrop for an intensification of racial identification and strife. Tensions between Han, Hakka, and Manchus surged. Cantonese-Hakka relations also took a violent turn for the worse. Local practice limited Hakka residential choices, and they frequently lived in segregated villages within counties. This initially seemed a productive relationship, as Hakka labored on previously unworked land and produced consistent harvests. Suffering in economic crisis, however, ordinary Cantonese came to resent the growth and prosperity of these allegedly alien Hakka communities.

Meanwhile, those with resources began to assert ancient land claims, claims they pursued in court so they could take ownership of lands Hakka worked and charge rent. Hakka, in turn, resisted this strategy, first in court and then with violence. As the economy contracted, Cantonese landlords (*punti*) became increasingly rapacious in their dealings with Hakka tenants. A war between Punti and Hakka, centered in Sze Yup, broke out in the mid-nineteenth century. As many as two hundred thousand people died on each side of the conflict in battles between armed peasants and their landlords' hired soldiers.[26] The Hakka-Punti War wasn't the only episode of mass mobilization and bloodshed in the region at midcentury. Tensions between Hakka, Manchus, and Han also produced the Taiping Rebellion (led by Hakka and targeting Manchus), which began west of Guangdong and swept north and east, and the Red Turban uprising of 1854–55 (initiated by Cantonese and targeting Manchus).[27] Meanwhile, imperial entanglement with and resentment toward Europeans peaked.

This period of intensified crisis and heightened racial tension in the mid-1800s—changing from covert to overt along the Han-Manchu axis, explicitly overt along the Han-European axis, and violent along the Cantonese-Hakka axis—was the moment at which hundreds of thousands of men from Sze Yup traveled overseas in search of new opportunities for work in North America and Southeast Asia. Those who came to California between 1850 and 1882 thus arrived with a fairly well-developed sense of identity and a great deal of experience with racial projects at the social, political, and institutional levels. Tangren would have been empowered in Cantonese/Hakka relations and would have felt similarly aggrieved for holding the short end of the stick in Manchu/Han relations. For Hakka migrants (fewer in number to California than to Hawai'i and Southeast Asia), the reception they found in California must have seemed like more of the same, if only imposed by a far more objectionable group of Europeans. For Tangren arriving in the United States, the rapid reversal of power in racial discourse might have been as jarring as the transnational dislocation because they experienced the other side of the racial prism.

Transnationalism, Diaspora, and Plasticity:
Becoming Chinese in the United States

The vast majority of Chinese migration east across the Pacific Ocean during the second half of the 1800s originated in the Pearl River delta, especially among the ethnically Cantonese Sze Yup and Sam Yup. In this region, the same forces—economic, political, and social—that caused fluid social formations also nurtured dynamic commercial habits, including frequent movement and migration. Since the Tang dynasty, people throughout the Pearl River delta had maintained global, cosmopolitan economic ties. By the mid-nineteenth century, migration and diverse economic strategies had become the norm. Contrary to a general perception, one that developed first among contemporaries and later among scholars, the flood of Tangren out of the Pearl River delta should be considered extraordinary in terms of scale but not in terms of form. According to historian Haiming Liu, Chinese understood migration as an opportunity "to maintain or improve their social and economic status at home" and had chosen migration as an economic strategy for generations prior to the nineteenth century. Moreover, Liu argues, Chinese Pacific crossings were rational decisions undertaken as "family-oriented, group-sustained, and socially embedded" events tied to kinship and other social relations. By the mid-nineteenth century in Guangdong, it had become normal for "young, able-bodied men, many with families" and a majority hailing from the middle and lower-middle classes, to choose "migration to improve familial circumstance." The conversion from self-sufficient to cash-crop farming in the Pearl River delta along with increasing connections to a wider world had made migration one normal choice among many in the region.[28] Perhaps because overseas migration reflected cultural continuity rather than rupture, numerous social and economic institutions stretched across the expanse of the Pacific Ocean to bind American Chinese to each other and to their home communities.

Two decades of active labor have generated a substantial body of scholarship on the transnational elements of Chinese migration to and residence in North America, including studies of the institutions that made it possible for Chinese crossing the Pacific to remain tied to their families and places of origin.[29] As I argued above, ancestry and location provided critical frameworks within which Tangren understood their own identities and through which they compared themselves to others as they molded and nurtured specific racial worldviews. Two of these institutions, *jinshanzhuang* and *huiguan*, afforded American Chinese ample opportunities to remain connected to the people and places their bodies left behind when they crossed the Pacific.

Merchants and traders were among the first immigrants from China to California during the early years of the gold rush. This small cadre of businessmen, who alighted in San Francisco and then fanned out into the gold districts, founded what became both transpacific and transcontinental businesses, or *jinshanzhuang*. Anchored in Hong Kong, many began as small businesses carrying grocery and other specialty goods between China and the United States. Quickly, however, they expanded to offer postal and financial conduits that allowed their "customers overseas to maintain contact with their families and native places."[30] As the trickle of immigrants from the Sze Yup and Sam Yup became a human stream crossing the Pacific Ocean—the official record of immigrant Chinese entering the United States through San Francisco rose from 325 in 1849 to 2,716 in 1851 to 20,026 in 1852— the *jinshanzhuang* dramatically increased the scale and scope of their activities. Eating foods from home and exchanging letters and money allowed American Chinese an opportunity to maintain ties to place and kin that defined their identities. However, as historian Madeline Hsu notes, these trade networks "did more than bring salted fish and rice to Chinese overseas." They reveal "the flexible nature of the social and cultural resources that Chinese brought to their encounters with Western cultures, the changes in their values and identities as they adapted to a capitalist world economy, and the role of the village and family networks in directing or at least mediating such changes."[31] As their roster of mail, remittance, and banking services grew, the *jinshanzhuang* developed the capacity to connect individual American Chinese to their home communities in villages throughout the Sze Yup and Sam Yup. More than goods, letters, and currency flowed through the *jinshanzhuang*, as ideas and values resupplied and replenished migrants, keeping them from emotional, intellectual, and ideological isolation. Along these transpacific sinews the experiences of life abroad could also reverberate back home, where they could be validated in ways that eased adaptation to life in the United States.

To an even greater extent than the *jinshanzhuang*, the *huiguan* kept American Chinese connected to each other and to their places of origin.[32] Before any Chinese crossed the Pacific to work in California, individual communities throughout China had already developed a tradition of hometown associations to aid travel throughout the empire, and these organizations in some cases served merchants and in others catered to men traveling to major cities in order to undertake civil service examinations. For example, a charitable estate in the Panyu district of Guangdong annually directed a sizeable outlay of silver to the Panyu *huiguan* in Beijing to support educational activities and pay the travel expenses of candidates traveling to the metropole to take tests.[33] Chinese migrants carried their *huiguan* across the Pacific, providing communal gathering spaces, hot meals, private rooms, postal services, Chinese newspapers, and other facilities.

The *huiguan* changed slightly in their new context, expanding to serve people from generally contiguous areas in China who spoke the same Cantonese dialects. Merchants formed the first two U.S. *huiguan* in 1851: the Sam Yup and the Sze Yup associations, representing the two largest regions sending Chinese immigrants to the United States. As the number of Chinese in the United States rose and as migrants came from new places, *huiguan* proliferated. By the early 1860s, six *huiguan* dominated the landscape, including the Yan Wo Company, which consisted principally of Hakka immigrants. In 1862 a meeting of the leaders of these six *huiguan* led them to become known collectively as the Chinese Six Companies. This loose, San Francisco–based confederation of merchants ultimately merged as the Chinese Consolidated Benevolent Association in 1882 and expanded to Chinese communities across the country thereafter.[34] To be sure, connections to specific places and familial descent were important building blocks of self-identity in China and beyond. Therefore, *huiguan* attachments allowed immigrants the chance to maintain a critical link to their personhood in official and informal terms while living abroad. As the number of *huiguan* along the Pacific coast grew, so too did the number of chapters in Los Angeles.

Through the 1860s, Los Angeles's small Chinese community participated primarily in one *huiguan*, the Sze Yup Company. By the 1870s, Los Angeles Chinese participated in the Kong Chow Company (the successor of the original Sze Yup Company), the Nin Yung Company (a rival group that had seceded from Sze Yup), and the Sam Yup association, among others.[35] *Huiguan* ties fostered a sense of collective local identity, and those ties to place and ancestry likely kept members connected to the geospatial origins of their family identities and anchored them to a place besides Los Angeles. Since many Chinese Angelenos lived in the houses of those for whom they worked, the *huiguan* provided a physical space that remained tied to home. Additionally, the *huiguan* bound American Chinese to each other. Beyond fostering individual attachments to home, they created a locus of collective identity formation, shaping the ways Chinese located themselves within Los Angeles's community.

Jinshanzhuang and *huiguan*, which became connected to each other as *jinshanzhuang* merchants founded and led California *huiguan*, likely promoted the maintenance of migrants' social identities and racial worldviews. As historian Richard Belsky has argued, the physical spaces *huiguan* owned and occupied generated the meaning they imparted. In places like Beijing and Shanghai, *huiguan* owned substantial parcels and built complex compounds with residential, communal, and ritual spaces. In the contested borderlands of the Pacific coast, physical space often shrank. Even when renting in rigidly segregated districts, *huiguan* erected altars and built temples, usually in back rooms on upper floors—spaces Whites wrote off as "joss houses." *Huiguan* also controlled small plots in segregated cemetery areas. In doing so, *huiguan* "recreated native-place space" or "recreated pockets of regional territory" on the other side of the Pacific Ocean. As Belsky argues, it "is tempting to think of the lodges as 'native-place theme parks' where the enjoyment of dialect, culture, and cuisine of one's native place satisfied nostalgic desires for a taste of home." However, "the ritual efficacy of such space, seen most clearly in respect to the altars and cemeteries," meant that migrants could stay connected to their regional deities and that "the soil of the huiguan cemetery" meant migrants' bodies could be buried somewhere their compatri- ots would properly perform annual sacrifices to the dead and ensure that their ghosts "would never go hungry."[36] The connections these institutions provided to specific places and ancestors meant that the same connections that served as a touchstone for identity formation among Sam Yup and Sze Yup residents in China remained central to their experience as transpacific migrants. At the same time, *huiguan* afforded the opportunity to connect with and share time and space with other migrants.

The opportunity for a diverse group of migrants to interact also created an affordance for some plasticity within the American Chi- nese community. The formation of the Six Companies and Consoli- dated Benevolent Association also indicates that the changed context of transnational migration provoked shape shifting, as people claim- ing distinct social identities tied to ancestry and place organized with increasing frequency around a more generic Chineseness. Spickard's introduction notes a similar process at work for immigrants from Cal- abria, Sicily, and Genoa who became Italians. Dawn Mabalon similarly writes of immigrants from various tiny Pacific Islands who spoke dif- ferent languages but became in a short time simply Filipinos.[37] Con- sidering the poor state of relations between Tangren and Hakka in China, the combination of their *huiguan* into a single umbrella orga- nization suggests that sharing the struggle of life in the United States provoked a kind of ethnoracial plasticity that superseded Han/Hakka antagonisms.

The Challenges of New Circumstances: Shape Shifting in Los Angeles

Even if strong social identities, buttressed by the *huiguan* and *jin- shanzhuang*, allowed American Chinese to preserve much of their Sze Yup and Sam Yup lives in Los Angeles, that worldview had to contend with new circumstances. They faced a new life in the borderlands of southwestern North America. Most Chinese in Los Angeles occupied a densely populated area near the city's historic core, limited to the few dozen buildings that European Americans would rent them. The space itself endured ceaseless efforts at regulation and outright destruction: a mob destroyed the Coronel Adobe (in which dozens of Chinese lived and several key businesses operated) during the 1871 anti-Chinese massacre, and firebugs repeatedly tried to burn and finally succeeded in burning part of the Chinese district in 1887. The Los Angeles City Council joined the efforts of private citizens to drive Chinese residents out of the city's fire limits, and preferably farther afield. The council strictly regulated Chinese residential and commercial districts and staged several failed attempts to exclude Chinese from the city's fire limits. In January 1888 the superintendent of streets bulldozed half of the Chinese district, provoking a major relocation, and the city destroyed Chinatown a second time at the turn of the twentieth century.[38]

American Chinese surely recognized both the discriminatory public policies and the racializing public discourses deployed to circumscribe their community in Los Angeles. As the Los Angeles City Council restricted Chinese people, so too had Tangren in Sze Yup spatially restricted Hakka. In China those claiming Han identities for themselves insisted that they differed racially from Hakka in part because the Hakka were sojourners detached from a fixed place of origin. In Los Angeles elite European and Mexican Americans similarly complained that the Chinese were shifty, worked for low wages, and concentrated themselves in closed enclaves. Just as the Tangren in Sze Yup held Europeans to be *yi* or *fan gui*, European and Mexican American Angelenos regarded immigrant Chinese as barbarian heathens with inappropriate gender norms, work habits, and lifestyles. Aside from the irony of this transnational symmetry, it meant that American Chinese in Los Angeles had to negotiate the very same kinds of social, spatial, and legal restrictions their countrymen and neighbors had imposed on the Hakka back in China. Chinese Angelenos, therefore, must have understood clearly the practice of de facto segregation and the potential for racial subjugation. Based on their previous experience as architects of an unequal, racialized society back home in China, migrants to Los Angeles should have understood that here they had become the individuals struggling for fairness and equality.

Evidence for just how American Chinese confronted the challenge of migrating to a place where they alighted on the wrong side of a racial contest suggests a complex array of choices made by individuals and groups across the class spectrum. Although direct evidence of Chinese racial reckonings in the form of words spoken or written remains rather elusive in Los Angeles's archives, the court cases considered here reveal a range of relationships that developed between Chinese and other Angelenos. The following analysis draws on 105 court cases between 1871 and 1883. Interpreting the raw evidence the court cases provide and the relationships they reveal does not proceed in as straightforward a fashion as one might like. To be sure, the city's court records offer one place where Chinese action is most legible. Lawsuits filed, criminal charges pressed, and testimony given provide one opportunity to hear Chinese voices. In most cases, however, translators mediate these voices. The courts used interpreters when Chinese people testified, and the translators seemingly omitted significant diacritical markers of racial identity.

The one case in the present study in which an affidavit written in Chinese survives in tandem with a translated copy reveals this challenge. In the case *People of Los Angeles v. Louis Spinner*, a witness named Ah Boy referred to all of the Chinese he wrote about as Tangren and all Americans as *fanren*. Harking back to the discussion of language above, *fanren* translates literally as "foreign man," but in the context of mid-nineteenth-century parlance, *fan* carried a weight closer to "barbarian" and often appeared in the phrase *fan gui*, or "foreign devil." The official translator, however, interpreted Tangren as "Chinamen" and *fanren* as "American."[39] In thinking further about whether to judge *fanren* as a relatively neutral appellation or a likely racial epithet, it seems unlikely that an immigrant to the United States would refer to a resident American as "foreign" in a purely descriptive fashion, as Americans in the United States were not "foreign" but local.

Whether intended with malice or simply uttered out of habit, the use of *fanren* to describe an American on U.S. soil carried at the very least a set of passive racial identifiers distinguishing Han from European and likely carried the more common racial aspersion. In addition to obscuring Ah Boy's use of the potentially racialized *fanren* to refer to non-Chinese (a decision that might have been informed by the pro-hibition of words like *yi* in China), the translation also hid the appel-lation Tangren, which carried weight in Guangdong and seemingly for Ah Boy was a way to signify the specific Han identity of the Chi-nese to whom he referred. It is also worth noting that Ah Boy was not a merchant or other leader but an ordinary Chinese laborer incar-cerated on charges of larceny. All recorded testimony in translation, in every case I saw, similarly used the English words "Chinaman" and "American." The specificity of the original Chinese verbiage—whenever else it might have been used—is lost. Although only a single example, this document suggests that at least one Chinese immigrant brought the racial animosity toward Europeans from Guangdong to the United States.

Another case with clear racial overtones also turns on speech, in this instance, issuing from the mouths of Mexican American teen-agers Guillermo Moreno and Ramon Barelas. As Lee Ling and Ah Ying walked up Main Street to look for work on July 30, 1873, Moreno and Barelas shouted, "Where are you going, John?" One of the Chi-nese replied, "Go to hell, you son of a bitch!" and a brawl ensued. In this episode, Ling and Ying resisted the racialized barb "John" and probably also rejected Moreno and Barelas's assertion of social power expressed in the interrogative "Where are you going?" Refusing to be subject to the whims of others, they fought to assert their freedoms. The records of the ensuing trial are frustrating: the Mexican Amer-ican teens did not explain their word choice, the Chinese men did not testify as to why they responded with violence, and no evidence exists as to whether the query was issued in English or Spanish.[40] Yet the silence might be instructive. Perhaps efforts to antagonize and control Chinese movement were so common that they needed no exploration during the trial. Perhaps too, more covertly, Europeans

and Mexican Americans understood the use of "John" and/or the presumed control over the two men's movements to be sufficiently con-
frontational to provoke a violent response. The trial turned on the
theft of Ah Ying's watch, not on the provocation of the two Chinese
men or the legitimacy of their response. Seemingly, all of the parties
and the court agreed that Barelas and Moreno intended to antagonize Ling and Ying and agreed that this antagonism provoked the subsequent assault. Ling and Ying certainly understood that they were
the targets of a racial epithet, indicating that they had learned something of the racial landscape and lived in it as active agents willing
to contest and police its boundaries. If they, like Ah Boy, held Mexican Americans in contempt as *fanren*, their response might be understood to be part of a similar if opposite racial project: teaching the
Mexican American teens where they belonged in the American Chinese racial world. Either way, Ah Boy in words and Ying and Ling in
deeds flatly rejected subordination to Whites and Mexicans. Nevertheless, we must bear in mind that such resistance was itself a borderlands adaptation and a new cultural form, as Tangren in Sze Yup and
Sam Yup held the upper hand.

Life in the borderlands also meant negotiating new spaces and
social relationships, especially as early Chinese settlers likely forged
relationships with English- and Spanish-speaking Angelenos.[41] Dolores
Dominguez, a Mexican American who did not speak English, testified
for the prosecution at an attempted murder trial that he was friends
with a few Chinese. Under cross-examination, the defense attorney
asked Dominguez what he was doing in the Chinese district. Dominguez said, "The barber is a friend of mine and I just went there to pass
the time." Incredulous, the lawyer hounded him:

DEFENSE ATTORNEY: Is he [your friend] a Chinaman?

DOMINGUEZ: Yes, sir.

DEFENSE ATTORNEY: You went to converse with him?

DOMINGUEZ: No sir, just went there for a walk to kill time.

DEFENSE ATTORNEY: Were you shaved while you were there?

DOMINGUEZ: No sir. I am not a Chinaman.

DEFENSE ATTORNEY: However you associate with Chinamen, don't
you. This Chinaman [pointing to complaining witness] was your
friend?

DOMINGUEZ: This Chinaman [pointing at complaining witness] is a
neighbor of mine and washes my clothes. It is another Chinaman
that lives adjoining the barber shop [who is my friend] and I went
to the barber shop to pass a little time [with him].[42]

This section of the testimony offers a brisk exchange on the boundaries of language, race, and friendship. Dominguez said he did not go
to converse because he does not speak Chinese, but he did go there to
pass time with a friend, both articulating a relationship and clarify-
ing the nature of the friendship. Nevertheless, Dominguez responded
that he did not get shaved because he is "not a Chinaman." The ethnic Manchus who controlled China during the Qing Empire required
men throughout the kingdom to wear a queue, a classic Tartar hair-
style. Accepting the queue was in fact one way that Han and other
Chinese showed their acceptance of the Manchu conquest and submission to the Qing rulers. As part of consolidating and maintaining
imperial control, Qing officials required careful queue maintenance
and enacted severe punishment for resisters. Maintaining the queue
requires the wearer to shave all around the head save the crown and
to allow hair from the crown to grow long and be braided. The bald
area had to be shaved every three or four days to be in compliance.
Consequently, Chinese barbers did a brisk business.[43] It is thus possible that Dominguez said, "I am not a Chinaman," when explain-
ing why his friend did not cut his hair because he had no intention
of shaving his hair and leaving a queue. Dominguez might also have
been illuminating a boundary that limited the services provided by his
friend the barber to Chinese customers. Perhaps, despite their friendship, shaving took place within a cultural context to which Dominguez did not have access. Regardless, Dominguez testified that he and
his Chinese neighbor could be friends and spend time together even
though he could not be his friend's customer. Such nuances suggest a

complicated network of permissible and impermissible behavior across the boundary between Mexican and Chinese Angelenos.

When asked why he didn't know the names of many Chinese, Dominguez said, "It is natural for a person to know a person that he sees frequently. I know many Chinamen but don't know the name of a great many." The lawyer persisted, asking Dominguez if he knew them because he had "met them on the street." Dominguez, through his interpreter, replied testily, "I have known them because I have frequently met them, not because I met them upon the street," implying that he spent time with these men socially. The lawyer remained flummoxed that Dominguez spent social time with Chinese men and that he could tell one from another by sight even though he didn't know their names. Dominguez said, "I can't tell the name sir because they are such strange names that I can't tell them even after hearing them. I know him by the name of John. That is what I always call him."[44] This answer at last satisfied the lawyer, perhaps because Dominguez finally said something that made sense to him: like almost everyone else, Dominguez lumped all his Chinese acquaintances together as John. But Dominguez's answer reveals something more interesting: whereas being called "John" by two Mexican American teenagers provoked Lee Ling and Ah Ying to violence, Dominguez could call another man "John," and they considered each other friends. This speaks to the permeability of the boundary separating American Chinese and Mexican and European Americans in Los Angeles. For the cross-examining lawyer, a friendship between Dominguez and a Chinese immigrant was positively unthinkable; so too would it have been a transgression for the Chinese barber to befriend a man designated *fanren* by his countrymen. Even though they had trouble conversing, and even though he used a rather derogatory moniker, Dominguez and his (unfortunately unnamed) Chinese friend worked around the social boundaries that otherwise prevented such a relationship.

Ah Boy's affidavit, Lee Ling and Ah Ying's assault on two Mexican youths, and Dolores Dominguez's testimony stake out opposite ends of a continuum of possible relationships between English-, Spanish-, and Chinese-speaking Angelenos. Between these two poles of positive and negative personal associations, court records reveal a variety of economic relationships between American Chinese and other Angelenos. Only those business arrangements that soured ended up in court. Seventeen times between 1873 and 1883 Chinese Angelenos filed civil suit against non-Chinese over failed economic arrangements, demanding redress of property unlawfully lost or payment according to contract for services rendered. Although these cases are instances of business gone bad, the evidence in a few of them tells a longer story of productive regular commerce.

Ah Foulke, Ah Chitte, Ah Sam, Ah Sears, and Ke Fo separately filed suit against Henry Hancock on February 2, 1882. The men, representatives of the Ah Young Company and another unnamed Chinese-owned business, demanded Hancock make good on debts in excess of $500. In supporting their claims, the American Chinese plaintiffs submitted detailed business records in Chinese and English that indicated a steady pace of economic intercourse lasting no less than five years, from early 1877 to the end of 1881. In nearly weekly transactions, Foulke, Chitte, Sam, Sears, and Fo engaged in a trade with Hancock that included various alcoholic beverages (whiskey, wine, aguardiente, and port), hogs, ducks, rice, shovels, socks, boots, and Hancock's famed *brea* (asphaltum). Quantities and prices ranged from single items costing a few cents to tonnage of asphaltum valued in the hundreds of dollars. The account ledgers also indicate payment for labor contracting for work including shipping and deliveries, *brea* removal, and other tasks. In charting the exchange of goods and labor, these records reveal a still wider world of economic exchange between the Chinese litigants, Hancock, and others in the area, including noted merchants Harris Newmark, Ah Sing, Yuck Wah, and other European Americans and American Chinese. In all, a rather large cadre of American Chinese orchestrated the business of tar extraction and in turn all of the development of the city's urban landscape to which Hancock is known to have contributed.[45]

Indeed, manuscript census records and other evidence reveal the extent to which Chinese immigrants became entwined in Los Angeles's economy during the 1870s and 1880s. American Chinese labored throughout Los Angeles in public places like restaurants, hotels, and laundry shops and in the private homes of dozens of European and Mexican Americans as cooks and domestics.[46] From this perspective, the ledgers submitted in the suits against Hancock offer only a fractional view of the larger integration of American Chinese into Los Angeles's economic life during the period.

What then to make of these economic ties in terms of Chinese subjectivity? At the macro level of structural analysis, participation in the local economy likely required American Chinese to modify their racial worldview. Economic dependence upon and requisite subordination to European Americans as clients or bosses in order to make a living would have certainly complicated a view of U.S. residents as *fanren*. If we think about these instead as a concatenation of individual relationships, then labor relations in Los Angeles meant that many Chinese worked not only for but also in the homes and businesses of European and Mexican Americans, especially as cooks, domestics, and physical laborers. Many others sold vegetables and wares to households and restaurants from wagons. Consequently, work involved regular contact and exchange, sometimes in public and sometimes in private spaces. While these work relationships did not necessarily translate into social integration, they nevertheless offered opportunities for daily contact between Chinese and non-Chinese in Los Angeles, sometimes in rather intimate settings.

Histories of Black domestic work in White homes and Black/White economic relationships in the South following the Civil War demonstrate that such regular contact did not necessarily nurture positive social relations or energy for racial equality. Nevertheless, Susie Lan Cassel has analyzed the diary of American Chinese Ah Quin, one of the few extensive diaries written in California by a bilingual Chinese that survives from the 1860s and 1870s. Quin chronicled his connection to those with whom he worked for several decades, and his experiences suggest the range of potential interactions and relationships that could develop in the course of domestic employment. Quin's entries reveal that he had both positive and negative exchanges with White bosses during his time as a cook and domestic. While we might expect mostly negative entries, Cassel shows that Quin instead emphasized moments of fraternity and joviality with his White employers. Quin recorded pleasant conversations, jokes, and gifts exchanged between him, his bosses, and other White men in his orbit. Although Cassel stresses that the general theme of this diary is one of adaptation, Quin's writings offer one first-person account of the potential for situationally specific friendship and borderlands exchange.[47] The well-known story of macro-level social relations in Los Angeles during the 1870s and 1880s makes clear that friendships did not form in such numbers to prevent the social, political, and spatial marginalization of American Chinese. However, the pervasiveness of face-to-face economic exchange likely introduced an element of dynamism in the ways American Chinese understood themselves and other Angelenos in terms of race and social identity.

Although a close review of a decade of court cases and other sources offers tantalizing rather than convincing evidence for American Chinese subjectivity (language and inconsistency mean there are no "smoking guns"), taking a step back and considering the culture of legal activism among American Chinese offers a different and perhaps more enlightening vantage. Analyzing American Chinese legal practices offers another way to listen to Chinese voices speak about their place in society. In Guangdong legal activism was a prominent characteristic of public life. Officially, the courts preferred to deal with criminal/penal and administrative issues, leaving "civil" matters to be mediated informally at the direction of kin associations or other extrajudicial processes. Nevertheless, according to Philip C. C. Huang, more than one-third of all cases during the late Qing period were of a civil nature, many of them involving ordinary people. Huang argues that "enough simple peasants turned to the courts to make lawsuits part of the collective memory of most villages." Moreover, the judges hearing these cases adhered closely to formal codes of law. Litigants could also expect outcomes relatively free of local political entanglements, as Qing rules required magistrates to serve outside their home counties.[48]

Migrants from Sze Yup and Sam Yup to Los Angeles specifically (and the Pacific coast generally) sustained this tradition, using the courts to assert social, legal, and economic claims. Ordinary and elite Chinese frequently used the courts to engage each other and non-Chinese Angelenos in civil and criminal complaints. Between 1873 and 1883 Chinese Angelenos filed more than twenty-two civil suits. When American Chinese turned to the courts, their actions necessarily implied certain claims of equality and belonging. As a set of rules and regulations adjudicated and enforced by non-Chinese, the U.S. legal system constituted foreign territory for Chinese litigants. Anticipating fair treatment and protection from the courts when the opposite was so obviously forthcoming from ordinary European and Mexican Americans indicates that Chinese expected the law to filter out social prejudice and treat Chinese participants as equals. While legal customs promoting fairness in legal decisions in China might have prefigured American Chinese faith in the courts, the legal system was different in the United States. Active court use, therefore, should be understood in itself as a claim to civil rights and legal equality and consequently marks a declaration by Chinese litigants of their claim to the rights of citizens, at least in the eyes of the law.

In one of the era's more interesting legal cases, Los Angeles's Chinese vegetable peddlers turned to the courts to resist city policy that targeted their business. Since its time as a Spanish and then Mexican pueblo, the Los Angeles city government had collected licensing fees from those doing business around town. By the late 1870s between twenty-seven and thirty Chinese vegetable peddlers paid license fees in the amount of two dollars per month for permission to supply Los Angeles's homes, markets, and restaurants with fresh vegetables from the backs of their wagons. In February 1879, against the backdrop of a growing statewide anti-Chinese movement, the Los Angeles City Council raised vegetable peddling license fees from $2.00 to $12.50 per month. One of the peddlers, Lee Bung, purposely ran afoul of the new law, plying his trade without proper paperwork. After citation and arrest, Bung mounted a legal challenge that ultimately went before the California Supreme Court. Throughout, Bung and his legal team argued that the law was usurious and constituted an unreasonable restraint on trade. Only high-volume liquor stores and merchants with monthly receipts above $10,000 paid equal or higher fees. Bung and others testified that as vegetable peddlers they earned between eight and ten dollars per month, less than the fee to operate. Most interestingly, Bung "by his counsel" implied that the policy was racially motivated, as neither the receipts of their businesses nor the relative relationship to other license charges factored into the policy. The California Supreme Court agreed, declaring the tax unconstitutional as "unreasonable and oppressive" and setting aside Bung's conviction.[49] Among the arguments made and the legal issues addressed in the supreme court's decision were laws about commerce, fine-grained arguments about reasonable taxation, and the responsibility municipalities bear to be fair both to the state and to their own residents. Although proffering sound legal arguments, the entire case rested on one unspoken principle: that American Chinese in Los Angeles had standing before the court despite being foreigners and that they had the right to be afforded the protections granted exclusively to citizens of the United States.

In their legal activism, American Chinese insisted on being treated as equals in the eyes of the law, and they trusted officers of the state courts to agree. In doing so, Chinese litigants demonstrated their sense of racial equality with non-Chinese and put their faith in officers of the court to treat them as such. One might also speculate that submitting to the authority of the courts required a modification in the estimation of all European and Mexican Americans as barbarians, especially those who worked as lawyers and judges. By the standards of race in contemporary Guangdong, trusting one's legal fate to the officers of the U.S. legal system would have been tantamount to leaving ignorant barbarians to direct the future. Allowing such debased people power to make binding decisions, especially in disputes among Chinese, seems unlikely otherwise. In the opposite case, it is difficult to imagine that self-described Whites would have submitted to a court administered by American Chinese unless the racializing language around Chineseness had changed. Consequently, frequent resort to the courts required a certain degree of racial plasticity on the part of American Chinese, as it required them to accept Anglo and Mexican legal officers as at least minimally fit in terms of race in order to hear and judge these cases fairly.

A Way Forward

Dolores Dominguez could not have been the only Mexican American who frequently mingled with his Chinese neighbors. Indeed, one can easily imagine that the combatants in the "Where are you going, John?" case might have expressed a contempt bred by familiarity rather than anonymity. These two expressions reflect the full range of possible relationships that likely emerged in the densely populated urban space Chinese and Mexican Angelenos shared. Reckoning the social identity of American Chinese remains challenging; hopefully, the approach here offers one way forward. Most immigrants to Los Angeles left Sze Yup with a sense of themselves as Tangren, civilized, proper Han Chinese and already reckoned European Americans as barbarians. These ideas made it across the ocean to at least a limited extent. Some, and perhaps many, migrants from Sze Yup brought their racial worldview with them to the United States. The *jinshanzhuang* that the *huiguan* fostered continued attachments to ideas of Tangren identity, and ordinary Chinese referred to their countrymen as Tangren and Americans as *fanren*. However, I find it unlikely that Chinese alone, among all transnational migrants to Los Angeles, preserved their social identity and racial worldviews in a pristine and unmodified form. In Los Angeles and throughout the Cantonese Pacific, evidence of contact, interaction, and borderlands innovations abounds. The boundaries between immigrant Chinese and other Angelenos became at least somewhat porous as Chinese immigrants engaged European and Mexican Americans in commercial and social relationships.

To be sure, as Madeline Hsu reminds us, American Chinese did not necessarily assimilate, nor, I would add, is assimilation a useful standard for judging how Chinese migrants formed their own subjectivity. Yet as they forged economic opportunity and contested their right to social and economic equality, American Chinese modified both their strategies and their ideas from what they had been in Guangdong. In Sze Yup, Tangren and Hakka waged a bloody civil war; in California, *huiguan* representing the two groups ultimately came together in forming the Consolidated Benevolent Association. Back in China, Tangren held Hakka in contempt even as they profited from them as landlords and labor overseers. Perhaps a similar exceptionalism allowed American Chinese to exploit economic opportunities (to the point of working for barbarians) in order to reap profits. Chinese Angelenos also defended their right to participate in the local economy in court and resorted to violence when necessary to assert the same equality. Contrasting these tense exchanges, some Chinese developed harmonious work and social relationships with the non-Chinese among whom they lived.

The varied choices these immigrants made as they maintained and modified their own boundaries marking space and identity in Los Angeles offer an emerging, if hazy, outline of shape shifting among American Chinese. Those same choices also offer at least a degree of racial plasticity in terms of how American Chinese reckoned other migrants from China and non-Chinese among whom they came to live. For some migrants, the dim view Chinese held of European Americans in China survived the Pacific crossing intact. The strong sense of self-identity and rights to treatment as socially equal people also survived the crossing, as evidenced by the frequency with which American Chinese used Los Angeles's courts to redress mistreatment. Yet these prima facie examples of a rather rigid, mutually agreeable segregation do not always withstand closer scrutiny. Economically, American Chinese in Los Angeles became deeply entangled in the local economy as storeowners, domestic workers, and vegetable peddlers. These occupations produced frequent and often close contact with employers and neighbors, proximity that in the case of Dolores Dominguez led to friendship with one particular Chinese Angeleno and a general sense of familiarity with others. In short, while American Chinese in Los Angeles defended the value of their own Chineseness, they opened themselves up to wider interactions with those with whom in China much interaction would have been scandalous.

Admittedly, the evidence thus far is frustratingly scant, consisting of veritable fragments of information. Yet more work must be done to reckon American Chinese as active participants in the racial contests that shaped the histories of cities all along the Pacific coast. Rather than simply understanding the ways that Whites and Mexicans negotiated their own identities through the prism of the Chinese they held in such contempt, we must begin to consider the Chinese as participants in these contests. Specifically, it is all too likely that they also considered those with whom they shared the densely packed urban cores as socially inferior, a fact that must necessarily alter our interpretive calculus.

Methodologically, an emphasis on the archive as a site of knowledge production also demonstrates a significant degree of shape shifting. American Chinese crossed the ocean, circulated along the Pacific coast, rebuilt and relocated when Whites and Mexicans burned and bulldozed their communities. These markers of resilience and malleability emerge when we consult legal records, municipal archives, census data, and fire insurance maps. This evidence of plasticity, combined with a parallel dynamism in the Pearl River delta region from which most immigrants hailed, further indicates the value of breaking through the Orientalist veil that maintains American Chinese as objects in our histories. But we must do more: we must find new ways to learn what motivated, organized, and sustained the determination to persevere; to recover the texture of that determination; and to apprehend the individual and collective sense of self and community that framed American Chinese resistance, persistence, and legal activism. By allowing our explorations into the past to allow for a greater plasticity in the nature of American Chinese conceptions of social identity, we can begin to shift the shape of scholarly production in ways that afford a view out onto the streets of U.S. cities through immigrant Chinese eyes.

Notes

A Huntington Library Fellowship supported my research in the Los Angeles Area Court Records, and I benefited greatly from the expertise of Peter Blodgett and the late Bill Franks at the Huntington. Colleagues at the Center for the Humanities and Global Asia Merced (GLAM) at the University of California Merced commented on earlier versions of this chapter. Jayson Beaster-Jones, Ignacio Lopez-Calvo, Eli Jelly-Schapiro, Christina Lux, Kit Meyers, Ma Vang, and Kenichi Yoshida offered valuable comments. At the "Shape Shifters" conference, Kariann Yokota, Lily Welty Tamai, and others offered substantive input. I am also indebted to William Deverell, David Igler, Paul Spickard, Christina Torres-Rouff, and the esteemed editors of this volume for their guidance. Portions of this essay were published previously under the title "Men of Tang among Fanren: Chinese Self-Representation in Los Angeles, 1860–1895," *California History* 93, no. 1 (Winter 2016): 45–63.

1. Henry E. Huntington Library, *Scenes of Altadena, Los Angeles, and Southern California*, PHOT CL 403b, n.d. The finding aid indicates that the image was taken by a Kodak Bulls-Eye camera and forms part of "an amateur album possibly taken by a relative of the McNally family." Kodak introduced the Bulls-Eye in 1896, and it became a runaway success. Given the lighting of the image, the sharpness of the shadows, and the tree in the background, which is barren of leaves, I am assuming this is a sunny winter day.

2. In this article I conscientiously use the term "American Chinese" rather than "Chinese American." I do so to leave open the question of the degree to which immigrants from China to the Pacific coast in the second half of the nineteenth century did or did not embrace acculturation, and to highlight the ways that U.S. law and policy prohibited legal assimilation to the contours of an immigrant community that did not develop a numerically robust U.S.-born second generation. At the same time, I use "Chinese Angelenos" to refer to people physically living in Los Angeles, as that term does not carry the same implication of assimilation and acculturation.

3. For studies of Chinese in Los Angeles, see David Torres-Rouff, *Before L.A.: Race, Space, and Municipal Power in Los Angeles, 1781–1895* (New Haven CT: Yale University Press, 2013), chap. 6; Joshua Paddison, *American Heathens: Religion, Race, and Reconstruction in California* (San Marino and Berkeley: Huntington Library Press and University of California Press, 2012); Scott Zesch, *The Chinatown War: Chinese Los Angeles and the Massacre of 1871* (Oxford: Oxford University Press, 2012); Isabella Seong-Leong Quintana, "National Borders, Neighborhood Boundaries: Gender, Space, and Border Formation in Chinese and Mexican Los Angeles, 1871–1938" (PhD diss., University of Michigan, 2010); Cesar Lopez, "El Descanso: A Comparative History of the Los Angeles Plaza Area and the Shared Racialized Space of the Mexican and Chinese Communities, 1853–1933" (PhD diss., University of California, Berkeley, 2002); and Raymond Lou, "The Chinese American Community

in Los Angeles, 1870–1900: A Case of Resistance, Organization, and Participation" (PhD diss., University of California, Irvine, 1982).

4. Lisa Lowe, "The Intimacies of Four Continents," in *Haunted by Empire: Geographies of Intimacy in North American History*, ed. Ann Laura Stoler (Durham NC: Duke University Press, 2006), 191–212, 208.

5. Audrey Smedley defines a racial worldview as "a cosmological ordering system structured out of the . . . ideologies, distinctions, and selective perceptions that constitute a society's popular imagery and interpretations of the world." Smedley argues that "people in all societies comprehend the world through prisms that their cultures and experiences proffer to them" and in turn "impose meanings on new discoveries and experiences that emanate from their own cultural conditioning" (*Race in America: Origin and Evolution of a Worldview* [San Francisco: Westview Press, 1999], 25).

6. Madeline Y. Hsu, "Transnationalism and Asian American Studies as a Migration-Centered Project," *Journal of Asian American Studies* 11, no. 2 (June 2008): 185–97, 185.

7. Lowe, "Intimacies," 196 ("following Foucault, Said, and Stoler"); Helen F. Siu and Liu Zhiwei, "Lineage, Market, Pirate, and Dan: Ethnicity in the Pearl River Delta of South China," in *Empire at the Margins: Culture, Ethnicity, and Frontier in Early Modern China*, ed. P. K. Crosley (Berkeley: University of California Press, 2005), 285–310, 289.

8. Torres-Rouff, *Before L.A.*, esp. chaps. 5–6.

9. Madeline Y. Hsu, *Dreaming of Gold, Dreaming of Home: Transnationalism and Migration between the United States and South China, 1882–1943* (Stanford CA: Stanford University Press, 2000).

10. Him Mark Lai, *Becoming Chinese American: A History of Communities and Institutions* (Walnut Creek CA: Altamira Press, 2004), 15.

11. Frank Dikötter, "Racial Discourse in China: Continuities and Permutations," in *The Construction of Racial Identities in China and Japan*, ed. Frank Dikötter (Honolulu: University of Hawai'i Press, 1997), 12–33, quotes 13–14.

12. Sow-Theng Leong, *Migration and Ethnicity in Chinese History: Hakkas, Pengmin, and Their Neighbors*, ed. Tim Wright (Stanford CA: Stanford University Press, 1997), 21.

13. Siu and Zhiwei, "Lineage," 297.

14. Liu Zhiwei, "Women's Images Reconstructed: The Sisters-in-Law Tomb and Its Legend," in *Merchants' Daughters: Women, Commerce, and Regional Culture in South China*, ed. Helen F. Siu (Hong Kong: Hong Kong University Press, 2010), 25–44.

15. Siu and Zhiwei, "Lineage," 289.

16. Leong, *Migration and Ethnicity*, 20–71; Lai, *Becoming Chinese American*, 4–16.

17. Leong, *Migration and Ethnicity*, 20–71.

18. Helen F. Siu and Wing-hoi Chan, introduction to Siu, *Merchants' Daughters*, 1–22, 4.

19. Leong, *Migration and Ethnicity*, 20–71, quotes at 71 and 60–61; Lai, *Becoming Chinese American*, 4–16.

20. Mark Elliott, *The Manchu Way: The Eight Banners and Ethnic Identity in Late Imperial China* (Stanford CA: Stanford University Press, 2001), xv.

21. Frank Dikötter, *The Discourse of Race in Modern China* (London: Hurst Publishers, 1992); Lydia He Liu, *The Clash of Empires: The Invention of China in Modern World Making* (Cambridge MA: Harvard University Press, 2004), esp. chaps. 2 and 3.

22. Dikötter, *The Discourse of Race*, 14.

23. Liu, *The Clash of Empires*, chap. 2 and 96–99.

24. Dikötter, *The Discourse of Race*, 38.

25. Liu, *The Clash of Empires*, 99.

26. Leong, *Migration and Ethnicity*, 70–74; Lai, *Becoming Chinese American*, 15. Few Hakka came to California before 1965, making an analysis of Hakka/Tangren relations in the overseas context more challenging.

27. For an analysis of the least known of these, the Red Turban uprising, see Jaeyoon Kim, "The Heaven and Earth Society and the Red Turban Rebellion in Late Qing China," *Journal of Humanities and Social Sciences* 3, no. 1 (2009): 1–35.

28. Haiming Liu, "The Social Origins of Early Chinese Immigrants: A Revisionist Perspective," in *The Chinese in America: A History from Gold Mountain to the New Millennium*, ed. Susie Lan Cassel (Walnut Creek CA: Altamira Press, 2002), 21–36, quotes at 23 and 24.

29. The transnational turn has generated a growing body of excellent scholarship placing Chinese communities at the center of the research, even though Chinese subjectivity in the arena of racial formation is not a core subject. See, among others, Elliott Young, *Alien Nation: Chinese Migration in the Americas from the Coolie Era through World War II* (Chapel Hill: University of North Carolina Press, 2014); Grace Peña Delgado, *Making the Chinese Mexican: Global Migration, Localism, and Exclusion in the U.S.-Mexico Borderlands* (Stanford CA: Stanford University Press, 2012); Julia María Schiavone Camacho, *Chinese Mexicans: Transpacific Migration and the Search for a Homeland, 1910–1960* (Chapel Hill: University of North Carolina Press, 2012); Hsu, "Transnationalism"; Sucheng Chan, ed., *Chinese American Transnationalism: The Flow of People, Resources, and Ideas*

between China and America during the Exclusion Era (Philadelphia: Temple University Press, 2006); Erika Lee, *At America's Gates: Chinese Immigration during the Exclusion Era, 1882–1943* (Chapel Hill: University of North Carolina Press, 2003); Yong Chen, *Chinese San Francisco, 1850–1943: A Trans-Pacific Community* (Stanford CA: Stanford University Press, 2002); and Hsu, *Dreaming of Gold*.

30. Madeline Y. Hsu, "Trading with Gold Mountain: *Jinshanzhuang* and Networks of Kinship and Native Place," in Chan, *Chinese American Transnationalism*, 22–33, quote at 22.

31. Hsu, "Trading with Gold Mountain," 28, 22–23.

32. Lai, *Becoming Chinese American*, 39–50.

33. Richard David Belsky, *Localities at the Center: Native Place, Space, and Power in Late Imperial Beijing* (Cambridge MA: Harvard University Press, 2006), 71.

34. Lai, *Becoming Chinese American*, 39–50.

35. For a detailed discussion of the *huiguan* in California, see Lai, *Becoming Chinese American*, chaps. 3–4. On the *huiguan* in Los Angeles, see Zesch, *The Chinatown War*; and Lou, "The Chinese American Community."

36. My analysis of *huiguan* space follows Belsky, *Localities*, 116. In San Francisco, *huiguan* ultimately purchased considerable real estate. Lai, *Becoming Chinese American*, chap. 4. An 1888 fire insurance map of Los Angeles depicts the Kong Chow Company Joss House at the rear of a storefront on North Los Angeles Street. *Huiguan* also controlled space in Los Angeles's Evergreen Cemetery during the nineteenth century.

37. Dawn Bohulano Mabalon, *Little Manila Is in the Heart* (Durham NC: Duke University Press, 2013).

38. Torres-Rouff, *Before L.A.*, 232–39.

39. *People of Los Angeles v. Louis Spinner*, Los Angeles County Court, case 1851, November 21, 1879, Los Angeles Area Court Records, Huntington Library, San Marino CA (hereafter LAACR). I am grateful to Dr. John Williams (Colorado College) for his translation and etymological expertise. In addition to its contextualization as close to "barbarian," the use of the literal term "foreign man" inverts the relationship of "immigrant" Chinese to "local" European Americans. The distinction between Tangren and *fanren* appears anecdotally in other venues. Writing about Chinese herbalists and Chinese medicine in Los Angeles and other Chinese communities along the Pacific coast, Haiming Liu notes that those serving exclusively Chinese clients were referred to as "Tang Doctors" and those who ministered to White and Latina/o customers as "Tang Fan Doctors" ("Chinese Herbalists in the United States," in Chan, *Chinese American Transnationalism*, 136–55, quote at 137).

40. *People of Los Angeles County v. Moreno and Barelas*, Los Angeles County Court, case 1248, November 12, 1873, LAACR; also cited in Quintana, "National Borders," 25–28.

41. Writing about Chinese migration to Mexico, Grace Peña Delgado notes that "in the absence of generational ties on which to draw," the earliest immigrants "were compelled to create alternative mechanisms to establish connections to their new home and neighbors," and so their "sense of social belonging and residential permanency was initially tethered to relationships mostly with Mexicans" ("Neighbors by Nature: Relationships, Border Crossings, and Transnational Communities in the Chinese Exclusion Era," *Pacific Historical Review* 80, no. 3 [August 2011]: 401–29, 406).

42. *People of Los Angeles County v. Ah Lung*, Los Angeles County Court, case 1568, January 28, 1887, LAACR, testimony of Dolores Dominguez.

43. Michael Godley, "The End of the Queue: Hair as a Symbol in Chinese History," *East Asian History* 8 (December 1994): 55–72. One could also imagine that just as herbalists and sex workers served either exclusively Chinese or exclusively American clients, the same could have been true for barbers.

44. *Ah Lung*, case 1568, testimony of Dolores Dominguez.

45. *Ah Foulke v. Henry Hancock*, Los Angeles Superior Court, case 1343, February 6, 1882, LAACR; *Ah Sam v. Henry Hancock*, Los Angeles Superior Court, case 1344, February 6, 1882, LAACR; *Ke Fo v. Henry Hancock*, Los Angeles Superior Court, case 1345, February 6, 1882, LAACR; *Ah Sears v. Henry Hancock*, Los Angeles Superior Court, case 1346, February 6, 1882, LAACR; *Ah Chitte v. Henry Hancock*, Los Angeles Superior Court, case 1347, February 6, 1882, LAACR. The names here, as elsewhere, suggest the possibility of satirical hostility and dehumanization. The expletives uttered when enunciating Ah Foulke and Ah Chitte might give clues as to the intentional mishandling of the plaintiffs' names, given the nature and target of their legal action. My thinking on this grows from Michelle Arnold, "Legal Dimensions of the Chinese Experience in Los Angeles" (BA thesis, California Institute of Technology, 2000), esp. 79–82. I am grateful to William Deverell for sharing the paper with me and bringing Arnold's analysis of names to my attention.

46. Of the 221 Chinese who lived on Calle de los Negros—the core of the city's Chinese residential district—in 1880, 78 worked as "laborers" and another 42 worked as cooks. Census Office, *Tenth Census*, 1880, Manuscript vol. 67, pp. 13–16. Manuscript census for Los Angeles is divided between reels 66 and 67, with the Chinese districts at the beginning of reel 67. Electronic access can be found at https://archive.org/details/10thcensus0067unit (last accessed December 29, 2018). Calle de Los Negros scans on pages 19–24.

47. Susie Lan Cassel, "To Inscribe the Self Daily: The Discovery of the Ah Quin Diary," in Cassel, *The Chinese in America*, 54–74.

48. Philip C. C. Huang, *Civil Justice in China: Representation and Practice in the Qing* (Stanford CA: Stanford University Press, 1996), 10–14, quotes at 11. See also Huang, *Chinese Civil Justice, Past and Present* (Plymouth: Rowman and Littlefield, 2010).

49. *People of Los Angeles County v. Lee Bung*, Los Angeles Criminal Court, case 01798, April 12, 1879, LAACR. Raymond Lou reports that members of the anti-Chinese Workingmen's Party had taken control of the Los Angeles City Council and that they in fact raised fees to twenty-five dollars per month. Lou, "The Chinese American Community," 136.

5

Becoming Mixed Race

Northern California and the Production of Multiracial Identities

Alyssa M. Newman

The fluid and contextual nature of identity has been a central theme of this part, and we have seen examples of how by circumstance, location, or intent shape shifters move across new contexts and into different identities. In this chapter, I will examine instances in which these changes in context not only offered new identity choices but also prompted new considerations of self-identification in the shape shifters themselves. What is significant about the instances of shape shifting that I explore is that they involve an emergent, malleable, and evolving racial category that is changing rapidly over the lifetime of these subjects in ways that are being adopted unevenly across the United States. Not only is the identity category itself changing, but so is the context within which these subjects adopt, claim, and are ascribed identities that were not available to them before.

There is a long history of confusion and ambiguity around the categorization of mixed race people in the United States because they are situated somewhere between existing racial categories. Rather than address the source of this ambiguity, the rigidity of the racial order has stubbornly adhered to a monoracial imperative, and mixed race people have been classified according to hypodescent or, in extreme form, the one-drop rule.[1] Over the last few decades, however, this has been changing. Due in large part to contestation on the part of mixed race people and interracial couples, the mandate to identify with only one racial category has been easing.[2] In fact, the census of 2000 was the first in history to allow respondents to indicate more than one box for race.[3]

Although the categories themselves have been changing, movement through space carries its own consequences for race and identity.[4] The ways in which a multiracial person may be read vary greatly by region and context. While a multiracial person may receive different racial interpretations within the same place in the same day, changes in surroundings introduce different sets of demographics and racial relations that impact how one is read and racially located. This chapter will focus on the stories of a handful of multiracial Americans whose moves in location from various regions of the United States prompted shifts not only in how they were read but also in their racial self-identification. Specifically, each of these shifts was from a monoracial identification to a multiracial one, and each of these individuals moved from elsewhere in the United States to Northern California.

California's multiracial population has been noted by scholars looking ahead at the projected growth of interracial marriages and mixed race children. For example, sociologists Jennifer Lee and Frank Bean discussed rising intermarriage rates as producing a visible and growing multiracial population: "Nowhere are these changes more apparent than in the West, where 40 percent of the multiracially identified population resides, and most prominently in California—the state that leads the country with the highest level of multiracial reporting and the only state with a multiracial population exceeding one million."[5] As a place that has already begun to experience the demographic changes that have been slower to arrive in other parts of the country, California provides an ideal place to examine what will happen when many multiracial people are able to live and interact in their schools, neighborhoods, workplaces, and politics.

While there is much existing work that addresses multiracial identity, much of this scholarship has assessed the various identities asserted by multiracial individuals.[6] Although this work has taken into account the role of context and the fluid nature of multiracial identities and identification, little work has been dedicated to exploring the role of geography and region in the formation of multiracial identities.[7] In this chapter, I examine how Northern California produces new multiracial identifications. Specifically, I document the influence of the substantial multiracial population and how through interaction, multiracial identities were ascribed, fostered, and newly inhabited there.

The site producing these new multiracial identifications is a region in Northern California that demographers have termed the "multiracial belt" of the state.[8] For the mixed race people whose narratives I share, their experiences and interactions in the region served to reinforce multiracial identity. These narratives come from interviews conducted for two different projects about multiracial collective identity. The first one, a high school case study based at a school in the multiracial belt, included interviews conducted with adolescents of part-Black ancestry in the spring and fall of 2011. The second project included interviews conducted in late 2013 and early 2014 of adults representing various multiracial backgrounds who were currently living or who had lived in the multiracial belt counties. Although this project expanded the scope of the study to a broader range of Northern California, interviewees were primarily recruited from the San Francisco Bay Area, Sacramento, and Stockton.

Viewing these narratives of identity shifts that occurred in Northern California together, a portrait emerges of a region with a long history of racial mixing. A familiarity with and normalization of multiraciality creates a context fertile for both phenotypically identifying individuals as multiracial and accepting multiracial identifications. In fact, multiracial identifications were not only accepted but also *expected* for those with mixed race backgrounds.[9] For those moving to the region (or within the region to more diverse neighborhoods) who either had their multiracial identities challenged or had not experienced much space to consider their multiraciality, the move to Northern California made a multiracial identification possible for the first time.

Aside from demographics contributing to familiarity with multiraciality, however, I argue that there is also a *cultural* account for the assertion and acceptance of multiracial identities. This represents a shape shifting context based on the "categories change" circumstance as described in the introduction to this volume. Although the 2000 census introduced the option to assert multiracial identity and created that precedent in federal data collection, the Pew Research Center found in 2015 that 61 percent of adults with a multiracial background do not consider themselves to be mixed race.[10] Thus, although the multiracial category exists nationally, a majority of adults with multiracial backgrounds do not assert the identity. However, in Northern California, the "menu of identities" not only allowed individuals to assert multiracial identities and have them be accepted but also actually encouraged and produced multiracial identifications.[11] In other words, a multiracial background alone does not necessarily correspond to a multiracial identification—the social and cultural context of multiraciality in Northern California was critical for prompting the instances of shape shifting documented in this chapter.

Identity Development over the Life Course

The category of multiracial has been inflected with new meaning since the existence of the identity was brought to the consciousness of the nation and since the federal government granted it sanction through the census of 2000. Undoubtedly, the relative recency of this change has produced generational differences in how multiracial people relate to this identity and have asserted it (or not) over time.[12] These shifts in signification and meaning have been occurring over the lifetimes of both the youths and the adults whom I interviewed.

The identity development process has been mapped out as a progression through predictable stages at adolescence, which has been identified as being a particularly important moment of identity negotiation.[13] College was noted by scholars as another moment in which identities are often reconsidered due to an exposure to new thoughts, worldviews, and, frequently, demographics.[14] Identity shifts in adulthood are considered unlikely because adults have already progressed through that stage in their development. Adults' experiences with being racialized, developing a worldview, and settling into their identities mark a completed process, barring the discovery of new information. The existence of generational differences in the embrace of multiracial identity makes clear that despite shifting racial terrain and paradigms, the hegemonic racial order that was formative in shaping one's racial identity still governs the way one sees oneself later in life.[15]

Interviewees had varying relationships to multiraciality and their conceptions of their own racial identities. However, both the youths and the adults I interviewed had experiences upon moving to Northern California that affirmed their multiraciality in ways they had never encountered before. Their moves from various regions of the United States prompted shifts in how they were read, which in turn impacted their relationship to multiraciality and multiracial identity assertion. The role of surrounding demographics was significant not only for interviewees' experiences in California but also for their experiences in the places they were from or in which they had lived. These experiences informed interviewees' previous monoracial identifications. Thus, the impact of the move to Northern California on interviewees' racial identities and identifications underscored the region's role in prompting identity reconsiderations, regardless of interviewees' age and their stage in the identity development process.

The Demographics of Northern California

Considering the United States as a whole, the West is the region with the most multiracial people in both number and percentage. As of the 2010 census, the multiracial population comprised 2.9 percent of the country itself but 4.7 percent of the West and less than 2 percent in all other regions. As a percentage of the total population, California was ranked as the fourth most multiracial state (4.9 percent) behind Hawai'i (23.6 percent), Alaska (7.3 percent), and Oklahoma (5.9 percent). In terms of how the country's multiracial population was distributed, 20.2 percent of the United States' multiracial population resided in California (for comparison, Texas had the next highest proportion, 7.5 percent). The concentration of multiracial people is important, however, for exploring the consequences of the local population for racial dynamics and multiracial identity. In this respect, Northern California is unique and highly distinctive. A brief released by the Census Bureau (also utilizing data from the 2010 census) included a ranking of the ten most multiracial places in the country. In this list, seven of the ten places were located in Northern California.[16]

Following the 2000 census, a group of demographers analyzing the multiracial population of the state also noted something distinctive about Northern California. These demographers identified a "multiracial belt" within the state in which there was "a concentration of counties with higher percent multiracials in the Central Valley and the Greater Sacramento regions"; these counties included Yuba, Yolo, Sacramento, Solano, San Joaquin, Alameda, Stanislaus, Merced, and Madera.[17] All of the interviewees included in the analysis that follows moved from different parts of the state or country to the multiracial belt. While the demographers included in the belt counties with a multiracial population of 5.2 percent or higher, the neighborhood of the high school examined in this study was 7.3 percent multiracial.[18]

To be sure, local neighborhood context varies, and large representations of multiracial people hardly indicate a utopic environment that universally generates affirming experiences for all multiracials living and visiting there. However, the demographic setting certainly sets a powerful context for the development of racial identity. Indeed, demographers have noted how in some communities, especially in Hawai'i and California, "it would not be surprising if the average person were to conclude that intermarriage and multiracial and multiethnic children are the norm."[19]

Thus, it was within such a setting that the adolescents and adults I interviewed partook in these experiences of shape shifting. Although they were expected to be in different stages of the identity development process, the narratives of the adolescents and the adults had striking similarities. The rapidly shifting context of multiraciality, which has transformed over the life course of both groups, was deeply impactful in these experiences of shape shifting in addition to the role of place and social interaction in Northern California.

The Teenagers

The growth of the mixed race population is often attributed to the current generations of youth, credited with representing the future of

U.S. demographics in which multiraciality represents the new typical face of the nation.[20] Indeed, these generations were born following the multiracial movement's contestation of census racial categories in the late 1980s and early 1990s and thus inherited a context within which multiraciality was more normalized, institutionalized, and (especially after the 2000 census) more legitimated than ever before. Thus, the youth growing up in the contemporary moment not only are part of a rapidly growing young multiracial population but also have more possibilities to assert their multiracial identities than previous generations.[21] While increasing birth rates certainly contribute to the growing multiracial population, larger numbers also reflect a greater portion of multiracial people electing to identify themselves as such.[22]

Despite their youth, the adolescents I interviewed had experienced challenges to their self-understanding or assertion of a multiracial identity. The environmental factors that influenced how these multiracial Black high school students identified came to the fore when I interviewed students who had moved to the school from elsewhere.

Jason

As a first example, Jason, whose mother is a Black-White biracial, grew up in Michigan exclusively around the White side of his family. He was distinctly disconnected from his Black family and broader Black heritage, as his mother did not even know the name of her Black father, and Jason's own Black father was a man he had never met. Growing up in those surroundings, he had always considered himself White:

> When I was little, I'm not gonna lie, there's me, my mom, and my niece and nephew; out of [everyone on my mom's side] in our family, we're maybe the only four dark-complexion-skinned people in our family. And when we lived in Michigan that was all I knew. I mean, we were in the snow, we liked to ride in snowmobiles, dirt bikes, quads, camping in the forest, hiking, hunting with my uncles and stuff, and my grandpa. So you know, when I was with them, I considered myself white, and that's what everybody took me in as. I mean, yeah, they looked at me as I'm light skinned, I'm mixed. But

when I was younger that's what I considered myself as—I was 100 percent white. There was no way anybody could tell me, oh no, you're part black. And I was like, I'm light skinned, but I'm full white, to the fullest.

Of note in Jason's description of his racial identification is the extent to which he conflated hobbies and activities with racial identity. Certainly, for adolescents the performance of race is highly scrutinized, as many other identities (skater, stoner, athlete, etc.) may also be highly racialized. However, it was a combination of shifting hobbies and interactions with his new peers and classmates at Grovedale High that prompted Jason to rethink his identity.

Jason's racial identification was largely tied to his surroundings and environment, and in Michigan he was socialized in a virtually all-White sphere. The move to California not only forced Jason to shift his hobbies, as there was no snow for him to go snowmobiling in and no hockey team for him to join, but also prompted a shift in the way he viewed his racial identity. In Jason's conception, the move away from Michigan "changed a lot":

I mean, cuz at first that's what I was doing, I was hockey and baseball. And I was good at it. And when I first moved out here, it kinda shocked everybody because when it came up for sign-ups at the new school for sports, you would see all the black people—boom—football and basketball list instantly. And I would look for baseball and hockey, and I would see no hockey, and I'm wondering like, where's the hockey team at? And then when it came to baseball, I'm not gonna lie, the first time I stepped on the baseball field out here I kinda looked and I was like, why am I the only dark-skinned boy out here playing baseball? And it came to me. I was like, I'm really not white like I thought I was. Like when I first thought I was 100 percent white it was based on all the activities and things that the family did together and the way I was dressin' and the stuff that we did. And then I really started to realize, like wow. . . . And for a minute I was thinkin' like, what am I? Am I more white than I am black, or am I more black than I am white? So I started to adapt into it more.

In the above quotation, Jason worked through stereotypical behaviors he associated with being Black or White and the culture shock he suffered when transitioning from Michigan to California. In recognizing his difference for the first time on the baseball field not only in terms of region but also in terms of race, Jason began to question his racial identity. With few options except to explore the stereotypically "Black" sports while remaining dedicated to the hobbies he engaged in while living in Michigan, Jason began to view these dual interests as the different sides of his racial heritage being expressed. He then merged these interests, believing he could remain interested in one without excluding the other, and began to view himself as biracial instead of White.

Jason's identity shift was also supported by his interactions with peers at his school. In contrast to Michigan, where his skin tone and racial difference were not topics of discussion with his family, at Grovedale Jason received inquiries about his background. However, the question most often took the form of "What are you mixed with?"—implying an assumption that Jason was indeed mixed and a framing that expressed a consciousness that was very open to mixture. As the next example will illustrate, the normalization of mixed race on the Grovedale campus and the ways in which people in the space readily interpreted others as multiracial contributed greatly to the production of multiracial identities within Northern California.

Keisha and Kendra

Biracial Black-White sisters Keisha and Kendra were also transplants to Grovedale High but had grown up in a predominantly White rural county located two hours away. Two years before moving to Grovedale, their family moved within the county from Lakeport to Middletown, a new town with the same rural White demographics. Most of the locals had gotten to know the sisters when they were growing up in Lakeport, but in Middletown their Blackness was immediately salient—and threatening. Keisha explained:

> When I moved to Middletown, there's like, in Middletown there's not a lot of anything besides white people. So when they saw me they were

like, "Oh she's black, I'm scared of her." Like a lot of people told me that, [and] after they got to know me they were like, "I was scared of you when you first started going here cuz you were black." And I was like, "I'm not even full black, I have white in me too." And they were like "Oh." But in Lakeport I started going there when I was in first grade, so everybody had already knew me, and it was like already . . . before they even realized I was black it was like, "Oh she's cool."

Keisha described both a lack of racial awareness or consciousness of race among her peers ("before they even realized I was black"), as well as the importance of getting to know her instead of exclusively reading her through the lens of a stereotype. Although the Blackness and otherness that were front and center in Middletown could understandably have affected the way that Keisha and her sister Kendra thought about their own racial identities, both sisters reported that their parents reinforced a biracial identity at home. Their Blackness, Whiteness, and mixedness were all affirmed and emphasized by their parents. Thus, the sisters retained a multiracial internal identity despite the demonstrated influence of reflected appraisals and the lingering salience of the one-drop rule.[23] I asked Keisha how her assertion of shared Whiteness was received by her peers at Middletown, and Keisha responded, "They never really thought of it as I was half white. Because, I mean, I'm not that dark, but I look black. So they're like, 'Oh she's just black.' They never acknowledged the white side."

Although Keisha and Kendra had developed a firm identity and sense of themselves as biracial from having parents who spoke to them about race and identity, their new demographic and cultural surroundings at Grovedale were still profoundly impactful. Among the many salient differences, the way their multiraciality was reacted to was especially significant. In fact, in this new context they did not even have to volunteer information about their multiraciality; it was often already ascribed to them. Even receiving inquiries about their racial background was entirely new to them:

ALYSSA: Okay, so either in Lakeport, Middletown, or here, do people ever ask you about your racial background, like what are you, what are you mixed with, any of those types of questions?

KENDRA: Yeah. Um, recently I would say just this year people have always been asking me what am I, and they always confuse me with like black and Filipino or something. And I have to let them know like, I'm black and white.

ALYSSA: So just this year. What about in Lakeport or Middletown, did you get those questions too or—

KENDRA: No. They just, they just assumed I was black. They didn't really ask.

Being Black and another race was a new identity option that did not exist in Lakeport and Middletown. In those places, multiracial was not something that Keisha and Kendra were allowed to be—it did not exist as an identity category within that local context. The dismissal of Keisha's assertion of her White side indicated that hypodescent was in full effect, and her discernible Blackness was determinative in others' interpretations of her exclusively as Black.

The new Grovedale setting affirmed an identity that Keisha and Kendra already possessed within the family but that they had not previously been able to access publicly. For Jason, this exposure to a more demographically diverse setting was also an exposure to a setting that was not monocultural, prompting his reconsideration of his racial identity, which was heavily steeped in participation in racialized activities and the performance of race. In a previous study at a neighboring high school, I found that the role of peer interactions took the affirmation of multiracial identities even a step further, correcting a student's monoracial identification to one that was multiracial. This high school, located less than ten minutes from Grovedale, had very similar demographics. A Black-White biracial student there had moved from a predominantly White suburban setting and, like Keisha and Kendra, was seen as exclusively Black there. When continuing to identify as Black at the new school near Grovedale, this student was told by another: "If you're fifty percent black and fifty percent white, how can you go around and say that you're only one?"[24] Thus, in this one notable and perhaps extreme example, it was more than creating a friendly context for identifying as multiracial that helped produce and foster multiracial identities in the Grovedale area of Northern California; it was also expecting a multiracial identification and rejecting a monoracial one.

The Adults

Like the adolescents discussed in the previous section, the adults had varying relationships to multiraciality and their conceptions of their own racial identities. However, in the stories I will share below, they each had experiences upon moving to Northern California that affirmed their multiraciality in ways they had never encountered before. Although the regions they moved from and their ages varied widely, the impact of the move to Northern California on the established racial identities and identifications of these adults underscores the region's role in prompting these shape shifting transformations.

Margit

The daughter of two immigrants, Margit was a thirty-eight-year-old woman who had been in California for the past thirteen years. Originally born in Arizona, she spent the first years of her life in Norway, where her father was from, followed by several moves along the East Coast between Maryland and Virginia. It had taken her some time to uncover her full background due to a secretive family history haunted by war, abandonment, and trauma. Her Norwegian ancestry from her father was clear, but her mother, who was from Indonesia, had a long family background of racial mixing between Indonesians and Dutch under colonization. Carefully deliberate and measured in her answers, Margit was delightfully excitable in specific moments, such as when recalling details about her identity development process or when offering to follow up with her mother about some of my questions.

It was not until she was much older that Margit discovered her mother's Japanese ancestry, the result of an intimate relationship (amorous or coerced) between Margit's grandmother and a Japanese soldier occupying her home during World War II. Following the war, the

departure of the Japanese soldier, and the return of Margit's grandmother's husband, Margit's mother was sent to live with other family
and eventually ended up in an orphanage. After some time, Margit's
mother was found by an uncle and taken along with another war baby
to Holland, where she would grow up and come to identify with being
Dutch. Uncovering this family history influenced Margit's racial identity, but I also spoke to her about other formative factors that shaped
her racial self-conception. She explained:

> MARGIT: So it wasn't until I got to college, when I started taking
> some courses around identity, race, class, politics, things like that,
> that I started to question my mother and dig into the family his-
> tory. And that's when I started developing consciousness around
> being a mixed-race person.
>
> ALYSSA: Okay. And so before that do you think that you thought of
> yourself as white or just—
>
> MARGIT: Yeah, I thought of myself as white. And I think a lot of that
> has to do with the fact, it has to do with because of how we were
> raised, and we didn't really incorporate any Asian ethnic activities,
> cultural events, things like that into our lives. But I think it also
> had a lot to do with how people perceived me. So people perceive
> me as white, even now that I have a mixed-race identity or I iden-
> tify as Hapa, most people view me and perceive me as white. And
> so that I think has a lot to do with how my own personal identity
> was shaped. If I looked more Asian, which some of my cousins do
> who are also mixed, I don't think I could have perceived myself as
> white, because other people's perception would have informed my
> identity.

Margit's college experience prompted a desire to finally learn this
family history and allowed her to develop a consciousness around
being a mixed race person for the first time. However, her surrounding social context and how she was racially interpreted by others also
had a powerful impact. As she mentioned, she is still often perceived as
White, but she holds on to her own secure self-identification as Hapa.

How Margit came to identify as Hapa was profoundly shaped by racial interpretation too. Indeed, Margit pointed to a very specific instance of the first time she was recognized, via a photograph, as mixed race. She was still in college but visiting a friend in Los Angeles. There was a photograph of her in the friend's home, and while Margit was not present, someone saw the picture and asked the friend if Margit was mixed. Although none of this experience had happened firsthand, Margit held on to this first instance of being recognized as mixed race as validation of her multiraciality. This experience was rare for her both before and after her identity shifted, but she noted that it was something that had "only happened in California" and that "a couple people, very few people have asked me if I was Hapa, have asked me if I was mixed Asian, if I had any Asian in me. And generally I have found the people who have asked me that know other Hapa people." The presence, visibility, and established mixed race identifications were critical in making California a place where Margit could find her mixed race identity affirmed.

When I asked Margit to explain how she learned about the term "Hapa" and when she began to affiliate herself with that identification, Margit offered another specific incident: "I learned about Hapa when I came to Northern California. So when I came to California and I started working for a nonprofit organization in San Francisco, and there was a Hapa woman who worked in the organization. And so once we started talking about our backgrounds she said, 'Oh you're Hapa too.' And I was like, 'What's Hapa?' And so she educated me in the land of Hapa, and that's when I started to take on that identity, I guess, to use that term to describe myself." Importantly, Margit's realization was not brought about by someone phenotypically recognizing Margit as mixed race; instead, it occurred during a discussion about backgrounds that made Margit's mixed heritage known. During this occasion Margit's shared background was marked by her coworker, and the two women built a connection over this commonality, opening up a new term and identification for Margit.

Beyond Margit's discovery of new terminology and language, her identity shift was prompted by new knowledge about her family background, the development of her mixed race consciousness, and a handful of experiences in which her mixed race background was readily interpreted and/or affirmed. Upon coming to California, not only was Margit recognized as mixed race for the first time, but she also could meet and connect with other mixed race people. After describing how she did not have any mixed race friends in college, Margit added, "And then all of a sudden, you know coming to California it was like I could see myself in a number of people, I could see that sort of Hapa look in a number of people, and that was great." I had been connected with Margit for an interview through a previous interviewee who I discovered was part of a network that included many mixed race women involved in working toward racial and social justice issues. Indeed, Margit had built a mixed race community in the Bay Area, especially among those whom she connected with through working on racial and social justice efforts.

Lewis

Lewis was a thirty-three-year-old Black and Korean student affairs professional from Oklahoma. At the time of our interview, he had been living in Northern California for ten months. His newness to the region provided him valuable insight into the differences in his racialization, the salience of his background, and the overall subtle changes in his everyday life that were a result of the demographics and social conditions in his new setting.

Lewis spent his early school years in a small, rural, predominantly Black town before the family moved to a "pretty much all-white" neighborhood of Tulsa when he was nine or ten. His parents had met in South Korea, where his father, a Black serviceman, was stationed. After his older brother was born in Korea the family moved to the United States, traveling around for different assignments until they ultimately landed in Oklahoma when Lewis was in kindergarten. During his childhood Lewis was raised in the Korean Baptist Church, where there were a handful of other biracial children, mostly White and Korean; he and his brother were the only ones who were part Black.

In both the predominantly Black and the predominantly White

places in which he grew up, Lewis's Black identity was expected and reinforced. For instance, when he was in the fourth grade he and another Black male were the only Black students in his homeroom. One day, a new girl was added to the homeroom, and she was also Black. Instantly, all of Lewis's friends encouraged him to try to be her boyfriend "because the two black people who are the endangered species in the room should get together, that's what should happen." Despite this clear assignment to Blackness, however, Lewis was also challenged on his Black identity. When Lewis entered high school he was in honors and AP classes and was frequently the only Black student in those spaces. His relative isolation from the rest of the Black population prevented him from forming friendships with other Black students and led them to question whether or not he was "down." Whenever he was confronted with those challenges Lewis would try to prove himself, such as defending his choice to wear plaid, supposedly a pattern associated with White fashion, by referencing the matching outfits of the all-Black male group Boyz II Men. Ultimately, Lewis reconciled his claim to Blackness within himself as he matured and no longer needed external verification.

When Lewis was recognized as mixed race within Oklahoma, perceivers often interpreted him as Black and White or Black and Native American. He was bothered by the erasure of his Asianness through those interpretations but also recognized how as he moved through space those interpretations shifted. On the East Coast, for instance, he was read as Puerto Rican or Dominican but for the most part always "brown or black." As it was for Margit, college was an important moment for Lewis in sorting out his racial identity, in part influenced by the way his phenotype was read and also through his interactions in different racial community spaces. He explained:

> So then I think that shifted for me in college to where I was exploring my own identity. Because I was in a culture identifiable as having, you know, brown skin and looking less stereotypically Asian, I found myself associating closer to other multiethnic people or to other black people in college. I ended up joining a historically black

fraternity and finding myself being more distanced from my Korean heritage I think because of how people perceived me, and that influence, particularly with a moment in which I was made to feel unwelcome at another Korean church I was trying to join when I went to college two hours away from my home. So that was the first time I was made to feel like a stranger in a church. And that did not feel good for me. And it almost was a reminder that, okay, it's another reminder that you are, no matter what you do, you can try to affirm how you are and how you want to identify, but others will try to consistently influence how you are seen by the world and remind you that you're a person of color, you're a brown person.

Although Lewis stayed in Oklahoma, this move to a new metropolitan area exposed him to a community different from the one he was raised in. This sense of rejection, coupled with his Asianness not being reflected in the way others racially interpreted him, caused him to more firmly locate his racial identity within his Blackness.

Following a discussion of how Lewis was racially interpreted differently in Oklahoma versus the East Coast, where he lived for a few years while finishing up graduate school, I prompted him to talk about his experience during his short time in California.

In terms of multiethnic identity, I think, I get less questions here. It almost seems like it's umm, it's more normal in that you're going to see mixed-race folks here period. And it's not gonna change your value base and how you interact with them. So at least that's what I've noticed. Umm, but then if I do find opportunities to inject that I'm Korean, that identity has almost shot up in terms of level of relevance here just because of the large Asian population here. . . . So I do feel that here, because numerically speaking there's fewer African Americans here, but there's a rich history of African Americans here, it's a different type of experience for me in terms of how I lead with my identity. And it's sometimes refreshing in some ways to kind of be able to think about more about my Korean identity. And that's more valued here than other places I've been. And I don't know where

I'm going with this, but I think I guess probably the population here has probably played a different role in how I identify.

Despite a Black population smaller than what Lewis was used to, he felt that the impact and history of the Black population on where he lived were very present and relevant. For the first time, however, he was around a large Asian community, one that was differentiated such that "Asian" did not just mean one homogenized group; instead, it meant one could be Filipino, Japanese, Chinese, Korean, and more. For Lewis, this exposure to a large and varied Asian population was meaningful:

> The other thing that I think it is amazing here is the type of engagement that Asian Americans in general have here in society versus where I grew up and other places. So for example, where I grew up in Oklahoma I never saw an Asian American person who, like, worked in sanitation, worked in the grocery store bagging groceries. That's not something that we saw in my community in Oklahoma because there were so few. Here, which actually I appreciate, is that it's not the model minority everywhere. It's like you see Asian Americans doing everything. Everything from being doctors to honestly just, you know, cleaning toilets or just doing whatever work they wanna do. They're everywhere. And that was actually refreshing to me because that was the stereotype that was perpetuated in terms of model minorities growing up in Oklahoma which actually made me feel like I wasn't Asian enough. I wasn't a straight-A student, but I wasn't dumb, like, I wasn't trying to reduce myself in terms of how I achieved in the classroom. I was always in the space of where I wasn't black enough because I was in the AP class. But I wasn't the valedictorian, I never was of that high achiever, I never was. And so in many ways that made me feel like I wasn't Korean enough, because I wasn't the kid that my parents bragged about in terms of my grades. You know, I made a few C's and D's here and there [laughs].

Thus, Lewis's move to Northern California provided a demographic and social context that affirmed both his Blackness and his Koreanness and allowed him to explore both identities. Even though he sometimes had to inject his background into a conversation, he felt that both of his backgrounds were relevant, salient, and recognized. Although he had only lived in the region for less than a year, his experiences of claiming both Blackness and Koreanness were accepted in his interactions despite his appearance or how he was racially interpreted.

The role of the larger Asian population was salient for a number of other interviewees as well. Margit's parents had considered retiring to the Bay Area because her mother reportedly loved visiting and "seeing people who look like me." Other interviewees felt that instead of being lumped into a Pan-Asian category, being Filipino or Vietnamese was distinctive and meaningful within the broader social context for the first time.

Discussion

The juxtaposition of teenagers and adults in this chapter offers a revelatory variance of perspective on the role of place in mixed race identity development. Certainly, the meanings assigned to race differed for the two groups, with the youth more intimately tying performance to their conception of race than the adults, who had generally matured past their compulsion to prove their identity and belonging to others. In some ways their different moments in the identity development process were an expected consequence of their age, but other differences were indicative of a shifting social context in which mixed race has undergone extensive resignifications.

This chapter explored the narratives of several individuals whose shifts in racial identity were related to a change of place. While the context from which they moved varied greatly, they all shared a move to Northern California and a shift in the direction of multiracial identification. Sometimes this move and shift supported an identity that was already there, and other times this shift opened these individuals to new identifications or ones they had not explored before.

Throughout each of these narratives, Northern California was a context that supported, affirmed, and encouraged multiracial identities. This was facilitated by two different factors: interaction and demographics. Many of the interactions that affirmed or encouraged multiracial identities for these interviewees were ones in which the interviewee was racially interpreted as multiracial. For some, such as Keisha and Kendra, this was unusual, as they had always been interpreted monoracially. For those girls, however, that was related to the hypodescent that prevailed in their previous local context. Their Blackness was always visible and affirmed; their Whiteness and mixedness were not. For others such as Margit who were also typically interpreted monoracially, their first experiences of being visibly recognized for what was hidden within their phenotype were extremely meaningful. Margit was accustomed to being read as White, and being racially interpreted as Hapa not only affirmed her Asianness and mixedness, which she had longed to have recognized, but also exposed her to a new way of identifying that she felt more accurately reflected and categorized her.

Other interactions that affirmed multiracial identities were when interviewees asserted parts of their identity that were not visible or discernible to observers and had those identifications accepted. For instance, Lewis mentioned how he would bring up his Korean ancestry in conversation as often as possible. He had often felt that his Asianness was not visible and even felt distanced from the Korean community when his appearance betrayed his shared ancestry. However, in Northern California he could assert his Koreanness and Asianness, and his multiple backgrounds were accepted at his word rather than rejected outright.

Another reason Lewis found his Koreanness to be more easily accepted after his move to Northern California was because he experienced his Korean identity as more salient within that context. The demographics of Northern California made being Korean meaningful, as the Korean population was substantial enough that the rest of the community was familiar with their presence. They were well represented enough that individual Koreans were not treated as the token representatives of their background. Lewis and several other interviewees in my study shared how their move to Northern California was the first time that they were actually exposed to other Asians who did not conform to one stereotypical way of being, even as they were only exposed to certain representations of Asianness.

The demographics also contributed to the interviewees' sense of being more normal, typical, and affirmed in multiple aspects of their identity due to the diversity of the region. Lewis mentioned how the history of Blackness in the area, despite a Black population that was smaller than he was used to, allowed him to feel his Blackness was salient. At the same time, the larger Korean and Asian populations made his Korean identity salient. He could affirm and nourish each of these aspects of his identity in the diversity and history of Northern California. The politics of representation and visibility presented a set of power dynamics different from that determined by a White or monoracial gaze. Margit's mother had also felt more normalized in the Northern California context and appreciated her visits to the region because she could recognize herself in others there. Similarly, Margit's phenotypically White appearance could be dissected more carefully and precisely in Northern California. Although she was still read as White in many settings, she also encountered others who recognized themselves in her and affirmed her Hapaness by accurately racially interpreting her.

The commonsense norm of multiracial identification was made apparent to the teenagers and adults who moved to Northern California through their interactions with those already living in the region. However, Northern California had also moved forward the discourse on multiraciality beyond simply recognizing and accepting multiracial identification. Amelia, a thirty-four-year-old Mexican and White interviewee, was completing a master's program in Iowa and had flown out for an interview at a university near Sacramento. The contrast she observed between the degree of development of multiracial identity and discourses around it was stark:

> When I was at the University of Iowa, like, one of my last weeks there, I was so ready to get out of Iowa. And I had been out here to interview for the position here, and when I had come out for the interview it was mixed heritage week some years ago, and I was like, oh

this is awesome. I had gone to the exhibit and connected with people, and then I went back to Iowa, and there was this article on the front page that basically felt like it was saying "Did you know: mixed race people exist!" It was such a contrast . . . this difference between being well established and kind of known and we're at this point of kind of like maybe some political organizing or community building versus like "Breaking news!" So the conversation is at very different places, I think, depending where in the country and maybe even where in the state.

Amelia's observation drives home the point that across the United States the recognition, acknowledgment, and existence of multiracial identity stand at really different points and may lag far behind the development of the identity in Northern California. While college students at the university where she interviewed were at the point of being able to engage in community building and organizing, the conversation in Iowa was only at the point of simply acknowledging that multiracial people exist. In many places in Northern California, being multiracial is not particularly unusual or necessarily of note. Thus, multiraciality is more deeply interwoven into the fabric of everyday interactions in the region. From events as special as a heritage week to the acceptance of their multiracial identification, those interviewees reviewed in this chapter had experiences in Northern California that normalized their multiraciality to a degree they had never encountered before.

The culmination of those interactions and experiences, large and small, that affirmed multiracial identity produced in some cases a multiracial identification that the interviewee had not previously asserted. For others, these affirmations allowed them to embrace and explore their multiraciality or different backgrounds to a greater degree. Even though the adults especially had a well-developed sense of self and identity, these encounters in Northern California prompted a reconsideration of their identity and opened new possibilities for their multiracial identification, as well as their racial self-conception.

When the demographics of Northern California are compared to much of the rest of the country, perhaps the actual numbers of individuals of mixed race ancestry are not at all distinctive or unusual. However, the ways in which the region produces multiracial identification—by allowing or expecting multiracial individuals to identify as mixed race—is a unique cultural context that richly offers much to explore about the role of place and racial identification. The dynamics of power and racial relations among this distinctive set of dynamics and politics of representation and racial visibility have generated tremors that reverberate along the structure of a U.S. racial order built upon a monoracial imperative that has increasingly allowed a multiracial identification to break through. In a shifting U.S. demographic landscape in which the multiracial population is rapidly growing, the Northern California context, in which multiraciality is well developed and normalized, provides an ideal setting for exploring the consequences of the entrance of the multiracial category of people into the racial order.

Notes

1. G. Reginald Daniel, Laura Kina, Wei Ming Dariotis, and Camila Fojas, "Emerging Paradigms in Critical Mixed Race Studies," *Journal of Critical Mixed Race Studies* 1 (2014): 6–65; F. James Davis, *Who Is Black? One Nation's Definition* (University Park: Pennsylvania State University Press, 1991).
2. G. Reginald Daniel, *More Than Black? Multiracial Identity and the New Racial Order* (Philadelphia PA: Temple University Press, 2002); Kim M. Williams, *Mark One or More: Civil Rights in Multiracial America* (Ann Arbor: University of Michigan Press, 2008).
3. Kimberly DaCosta, *Making Multiracials: State, Family, and Market in the Redrawing of the Color Line* (Stanford CA: Stanford University Press, 2007).
4. David L. Brunsma, "Public Categories, Private Identities: Exploring Regional Differences in the Biracial Experience," *Social Science Research* 35 (2006): 555–76; France Winddance Twine, "Brown Skinned White Girls: Class, Culture and the Construction of White Identity in Suburban Communities," *Gender, Place and Culture* 3, no. 2 (1996): 205–24; Richard Wright, Serin Houston, Mark Ellis, Steven Holloway, and Margaret Hudson, "Crossing Racial Lines: Geographies of Mixed-Race Partnering and Multiraciality in the United States," *Progress in Human Geography* 27, no. 4 (2003): 457–74.

5. Jennifer Lee and Frank Bean, "America's Changing Color Lines: Immigration, Race/Ethnicity, and Multiracial Identification," *Annual Review of Sociology* 30 (2004): 236.

6. Daniel, *More Than Black?*; Kristen A. Renn, *Mixed Race Students in College: The Ecology of Race, Identity, and Community on Campus* (Albany: State University of New York Press, 2004).

7. Kerry Ann Rockquemore, David Brunsma, and Daniel Delgado, "Racing to Theory or Retheorizing Race? Understanding the Struggle to Build a Multiracial Identity Theory," *Journal of Social Issues* 65 (2009): 13–34; Brunsma, "Public Categories."

8. Julie Park, Dowell Meyers, and Liang Wei, "Multiracial Patterns in California by County," Public Research Report No. 2001-3, Race Contours 2000 Study, University of Southern California and University of Michigan Collaborative Project.

9. Alyssa M. Newman, "How Can You Say You're Only One? Identity and Community among Mixed Black High School Students," *Eleven: The Undergraduate Journal of Sociology* 1 (2010): 3–28.

10. Pew Research Center, *Multiracial in America: Proud, Diverse, and Growing in Numbers* (Washington DC, June 2015).

11. The "menu of identities" is referenced in the introductory chapter to this volume, "Shape Shifting: Reflections on Racial Plasticity" by Paul Spickard.

12. Maria P. P. Root, "From Exotic to a Dime a Dozen," *Women & Therapy* 27, no. 1 (2004): 19–31.

13. Erik Erikson, *Identity and the Life Cycle* (New York: W. W. Norton, 1959).

14. Renn, *Mixed Race Students*.

15. Kathleen Korgen, *From Black to Biracial* (New York: Praeger, 1998).

16. Nicholas A. Jones and Jungmiwha Bullock, "The Two or More Races Population: 2010," U.S. Census Bureau (2012), C2010BR-13. According to definitions available on the U.S. Census Bureau's website, "Places, for the reporting of decennial census data, include census designated places, consolidated cities, and incorporated places" (http://www.census.gov/geo/www/geo_defn .html#Place). In this census brief, places were confined to only those with a population of one hundred thousand or more total population.

17. Park, Meyers, and Wei, "Multiracial Patterns," 2.

18. 2010 Census Bureau for neighborhood, "American Fact Finder," www .factfinder2.census.gov.

19. Sharon M. Lee and Barry Edmonston, "New Marriages, New Families: U.S. Racial and Hispanic Intermarriage," *Population Bulletin* 60, no. 2 (2005): 33.

20. Lee and Edmonston, "New Marriages," 33.

21. Karen R. Humes, Nicolas A. Jones, and Roberto R. Ramirez, "Overview of Race and Hispanic Origin: 2010," U.S. Department of Commerce, Economics and Statistics Administration (2011), U.S. Census Bureau; Root, "From Exotic."

22. Pew, *Multiracial in America*.

23. Nikki Khanna, "If You're Half Black, You're Just Black: Reflected Appraisals and the Persistence of the One-Drop Rule," *Sociological Quarterly* 56 (2010): 96–121.

24. Newman, "How Can You Say," 20.

6

"You Are the Shame of the Race"

Dynamics of Pain, Shame, and Violence in Shape Shifting Processes

Angelica Pesarini

"Colorism" is a process of discrimination that grants advantages and privileges to lighter-skinned members of the same racialized group over those with darker complexions.[1] A great deal of research traces the genealogy of such a practice, whose origins in the United States stem from European colonialism and slavery. Since the creation of the first colony in Virginia in 1607, unconsented sexual intercourse occurred within plantations between White slave owners and enslaved Black women, giving birth to generations of so-called mulattos.[2] Despite strict regulations on miscegenation, records highlight the privileges and skills these lighter-skinned individuals gained over their darker counterparts due to the social meaning attributed to their lighter complexion and their more European-looking features within what Margaret Hunter calls "skin colour hierarchies."[3] Similarly, the practice of "passing"—often associated to colorism—would provide a few lighter-skinned people with advantages and opportunities denied to darker members of the same racialized group, especially in periods of racial segregation, such as under the Jim Crow era.[4]

Although the majority of the scholarship on colorism and passing in colonial settings seems to be concerned mainly with the privileges and higher status of lighter-skinned Blacks, little attention has been paid to those moments when a lighter complexion triggered a situation of disadvantage, shame, and pain and when an imposed change of racial identity became a source of violence rather than an asset. This invites us to reconsider concepts such as passing itself, easily explained by some as racial imposture or as a simple and rational denial of a specific ancestry.[5] In this regard, *shape shifting* can be seen as a conceptual tool able to highlight the complexities and the ambiguities of preconceived and crystallized etiquettes attached to people's bodies and identities. As Stuart Hall explains, "race" itself is a floating signifier, suggesting that it does not work in exactly the same way everywhere; instead, race is a contingent and fluid set of discursive practices operating in specific contexts and constantly being "resignified."[6] This means that racialized subjects find themselves surrounded by and immersed in sets of changing racializing dynamics over which, at times, they may have some power and that they can partly transform, resist, and subvert according to the negotiations they operate in their everyday lives.

In his theorization, Paul Spickard identifies several situations or contexts in which the racialized subject becomes a *shape shifter*. One of these concerns compelled or rational identity shifts triggered by changes of social and racial circumstances, such as in the case of migratory processes. As Spickard explains, "Most often, people change their identities in response to changes in the social systems around them. In new social settings, there are different menus of identity options, and people must find new ways to locate themselves."[7] However, this is not an easy matter. As I show in this chapter, it is not the simple fact of migrating somewhere that necessarily causes an identity shift. Changes in identification processes may be the result of a sudden awareness of racializing practices in place; therefore, a set of new responses and strategies must be adopted to face racism and discrimination. I have called these responses "color strategies."[8] These refer to the ways racialized subjects juggle and interact with racial categories in order to negotiate a space of existence in specific racialized environments. The analysis of color strategies highlights the fact that the negotiations put in place by racialized subjects are never easy or pain free, as I discovered in my study on mixed race identities in Fascist East

Africa and postcolonial Italy. As this chapter shows, shame, violence, and pain may be at the core of everyday life for those who shape shift.

To examine these issues, I focus on the identification processes of two mixed race Italian women born in the former Italian colonies in East Africa.[9] The first story belongs to Isabella Marincola, who was born in Somalia in 1925 to the Italian colonial officer Giuseppe Marincola and a young Somali woman named Ashkiro Assan. The second story is about Bruna, born in Eritrea in 1940 to an Ethiopian mother and an Italian father who never recognized her.[10] These two stories show how dynamics of shape shifting may differ according to the social settings in which they take place and the different degrees of power racialized subjects may exert by using their color strategies. In relation to power, Rebecca King-O'Riain aptly highlights how practices of shape shifting are determined by the agency of social actors and the fact that they shape shift in different ways according to the degree of power with which they are provided.[11] Before introducing the two stories, however, it is necessary to illustrate the specific historical and political context in which these stories are located, namely, Italian colonialism and Fascism in East Africa.

Italian Colonialism in East Africa

Formal Italian domination over East Africa started in 1890, when all the Italian possessions gained up to that time were legally consolidated into a single political entity named Eritrea, which ended officially in 1941. The first Italian possession in East Africa dated back to 1869, when an Italian shipping company bought the Bay of Assab, on the coast of modern Eritrea. Later, the bay was sold to the Italian state and declared an Italian colony in 1882. In 1885 Italy started to enlarge its possessions in Eritrea, occupying the coastal town of Massawa and trying to expand into the Ethiopian highlands. This first invasion was temporarily stopped by the Ethiopian army, which defeated the Italians in the Battle of Dogali in 1887. In 1889 the new emperor, Menelik II, signed the Treaty of Wichale and agreed to Italian expansion in the north of Ethiopia. Despite the agreement, Italy kept on expanding beyond the limits imposed by the treaty. In 1896, during the Battle of

Adwa, the Ethiopian troops managed to definitively defeat the Italian army, making Adwa the biggest European defeat in the history of colonial Africa. Despite this massive defeat, Ethiopia still remained the ultimate target for the Italians. The "shame" of Adwa was avenged in 1936 at the end of the second Italo-Ethiopian War, when Mussolini announced the birth of the Empire of Italian East Africa—Africa Orientale Italiana—formed by the merger of Italian Somaliland, Italian Eritrea, and occupied Ethiopia. The empire was short-lived, though, given that it lasted only until 1941, when the Fascist army was defeated by the British during the Battle of Keren.[12]

Before the introduction of racial laws in the empire (1937–40) and despite the presence of prostitutes and state-controlled brothels, Italian long-term residents usually had relationships with local women within a practice known as *madamato* or *madamismo*, literally, "having a relationship with a *madama*."[13] This term applied to concubines who would temporarily live with Italian men, "performing domestic and sexual services and being rewarded in kind and/or money."[14] *Madamato* was apparently built on an existing form of temporary marriage in Eritrea known as *demoz*, consisting of an Eritrean woman, normally a Coptic Christian, who "commits herself, directly or through her family, to live in conjugal union with a man, for a given length of time, and for the payment of a given sum."[15] According to Eritrean customary norms, the father of the children had to provide economic support to his partner and their offspring.[16] Nevertheless, historical research and archival studies, like the ones conducted by Giulia Barrera and Gianluca Gabrielli, show that many Italian men dismissed such norms, abandoning women and children. This was especially true of military officials and men whose tenure in Africa was temporary.[17]

Until the creation of the empire, the colonial authority did not consider those unions particularly dangerous, and they gave birth to a generation of children considered "Italian" in East Africa. Although interracial marriages were legally possible until 1937, and although there was an enormous number of interracial relationships, very few Italian men decided to legally acknowledge their relationships with their African partners.[18] The rarity of these marriages was partly caused by the fact that many men were already married in Italy and did not plan to stay in Africa. Furthermore, the impact of scientific racism and racial classifications played an important role. For many European men, Africa was a "porno-tropic," to use Anne McClintock's words, "a fantastic magic lantern of the mind onto which Europe projected its forbidden sexual desire and fears . . . the quintessential zone of sexual aberration and abnormality."[19] By the end of the eighteenth century, the inferiorization and the reduction of Black people to the realm of animals added to racial stereotypes produced by the Western scientific community, which framed the sexuality of Blacks as "deviant." Black women were seen as so hypersexualized that they would copulate with apes.[20] Therefore, also in the case of Italian colonialism, Eritrean women were often considered good for sex but not suitable as life partners owing to their lack of "womanhood," as argued by Renato Paoli, an Italian journalist who visited Eritrea in 1936. In his private correspondence, he complained about the lack of "women" in the colony, stating that "there are black females, exuberant and generous; but women are missing and women can only be white."[21]

"You Are the Shame of the Race": What Race?

Isabella Marincola's (1925–2010) life is a fascinating piece of Italian history. Her story lies at the intersection of the multiple and complex identities she negotiated, resisted, and at times subverted over a seventy-five-year period of Italian history. Isabella was an Italian mixed race woman born in colonial Somalia and raised in Fascist Italy who lived the majority of her adult life in a so-called postcolonial historical phase both in Somalia and in Italy. She went through the declaration of the empire of Africa Orientale Italiana by Mussolini and the racial laws; she was a young woman in the aftermath of World War II; and she experienced the period of terror due to Mohamed Siad Barre's coup when she went to Somalia. At the end of her life Isabella went back to Italy and struggled to be recognized as a Black Italian. She died in Bologna in 2010. Her lucid analysis of intergenerational racism shows the problematic ties that Italy still has with its former colonies and how a selective and hegemonic historical memory may deem some individuals outside the realm of the nation.

Isabella told her life story to her son Antar and the writer Wu Ming 2. The three of them took part in what they called a "collective autobiographical work," published by Einaudi in 2012 and titled *Timira: Romanzo meticcio*. The novel is loyal to Isabella's narratives, which were recorded by Wu Ming 2 during their regular encounters. As it is explained in the book, "The aim of this publication is not to tell an 'absolute truth' rather to tell Isabella's truth and her point of view on the experiences she had and the people she met."[22] Therefore, I base my account of Isabella's life story on several sources. First, I will use the book Isabella herself, her son Antar, and Wu Ming 2 wrote together. Second, I will integrate this with a long interview I conducted with Antar in Bologna in 2012.[23] Finally, I will use a video interview of Isabella conducted by the Italian director Aureliano Amadei and titled *Quale razza?* (What race?).[24]

Isabella was born in 1925 in Somalia, the second child of Giuseppe Marincola, an Italian colonial officer, and Ashkiro Assan, a Somali woman born in Harardere, a small fishing village four hundred kilometers northeast of Mogadishu. Isabella and her brother Giorgio came into the world at a historical turning point for both Somalia and Italy.[25] In 1922 the Fascist Party organized the famous march on Rome, which took place from October 22 to October 29. In 1923 Cesare Maria de Vecchi di Valcismon, one of the organizers of the march, was nominated the new governor of Italian Somaliland.

Isabella left Somalia and her mother in 1927 at the age of two. Giuseppe Marincola, unlike many others, recognized both children and decided to bring them both to Italy. While he sent Giorgio to the south of the country to live with some relatives who had no children, he took Isabella to his house in Rome, where he lived with his wife, Flora Virdis, and their two children.[26] Of course, the child who was introduced into the household was not just *a* child. Isabella was a Black child. This unusual situation gave rise to complex heteropatriarchal dynamics that profoundly affected the lives of Isabella, Flora, and Ashkiro.[27]

On the one hand, within the Somali "porno-tropics" Marincola had a public relationship with a Black woman, and unlike many other Italian men in his position, he legally recognized the children born from this union.[28] Yet one has to bear in mind the unbalanced structures of power, violence, and segregation at the core of the colonial life. Precisely because of these, Ashkiro was considered a *female* but not a woman, certainly not a mother able to raise Marincola's *Italian* children. On the other hand, in Italy there was a White woman, the ideal wife and mother, who seemed to perfectly reflect the principles of female domesticity. In this situation, Marincola felt entitled to impose the presence of his Black daughter, born in adultery, on his wife, while he considered the biological mother of the child, an African woman, as inadequate and not capable of properly raising his Italian children. This decision triggered, inevitably, a series of painful consequences. Flora, unlike other women in her situation, could not conceal her husband's infidelity by pretending fictitious maternal links with the child. Isabella's reified physical appearance embodied the sign of Marincola's infidelity with a Black woman. Thus, the child's impossibility to pass as White made things extremely complicated. As Isabella writes about her stepmother: "She hated me from the beginning because I couldn't blend in. If she could have said around that I was her daughter, maybe, sooner or later, she would have ended up loving me. But instead I had dark skin, the permanent sign of my father's fling with an African whore."[29] On the other side, Ashkiro, the biological mother of Giorgio and Isabella, saw her children being taken away from her. She would never have the chance to see Giorgio again, considering he died in 1945 at age twenty-two, and she would meet Isabella only in 1956, twenty-nine years after their separation in 1927.

What is striking in Isabella's account is her unawareness of her Blackness until the age of twelve, when her stepsister showed her a picture of Ashkiro and told her that the Black woman portrayed in the picture was Isabella's real mother. As Antar, Isabella's son, noted: "Whenever she would ask her father, 'Dad, why am I so dark?' he would say, 'Because you caught too much sun in Somalia!' If she would ask, 'Why is it written on my documents that I am the daughter of

Ashkiro Assan?' the reason given was that 'this is the Somali translation for Flora Virdis.' Thus, you see, she was raised in a climate of cultural deflection."[30] However, if Isabella was a color-blind child, her stepmother was certainly not, and she could perfectly see Isabella's skin shade. This was one of the main reasons lying at the core of their very conflictual relationship, characterized by tensions, verbal abuse, and physical violence inflicted by Flora on Isabella. The book includes descriptions of the many episodes of harsh physical violence experienced by Isabella, who was beaten up and whipped by Flora from a very young age.

According to Antar, his mother was color-blind because, as he affirms, "she really couldn't see the color of her skin because nobody had ever *taught* her to know, *to see* things."[31] This seems to be a crucial point that unpacks the dynamics of power at the core of the relationship between seeing and knowing. Isabella's body was clearly shaped by histories of colonialism; therefore, her color was a social and bodily given inherited by those stories. However, when she was a child she could not see the meanings or the history inscribed on her colonial body. When she suddenly started *to see* her color, this new knowledge gave her power. Her world drastically changed, giving rise to a painful shape shifting process. She was no longer just a child. She was a Black child, born in the colonies from her father's African lover, as she would further realize after having met and spoken to her biological mother for the first time in 1956:

> But now that I listen to my mother, now that she can speak, I have to acknowledge it. I am the daughter of violence, and I would be anyway, even if my parents would have loved each other, like in a nice *fotoromanzo*. Love at the time of colonies is embedded with ferocity. A sharp knife threatens and kills you anyway, even if one spreads honey on it. I am the daughter of a racist, someone who looked for oblivion all along his African adventure. Someone who ruined six people's lives because of his lies, Flora Virdis included. Who knows what Mrs. Marincola would have said to me if someone could have translated her whips into words. Who knows what she would have

said if I could have asked her how she felt when they brought her home someone else's children, furthermore, black.[32]

Despite the shock and the pain of this discovery while she was a child, it is precisely through her "racial learning" and through a sudden awareness of her Blackness inscribed on her body that Isabella started to shift and challenge dynamics of power and respond to her stepmother's violence by using what I called "color strategies."[33] One of these responses would consist in strategically using her color, indeed, by loudly exposing Flora's most intimate feelings of shame caused by the presence of a Black child within her household. The following passage taken from *Timira* can further clarify Isabella's strategies: "Mum? Who knows why Giorgio would persist in calling her that. I would prefer using 'My father's wife,' 'Mrs. Marincola,' sometimes the ironic 'Dear Mummy.' When I would really want to get her mad, I would say 'Madama Flora' or just 'Madama,' which is the same name they used to call partners of Italian men in the colony. Women like my real mother. These are the women whom Mrs. Marincola would enjoy calling whores."[34] In this passage, we can see how Isabella was aware of the reasons why her stepmother felt ashamed, but now she could use those same feelings as a weapon against her stepmother. If *madamas* like Isabella's mother who were with Italian men in the colonies were labeled "whores" by Flora, Isabella could reappropriate and subvert the meaning of such a word. She could throw it against Flora herself, calling her "Madama Flora."

We can notice a further shape shifting process in Isabella's identity and consequent new color strategies when, as an adult, she turned the White male fetishization of her body to her own advantage in order to achieve a better lifestyle and to survive independently without the help of her parents. The autumn of 1945 seems to have been a crucial year in her life. Giorgio, her beloved brother, died on May 4, just a few days before the end of World War II. In October of that same year, when she was twenty and had enrolled in her second year of natural science studies at the University of Bologna, Isabella left her house as the result of a ferocious argument with Flora, who ordered Giuseppe to make a choice between his wife and his daughter. Having no money and living in precarious conditions, Isabella started working first as a nude model and then as an actress, featuring in some major films in the history of Italian cinema such as *Riso amaro* by Dino Risi. Her career turned out to be very successful, to the extent that as a model she posed for artists such as Assen Peikov and Renato Guttuso. She started to be known in the field, and her fame was due also to the fact that she was not just one of the very few mixed race Italian female models in Rome at the time but also one of the very few Black Italians in the whole country.[35] As Isabella explained, White Italians seemed to be fascinated by this "beautiful Abyssinian" who was able to speak perfect Italian; thus, she often felt she was seen as the "icon of the colonial adventure" and was cosseted like a "trained monkey." Isabella well described the racialized and gendered looks she got while walking on the streets of Rome in the late 1940s: "Over time, those sweet cuddles turned in the opposite direction. On the one hand, the explicit and offensive sexual approach. On the other, the inappropriate looks, filtered like the branches of a hedge. 'Look at her lips, look at her hair, look at her skin. She is a mulatto.' Then I would turn, and I would spit my precooked answer, the discomfort that turns into cockiness: 'Yes, madame, I am like you say. But I am not deaf.'"[36]

"I Do Apologize, but in Africa It's Different"

The fact of seeing a Black woman portrayed as an icon of beauty triggered contrasting opinions. If some identified in her image the portrayal of a princess (after all, how could an African woman be so beautiful if she were not gifted with royal blood?), others would associate her with the animal kingdom and an insatiable sexual appetite, the heritage of nineteenth-century scientific racism.[37] In this regard, it is interesting to notice that some of the moral norms respected in the metropolitan territories were not always applied in the colonies.[38] This was evident, for instance, in relation to sexual abuses perpetrated against Black children in East Africa by Italians. In 1898 the governor of Eritrea, Ferdinando Martini, sent back to Italy an officer "whose main occupation, or at least one of his favourites, was to raise little girls with *minuzzoli di pane* [scraps of bread] in order to later make them concubines for himself and his comrades," as the archival research conducted by Giulia Barrera shows.[39] Yet because of the construction of African women as available and sexually insatiable, even the law would sometimes justify such abuses. There was the case of an Italian man accused of raping a nine-year-old girl in Massawa who was released by the court because of "Eritrean easy virtues" and "different meaning attached to morality."[40] Such constructions of Africa and its Black virgins characterized the perception of Italian colonialism long after the end of colonialism, something that Isabella experienced throughout her life. What is interesting, though, is the nature of the racialized look at her body and her responses to it. A peculiar episode that clearly shows the construction of the female Black body projected on Isabella concerns the encounter she had in Rome with the famous journalist and historian Indro Montanelli while she was posing in Peikov's studio one morning in 1946.

Montanelli, considered one of the most respected Italian journalists of the twentieth century, was initially a supporter of Fascism, and in 1935 he took part in the invasion of Ethiopia as a voluntary conscript, leading a troop of Askari.[41] From 1965 he participated in the debate on the colonial legacy, arguing for the "humanity" of Italian colonialism in comparison to other colonial powers.[42] Despite his actions being fully documented by the historian Angelo Del Boca, for more than thirty years Montanelli firmly denied the use of chemical weapons by the Fascists during the invasion of Ethiopia. He publicly apologized only in 1996, when the minister of defense, Domenico Corcione, showed archival evidence on this matter.

During his stay in East Africa, from May 1935 until October 1936, Montanelli, at the time a twenty-six-year-old man, took a so-called wife, a twelve-year-old Bilen child called Fatima or Destà and defined by Montanelli himself as a "docile little animal" whom he had "legally bought" from her father.[43] During a live TV show in 1969, when the journalist Gianni Bisiach asked him about the beauty and the age of the little girl, Montanelli proudly said, "Yes, it seems I made a good choice. She was a beautiful Bilen girl, aged twelve. [He stops for a few seconds and, looking at the studio audience, smiles.] I do apologize, but in Africa it's different [audience laughs]. I had regularly married her, in the sense I had regularly bought her from her father, and she joined me along with the other Ascaris' wives."[44] On a different occasion he explained the difficulty of performing sexual acts with the child due to the fact that she had been infibulated. As he wrote, this physical condition, which caused Desta's physical numbness, put up an almost "insurmountable" barrier to his sexual desire, to the extent that the "brutal intervention" of the child's mother was needed in order to *break* that barrier.[45]

When Montanelli met Isabella in 1946, she was posing for Peikov's latest sculpture, titled *The First Woman*. Interestingly, by reading their brief dialogue one may notice the impact of scientific racism in 1940s Italy. Discussing with Peikov the sculpture and looking at Isabella, Montanelli pointed out that something was missing. Considering that the subject of the sculpture was supposed to be the first woman, Peikov assumed Montanelli was referring to Eve and her infamous apple. Yet the journalist had in his mind something slightly different. Referring directly to Isabella, he said, "No, not an apple. Rather a banana, uh? Or maybe peanuts? Do you like peanuts, Miss, right?" Although later on Isabella confessed how shocking she found the experience of being directly compared to a primate in front of this man wearing a black hat, she made use of her sharp irony, a powerful weapon she had learned to use during her life. "To be honest, I never had any," she replied. "But if you buy me a bag, I am happy to try some." It seemed that Montanelli grumbled something and quickly left. That morning, in order to comfort Isabella after the difficult experience she had just gone through, Peikov decided to take her on the mezzanine of his studio where there were two mattresses. She let him do it, although her considerations about this episode are quite bitter: "His approach had been too docile to reject it with the usual shouts. He knew that the man with the black hat had hurt me, and this was his way to offer me a distraction. The result was that I felt a big sadness. I considered Assen a good friend, and the only way he had found to cheer me up was to *delicately* jump on me. He noticed I was crying, so he took me back downstairs, and he paid me for the whole morning."[46]

The episode with Montanelli, followed by Peikov's behavior, shows how Isabella was someone whose body was loaded with a history she suddenly, and painfully, became aware of. Similar to Destà, a child bought by an adult Italian male and temporarily used as a wife because "in Africa it's different," Isabella, while posing naked for several artists, noticed how "in front of a *negro* even honesty could go on holiday."[47] As she clearly reiterates in the book, getting naked for her was merely a job; however, one can read the numerous episodes of sexual harassment she went through with White Italian men and women, who would often assume that such behavior was acceptable given her skin tone. Nonetheless, it was precisely the awareness of the meaning inscribed on her body that helped Isabella to shape shift toward a new identity and to respond to, challenge, and sometimes subvert racializing practices already in place. This last point, the subversion of racializing practices, turned out to be particularly helpful for her psychological well-being and self-esteem during her short career as an actress. Used on the streets to getting inappropriate and dissecting looks, onstage Isabella felt empowered. She found there what she defined as an "antidote" against the looks:

> For the first time in my life people were looking at me because *I* had decided to impose myself on their attention. On the streets people would look at me furtively, and I couldn't prevent it. I had endured that scrutiny, repeating every day to myself that they could look at me, poor fools; anyway, the most precious part of my body was not visible, unlike my mixed skin. . . . Onstage I discovered that there is also another antidote to the poison of the looks, not only to take a step back in order to take refuge in the barricade of your own skin but also to take a step forward, showing yourself, shouting: "Look at me now, as there's nothing else you can do." I am here; you have to accept me. You shut up, finally, and I speak.[48]

Interestingly, if on the streets Isabella couldn't avoid being stared at, onstage she was the one imposing her presence on the viewer. This seems to be an important aspect in order to understand color strategies, or, more precisely, how racialized subjects respond to, resist, and subvert imposed identities and racial stereotypes passing through their skin. In Isabella's case, power seems to temporarily come from the subversion of the viewer's look. She made use of her colonial skin, considered by Homi Bhabha as "the most visible of fetishes," in order to earn an income and to be in control.[49] Nonetheless, it is crucial to bear in mind that the negotiations enacted by racializing subjects in order to respond to racism and discrimination are never easy to define, and they may carry a huge amount of pain and violence, as in the case of Isabella. Talking about her childhood as a Black Italian, raised in a White Fascist society and the desire she triggered in men as an adult, she lucidly said:

> In Rome some people would say, "She is a massive whore! . . . She has slept with everyone but the Pope and Togliatti." When my husband met me, this was the gossip going on. It wasn't true, though. I was really scared of sex, but all these promises, who knows! Maybe because one is Black, [they think] she can give you Nirvana, she can really pleasure you. I never understood that. Like if I were a world to discover, like if I had hidden talents . . . [people would say,] "How appetizing this black Lolita is!" And I would turn, smiling. This is a very sad memory I have of myself. . . . You cannot imagine the appetite I would raise in men because of my black skin. . . . I suffered the terrifying condition of being a person whom everyone looked at, whom everyone would talk about, of being such a weird animal. . . . I was the daughter of a whore, I was the daughter of a slut, I was a smelly nigger. I was, really, society's garbage. This was my childhood.[50]

This painful awareness of her color gave to Isabella the tools to shape shift into something different. At a very young age she suddenly had to reckon with who she was and the history inscribed on her body. This knowledge provided her with power and a greater degree of agency, which allowed her to survive in a racialized and segregated context such as Fascist and postcolonial Italy. Nonetheless, the new identity she embodied and the new knowledge she gained became a source of pain she would have to carry throughout her life. As she said in her interview with Amadei, "Once I was told, 'You are the shame of the race.' I asked, 'What race?'"[51]

Feelings of shame and pain in dynamics of identity shift, in a racialized context, will be further illustrated in the next section through the story of Bruna.

"You Were Too White. I Was Ashamed!"

Bruna is an Italian mixed race woman born in Eritrea in 1940 from an Ethiopian mother and a White Italian father who never recognized her. "Shame" was a recurrent word in the interview I had with Bruna, who often mentioned this term in relation to her color.[52] Because of her very light complexion and blond hair, she consistently was racialized as White. In periods of formal racial segregation, in some settings passing as White provided lighter-skinned individuals with advantages and opportunities denied to darker members of their same racialized group, and it was also considered a way to subvert and resist racist/racial norms.[53] In the case of Bruna, her imposed White identity in Fascist Eritrea had a dramatic impact on her life. One has to bear in mind that this participant was born in 1940, at the pinnacle of racial segregation in East Africa when so-called *meticci* (mixed race people) were not considered Italians anymore but just Africans.

In 1937 a new decree stated that Italian citizens having relationships of a "conjugal nature" with colonial subjects might face imprisonment from one to five years.[54] The aim of the decree was to prevent sexual relationships, usually between African women and Italian men, in order to stop the procreation of *meticci*, who were regarded as contaminating Italian blood. Therefore, interracial relationships, which had been tolerated until the creation of the empire, were declared illegal in 1937. In addition, a system of racial segregation imposed a separation in housing, in social life, in transportation, and at sites of public entertainment.[55] In 1938 the "Manifesto della razza" (Race manifesto) was published. This text, written by a number of anthropologists under Mussolini's precise instructions, illustrated in ten sections the "material existence" of human races, the different "racial compositions" of human beings, and the purity of Italian blood. Moreover, the document invited Italians to consider their responsibility as "members of a pure race" and exhorted them to proclaim themselves "frankly racist."[56] Following the publication of the manifesto, in 1940 the regime introduced a specific corpus of norms targeting mixed race children.[57] The new regulations denied these children the possibility of gaining Italian citizenship by declaring them as "natives," owing to the presence of an African parent, and by prohibiting Italians to recognize or adopt them. In this way, mixed race Italians could not receive Italian citizenship and had to be raised and supported exclusively by their native parent. This is when Bruna was born.

In 1940 Asmara, the capital of Eritrea and one of the main centers of the empire, was a racially segregated space, as Bruna remembers: "Blacks couldn't come to [the center of] Asmara! They were all relegated in Ucria [a neighborhood located in the periphery of the city]. Asmara belonged only to Whites!"[58] Having a White child was particularly difficult for Bruna's mother, who was a young Black woman and who had been left by an Italian partner who did not recognize their daughter. The violence of the racial segregation occurring at that time is made clear by Bruna through an episode she told me during the interview I conducted with her: "My mum would tell me that buses were divided. Behind there was a little space for Blacks, and it was like in America. If you tried to sit in the front, they would beat you up, they would kick you out! And my mum told me that once we were on a bus and this guy told her: 'This child is White; put her in the front! You stay behind' because he thought that she worked for an Italian family."[59]

Nevertheless, for Bruna, being racialized as a White child did not turn out to be an advantage or a source of protection; rather, this imposed Whiteness became a source of shame and pain. Given Bruna's nonassimilability in her mother's Eritrean community because of her appearance and the difficulty her mother experienced raising a "White" child alone, Bruna's mother decided to leave her in a *collegio*. These institutions, ruled by Catholic missionaries, were for unrecognized or abandoned mixed race Italian children. The colonial government felt the need to conceal the shame of the empire, and the placement of mixed race children into these institutions supported that purpose. Bruna seemed to be clearly aware of the construction of her embodiment as a source of shame for the Italians and thus the need for it to be concealed, as she clearly affirmed: "They would lock us there because we couldn't be the shame of Whites!"[60] Nevertheless, although some Eritrean women felt shame because of the social stigma attached to their children's color, these same women encouraged the "Italianization" of their children, despite the absence of their Italian fathers.[61] As Barrera notices, in Eritrean customary laws, which were similar to Italian customs at that time, the father was the one responsible for the children and the one who provided them with social identity. Children had to speak their father's language and practice his religion.[62] In this process, an Italian education played a central role, and this was provided within these single-sex institutes for abandoned or unrecognized mixed race Italian children called *collegi*.[63]

The interviews I conducted highlight how the *collegi* fulfilled an important role of social control and "docilization" of the mixed race body.[64] Starting in 1928, owing to the high rate of abandoned mixed race children living in the streets of Asmara, the colonial government decided to place these children within the *collegi* using treasury funds.[65] Yet it is important to bear in mind that once inside the *collegio*, a child would go under the care and control of the government, which decided if and when the child could leave the premises of the institute.[66] Therefore, when a mother decided to leave her children in a *collegio*, she would immediately lose any authority over them. Mothers were allowed to visit their children once a month, and the children could never leave the institute to visit their families. Despite such strict restrictions, for many young single mothers with very limited economic resources, this was not an unusual choice, combined with the fact that they wanted an Italian education for their children. This seems to be partly confirmed by Bruna's words: "[My mother] put me there because they would say, 'She is White, and so it's better for her being with other Italians and going to school.' . . . She says, 'You know, I brought you there because you were with Italian nuns, you had to learn Italian!'"[67]

Bruna was left in a *collegio* when she was only two years old, the minimum age to be accepted. From archival research it appears that very rarely children were placed in a *collegio* before the age of four or five.[68] On average they entered these institutions when they were seven or eight years old. Therefore, it seems that Bruna's mother had a compelling need to leave her daughter with the missionaries. Furthermore, once she left her child in the *collegio*, she moved to Ethiopia, and their relationship for the following sixteen years was reduced to an annual half-hour visit.[69]

Once inside the *collegio*, Bruna made an important discovery. She quickly perceived the existence of an internal racialization of girls imposed by the nuns and based on shade. Due to her lighter skin tone, she noticed, she received some positive attention. For instance, she was the one chosen by the nuns to read the prayers in front of the bishop of Asmara whenever he visited the children. Furthermore, her being White was associated with positive aesthetic codes that prevented Bruna from being physically abused and verbally harassed as much as darker-skinned girls. This appreciation of her Whiteness made her reproduce the same racializing and racist attitudes toward darker children, as she affirms: "Because you know, in the *collegio* I was one of the *prettiest* girls, one of the *whitest*, and we would insult darker girls because of the nuns!"[70] In this extract, she openly attributed her beauty to her light complexion and illustrated the construction of racializing aesthetics based on the deployment of European beauty paradigms.[71] This passage reveals the use she made of her color and how she adapted herself to a hostile and violent environment. Like Isabella, Bruna clearly negotiated color hierarchies already in place in order to turn them to her own advantage. Nonetheless, growing up, she felt ashamed of her conduct after she became aware of the dynamics of violence and racism within the institute: "But then I suffered thinking about that, as I said to myself: 'What the heck! I hurt my friends!' . . . We were all mixed girls, daughters of Italians, but there were some who were lighter, some were darker, others were White with frizzy hair, some were Black with straight hair."[72] This illustrates the fluidity and contingency of the negotiations of color enacted by racialized subjects.

If Bruna initially used the color hierarchies already in place within the *collegio* and used by the nuns to create boundaries between the girls, growing up she reconfigured these by privileging solidarity and friendship with the other girls living in the same condition, regardless of their skin color. By witnessing everyday violence in the *collegio*, she understood that her lighter skin was not enough to guarantee her better treatment. Lighter or darker, they were still the daughters of their fathers' "whores," as the nuns used to tell them.[73]

Bruna understood the reasons why her mother "abandoned" her—as she said—only when as an adult Bruna left the *collegio* and started to build up a relationship with her mother. Bruna realized that her mother had a wealthy lifestyle in Ethiopia, considering she owned two houses. Therefore, she could not explain to herself why her mother abandoned her in that institute. As Bruna explained in the interview, one day she decided to clearly ask:

> "Mum, why didn't you take me to Ethiopia with you?" And you know what she said to me? "Because I was ashamed! You were too white!" This is what she said to me! And imagine that she never introduced me to her mother and father. She told them that she had a baby girl, but she never said I was *meticcia*! . . . Sometimes I tell her about the *collegio*, but it hurts her, as she feels bad for abandoning me while she instead looked after her nephews, her brothers and sisters, and she threw me away![74]

As one may ascertain from this passage, Bruna sounded astonished by her mother's answer. She realized not only that her mother was ashamed of her daughter's color but also that she had excluded her from entering the circle of the family. Bruna's mother acknowledged the existence of a baby girl, but she omitted to say that she was a *meticcia*, as this would have implied admitting that Bruna's mother had had a sexual relationship with a White Italian man who left her afterward.

Due to increasing levels of violence in the early 1970s between Ethiopia and Eritrea, many Eritreans and Italians, including Bruna, decided to go to Italy. In Italy she found herself forced to make a profound reconsideration and a consequent shift in her identity. When she lived in the *collegio*, she realized that despite their different complexions, her friends in the orphanage were all daughters of Italians. This was one of the very few certainties mixed race children could count on. They were Italian because they had an Italian father and an Italian name and they spoke Italian. Therefore, despite the difficulties they had to face in Eritrea because of their "difference," their Italianness was not in question. Once Bruna arrived in Italy, however, this firm certitude just crumbled. She remembers very well how it happened. As she told me: "One day I was walking down the street when a woman said, 'Hey you! Negro!' I turned around and saw no Negroes, and at that time in the 1960s you wouldn't see many around. Again, she said, 'Hey you, Negro! I am talking to you!' I turned and I said, 'Are you talking to me?' and she says, 'Well, do you see any other Negroes around?' My God, I flooded with tears! Just like this, in the middle of the street. And from that moment I started to understand many things."[75]

Bruna was physically affected by this experience. She burst into tears, shocked by the violence of the White woman's talk. When she was first addressed, she seemed surprised and confused due to her own internal racial classification. Like the White woman, Bruna also thought that there were "Negroes"; but she never imagined she could be one of them, which is why she struggled to understand whom this woman was addressing. When she heard the same word repeated again in her direction, she couldn't prevent herself from genuinely asking, "Are you talking to me?" When the Italian woman, ironically, invited the respondent to look around in order to see if there were "other Negroes around," Bruna suddenly understood. She was the "Negro." Such a sudden awareness—the fact of perceiving herself through the eyes of that White woman—deeply shook Bruna's existence. This experience forced her to enter a process of identity reconfiguration, or shape shifting. Like Isabella, Bruna also gained a new knowledge by painfully realizing that she was not who she thought she was. She discovered her Blackness in a violent way, being racially abused "like this in the middle of the street." Again, the relationship of power to knowledge is essential here. In Bruna's case, the White

woman verbally abusing her seemed to embody the "locus of power/
knowledge of white racist supremacy," able to deem her outside the
borders of the Italian nation.[76]

These two stories reveal several important issues in relation to identity
formation and identity shifts. The analysis highlights how practices
of shape shifting may differ according to the social context in which
they take place and the different degree of power shape shifters may
have in a specific environment. Also, it reveals the importance of the
social, geographical, and historical contexts where social actors shape
shift. Isabella spent her childhood and part of her young adult life in
Fascist Italy, being pointed at and singled out for being one of the very
few non-White Italians at that time. Apart from her brother, she did
not know anyone having her same skin tone. Despite this apparently
obvious physical feature, she was unable to "see" her Blackness until
the age of twelve, when she was confronted by a picture of her biological mother. In contrast, at a very young age, Bruna became aware
of her pale complexion and blond hair, which affected her life tremendously. Her "shameful" Whiteness and her inability to blend in
(similar to Isabella) were among the reasons why her mother put her
into an orphanage. Therefore, the bodies of these two children seem
to be located at the complex intersection of categories such as color,
race, gender, identity, and citizenship that are inscribed on their own
skin. On the one hand, there is a child, Isabella, who despite being
Black also has "Italian blood" in her veins; thus, she cannot possibly
be raised by her uncivilized Black mother in Africa. Once she arrives
in Italy, however, this child is suddenly too Black to blend in and be
considered Italian. On the other hand, there is another child, Bruna,
who is too White to be raised by her Black mother; therefore, she is left
in a Catholic orphanage run by White Italian nuns in order to make
her an *Italian*. Also in this case, when she goes to Italy she is suddenly
a *negra*, and all of her Italian heritage and cultural capital is erased in
favor of a biological reading of her body. Once they become aware
of the racializing practices dissecting their bodies, the two women
respond by using contingent and specific color strategies. Owing to

the multitude of mixed race girls' skin colors and the internal hierarchy of colors reigning within the *collegio*, Bruna has to reckon with her Whiteness, and she decides to turn it to her own advantage. To do so, she exploits the power given to her by the meaning attributed to her skin tone in order to achieve a less violent and abusive lifestyle.

Isabella operates in a different way. Once she realizes the history inscribed on her body, she decides to use her new identity to openly respond to her stepmother's violence, and she uses her skin and her adulterous conception in order to shame Flora. Furthermore, as an adult, Isabella uses the sexual desire her body triggers in men in order to live independently and achieve a better lifestyle.

These two stories show us the complexities of identity reconfigurations and how shape shifting processes may provide racialized subjects with some power and awareness in order to face everyday life. Nonetheless, we should not underestimate the pain, violence, and shame that may come with this power and the ways they inform an individual's ability to shape shift, whether by his or her own accord or because of societal pressure.

Notes

1. Margaret Hunter, "The Persistent Problem of Colorism: Skin Tone, Status, and Inequality," *Sociology Compass* 1, no. 1 (2007): 237.
2. Taunya Lovell Banks, "Colorism: A Darker Shade of Pale," UCLA *Law Review* 47, no. 6 (August 2000): 1706–45. See also Deborah Gabriel, *Layers of Blackness: Colourism in the African Diaspora* (London: Imani Media Ltd., 2007).
3. Margaret Hunter, "If You're Light, You're Alright," *Gender & Society* 16, no. 2 (2002): 176.
4. Nikki Khanna, "'If You Are Half Black, You Are Just Black': Reflected Appraisal and the Persistence of the One-Drop Rule," *Sociological Quarterly* 51 (2010): 96–121. See also G. Reginald Daniel's chapter in this volume.
5. See Paul Spickard's introduction to this volume, "Shape Shifters: Reflections on Racial Plasticity."
6. Stuart Hall, "Race, the Floating Signifier," 1997, http://www.mediaed.org/transcripts/Stuart-Hall-Race-the-Floating-Signifier-Transcript.pdf.
7. Spickard, "Shape Shifters."

8. Angelica Pesarini, "Colour Strategies: Negotiations of Black Mixed Race Women's Identities in Colonial and Postcolonial Italy" (PhD diss., University of Leeds, 2015).

9. See also Angelica Pesarini, "Madri nere figlie bianche: Forme di subalternità femminile in Africa Orientale Italiana" [Black mothers, White children: Expressions of subaltern identities in Fascist East Africa], in *Subalternità italiane*, ed. Valeria Deplano, Lorenzo Mari, and Gabriele Proglio (Ariccia: Aracne, 2014).

10. Pseudonyms are used throughout the chapter to respect the privacy of each respondent.

11. Rebecca Chiyoko King-O'Riain, "Plastic Paddies, Citizenship Tourists, and Migrants in Ireland: Will the 'Real' Irish Please Stand Up?," paper presented to the Collegium for African American Research, Liverpool, June 25, 2015.

12. On the history of Italian colonialism and Fascism in East Africa, see, for example, Jaqueline Andall and Derek Duncan, eds., *Italian Colonialism: Legacy and Memory* (Oxford: Peter Lang, 2005); Ruth Ben-Ghiat and Mia Fuller, eds., *Italian Colonialism* (New York: Palgrave Macmillan, 2008); Paolo Cannistrano, ed., *Historical Dictionary of Fascist Italy* (Westport CT: Greenwood Press, 1982); Angelo Del Boca, *Gli italiani in Africa orientale* (Roma-Bari: Laterza, 1976); Angelo Del Boca, *Italiani brava gente? Un mito duro a morire* (Vicenza: Pozza, 2005); Luigi Goglia, *Il colonialismo italiano da adua all'impero* (Bari: Laterza, 1981); Nicola Labanca, *Oltremare: Storia dell'espansione coloniale italiana* (Bologna: Il Mulino, 2002); Cristina Lombardi-Diop and Caterina Romeo, eds., *Postcolonial Italy: Challenging National Homogeneity* (New York: Palgrave Macmillan, 2012); Tekeste Negash, *Italian Colonialism in Eritrea, 1882–1941: Policies, Praxis and Impact* (Stockholm: Uppsala University Press, 1987); Patrizia Palumbo, ed., *A Place in the Sun: Africa in Italian Colonial Culture from Post-Unification to the Present* (Berkeley: University of California Press, 2003); Alberto Sbacchi, *Legacy of Bitterness: Ethiopia and Fascist Italy, 1935–1941* (Asmara, Eritrea: Red Sea Press, 1997); Robert Grillo and Jeff Pratt, eds., *The Politics of Recognizing Difference: Multiculturalism Italian-Style* (Aldershot: Ashgate, 2002); Alessandro Triulzi, "Italian Colonialism and Ethiopia," *Journal of African History* 23 (1982): 237–43; Alessandro Triulzi, "Displacing the Colonial Event," *Interventions* 8 (2006): 430–43; Valeria Deplano and Alessandro Pes, eds., *Quel che resta dell'Impero: La cultura coloniale degli Italiani* (Udine: Mimesis Edizione, 2014); Valeria Deplano, *L'Africa in casa: Propaganda e cultura coloniale nell'Italia fascista*, Quaderni di Storia (Milan: Le Monnier, 2016); Gian Paolo Calchi Novati, *L'Africa d'Italia: Una storia coloniale e postcoloniale* (Rome: Carocci, 2011); Centro Furio

Jesi, ed., *La Menzogna della razza: Documenti e immagini del razzismo e dell'*
antisemitismo fascista (Bologna: Grafis Edizioni, 1994).

13. Giulia Barrera, *Dangerous Liaisons: Colonial Concubinage in Eritrea (1890–1941)*,
    PAS Working Papers No. 1 (Northwestern University, 1996), 7. For a history
    of *madamato*, see also Barbara Sòrgoni, *Parole e corpi: Antropologia, discorso*
    giuridico e politiche sessuali interraziali (Naples: Liguori, 2006); Sandra Pon-
    zanesi, "Beyond the Black Venus: Colonial Sexual Politics and Contempo-
    rary Visual Practices," in Andall and Duncan, *Italian Colonialism*, 165–88;
    Gianluca Gabrielli, "La persecuzione delle 'unioni miste' (1937–1940) nei
    testi delle sentenze pubblicate e nel dibattito giuridico," *Studi piacentini* 20
    (1996): 83–140; Gianluca Gabrielli, "Un aspetto della politica razzista nell'im-
    pero: Il 'problema dei meticci,'" *Passato e presente* 15 (1996): 77–105; Ruth
    Iyob, "Madamismo and Beyond: The Construction of Eritrean Women,"
    Nineteenth-Century Contexts 22 (2000): 217–38; Silvana Palma, "Fotografia di
    una colonia: L'Eritrea di Luigi Naretti," *Quaderni storici* 37, no. 109(1) (April
    2002): 84–115; Giulietta Stefani, *Colonia per maschi: Italiani in Africa Orien-*
    tale; Una storia di genere (Verona: OmbreCorte, 2007).

14. Barbara Sòrgoni, "Racist Discourses and Practices in the Italian Empire
    under Fascism," in Grillo and Pratt, *The Politics of Recognizing Difference*, 45.

15. See Barrera, *Dangerous Liaisons*, 19; Sorgòni, *Parole e corpi*.

16. Gabrielli, "Un aspetto," 77.

17. Giulia Barrera, "Patrilinearity, Race, and Identity: The Upbringing of Italo-
    Eritreans during Italian Colonialism," in Ben-Ghiat and Fuller, *Italian Colonial-*
    ism, 100; Gabrielli, "Un aspetto," 78. See also King-O'Riain, "Plastic Paddies."

18. Barrera, "Patrilinearity," 32.

19. Anne McClintock, *Imperial Leather: Race, Gender and Sexuality in the Colo-*
    nial Contest (New York: Routledge, 1995), 22.

20. See Sander Gilman, "Black Bodies, White Bodies: Toward an Iconography
    of Female Sexuality in Late Nineteenth-Century Arts, Medicine and Litera-
    ture," *Critical Enquiry* 12 (1985): 204–42. See also Noel Carrol, "Ethnicity, Race
    and Monstrosity: The Rhetoric of Horror and Humor," in *Beauty Matters*,
    ed. Peg Zeglin Brand (Indianapolis: Indiana University Press, 2000); Win-
    throp D. Jordan, *White over Black: American Attitudes toward the Negro, 1550–*
    1812 (Chapel Hill: University of North Carolina Press, 1968), 3–43, 136–78.

21. Renato Paoli cited in Barrera, *Dangerous Liaisons*, 14.

22. Wu Ming 2 and Antar Mohamed, *Timira: Romanzo meticcio* (Torino: Ein-
    audi, 2012), 504, 505. Wu Ming 2 (Giovanni Cattabriga, Bologna, 1974) is one
    of the writers belonging to the Wu Ming Collective, a collective of writers
    founded in Bologna in 2000. For further information, please have a look at

the webpage of the collective: https://www.wumingfoundation.com/giap /what-is-the-wu-ming-foundation/.

23. Antar Mohmed, interview by the author, June 2012, Bologna, Italy, tape recording. All the interviews quoted in this chapter were conducted in Italian and translated into English by the author.

24. *Quale razza?*, prod. Motoproduzioni, dir. Aureliano Amadei, 10 min., 2008, https://www.youtube.com/watch?v=ivqZeYkMCm0, my transcription and translation.

25. Giorgio Marincola was born in 1923 and became known as the first Black Italian partisan during World War II. He was killed in Stramentizzo during the last massacre by the Nazis in Italy on May 4, 1945, just a few days before the end of the war. He was twenty-two years old.

26. Flora Virdis is the pseudonym used in the book. The real name of Isabella's stepmother was Elvira Floris.

27. Heteropatriarchy can be defined as "social systems in which heterosexuality and patriarchy are perceived as normal and natural, and in which other configurations are perceived as abnormal, aberrant, and abhorrent" (Maile Arvin, Eve Tuck, and Angie Morrill, "Decolonizing Feminism: Challenging Connections between Settler Colonialism and Heteropatriarchy," *Feminist Formations* 25, no. 1 [Spring 2013]: 8–34).

28. McClintock, *Imperial Leather*, 33.

29. Ming 2 and Mohamed, *Timira*. All the quotes from *Timira* used in this chapter have been translated from the original Italian into English by the author.

30. Mohamed, interview.

31. Mohamed, interview, my emphasis.

32. Ming 2 and Mohamed, *Timira*, 375.

33. "Racial learning" is from Linda Alcoff, *Visible Identities: Race, Gender and the Self* (Oxford: Oxford University Press, 2006), 192.

34. Ming 2 and Mohamed, *Timira*, 126.

35. For the presence of Eritreans, Libyans, and Somalis in Italy in the aftermath of World War II, see Valeria Deplano, *La madrepatria è una terra straniera: Libici, eritrei e somali nell'Italia del dopoguerra (1945–1960)* (Milan: Mondadori, 2017).

36. Ming 2 and Mohamed, *Timira*, 169.

37. For the stereotype of the Somali princess, see Deplano, *La madrepatria*, 148–49. See also Gilman, "Black Bodies."

38. See Giulia Barrera, "Patrilinearitá razza e identitá: L'educazione degli Italo-Eritrei durante il colonialismo Italiano (1885–1934)," *Quaderni storici* 37, no. 109(1) (April 2002): 21–53; Ann Laura Stoler, *Carnal Knowledge and Imperial*

Power: Race and the Intimate in Colonial Rule (Berkeley: University of California Press, 2002).

39. Ferdinando Martini cited in Barrera, *Dangerous Liaisons*, 29.

40. Elisabetta Bini, "Fonti fotografiche e storia delle donne: La rappresentazione delle donne nere nelle fotografie coloniali italiane," SISSCO Conference, "Cantieri di Storia II. Lecce," 5. My translation from Italian to English.

41. In 2000 Indro Montanelli (1909–2001) was honored as a Word Freedom Press Hero. See http://ipi.freemedia.at/awards/press-freedom-heroes/indro-montanelli.html. From 1938 Montanelli worked for more than thirty years as a foreign correspondent for the Italian newspapers *Il Corriere della Sera*, documenting, among other things, the Spanish Civil War on the side of Francisco Franco's troops, World War II, and the Hungarian Revolution. In 1977 he was shot in the legs by the Brigate Rosse (Red Brigades), but he didn't report permanent damage. He died on July 22, 2001, at the age of ninety-two. The interested reader can find more about Montanelli's biography in Indro Montanelli, *Soltanto un giornalista* (Milan: Rizzoli, 2002); Sandro Gerbi and Raffaele Liucci, *Indro Montanelli: Una biografia (1909–2001)* (Milan: Hoepli, 2014); Gianluca Mazzuca, *Indro Montanelli: La mia Voce; Storia di un sogno impossibile raccontata da Giancarlo Mazzuca* (Milan: Sperling & Kupfer Saggi, 1995); Paolo Granzotto, *Montanelli* (Bologna: Il Mulino, 2004); Marco Travaglio, *Montanelli e il Cavaliere: Storia di un grande e di un piccolo uomo* (Garzanti: Milano, 2004). Askari were Eritrean soldiers fighting for the Italians. See Alessandro Volterra, *Sudditi coloniali Ascari eritrei 1935–1941* (Milan: Franco Angeli, 2005); Negash, *Italian Colonialism*.

42. Indro Montanelli, *Ventesimo battaglione eritreo: Il primo romanzo e le lettere inedite dal fronte Africano*, ed. Angelo Del Boca (Milan: Rizzoli, 2010), introduction.

43. Montanelli, *Ventesimo battaglione eritreo*; *Cento anni*, episode 5, "Ti saluto e vado in Abissinia," Fabbri video, 1993, YouTube, https://www.youtube.com/watch?v=iJBW4gFJ3n0; *L'ora della verità* (The hour of the truth), presented by the journalist Gianni Bisiach in 1969, TV show broadcast on the Italian national TV channel RAI, video available on YouTube, https://www.youtube.com/watch?v=MHVBk8qikWo. Bilens are one of the nine ethnic groups living in Eritrea.

44. *L'ora della verità*.

45. Indro Montanelli, "Quando andai a nozze con Destá," in La Stanza di Montanelli, *Corriere delle Sera* (February 2, 2000).

46. Ming 2 and Mohamed, *Timira*, 171, 174.

47. Ming 2 and Mohamed, *Timira*, 172.

48. Ming 2 and Mohamed, *Timira*, 203–4.

49. Homi K. Bhabha, *The Location of Culture* (London: Routledge, 1994), 112.

50. Palmiro Togliatti was an Italian politician (1893–1964) and general secretary and leader of the Italian Communist Party from 1927 until his death in 1964. In 1944 he served as deputy prime minister and from June 1945 as justice minister. He acted as vice premier under the De Gasperi government. Amadei, *Quale razza?*

51. Amadei, *Quale razza?*

52. Bruna, interview by the author, Asmara, November 2012. The interview was conducted in Italian and translated into English by the author.

53. Khanna, "'If You Are Half Black.'" As Paul Spickard points out in the introduction to this volume, in the cases of P. B. S. Pinchback, Herb Jeffries, and others, sometimes the advantage and opportunity for apparently mixed people were in choosing to identify as Black.

54. See Gabrielli, "La persecuzione."

55. Barrera, *Dangerous Liaisons*, 38; Centro Furio Jesi, *La Menzogna della razza*, 290.

56. The "Manifesto della razza" was published in 1938 in the journal *La difesa della razza* 1, no. 1 (August 1938).

57. Norme relative ai Meticci (Norms Concerning Children of Mixed Race), May 13, 1940.

58. Bruna, interview.

59. Bruna, interview.

60. Bruna, interview.

61. Barrera, "Patrilinearitá razza e identitá."

62. Barrera, "Patrilinearity," 103.

63. The official presence of the Italian catholic mission in Eritrea was registered in 1894 after the creation of the Colonia Eritrea. The main administrative and religious headquarters was in Keren, seventy-two kilometers (forty-four miles) north of Asmara. See Chelati Dirar, "Collaborazioni e conflitti: Michele Da Carbonara e l'organizzazione della Prefettura Apostolica in Eritrea," *Quaderni Storici* 37, no. 109(1) (April 2002): 148–88.

64. Michel Foucault, *Discipline and Punish: The Birth of the Prison* (London: Penguin, 1979), 137.

65. Barrera, "Patrilinearity," 105.

66. Barrera, "Patrilinearitá razza e identitá," 40.

67. Bruna, interview.

68. Barrera, "Patrilinearitá razza e identitá," 36.

69. Bruna, interview.

70. Bruna, interview.

71. Shirley Ann Tate, *Black Beauty: Aesthetics, Stylization, Politics* (Farnham: Ashgate, 2009); Carrol, "Ethnicity"; Gilman, "Black Bodies."

72. Bruna, interview.

73. Bruna, interview.

74. Bruna, interview.

75. Bruna, interview.

76. Shirley Ann Tate, *Black Skins, Black Masks: Hybridity, Dialogism, Performativity* (Aldershot: Ashgate, 2005), 107.

PART 2

Choosing Identity

7

William A. Leidesdorff

The Rise of a Shape Shifter and the Posthumous Fall from Grace of a Racial Imposter

Laura Moore

On May 20, 1848, the *California Star* reported: "One of the largest and most respectable assemblages ever witnessed followed the deceased from his late residence to the place of interment. . . . All places of business and public entertainment were closed, the flags of the garrison . . . were flying at half mast. . . . It is no injustice to the living, or unmeaning praise for the dead, to say that the town has lost its most valuable resident, and the feeling evinced by the community is an involuntary tribute to his merits as a man and a citizen."[1] This reverent description comes from the obituary of William Alexander Leidesdorff, a prominent San Francisco politician and businessman who unexpectedly died on May 18, 1848. Within a matter of a year of Leidesdorff's death, the high esteem with which the "most valuable resident" was regarded was diminished when it was alleged that he was a Black man deceptively passing as a White man.[2]

The perception that Leidesdorff deviously hid his Black racial ancestry originated when General Joseph Libby Folsom, the man vying for Leidesdorff's highly valued property, revealed that Leidesdorff's mother, Anna Marie Sparks, was an African-descended woman living on the island of Saint Croix. The accusation that Leidesdorff passed for White persists to this day and has as its basis the underlying viewpoint

Fig. 7.1. Portrait of William Leidesdorff, ca. 1845. Courtesy of the Bancroft
Library, University of California, Berkeley, BANC PIC 1956.014—DAG.

that Leidesdorff's economic and political successes were only achievable because he concealed his Black racial heritage.

This chapter examines the narrative of Leidesdorff's racial passing. Through emphasizing the significance of context—the time,
place, and circumstances in which Leidesdorff lived—I contend that

rather than accepting that Leidesdorff was a racial imposter, it is more accurate to describe his actions as shape shifting. By categorizing Leidesdorff as a shape shifter—an individual who negotiated his racial identification—this chapter argues that his racial identification was complex and fluid and that this racial fluidity defied static racial categories. It is imperative that we as scholars are judicious in the labels we assign to individuals. This is particularly true for people whom some call racial passers because of the underlying assumption that passers accept binary racial categorizations, refuse to acknowledge their true identity, and, in fact, deceive society.

Through a microhistorical analysis of Leidesdorff's life as a shape shifter, I propose that three dynamics played a significant role in contributing to Leidesdorff's success in shape shifting. The first was that his multiracial ancestry created a phenotype that was not visually determinable. His father was of Danish and Jewish heritage, while his mother was categorized as a mulatto in one record and a *castice* in another document.[3] According to various records, the combination of his mother's and father's genetics provided Leidesdorff with a phenotype that did not fit the binary categorization typically associated with Whites versus Blacks. This racial ambiguity provided him a degree of flexibility, for at different moments, depending on the space within which he found himself, he could negotiate his racial identity.

The second contributing factor to Leidesdorff's success in shape shifting was location. Throughout Leidesdorff's life, whether in Saint Croix during the 1810s, New Orleans and South America in the 1820s, and the Caribbean through the 1830s, or Yerba Buena (later San Francisco) preceding the American takeover in 1848, he resided in spaces that allowed for a greater degree of fluidity for mixed race individuals, unlike the American racial system, which defined him as passing. In each of these places, colonialism by the French, Spanish, and Danish altered the racial hierarchy.[4] Additionally, within some of these places, Leidesdorff encountered changing racial categories and different menus of identity.[5] Therefore, his movement through these various settings allowed him to negotiate his identity depending on what most suitably fit within the context of his social setting. I refer to this phenomenon as *spatially bolstered shape shifting*. As Leidesdorff encountered new social contexts in the varied destinations to which he traveled, his shape shifting challenged rigid boundaries of race.

The third dynamic that contributed to Leidesdorff's ability to shape shift successfully was his occupation as a shipmaster. This is *occupation/economics-bolstered shape shifting*. While sailing out of New Orleans, Leidesdorff's ships carried cargo to Boston, New York, Texas, Mexico, Havana, and Honduras. Working on a ship that rarely stayed in one port for a long period enabled Leidesdorff to avoid to some degree the social constraints of any one particular society. Throughout the nineteenth century, the crews working in the American shipping industry were multiracial, multiethnic, and international. Author Dean Hantzopoulos described these crews as "composed of Yankees from New England and Long Island, Native Americans, African Americans, Cape Verdeans, recent immigrants from many countries, and indigenous people from various ports of call on the whaling routes in the Pacific."[6] It was quite common to have a majority of a ship's crew members be foreign-born. As shipmaster, Leidesdorff was responsible for crafting crew and passenger lists for his voyages. These lists required a physical description of each crew member on board, including complexion and hair color. Although he diligently filled in the descriptions of his crew members, the evidence reveals that Leidesdorff did not provide a description of his own complexion and hair color.

These three factors of multiraciality, location, and occupation undergirded his ability to successfully shape shift from Saint Croix to California. Rather than suggest that Leidesdorff was a racial imposter, as the historical narrative suggests, this chapter demonstrates how he continually negotiated and renegotiated his racial identity depending on the social context of the space in which he existed.

The second part of this chapter explores the posthumous mischaracterization of Leidesdorff as a Black man who passed as White. When General Folsom first revealed Anna Marie Sparks's "African heritage" and accused Leidesdorff of having passed for White, the agency that Leidesdorff seized in shape shifting was eradicated. Instead, he became discredited as a man who deceitfully passed for White. In contrasting

Leidesdorff's shape shifting with the posthumous maligning of his reputation and classification as a racial imposter, this chapter reveals the extent and limits of human agency.

Leidesdorff's reputation was further maligned in the posthumous misrepresentations of him throughout the American press. In the sixty-plus years following his death, Leidesdorff's life story, but more specifically his multiraciality, was the subject of sensational stories in the press that portrayed him and his family in demeaning descriptions. For example, several of these stories characterized Leidesdorff as a tragic mulatto who suffered a catastrophic crisis because he was neither White nor Black. Rather than acknowledging that Leidesdorff's multiraciality provided him a sense of empowerment or control, these portrayals assumed multiraciality to be detrimental and an insurmountable obstacle. I suggest that these portrayals of Leidesdorff's multiraciality and Blackness found throughout the press account for one method by which race was socially constructed through negative connotations.

Furthermore, the posthumous racial categorization of William Leidesdorff continues through the work of historians. These scholars range from historians of Jewish history in the first decade of the twentieth century to scholars working in the growing field of Black history in the middle decades of the twentieth century. Despite different methods and interpretations, each of these scholars sought to restore Leidesdorff's maligned reputation. In restoring his reputation, they attempted to clarify his racial identity. In categorizing Leidesdorff's identity as Jewish, African, Afro-American, or Black, the scholars suggested a more binary or simplistic racial identity for a man who constantly defied strict racial boundaries and episodically negotiated his racial identity.

Leidesdorff is celebrated today for being the first African American diplomat and is referred to as the "African Founding Father of California."[7] However, what also remains part of this historical narrative is the accusation that he hid his African ancestry in order to achieve success in California. In allowing this notion of his passing to persist, we inaccurately depict him as a racial imposter rather than a man who saw his racial identity as malleable. Moreover, this narrative of passing incorrectly portrays racial identity in California before the American takeover.

Life as a Shape Shifter

William Leidesdorff's phenotype defied simple or binary categorization, which empowered him to negotiate his identity as a shape shifter. Leidesdorff was born on October 23, 1810, to a Jewish Danish man and a free woman of color in the Danish colony of Saint Croix. As an infant, William Leidesdorff was baptized in the Lutheran church. It is these baptismal records that first categorize Leidesdorff's race as *castice*.[8]

In conjunction with colonialism and the institution of race-based slavery, interracial sexual relationships—ranging from abusive master-slave relationships to common-law marriages—created multiracial offspring who spurred a continuous readjustment of official colonial categories. Wieke Vink outlines these constantly shifting categories: "While mixed-blood *mulattos* appeared as a separate category in early colonial documents, a more refined and sophisticated system of colonial classification appeared in the late eighteenth century, which came to include such categories as *castice* and *poestice*." A *castice* was categorized as a child of a *mustee* and White parents, while a *mustee* was a child of *mulatto* and White parents.[9] Individuals classified as *castice* and *poestice* were often phenotypically White, yet in most cases they were considered "colored," as Leidesdorff was in Saint Croix.[10] Leidesdorff's mother was listed as a mulatto and a "free-woman of color" in one record, while in a record dated 1831 she was listed as a *castice*.[11] His mother's changing racial categorization signifies how the colonial classification of race was in flux and in all likelihood influenced Leidesdorff's earliest understanding of racial identity and the fluidity of racial boundaries.

Leidesdorff's father, also named William, was born in Copenhagen in 1778. It is alleged that he migrated to Saint Croix in 1806 to begin work as an estate manager.[12] Andrew Gibb writes that the elder Leidesdorff "may . . . have immigrated to St. Croix in the pursuit of opportunities unavailable to him in the mother country" because he was Jewish. Although Denmark accepted Jewish migrants, full citizenship rights were not recognized until 1814. This denial of rights in Denmark resulted in increased Jewish migration to the Danish overseas colonies.[13] By 1820 the Danish West Indies had an estimated Jewish population that constituted approximately half of the entire White population in the islands. By the 1830s some visitors referred to the islands as the Jewish West Indies.[14]

With his mother described as a mulatto or *castice* and his father as a Jewish Dane, Leidesdorff's multiraciality enabled him a degree of racial ambiguity that assisted his shape shifting. The blurring of racial lines due to his mother's and father's genetics provided Leidesdorff with a phenotype that was more ambiguous than most. This uncertainty is evident in the descriptions provided by individuals who were asked to testify regarding the deed to his property. Their responses ranged from a physical appearance that was Hungarian, to White, to "unquestionably a half-breed West Indian," to "very dark, with the heavy features of the negro."[15] From these responses, it is clear that his racial categorization was not easily determinable, and his physiognomy provided him a degree of flexibility for defining himself as he saw fit.

Anna Marie Sparks, Leidesdorff's mother, and William Sr. were never married. They had six children during their relationship, and William Jr. was their oldest son. Interracial relationships that were consensual between Black women and White men were not an anomaly in the Danish West Indies. Anthropologist Karen Olwig describes this as "a differentiation in attitudes on the three islands that comprised the Danish West Indies. On St. John, sexual intercourse between the races was not a subject for public discussion. However, on Saint Croix, white males often paraded their black concubines before their compatriots."[16] In describing this phenomenon, Neville A. T. Hall writes, "A sexual modus vivendi between the races" emerged. Interracial sexual relationships became the "custom of the country" and were celebrated in the Danish West Indies. This view toward interracial intimacies was highly stratified by gender and race, for "the arbiters of the convention were exclusively the islands' white males." Interracial marriage was not legally recognized. However, with the "perennial shortage of white women" on the island of Saint Croix, interracial couples often lived together in common-law marriages.[17] This was the case for Sparks and Leidesdorff, who lived together for three decades but never formally married.

The numerous interracial relationships resulted in what Richard Haagensen remarked as "the evolving mosaic of colors" in reference to the varied skin tones of the Danish West Indies population. Haagensen, who lived in Saint Croix in the 1750s and published *Beskrivelse over eylandet St. Croiz* (Description of the island of St. Croix) in 1758, went on to explain "the calculus" of racial categorization: "[The] admixture of *mulatto* and white resulted in a 'mucediser'; that latter with a white produced an almost white person, known variously in the early nineteenth century as 'casticer,' 'pausticer' or 'griffe.'"[18] In addition to the blurring of racial lines, interracial relationships also contributed to an expanding population of free women of color. According to Hans West, "In 1792 . . . more than half of the 797 free non-whites in Christiansted [Saint Croix] were women."[19]

The degree of interracial sexual intimacies, the increase in the multiracial population, and the substantial population of free women of color on Saint Croix all speak to the significance of place in Leidesdorff's shape shifting. In Leidesdorff's formative years, he was in a space that was racially fluid. It is reasonable to presume that his childhood in Saint Croix contributed to his perception that the boundaries of race were fluid and therefore meant to be traversed as a shape shifter.

Throughout Leidesdorff's life, whether in Saint Croix, New Orleans, or Yerba Buena, he resided in spaces that were racially fluid. This fluidity was the result of a confluence of factors, including the identity of the colonizers, the demographics of a space, and the economic structure of a region. This confluence of elements in certain locations made shape shifting more feasible; I refer to this phenomenon as *spatially bolstered shape shifting.*

When Leidesdorff arrived in New Orleans during the early 1830s, he would have noticed the large population of multiracial free people of color occupying important economic and social roles in the city. The influence of French and Spanish colonialism preceding White

American settlement in New Orleans is significant, for it altered the racial system that emerged in Louisiana. As was the case in the Danish West Indies of Leidesdorff's youth, "interracial unions became such an accepted social practice in Louisiana that they developed into a well-established institution called *plaçage*," according to G. Reginald Daniel. This was due to the fact that the small White male settler population in the region formed relationships with Native women and then women of African descent. In addition, the Louisiana region offered a "comparatively favorable situation for multiracial" individuals. Daniel asserts that it was during the colonial period that the distant French monarch "saw Free Coloreds as a military 'balance-wheel' against independence-minded whites" and thus privileged them with "some protection of their rights." This resulted in multiracial free coloreds gaining an "intermediate status and privileges superior to those of blacks but inferior to those of whites, [and so] both the Crown and the colonists in 'Latin' North America won the loyalty of the free people of color while maintaining white domination and control."[20]

Under French and Spanish colonialism, the racial system of Louisiana allowed greater social opportunities to people of mixed heritage. This was the result of "shared bonds of ancestry and culture," suggests Daniel. He writes, "Since whites and most Free Coloreds shared bonds of ancestry and culture, whites viewed Free Coloreds as natural and valuable allies against the black slave majority." When the Spanish regained control of the region in 1769, the population of free people of color increased significantly because of natural increase and manumission policies. The system of *plaçage* continued and resulted in what Daniel calls the "mulattoization" and "Europeanization of Louisiana's free people of color."[21]

Despite the Americanization of the region after 1803, free people of color remained determined to "preserve their intermediate status, as they watched Louisiana's ternary racial order polarize into black and white."[22] In the decades preceding Leidesdorff's migration to New Orleans, the multiracial population continued to expand. For example, during the 1820s the population of free people "rose in numbers . . .

to account for almost one in four of the residents in and around the city." By 1830 their numbers had increased to almost two-thirds.[23]

Despite the degree of racial fluidity granted to free people of color and the "exceptional liberties, including freedom of movement and the right to testify in courts against whites," it is important to not ignore the reality that free people of color, according to Lisa Ze Winters in *The Mulatta Concubine*, "endured daily threats against their liberty."[24] This constituted mounting extralegal violence perpetrated against free people of color, including kidnapping and enslavement. Shape shifting became even more essential for free people of color when in the 1830s oppressive laws were enacted undermining their elevated status. These laws varied from outlawing the immigration of free Black people to arresting Black seamen who arrived at the docks of New Orleans.[25] It is in this social context that the decision to negotiate a new racial identity would have provided Leidesdorff with increased safety and opportunities.

It was in the midst of this hardening of racial boundaries in New Orleans that Leidesdorff applied for American citizenship in the city in 1834. In applying for citizenship in this southern city, he negotiated his racial identity to acquire a status unavailable to free people of color who immigrated into the city after 1830.[26] If Leidesdorff had forthrightly asserted his racial category, *castice*, at his baptism or stated his mother's mulatto designation, it is likely he would not have been naturalized. Thus, in applying for citizenship, Leidesdorff negotiated his racial identity to best fit the social setting within which he found himself. Alternatively, it is possible that he claimed Danish citizenship. According to ship manifests and testimony after his death, he spent time in Denmark being educated.[27] If these records are accurate, his language abilities would have buttressed a claim of Danish citizenship.

Leidesdorff's naturalization in 1834 generated significant opportunities for him. Most crucial to his success was the fact that American citizenship made Leidesdorff eligible to command an American merchantman.[28] As shipmaster, Leidesdorff was authorized to command international crews in foreign commerce and therefore control his own trajectory toward achieving success.

His shape shifting and subsequent citizenship also afforded him protection against the Negro Seamen's Law of 1830, which required "all out-of-state free black seamen to leave the state within thirty days or with their ships if these vessels were being prepared for outbound voyages."[29] Significantly, prior to his citizenship and command as shipmaster, his racial categorization was determined not by himself but by the ship captain who employed him. For example, when he served as a mate on the *Lucy Ann* of Baltimore, which sailed to New Orleans in August 1833, his complexion and hair were listed as dark.[30] Leidesdorff's stated birthplace and residence were listed as Baltimore, which illuminates one method by which he negotiated what was known about his heritage. In securing American citizenship and consequently the control to self-categorize on ship manifests, Leidesdorff empowered himself as a shape shifter.

It was during Leidesdorff's time as a shipmaster that he was able to negotiate his racial identity even more directly. As shipmaster, Leidesdorff had the discretion to describe his features, skin tone, and hair color as he desired. Martha Putney found that between 1834, when he became naturalized, and February 14, 1838, Leidesdorff was the shipmaster on eighteen crew lists; seventeen of these lists were for his ships that were registered in New Orleans and that departed from and returned to that city. Among these eighteen crew lists, there is only one that has descriptive information of Leidesdorff's physical appearance.[31] It lists his age as twenty-six, his complexion and hair as dark, and his residence as New Orleans. The list does not include his place of birth.

Leidesdorff's position as shipmaster meant that he was assigned the duty to detail his crew's complexion and hair color while enabling him to withhold detailed information on himself. This demonstrates what I refer to as *occupation-bolstered shape shifting*. Once Leidesdorff was promoted to shipmaster he could racially identify on his own terms. Beyond having the power to racially self-categorize, the continued movement involved in shipping allowed Leidesdorff to avoid, to some degree, the social constraints of any one particular society. When registered out of the port of New Orleans, Leidesdorff's ships carried cargo to Boston, New York, Texas, Mexico, Havana, and Honduras.

Relocating offered Leidesdorff a degree of racial fluidity, depending on the space in which he found himself. Leidesdorff's chosen occupation as a shipmaster served him well in his shape shifting.

After seven years in New Orleans, Leidesdorff signed on as shipmaster of a vessel bound for California. It is arguable that the heightened restrictions against people of African descent in New Orleans and in the South more broadly contributed to Leidesdorff's decision to relocate. Although he had success shape shifting in New Orleans during the 1830s, perhaps Leidesdorff recognized that more opportunities awaited him beyond the increasingly racially static southern city.

Becoming a Californio: Shape Shifting in California

The very opportunities that were becoming restricted in New Orleans opened to Leidesdorff on the distant islands of Hawai'i and the coast of California. These spaces provided both economic opportunity and the lure of a more racially fluid society. Within these contexts his occupation and ability to travel within spaces of racial fluidity enabled him to negotiate his own racial identity.

The racial fluidity that Leidesdorff witnessed existed in California long before his arrival in 1841. The first known people of African descent to travel to California arrived with Jesuit missionary expeditions during the late seventeenth century.[32] Under Spanish rule, the social system permitted the people of African ancestry to be "defined and redefined more flexibly than did the increasingly rigid dichotomies of Black and White in Anglo America." As Jack D. Forbes argues, race was not a mandatory badge of subordination for those inhabitants of the frontier regions who were of African descent or mixed race, because the smaller population on the frontiers of the Spanish Empire forced the colonizers to adapt their rigid social hierarchy to be more reflective of the predominantly multiracial population that existed. A person with mixed ancestry could rise in the social hierarchy of the California frontier. This is not to say that individuals of mixed race and African descent were not subjected to injustices, as it is clear that many were; however, they were not forbidden from rising to positions of power and wealth because of a perceived inferior racial status.[33]

In the Spanish Empire, a person's social status was "never fixed solely by race, but rather defined by occupation and wealth," as well as the notion of the purity of his or her blood—*limpieza de sangre*.[34] The system of *castas* was developed as an elaborate hierarchical classification based on race, ethnicity, and class and was used by the Spaniards to maintain their political and social control. This system had greater significance in urban centers of the empire, such as Mexico City, but often was not enforced in the northern frontier. Mulattos and mestizos frequently were soldiers in the northern frontier, and some rose to powerful positions despite their racial ancestry.[35] According to William Mason, "Castas in northern cities show up as tailors, armorers, and other supposedly prohibited positions, another indication that the restrictive laws were important only in central Mexico." Mason contends that by the eighteenth century "the castas in the northern frontier who held prominent positions were, for convenience purposes, labeled *españoles*."[36] Thus, many mixed race men and women in California did not formally acknowledge their African and indigenous ancestry and instead declared themselves *gente de razón* (people of reason).[37] With this racial fluidity on the California frontier, to a certain extent, people of mixed descent were permitted to determine their own racial categorization, with the result that they could successfully attain power and wealth.

Mexican independence brought to California new ideas of republicanism and liberty. As the existence of slavery became more defended in the southern states of the antebellum United States, it was abolished in the Mexican Republic in 1829. The republic, formed in 1824, extended full legal equality to all citizens regardless of color. People of African descent "found it much easier to secure land grants, wealth, and higher military rank under Mexican control." According to Forbes, most persons of African ancestry were assimilated into a more general identity as Californios or Mexicans.[38]

Race was not a rigid, static concept, and interracial marriage was common. For example, Santiago de la Cruz Pico, a mestizo (White and

Indian), and his mulatta (White and Black) wife, María de la Bastida, acquired the first rancho in what is now Ventura County. The grandchildren of Pico went on to become powerful leaders in Mexican-controlled California, including Governor Pío Pico. Manuel Nieto, a mulatto, is another example of a person of mixed African descent achieving wealth and power in California during Mexican rule. Nieto owned Rancho Los Alamitos and Rancho Los Cerritos, a total of 167,000 acres of grazing land. José Bartolomé Tapia, the son of Felipe Tapia, a mulatto, and Juana Cárdenas, a mestiza, owned Rancho Malibu. Tiberio Tapia, a grandson of a Black man and a mestiza, owned Rancho Cucamonga near Los Angeles and served three times as mayor of Los Angeles. María Rita Valdez, whose Black grandparents were among the founders of Los Angeles, owned Rancho Rodeo de Las Aguas. Because of the wealth these Californias inherited, Anglo-American men who arrived in the West just prior to and after the U.S. acquisition of California sought them out for marriage. According to Deborah Moreno, "California mission records show that approximately 15 percent of the marriages recorded in California during the Mexican period were intercultural." The majority of the men who married Californias were French and Irish immigrants who were Catholic, a precondition for marriage.[39] These marriages between Whites and Californias were such a common occurrence that by the end of the nineteenth century a majority of these Mexican inheritances were in the hands of families bearing such names as Richardson, Ord, Livermore, Baker, Fitch, Stearns, Hill, Robinson, Dalton, Hartnett, Den, Black, Burdell, and Cooper.[40]

Because Mexican California was not a racially rigid society, the fluid social circumstances within this space afforded Leidesdorff and other individuals of mixed ancestry the opportunity to negotiate their racial identity and social positions. This fluidity enabled Leidesdorff to settle in one place rather than continually remain on the move renegotiating his identity. It was in Mexican-controlled Yerba Buena, California, that Leidesdorff became a Californio and successful businessman.

In the course of his business ventures, Leidesdorff introduced the first steam vessel into San Francisco Bay waters, opened the first San

Francisco hotel, acquired a waterfront lot at the foot of California Street, and built a warehouse.[41] He became a naturalized Mexican citizen and was granted almost 35,500 acres along the American River. As a resident of Yerba Buena, he played a key role in the development of the young city.

The racial fluidity that was achievable in Mexican California enabled Leidesdorff to attain his position of power as a Californio and ultimately a highly regarded position from the U.S. government. While at this point Leidesdorff was a Mexican citizen, he was in favor of the U.S. takeover and in 1845 was appointed to the position of American vice-consul by President James Polk.[42] He was then elected to the city council, serving as treasurer.[43] Leidesdorff was then chosen to be chairman of the school committee, and he established the first public school in San Francisco and secured the services of Thomas Douglass of Yale as the schoolmaster.

Some scholars suggest that if his African heritage had been known, Leidesdorff would not have been appointed to such high positions of power. This, they claim, is proof of his racial passing.[44] This conclusion is too simplistic. In the racially fluid society of California, people were able to negotiate their racial categorization. I propose that what was of greater significance and what determined Leidesdorff's appointment to such positions was his wealth and prominence, which he established long before the American takeover. In all likelihood his mixed race ancestry, which made his race indeterminable, enabled him to blend into the Californio population, which was itself an amalgamation of races. Rather than acting as a racial imposter posing as a White man, Leidesdorff shape shifted his identity to fit his needs.

Discrediting Leidesdorff Posthumously

In the years after Leidesdorff's death, when he was accused of passing for White, his estate was the subject of a protracted battle in which the campaign to discredit him and his heirs served multiple purposes. This stigmatization of his supposed racial imposture continued into the twentieth century—more than sixty years after his death. He became a symbol of the potential horrors of invisible Blackness, multiraciality,

and miscegenation. It was through these mischaracterizations and racist portrayals of Leidesdorff and his heirs that racial difference, multiraciality, and Blackness were socially constructed.

Leidesdorff fell ill with typhus in May 1848 and died two weeks later
on May 18, 1848, at the age of thirty-eight. Within a few days of Leidesdorff's death, gold was discovered on his property near the American River, significantly increasing the value of the property. It was at
this point that General Folsom began his crusade to acquire Leidesdorff's property by sending his lawyers to the Danish West Indies to
locate and negotiate with Leidesdorff's heirs. Because Leidesdorff died
intestate, the distribution of the assets of his estate was a complicated
and lengthy legal matter. Forty years passed before the contested legal
affairs involving his heirs were finally resolved. This occurred within a
social climate of hardening racial boundaries in Californian society.[45]

The acquisition of California by the United States and the subsequent influx of thousands of White settlers during the gold rush marked
an end to the relative ease with which persons of part-African ancestry could assimilate into the Californio population.[46] It was no longer
easy for a person of African ancestry to attain a high social standing.
Instead, with Americanization came a stricter system of categorization. As Jack Forbes concluded, "Seemingly overnight, people of African descent arriving in California entered a society where their rights
were denied, their opportunities were limited, and their social position was set firmly apart."[47]

In 1848, at the start of the gold rush, there were just a few dozen
African Americans who had migrated from the United States and were
documented as living in California.[48] However, within four years, their
numbers had increased to more than two thousand.[49] Forbes argues
that "the Anglo American migration ushered in a new era for persons
of African descent in California—one that defined them rigidly and
restrictively as Blacks. It was from this time forward that they would
have to fight as a group for any measure of legal and social assimilation."[50] The arriving population of African Americans endured this
newly adopted restrictive racial system in contrast to the more fluid
system Leidesdorff had experienced.

The California Constitutional Convention of 1849 marked the formal legislative ending of the era of Mexican racial tolerance. The convention declared slavery as unacceptable within the boundaries of the proposed state. However, this was not a decision based on moral principles or persuasion; instead, it was due to the threat of economic competition posed by slavery in the gold fields. The prejudice against Blacks in California, which had been expressed so resoundingly during the Constitutional Convention, carried over into the first state legislature, and the momentum of this prejudice continued to build throughout the 1850s.

During the 1850s, California's legislators passed an extensive body of discriminatory laws against Blacks, including "the prohibition of testimony in civil and criminal actions involving whites; the institution of poll and property taxes; the invalidation of marriages between whites and blacks or mulattoes; exclusion from the state homestead law; and lapsing of legislation affecting free blacks' rights under Fugitive Slave laws." California statutes went so far as to exclude non-Whites from voting, from serving in the militia, and from testifying in court when Whites were involved. As was the practice in several midwestern states, California legislators attempted to exclude Blacks from settling in the territory during this time period.[51]

During the early months of 1858, events occurred that heightened the despair of Blacks in California. Laws were enacted that segregated public schools—the same public school system that Leidesdorff had helped to establish. The Archy Lee case, in which the California Supreme Court ordered the return of Lee to his master after Lee escaped, was symbolic for African Americans, as it was a sign that the South and its notion of White supremacy shaped their existence in the California territory. It was apparent that the safety and well-being of Blacks were constantly threatened in California. Thus, in response to the racist legislation that was being enacted and the rising influence of White supremacy ideology in the 1850s and early 1860s, a significant number "of dissatisfied free blacks—some of them forty-niners—pulled up roots once again and moved north to the British colony of Vancouver Island in search of freedom from racial discrimination." On April

20, 1858, the *Columbia*, *Golden Age*, and *Commodore* ships transported a large group of Black Californians to British Columbia in search of the racial fluidity that once existed in California.[52]

Significantly, similar racially determined restrictiveness took place in New Orleans during Leidesdorff's life. In response, Leidesdorff shape shifted and eventually migrated away from the restricting racial system. However, in death such adjustments were not possible. Thus, what occurred as a result of the Americanization process was that Leidesdorff's integrity was questioned, and his legacy was destroyed. This establishment of hardening racial lines in California is thus crucial to understanding the contours of the posthumous campaign to malign Leidesdorff as a racial passer. As Tomás Almaguer argues, "Race and the racialization process in California became the central organizing principle of group life during the state's formative period of development" during the second half of the nineteenth century.[53] This is evident in the controversy that surrounded the settling of Leidesdorff's will when his estate became the subject of extensive coverage by newspapers and other publications.

In one such publication, *An Epistle to Posterity* (1898), Mary Elizabeth Wilson Sherwood detailed her husband, John Sherwood's experience working as a lawyer for Folsom in Saint Croix. She recounts that Leidesdorff's "old mother, Anna Marie Sparks, who could neither read nor write, demanded boxes of jewels and barrels of gold. The price had gone up every hour since Captain Folsom made the first treaty. Should she allow her son's great fortune to escape her? So poor Captain Folsom kept paying, and other heirs sprang up." Rather than portray Sparks compassionately because of her son's death, Sherwood depicts her as greedy and lacking in integrity, while Folsom is characterized as the sympathetic victim with honorable intentions. Sherwood's account continues by describing her personal experience when she traveled with her husband to Saint Croix: "He drove me up a hill to a humble shanty where sat a drunken Danish soldier . . . awaiting his share, and it was paid to him—20,000 in gold. He was a brother-in-law of the late Captain Leidesdorff, and he drank himself to death in three months out of his bag of gold."[54] Sherwood's portrayal discredits Leidesdorff's heirs. These accounts are also steeped in a racist ideology of White superiority and served to justify the campaign to undervalue the claims of Anna Marie Sparks, who in Sherwood's description pursues her interests with no regard for the high esteem and honorable intentions of Sherwood's husband's client, Folsom.

Leidesdorff was also discredited posthumously through sensationalistic stories in the American press. Notably, these stories characterized him as a man who faced tragic consequences because he hid his true racial ancestry. Leidesdorff's supposed invisible Blackness and miscegenation became the focus of cautionary tales told through the first decades of the twentieth century.[55]

Although the fear of miscegenation was not a new public emotion, in the second half of the nineteenth century with the eradication of slavery, this fear was magnified, as "whites imagined 'social equality' as tantamount to forced sexual relations between black men and white women."[56] White Americans feared that miscegenation would undermine the racial hierarchy and result in the degeneration of the White race. As a result, in each state in which the population of Blacks increased to 5 percent of the total population, antimiscegenation laws were enacted. Consequently, by 1913 forty-two states had enacted statutory impediments to marital miscegenation.[57]

In addition to the fears that emerged over miscegenation in the post–Civil War period, there was growing concern among White Americans about the phenomenon of passing. Due to the rigid Jim Crow laws in American society in the 1880s, people of mixed African and European ancestry began attempting to cross the color line in greater numbers. This resulted in what G. Reginald Daniel calls the "great age of passing," which lasted from 1880 to 1925. Whites feared that "failures to police 'the line,' could engender an array of horrors— from the danger of lynching one's own brother, to apparent whites giving birth to black infants."[58] This included fear of "'racial Mongrelization' and the decline of Anglo-North American civilization."[59]

In this climate of intensifying fear over racial mixing, newspaper articles describe Leidesdorff as the perpetrator and his fiancée, a White woman, as the innocent victim. For example, the *San Francisco Call* published an article in 1913 that claimed that Leidesdorff abandoned his thriving business in New Orleans when his true racial ancestry became known to his White fiancée. While allegedly passing, Leidesdorff fell in love with "the daughter of an old and proud family of French descent and they became engaged." Supposedly, when his true racial identity was revealed, Leidesdorff received a note from the woman's father that motivated Leidesdorff to dispose of his property, purchase a ship, and plan his trip to California. However, "a day or two before he was ready for sea, while he was going to where his vessel lay, a funeral procession came in sight. To avoid it he stepped into a store, and asked the owner what funeral it was. The reply was, 'Oh, the funeral of the young lady, who came so near being married to a mulatto. She died yesterday, they say, from the shock.'"[60] After his death Leidesdorff was criticized as a racial imposter who should be held responsible for the death of the person he loved most—his fiancée.

In a similar accounting of Leidesdorff's supposed love affair, a Mrs. M. J. Scooffy asserted in the *Evening Sentinel*:

> One evening at a reception [Leidesdorff] met a beautiful and accomplished young lady of the most exceptional standing. . . . Their affection for each other was mutual, and their acquaintance soon ripened into love of the most intense type. . . . He had no idea that the secret of his birth would be revealed. . . . All arrangements for the wedding perfected, when in some mysterious way, the particulars of which I have never learned, the African tinge in the views of the ardent lover was divulged to the mother, and after one brief scene at her house he left New Orleans, and the climax of a social tragedy was apparently reached. But the end was not yet. Years elapsed, and one evening, when reading a newspaper, the older woman read that Leidesdorff was appointed Consul. . . . "My God!" she said. "Does that mulatto still live?" And then she fell unconscious to the floor.[61]

In both articles, Leidesdorff is the central character in a fearmongering campaign sixty-plus years after his death. It is his supposed passing and trickery of an innocent White woman that become the overriding legacy of a man who was revered at the time of his death.

Rather than seeing Leidesdorff's multiraciality as providing him a sense of empowerment in determining his racial identity in a fluid social context, these portrayals construct his multiraciality as facilitating his manipulation of others. The characterizations of Leidesdorff found throughout the press represent one method by which Blackness and multiraciality were socially constructed with negative connotations and supposed tragic consequences.

Immediately following his death and for many years after, Leidesdorff was condemned as a liar and as a person who deceived those around him because, it was alleged, he hid his true racial heritage. The portrayal that Leidesdorff internally suffered as a result of his multiraciality demonstrates the extent to which White Americans felt threatened by the blurring of racial boundaries. As a result of this fear, Whites desperately sought to instill the perception that mixed race people experienced angst and that if they decided to pass, they would face dire consequences, as in the death of a fiancée. They maintained and bolstered this myth in order to hold the line on race and preserve their power. If Leidesdorff's shape shifting empowered him, then the supposed racial boundary that maintained White supremacist power was destabilized. The mischaracterization of Leidesdorff's life was utilized to instill fear about racial miscegenation and shape shifting.[62]

The Role of Historians in Posthumously Classifying Leidesdorff's Racial Identity

The newspaper accounts and publications regarding Leidesdorff and his African-descended heirs, in particular Anna Marie Sparks, are not the only methods by which his race was examined posthumously. The efforts at categorizing William Leidesdorff's race persisted through the work of historians attempting to restore his maligned reputation. These historians range from scholars of Jewish history in the early 1900s to historians of African American history in the mid-twentieth century. Despite their contrasting objectives, these scholars sought to restore Leidesdorff's maligned reputation and did so by determining and imposing their own ideas about racial categorization on him.

For example, in 1906 *The Jewish Encyclopedia* included an entry on

William A. Leidesdorff. Within this account, the authors claimed that Leidesdorff's possible birthplace was "Szathmar[,] Hungary." They suggested that he was the "son of Mordecai Leidesdorff; his cousin Yitl (Henrietta) married Akiba Eger." The authors detailed his departure from home at the age of fifteen and claimed that "his family never heard from him again." According to the authors, he "passed as a native of Jamaica, of Danish extraction . . . [and] bore a high reputation for integrity and enterprise. He is said to have been 'liberal, hospitable, cordial, confiding even to a fault.'" The authors praised him for his acquired wealth and work in forming public schools in San Francisco. In describing Folsom and Anna Marie Sparks, the authors wrote: "Folsom visited Jamaica and found some 'relatives'—even a woman who claimed to be Leidesdorff's mother—and purchased the claims of all these people. But they obtained no standing in court."[63] By concluding with the dismissing characterization that Sparks had no standing in court, the authors revealed their projected narrative that Sparks lacked credibility. They dismissed the veracity of her maternal status, claiming that she lied about being Leidesdorff's mother. The disregard for Sparks and her legitimate status as his mother is similar to the portrayal of Sparks in the newspaper accounts. This historical account of Leidesdorff's life was an effort to restore his historical legacy and reputation—to counter the misrepresentation of him as a passer and deceitful man. However, implicit in this interpretation was the contention that if he was Jewish, he could not be Black. In claiming that Leidesdorff was born in Hungary, the authors essentially whitewashed him.

In contrast to this interpretation, a group of scholars working in the field of Black history emerged in the mid-twentieth century who produced scholarship that celebrated his accomplishments and asserted his Blackness. Their efforts have resulted in the most significant restoration of his legacy and have had the greatest success in shaping his memorialization, for he is celebrated and remembered today by the city of San Francisco Board of Supervisors and Californian legislature as the "African Founding Father of California."[64] In many ways these scholars were working in the mode of "compensatory history," which seeks to identify the accomplishments of extraordinary Black Americans.[65] This mode of scholarship is exemplified by Delilah Beasley's *The Negro Trail Blazers*, published in 1919.[66] It continued through the 1960s, 1970s, and 1980s with the proliferation of monographs on African American contributions to California society and culture. Notably, historical accounts found in these publications served an important public history role in that they informed the work of many journalists who contributed articles to the Black press. These columns and monographs served a monumental purpose in the Black liberation struggle of the mid-twentieth century, for they represented a school of historical writing that challenged Eurocentrism and provided historical investigations that had the ultimate goal of encouraging African Americans to have racial pride and self-respect.

The restoration of Leidesdorff's legacy reflected a broader effort in the 1950s, 1960s, and 1970s in which the writing of Black historians took on a new politicized element. According to William Wright, these publications "helped to produce the view that Black history was about the internal cultural and social development of Black people in America."[67] The promotion and celebration of Black history became a major component of the movement to assist African Americans in their "quest for self-determination and communal development that followed the legislative victories of the mid-1960s."[68] Thus, these historical accounts about William Leidesdorff served a political function and generated a sense of pride in the achievements and sacrifices of African Americans throughout America's history.

An early example of this historical scholarship is Sue Bailey Thurman's 1952 *Pioneers of Negro Origin in California*. She described Leidesdorff as "born in the Virgin Islands, the gifted son of William Leidesdorff, a Danish sugar planter, and Anna Marie Spark [*sic*], a native woman having Negro blood." She praised Leidesdorff by stating: "No nationality or racial minority migrating to the state could wish to have a more distinguished antecedent." Thurman concluded by stating: "Greater tribute may not be given the first pioneer of Negro origin who came to San Francisco, made his contribution and passed on. But the citizen of today—of whatever racial, creed or national origin, migrant like himself—may walk 'The City's' streets with dignity, knowing that Leidesdorff helped immeasurably to establish this right, a hundred years ago."[69]

Within twenty years of Thurman's publication, a distinguished group of historians working in the field of Black history sought to outline Leidesdorff's successes and contributions to society, as well as his Blackness. For example, in the first sentence of the section focusing on Leidesdorff in Jack Forbes's *Afro-Americans in the Far West*, Leidesdorff is labeled as "the most successful Afro-American arriving late in the Mexican period." This recognition is directly followed by a reference to his mother, who according to Forbes was a "St. Croix (Virgin Island) mulatto." Despite his description of Leidesdorff as an Afro-American, Forbes titled his section on Leidesdorff the "Quadroon Civic Leader of Early San Francisco." This reference to quadroon in the title is the only mention of his multiraciality. His father is not discussed in the excerpt.[70]

Like Forbes's work on Leidesdorff, Russell Lee Adams's *Great Negroes Past and Present*, published in 1969, celebrated Leidesdorff as a "business pioneer" and "maneuvering millionaire." Within the first sentence of his biographical sketch of Leidesdorff, Adams referred to Anna Marie Sparks as his "African mother."[71] As we know from records from Saint Croix, Sparks was classified as a *castice* and a mulatto. Despite these discrepancies between the categorization of the records and Adams's labeling and acknowledging of Sparks's Black heritage, these accounts are in stark contrast to the Jewish historians' account.

Similarly, in *Blacks in Gold Rush California*, Rudolph Lapp seeks to restore Leidesdorff's reputation while simultaneously proclaiming his Blackness and reiterating the passing narrative. Lapp referred to Leidesdorff as an "Afro-American" and described his heritage as of "West Indian of Danish-African ancestry." This again stressed his Blackness with no attempts at whitewashing. However, Lapp allowed the notion that Leidesdorff passed as White to continue historically when he wrote, "Contemporaries considered him white," suggesting that he was a racial imposter.[72]

William Sherman Savage's *Blacks in the West* presented a similar accounting of Leidesdorff's successes, his Blackness, and his racial passing. Savage stressed the certainty of Anna Marie Sparks's status as Leidesdorff's mother: "The feeble contention that William Leidesdorff was not the son of Marie Ann [sic] Sparks convinced no one, and the claim failed." Yet while emphasizing Leidesdorff's Black mother, Savage also stated: "[Leidesdorff] did not regard himself as a Black and probably was not so considered by many others; therefore, it was possible for him to have considerable influence in local government."[73] This juxtaposition presenting Leidesdorff's African ancestry in conjunction with his racial passing is a fundamental aspect of the narrative of his life and early California history.

During the height of the Black liberation movement, African American newspapers also sought to redress Leidesdorff's maligned reputation through the publication of historical biographies outlining his achievements in their columns. The publications asserted his Blackness and celebrated his many achievements. There were numerous stories in the Black press counteracting the negative reputation that Leidesdorff had up to that point. These publications served an important role in providing Black Americans with historical figures they could look up to. Not only did these publications celebrate tremendous accomplishments made by Black Americans in the past, but the newspaper articles assisted in the political fight for equal rights.

For example, Leidesdorff's history became a featured story in *Ebony Jr.* in 1978. The article was titled "Those Spirited Black Settlers of the Wild West!" and was written by Mary C. Lewis. The author included illustrations of the San Francisco Harbor and the portrait of Leidesdorff. She wrote, "Leidesdorff . . . was the super-doer of San Francisco." She explained Leidesdorff's heritage as being born to a "Danish planter and an African mother from the Virgin Islands." Lewis concluded by stating: "Thanks to super-doers like Leidesdorff, San Francisco grew into a strong city ready to take on the Gold Rush of 1850!"[74] For Black children, these stories served an important role by instilling pride in past heroism of Black Americans and providing an alternative historical narrative that resisted Eurocentric interpretations. Lewis's account mirrors the reverence displayed in the obituary of William

A. Leidesdorff. Crucial to her reverent description and his obituary is the excluding of the narrative of passing for White. As I have demonstrated, Leidesdorff was not a racial imposter; instead, he constantly negotiated his racial identity as a shape shifter.

Conclusion

Although it has been suggested that when the "most valuable resident of San Francisco" died in 1848 his African ancestry was unknown, this chapter has demonstrated that Leidesdorff's racial identity was much more complicated than that simplistic conclusion implies.[75] Living in California before the United States instituted a rigid racial system, individuals of mixed racial ancestry did blend into the Californio population and advanced economically and politically.

Leidesdorff is remembered today for being the first African American consul in San Francisco in 1848 and is often referred to as the "African Founding Father of California."[76] This legacy is the result of a conscientious effort to restore Leidesdorff's maligned reputation beginning in the 1950s and reaching its height in the 1960s and 1970s. It began with historians of Black history addressing the sensationalistic misrepresentations of Leidesdorff as a tragic mulatto who came from a cunning and dishonest family. During the height of the Black liberation movement, the Black press assisted in the restoration of his reputation by publishing articles that outlined his achievements. These publications boldly asserted and celebrated his Blackness and his African heritage, providing an alternative to the Eurocentric narrative.

Yet what also remains part of the narrative today is the mischaracterization of Leidesdorff as an individual who passed falsely as a White man and thus was afforded the opportunities to be successful. It is time to correct that misconception and to acknowledge that in California prior to 1848, mixed race individuals were not prohibited from attaining positions of power because of their race. Rather, Leidesdorff determined his racial identity as a shape shifter through racially fluid spaces and occupations that empowered him to negotiate his racial categorization.

In San Francisco today few residents know the impact of William

A. Leidesdorff. His legacy has been tarnished by the vicious attacks orchestrated by White Americans who utilized the ideology of White supremacy to their advantage. The controversy surrounding the legitimacy of his heirs stigmatized Leidesdorff's reputation. At the time of his death the residents of San Francisco had great reverence for this man. The life of William A. Leidesdorff provides insight into the nature of the racial fluidity of the frontier territory during its various incarnations. It is tragic that this man who was held in such high esteem in his lifetime and was revered by his fellow citizens of San Francisco upon his death would fall from public esteem in the years following his demise because of the revealing of his supposedly secret African ancestry. It is especially troubling when one considers that Captain Folsom, the very man who revealed this information, was the man who ultimately would gain the most when it was discovered. Tragically, Leidesdorff's property along the American River is now known as the town of Folsom, named after Captain Folsom.

Notes

1. Obituary, *California Star*, May 20, 1848, 3.
2. The details of William Leidesdorff's personal life were written about in newspaper articles for approximately six decades after his death. In this chapter I rely on these articles to tell the narrative of Leidesdorff's life. However, I am well aware that because of the sensationalistic nature of journalism in the mid- to late nineteenth century, the facts described in these articles must be viewed with skepticism. Despite these shortcomings of the newspaper articles, they are important because they illustrate the manner in which William Leidesdorff's life is portrayed in nineteenth- and early twentieth-century journalism and are evidence of the California cultural viewpoints surrounding race, mixed race individuals, and the phenomenon of passing.
3. In the Danish West Indies, a *castice* was the child of a White parent and a *mustee* the child of mulatto and White parents.
4. Mervyn Alleyne, *The Construction and Representation of Race and Ethnicity in the Caribbean and the World* (Kingston: University of the West Indies Press, 2002); G. Reginald Daniel, *More Than Black? Multiracial Identity and the New Racial Order* (Philadelphia: Temple University Press, 2002); Andrew Fisher and Matthew O'Hara, eds., *Imperial Subjects: Race and Identity in Colonial Latin America* (Durham NC: Duke University Press, 2009).

5. See the chapter by Paul Spickard in this volume, "Shape Shifting: Reflections on Racial Plasticity."

6. Dean Hantzopoulos, "Diversity in Whaling," last modified 2015, http://educators.mysticseaport.org/artifacts/diversity_in_whaling/.html.

7. California State Legislature, Assembly Concurrent Resolution No. 131, chap. 41, May 3, 2004.

8. Christiansted Lutheran Mission Church, Church Book, 1805–18, baptisms, pp. 51, 64.

9. Wieke Vink, *Creole Jews: Negotiating Community in Colonial Suriname* (Leiden: KITLV Press, 2010), 131.

10. According to Vink, on the island of Suriname *castices* and *poetices* were included in the White companies of the civil guard, demonstrating the more flexible racial structure (*Creole Jews*, 131).

11. Christiansted Free Colored Census, no. 987, 1816, located at the Rigsarkiv, the Danish National Archives, Copenhagen, Denmark. Accessed via Svend E. Holsoe's website on the genealogy of the Danish West Indies, http://www.vifamilies.org/home.html.

12. Rigsarkiv, the Danish National Archives, Copenhagen, Denmark, Vestindiske Lokal Arkiver, the West Indian Local Archives, found in the Danish National Archives, Copenhagen, Denmark, VI Guvernementet, Oaths of Allegiance, 1799–1807, p. 44. Accessed via Svend E. Holsoe's website on the genealogy of the Danish West Indies, http://www.vifamilies.org/home.html.

13. Andrew Gibb, "William Alexander Leidesdorff and the American 1847: Minstrelsy and Race in California before the Gold Rush," *Theatre History Studies* 34 (2015): 25.

14. Norman Berdichevsky, *An Introduction to Danish Culture* (Jefferson NC: McFarland & Company, 2011), 34–35.

15. "Postscript: The Leidesdorff Estate," *Sacramento Daily Union*, January 1, 1856; "Important Testimony in the Leidesdorff Estate," *Daily Alta California*, December 8, 1857; "The Leidesdorff Heirs: Claimants for Valuable Property in San Francisco and Sacramento," *Daily Evening Bulletin*, July 29, 1889; "Leidesdorff's Estate: Another Contest for a Dead Man's Effects Begun," *Los Angeles Herald*, July 26, 1889.

16. Karen F. Olwig, *Cultural Adaptation and Resistance on St. John: Three Centuries of Afro-Caribbean Life* (Gainesville: University of Florida Press, 1993), quoted in Eddie Donoghue, *Black Women / White Men: The Sexual Exploitation of Female Slaves in the Danish West Indies* (Trenton NJ: African World Press, 2002), xiii–xiv.

17. Neville A. T. Hall, *Slave Society in the Danish West Indies: St. Thomas, St. John & St. Croix* (Kingston: University of the West Indies Press, 1992), 151, 152.

18. Richard Haagensen, *Beskrivelse over eylandet St. Croiz*, quoted in Hall, *Slave Society*, 152.

19. Hans West quoted in Hall, *Slave Society*, 150.

20. Daniel, *More Than Black?*, 75, 76, 77.

21. Daniel, *More Than Black?*, 76, 77, 78.

22. Daniel, *More Than Black?*, 78.

23. Thomas Joseph Davis, *Plessy v. Ferguson* (Santa Barbara: Greenwood Press, 2012), 77.

24. Lisa Ze Winters, *The Mulatta Concubine: Terror, Intimacy, Freedom, and Desire in the Black Transatlantic* (Athens: University of Georgia Press, 2016), 161.

25. Winters, *The Mulatta Concubine*, 161.

26. National Archives and Records Administration, Fort Worth, Texas, RG 21, U.S. District Court, Eastern District of Louisiana, New Orleans, Declaration of Intention, 1834, 22. Accessed via Svend E. Holsoe's website on the genealogy of the Danish West Indies, http://www.vifamilies.org/home.html.

27. W. D. H. Howard, the administrator of the estate in 1848 and 1849, transcribed the deposition of a woman who testified that William Leidesdorff was "a native of the Danish West India island of Saint Croix, born illegitimately of a woman with whom his father lived for thirty years constantly as man and wife. The children of which woman, including W. A. Leidesdorff were formally acknowledged and legitimatized in a court of records at the place of their birth by the father." Another deposition taken by Howard is that of James W. Lachane, who knew William A. Leidesdorff in New Orleans. Lachane testified that "William A. Leidesdorff was always understood and believed by this defendant and by his acquaintances generally to have been a Danish subject by birth and to have been born in the Danish Island of Saint Croix." See William A. Leidesdorff Estate Papers, 1844–52, Bancroft Library, University of California, Berkeley.

28. A merchantman is any nonnaval vessel, usually a trading ship. Trade law required that shipmasters of American trading ships be American citizens.

29. Martha S. Putney, *Black Sailors: Afro-American Merchant Seamen and Whalemen prior to the Civil War* (New York: Greenwood Press, 1987), 66. See also W. Jeffrey Bolster, *Black Jacks: African American Seamen in the Age of Sail* (Cambridge MA: Harvard University Press, 1997).

30. Bolster, *Black Jacks*, 66. Putney's objective in researching Leidesdorff's crew lists was to find out information on his background: "Without

foreknowledge of Leidesdorff's origins, the researcher most certainly would have received no help from the lists on his racial identity" (*Black Sailors*, 66).

31. Bolster, *Black Jacks*, 66.

32. William Loren Katz, *The Black West: A Documentary and Pictorial History of the African American Role in the Westward Expansion of the United States* (New York: Harlem Moon, 2005), 109.

33. Jack D. Forbes, "The Early African Heritage of California," in *Seeking El Dorado: African Americans in California*, ed. Lawrence B. de Graaf, Kevin Mulroy, and Quintard Taylor (Seattle: University of Washington Press, 2001), 75, 77.

34. Forbes, "The Early African Heritage," 77.

35. The term "mestizo" is most commonly used to describe the offspring of a Spaniard and an Indian.

36. William Marvin Mason, *The Census of 1790: A Demographic History of Colonial California*, Ballena Press Anthropological Papers No. 45 (1998), 9, 10.

37. California Indians were *sin razón*, "without reason."

38. Forbes, "The Early African Heritage," 83, 89.

39. Deborah Moreno, "'Here the Society Is United': 'Respectable' Anglos and Intercultural Marriage in Pre–Gold Rush California," *California History* 80, no. 1 (Spring 2001): 3, 6.

40. Mario de Valdes y Cocom, "The Blurred Racial Lines of Famous Families: The Pico Family," *Frontline Documentary*, November 26, 1996, http://www.pbs.org/wgbh/pages/frontline/shows/secret/famous/.

41. Katz, *The Black West*, 110–13.

42. Rudolph M. Lapp, *Blacks in Gold Rush California* (New Haven CT: Yale University Press, 1977), 10.

43. Katz, *The Black West*, 112.

44. See Juliet E. K. Walker, *The History of Black Business in America: Capitalism, Race, Entrepreneurship, Volume 1, to 1865* (Chapel Hill: University of North Carolina Press, 2009), 124; Rudolph M. Lapp, *Afro-Americans in California* (San Francisco: Boyd & Fraser, 1987), 3; Rand Richards, *Mud, Blood, and Gold: San Francisco in 1849* (San Francisco: Heritage House Publishers, 2009), 153; Scott Malcomson, *One Drop of Blood: The American Misadventure of Race* (New York: Farrar, Straus and Giroux, 2000), 406; William Loren Katz, *Black People Who Made the Old West* (Trenton NJ: Africa World Press, 1992), 73; Lynn Maria Hudson, *The Making of "Mammy Pleasant": A Black Entrepreneur in Nineteenth Century San Francisco* (Urbana: University of Illinois Press, 2003), 134.

45. See Tomás Almaguer, *Racial Fault Lines: The Historical Origins of White Supremacy in California* (Berkeley: University of California Press, 1994); Albert Camarillo, *Chicanos in a Changing Society: From Mexican Pueblos to American Barrios in Santa Barbara and Southern California, 1848–1930* (Cambridge MA: Harvard University Press, 1979); Carlos Manuel Salomon, *Pio Pico: The Last Governor of Mexican California* (Norman: University of Oklahoma Press, 2012); Verónica Castillo-Muñoz, *The Other California: Land, Identity, and Politics on the Mexican Borderlands* (Berkeley: University of California Press, 2017).

46. Lawrence B. De Graaf and Quintard Taylor, "Introduction: African Americans in California History, California in African American History," in de Graaf, Mulroy, and Taylor, *Seeking El Dorado*, 8.

47. Forbes, "The Early African Heritage," 89.

48. Lapp, *Blacks in Gold Rush California*, 11–12.

49. "The California census of 1850 revealed fewer than 1,000 Black pioneers in a total population estimated at between 100,000 and 175,000. The number rose to 2,200 according to a special census taken in 1852 and to 4,086, including 2,062 mulattoes, in 1860. Only four of the state's counties had more than 100 Blacks in residence in 1860" (Malcolm Edwards, "The War of Complexional Distinction: Blacks in Gold Rush California & British Columbia," *California Historical Quarterly* 56, no. 1 [Spring 1977]: 36).

50. Forbes, "The Early African Heritage," 88.

51. Edwards, "The War," 37. Despite these racially restrictive laws enacted in California in the 1850s, Blacks were not barred from property ownership in the state.

52. Edwards, "The War," 37–38, 34, 39.

53. Almaguer, *Racial Fault Lines*, 7.

54. Mary Elizabeth Wilson Sherwood, *An Epistle to Posterity: Being Rambling Recollections of Many Years of My Life* (New York: Harper & Brothers Publishers, 1898), 73–74.

55. See Edward Cahill, "The Candid Friend: An Independent Review of Men and Things That Figure in the Contemporary Life of California," *San Francisco Call*, August 24, 1913, 21; M. J. Scooffy, "The Romance of William Leidesdorff," *Evening Sentinel*, August 10, 1901, 4.

56. Crystal Feimster, *Southern Horrors: Women and the Politics of Rape and Lynching* (Cambridge MA: Harvard University Press, 2009), 51.

57. Randall Kennedy, *Interracial Intimacies: Sex, Marriage, Identity, and Adoption* (New York: Pantheon Books, 2003), 219, 255.

58. Nella Larsen, *Passing: Authoritative Text Backgrounds and Contexts Criticism*, ed. Carla Kaplan (New York: W. W. Norton and Company, 2007), xvi.

59. Daniel, *More Than Black?*, 52.

60. Edward Cahill, "The Candid Friend: An Independent Review of Men and Things That Figure in the Contemporary Life of California," *San Francisco Call*, August 24, 1913, 21. There are no documents in the Leidesdorff papers at the Huntington Library that make reference to this engagement.

61. Scooffy, "The Romance," 4.

62. There is no record of Leidesdorff's fiancée in New Orleans or that any of these stories have any amount of truth to them.

63. Isidore Singer and Cyrus Adler, *The Jewish Encyclopedia: A Descriptive Record of the History, Religion, Literature, and Customs of the Jewish People from the Earliest Times to the Present Day* (New York: Funk & Wagnalls Company, 1904, 1906), 672.

64. City and County of San Francisco Board of Supervisors Resolutions between January 1, 2004, and December 28, 2004, http://www.sfbos.org/index.aspx?page=2291.

65. This term comes from Gerda Lerner's work on women's history, "Placing Women in History: Definitions and Challenges," *Feminist Studies* 3 (1975): 5–14.

66. Delilah Beasley, *The Negro Trail Blazers* (Los Angeles: Times Mirror Printing and Binding House, 1919), 107–13.

67. William D. Wright, "What Is Black History?," in *Critical Reflections on Black History* (Westport CT: Praeger, 2002), 17.

68. Nancy Maclean, "The Civil Rights Movement: 1968–2008," http://nationalhumanitiescenter.org/tserve/freedom/1917beyond/essays/crm2008.html.

69. Sue Bailey Thurman, "William Alexander Leidesdorff," in *Pioneers of Negro Origin in California* (San Francisco: Acme Publishing Company, 1952), http://www.sfmuseum.net/bio/leidesdorff.html.

70. Jack Forbes, *Afro-Americans in the Far West: A Handbook for Educators* (Berkeley: Far West Lab for Educational Research and Development), 19, http://files.eric.ed.gov/fulltext/ED025482.pdf.

71. Russell Lee Adams, *Great Negroes Past and Present* (Chicago: Afro-American Publishing Company, 1969), 76, 80.

72. Lapp, *Blacks in Gold Rush California*, 9–10.

73. William Sherman Savage, *Blacks in the West* (Westport CT: Greenwood Press, 1976), 132–33, 159.
74. Mary C. Lewis, "Those Spirited Black Settlers of the Wild West!," *Ebony Jr.* 14 (1978): 8–11.
75. Obituary, *California Star*, May 20, 1848, 3.
76. California State Legislature, Assembly Concurrent Resolution No. 131.

8

Indian, Civilizer, Slaveholder, and Politician

The Many Shapes of Peter Pitchlynn

Paul Barba

During an 1837 expedition west across the recently ceded Chickasaw territory in present-day Oklahoma, Peter Perkins Pitchlynn, a part-Choctaw, part-White man, encountered a small group of travelers camped on a dividing ridge between the Red and Washita Rivers. The all-White party consisted of a man by the name of Spaulding, a young woman, and three children, and their tales of travel and hardship left an indelible mark on Pitchlynn. As former "prisoners among the Pawnees," the young woman, her infant, and her two young brothers, age nine and seven, had just been sold to Spaulding and were on their way back to central Texas under his protection. As Pitchlynn and company interviewed the former captives, the "mournful look" on the young woman's face exposed to her listeners the horrors of watching her father, mother, sister, and brother murdered before her eyes, of the abuses and whippings she faced on a daily basis, and of being separated from her infant child.[1] Encounters such as this prompted Pitchlynn to conclude that the Native people of the West were "rude and wild," "a curiosity to any civilized man."[2] To modern-day readers, however, perhaps it is Pitchlynn's language that is most curious. As a part-Native man, Pitchlynn seems to have disparaged himself when he condemned the Native people of the North American West as wild and uncivilized. Naturally, one wonders, what compelled Pitchlynn to make such seemingly confident but self-deprecating declarations?

    This chapter investigates the shifting and sometimes contradictory
racial ideas of this multiethnic Choctaw man, Peter Pitchlynn. In many
ways, Pitchlynn was a remarkable individual whose lifespan—from
1806 to 1881—encompassed almost the entire nineteenth century and
covered some of the most pivotal years of Choctaw history, including
the formation of a politically unified Choctaw Nation; the emergence
of a strong Presbyterian missionary presence; removal from the Choctaw homeland; U.S. westward expansion; and Choctaw intervention
in the U.S. Civil War. Moreover, Pitchlynn seems to have had a hand
in nearly every Choctaw postremoval issue, conflict, and controversy.
In particular, this chapter explores how Pitchlynn navigated the various racial ideologies of his time, especially those relating to Native and
African American people. In this process of ideological navigation,
Pitchlynn positioned himself variously as an Indian man, a beacon
of civilization, a slaveholding patriarch, and a representative leader.
Thus, it was not uncommon for Pitchlynn to denounce the savagery
of his Native plainspeople neighbors while consuming the rhetoric
of the federal government, which sanctioned "uplift" programs that
targeted Choctaw people. In short, Pitchlynn was a shape shifter, a
person whose identity morphed and mutated according to changing
geographical, political, and cultural contexts. To a large extent, Pitchlynn's shape shifting was driven by social compulsion, as the racial
ideologies that flowered in the wake of Euro-American colonial expansion framed the broader outlines of his identity formation, especially
those that pitted White civilization against Indian and African savagery. Yet Pitchlynn was also a self-made shape shifter: he appropriated and performed multiple, sometimes unharmonious identities
to optimize economic, political, and cultural opportunities for the
Choctaw people, his family, and himself. Examination of Pitchlynn's
history reveals both the enduring elasticity and uncertainty of ideas
about race in nineteenth-century North America and the ability of
certain individuals to refashion those ideas on their own.
    Beyond the particularities of nineteenth-century North America,
Pitchlynn's ability to navigate externally imposed identity markers
and categories illuminates how shape shifting can serve as (1) a unique

offshoot to processes of displacement and relocation; (2) a viable individual response to ideologies of domination and exploitation; and (3) an alternative framework for scholars to understand the lived experiences of multiethnic people. The expulsion of Choctaw people from their ancient homelands in Alabama and Mississippi during the 1820s and 1830s meant that Pitchlynn and tens of thousands of others were suddenly in forced contact with communities of considerable political, economic, and cultural distinctness. In general, the removed Choctaw people had to figure out their place in this new foreign world of the southern Great Plains. Could they simply transplant their old lives here? Or would they spend most of their time contending with local dynamics and concerns? For some individuals, including Pitchlynn, it was in this context of abrupt cross-cultural interaction that older, more conventional identities took on new meanings and salience.[3]

But Pitchlynn's tendency to shape shift was not just the result of displacement and relocation: shape shifting allowed him to reconcile and adjust to seemingly contradictory ideas of control and conquest. Throughout his life, Pitchlynn was taught by government and educational agents that to be Indian was to be uncivilized, a notion that, on a rhetorical level, justified White American expansion and, on a practical level, fueled White American intervention and imposition. Pitchlynn, however, also came to value his Choctaw identity; he was proud to be an active member of the larger Choctaw community. Pitchlynn refashioned his sense of self in ways that both reflected and challenged conventional notions of Indianness and Choctawness. Depending on perspective, Pitchlynn could be many kinds of people at once. Yet shape shifting came with both great benefits and great costs. When Pitchlynn positioned himself as a civilized Native representative deserving of the benevolence of a paternalistic national government, he was able to curry the favor of U.S. officials. On the southern part of the Great Plains, where he built a life as an agriculturalist slaveholding patriarch, however, Pitchlynn was viewed by Native plainspeople as little more than an intruder and perhaps even as an agent of Euro-American colonial expansion.

Finally, a look at Pitchlynn's shape shifting offers scholars a useful model to interpret the histories of multiethnic people. Pitchlynn was born in 1806 to John Pitchlynn, a White American trader and government interpreter, and Sophia Folsom, a Choctaw woman. Among the Choctaws of the nineteenth century, Pitchlynn's heritage was not entirely unusual, as many other Choctaw families, such as the Folsoms, LeFlores, and Juzons, were the products of Choctaw-White unions. Nonetheless, scholars have struggled to situate these multiethnic men and women within the broader context of Choctaw society. How did Choctaw society receive these individuals? How did these individuals understand their own identities? What roles did these individuals play in bridging the worlds of Choctaws and Euro-Americans? Some scholars have argued that Pitchlynn and other multiethnic Choctaws were agents of vast historical change, harbingers of a new era of Choctaw decline and dependency. With their genealogical and cultural ties to Euro-America, these individuals supposedly were obsessed with reshaping the Choctaw people into market producers and consumers.[4] Other scholars, however, have dismissed the impact of nineteenth-century racial ideologies and paradigms on these multiethnic individuals. As Donna L. Akers has asserted, Choctaws were "unaffected by categories determined by white society outside the Choctaw Nation." "Most Choctaws," she has claimed, "defined people in a more traditional manner. If one lived like a Choctaw, acted like a Choctaw, and spoke Choctaw, then one was included in the community of Choctaw people."[5] And some writers, including Pitchlynn's twentieth-century biographer, W. David Baird, have reiterated the well-worn narrative of tragic racial betwixt-and-betweenness (which Paul Spickard outlines in the introductory chapter of this volume). According to Baird, multiethnic Choctaws were hybrid outcasts—isolated men and women who were torn between competing worlds and ultimately comfortable nowhere. Thus the individual lives of these part-White, part-Choctaw people were heartrending.[6]

Although recent scholarship has helped to debunk interpretations that link race to behavioral patterns, the persistent historiographical struggle to understand the identities and historical experiences of multiethnic people like Pitchlynn is in part a result of a lingering obsession with monoraciality—the notion that people can bear comfortably no more than one (racial) identity.[7] Yet individuals are not simply the sum of their ancestry; nor are they the resulting outputs of clashes between hegemonic identity frameworks that impose themselves upon individuals. They are, rather, the fluid and ever-changing products of multiple intersecting historical forces. As the following historical analysis of Pitchlynn illuminates, identities can be made, unmade, and remade over time and across space as experiences, interests, and perspectives change. Appreciation of shape shifting helps to account for the nuance and complexity inherent to identity formation.[8]

Ha-Tchoc-Tuck-Nee

Any analysis of Pitchlynn's identity must recognize the fact that he self-identified as a Choctaw man. Nothing made this more clear than his frequent use of the possessive pronouns "my" and "our" when speaking of the Choctaw people. Throughout his life, but especially as his political career progressed, Pitchlynn believed it was his responsibility to advance the welfare of *his* people, the Choctaws. In a letter to Israel Folsom dated February 15, 1858, for instance, Pitchlynn related his experiences in Washington DC, where he was advocating for the Choctaw Nation. His objectives, he claimed, were straightforward and simple: "My whole wish is to do all the good I can for my people."[9] Pitchlynn even had aspirations to author a sweeping history of the Choctaws, because "it is a book which our people should have." As a result, he spent considerable time gathering documents and other research materials. His findings, he believed, would resurrect a forgotten Choctaw past, histories that "the present generation of Choctaws know nothing of."[10] Pitchlynn's passion for and self-identification with the Choctaw people were undeniable.

But what exactly did it mean to be a member of the larger Choctaw community? According to James Carson Taylor, Choctaw identity was defined by adherence to a unique *moral economy*, a "[moral] system that sanctioned as proper or rejected as improper the outcomes of economic interaction." According to Taylor, "Choctaw culture . . . can be thought of as a grid that individuals carried in their heads and hearts and into which they fed received customs, personal knowledge, and perceptions of the present in order to determine appropriate and proper courses of action." Key to the Choctaw moral economy were four foundational structures of Choctaw culture: (1) chiefly political organization, (2) matrilineal kinship, (3) a gendered division of labor, and (4) a cosmological system based on the sanctity of a sacred circle that defined the limits of Choctaw society. From as early as the beginning of the eighteenth century, Choctaws were politically divided into three geographic districts, the Northeastern, Western, and Southeastern divisions, with each district under the influence of a single chief, who exerted control over the allocation of prestige goods. This political arrangement was important because it also highlighted broader cultural and historical divisions *among* the Choctaw people (e.g., the Six Towns people of the Southeastern district distinguished themselves from those of the other two districts by growing their hair long, flattening their heads, and tattooing their mouths blue). At times, district divisions even led to competing political alliances with non-Choctaw communities.[11]

Yet despite these differences, kinship practices kept Choctaws united. In Choctaw society, kinship was matrilineal: Choctaw children lived and identified with their mother's clan, or *iksa*, and it was the responsibility of the mother and any maternal uncles to raise the children. Furthermore, matrilineal ties influenced economic activity. Although agricultural land was subject to usufruct rights (open to common use, provided the land was not abused or wasted) and thus never owned in the Euro-private property sense, land distribution was based on matrilineal ties. And as women were in charge of the home, domestic property, and land, gender divisions characterized Choctaw labor. Therefore, economic matters were the concern of Choctaw women. On the flip side, it was the realm of men to engage in external matters such as diplomacy and warfare. Hunting was also an appropriate male behavior, but Choctaw men had to be careful when crossing the boundaries beyond the sacred circle of the "beloved people" (i.e., into the outside world). Only certain members of Choctaw society were permitted to venture beyond the boundaries of the Choctaw social

world. As Taylor has remarked, Choctaw society "demanded constant vigilance. To maintain balance between the three worlds and to
ensure order within the sacred circle, chiefs had to redistribute goods,
men and women had to follow the rules of kinship and do the work
appropriate for each gender, and all Choctaws had to avoid polluting
themselves and their society."[12]

Much of Pitchlynn's life reflects his grounding in this distinct Choctaw moral economy. Throughout his life, Pitchlynn was acquainted
with many of the standards, expectations, and values of the larger
Choctaw society. Even though Pitchlynn spent most of his early life
under the care of his White father, John, his home was located in
the middle of Choctaw territory. Most of the children with whom
Pitchlynn played were Choctaw, and his childhood friends named
young Pitchlynn Ha-tchoc-tuck-nee, or Snapping Turtle. This alone
suggested Choctaw efforts to incorporate Pitchlynn within the Choctaw social framework. Moreover, Pitchlynn and his friends enjoyed
ball playing, which was among the most prominent social activities of Choctaws during the eighteenth and nineteenth centuries.[13]
In at least these respects, Pitchlynn's youth was unremarkable for a
Choctaw child.

Evidence also suggests that from an early age, Pitchlynn perceived
himself as different from his White father and lighter-skinned siblings.
Reflecting on his childhood in a letter dated January 1835, Pitchlynn
commented: "My mothers children are all very white except myself
and sister. . . . [W]e show the Choctaw in our black eyes & hair." Here
Pitchlynn indicated an awareness of the power of physical characteristics in establishing the boundaries of group identity, and for him,
his dark features accounted for his inclusion in Choctaw society (and
exclusion from White America). Furthermore, Pitchlynn's mother,
Sophia, had long sent mixed messages to him about the value of speaking in the Choctaw language. According to Pitchlynn (who was the
eldest son), his mother's aversion to teaching her other children the
Choctaw language—even though "she would never speak English"—
convinced Pitchlynn that "none but myself have learned the Choctaw language perfectly." Yet Pitchlynn still invested much time and

energy into advancing his knowledge of the language, and he ultimately became among the first to write proficiently in the Choctaw
language.[14]

But Pitchlynn's mother was by no means his only source of Choctaw identity. Others also encouraged Pitchlynn to embrace his Choctaw ties throughout his life, including an older multiethnic Choctaw
man by the name of James McDonald. Through his frequent correspondence with McDonald, Pitchlynn expanded his knowledge of
Choctaw stories and storytelling, which reinforced his understandings
of Choctaw gender roles and other cultural conventions. McDonald
also encouraged Pitchlynn to consider the changing historical nature
of Choctaw identity. According to McDonald, traditional Choctaws
had an unparalleled linguistic gift for storytelling, that is, for describing the natural world in marvelously descriptive ways. But "in tales
of high imagination," he argued, "the Indians are deficient." It was
only through intergenerational contact with Euro-American colonists,
McDonald claimed, that Choctaws were becoming more intellectually
advanced. As deficient as the collective Choctaw high imagination may
have been at the time to McDonald, "it is, as I conceive, simply for the
want of improvement. They have the stamina, if in early life it could
be drawn out, cultivated, and polished." It is important to note that
even as he praised the "richness" of the English language, McDonald
consistently commented on the disruptive nature of Euro-influences.
From McDonald's perspective, the outside forces that had penetrated
the sacred circle of the Choctaw people were a cause for concern.[15]

Written toward the end of 1830, McDonald's letters to Pitchlynn
would not have been necessarily foundational to his identity, but the
correspondence between the two men demonstrated Pitchlynn's desire
to discover what it meant to be a Choctaw man—and how the experience of discovering one's identity is rarely a seamless, straightforward process.[16] Moreover, their correspondence also revealed some
of the ways in which Pitchlynn and his fellow Choctaws attempted
to reconcile and to understand the many, often contradictory messages they had been receiving from Europeans and Euro-Americans
for decades. For Pitchlynn, as for many other Choctaws of the first

half of the nineteenth century, these messages originated from two principal sources: Europeanized educational institutions and the U.S. government. Both sources were fundamental to Pitchlynn's understanding of civilization, and his appropriation of such messages speaks to his shape shifting abilities.

His Father's Son

Pitchlynn's father, John Pitchlynn, made every effort to provide his children with a European-style education. But aside from the visits from traders, travelers, and ministers to the Pitchlynn trading post along the Gaines Trace (the main road that connected the Tennessee and Tombigbee Rivers), few Europeanized educational opportunities existed for the Pitchlynn children prior to the missionary activities of the American Board of Commissioners for Foreign Missions (ABCFM) in the 1820s. In fact, it was not until 1820 that the elder Pitchlynn was able to convince both the ABCFM representative, Cyrus Kingsbury, and Choctaw leaders of the prudence of building an educational institution in the vicinity of the Pitchlynn trading house.[17] By this time, however, John Pitchlynn had already made plans to send his son Peter to a school in Tennessee. The Tennessee school, known as Charity Hall, was actually a Chickasaw school established by the Reverend Robert Bell in 1820. Built on the east bank of the Tombigbee River, the school brought together dozens of children from various Native locales and schooled Pitchlynn and at least two of his brothers in "the branches of Knowledge" such as "reading, Writing, Arrithmetic, & the English grammer [sic]," as well as "moral and religious" matters.[18]

Pitchlynn quickly took up the mantle of his father, and his educational aspirations eventually led him to a handful of other schools and universities. Even as he pursued his own studies, Pitchlynn made efforts to provide educational opportunities for other Choctaws. In November 1825, for instance, nineteen-year-old Pitchlynn aided in the enrollment of twenty-one Choctaw youths at Senator Richard M. Johnston's Choctaw Academy in Kentucky. According to Pitchlynn, he was in favor of such schooling beyond the limits of the Choctaw Nation "because I was educated in the bosom of our white brethren, in

Tennessee, and I know how to appreciate the inestimable blessings arising from an education among them."[19] Pitchlynn would later become
superintendent of the Choctaw Academy in the 1840s and would continue to figure prominently in the molding of Choctaw youths.[20]

Pitchlynn's contact with Euro-and Euro-American travelers, traders, ministers, educators, and missionaries was instrumental in framing his ideas about civilization and the nature of humanity. It was
through these conversations, school lessons, prayers, and sermons
that Pitchlynn was able to establish an intellectual foundation for
understanding the origins of humankind, one that emphasized the
common ancestry of all (i.e., monogenism). It was likewise through
this contact that Pitchlynn picked up on the interrelated nature of
Europeanized education and Christian instruction. At all these educational institutions—the ABCFM-led schools, Charity Hall, and the
Choctaw Academy—educating Choctaw and other Native students
meant civilizing them. The instructors of these institutions saw little distinction between schooling Indians in reading, writing, and
mathematics and teaching them how to act like so-called civilized
(i.e., Euro-American) people. As part of their education, Choctaw students were to learn proper cultivation of the land, Christian prayer,
and other facets of Euro-American social and economic protocol. In
an 1820 report on missionary efforts, the Reverend Cyrus Kingsbury
explained: "In addition to the common rudiments of education, the
boys are acquiring a practical knowledge of agriculture, in its various branches; and the girls, while out of school, are employed under
the direction of the female missionaries, in different parts of domestic labor. . . . All the children are placed entirely under our control."
For too long, educators preached, the Choctaws had suffered in their
state of savagery: "As a people, the Choctaws, like most other uncivilized tribes, are in total darkness on moral and religious subjects;
exposed to various imaginary terrors from supposed witchcraft and
other causes, addicted to the intemperate use of ardent spirits;—in
short, ignorant, degraded, and miserable."[21] The missionaries made
it clear that it was incumbent upon them as educators and guides to
lift the Choctaws out of their miserable state.

Furthermore, the missionaries—as well as many other Euro-Americans—believed that much of the Choctaws' supposed savagery lay in their inverted gender roles and illiteracy. Missionaries and other White American observers saw Choctaw women's responsibility for agricultural production in Choctaw society as evidence of Choctaw men's unmanliness. If Indians and Choctaws in particular were to advance in civilization, Choctaws would have to right their wrong gender roles. As the ABCFM Prudential Committee argued in 1821, "The education of females is justly considered as very important, in reference to the advancing of civilization of natives." And just as critical was instruction in written language. ABCFM officials lauded their missionaries' efforts: "They have put in the hands of barbarians this mighty instrument of a written language. . . . They have given a shape and a name to their barbarous articulations; and the children of men, who lived on the prey of the wilderness, are now forming in village schools to the arts and the decencies of cultivated life."[22]

Schooled under similar programs, Pitchlynn drew connections between religion, education, and civilization. For Pitchlynn, the rhetorical relationship between the binaries of ignorance and knowledge and of wilderness and civilization were clear. In a letter to Gideon Lincecum, Pitchlynn thanked his friend for sharing his civilizing wisdom with him: "We dwelt in a remote wilderness where the light of Science and civilization had never shot a single ray. Twas then you came and took me by the hand and led me by your council to the source of knowledge."[23] Pitchlynn often voiced his gratitude regarding his Europeanized education; to Pitchlynn, education was essential for Choctaw "improvement" and for fostering the qualities of a civilized man.

Such were the racialized ideologies that Pitchlynn encountered and imbibed during his schooling. He learned that Choctaws, like other Indians, were uncivilized. Missionaries regularly had pointed to a number of supposedly barbaric aspects of Choctaw culture, noting Choctaw witchcraft, their gender inversion of labor practices, and a deep moral ignorance. But all hope was not lost. Pitchlynn was taught—and truly believed—that Choctaws were full humans, descendants of Adam and Eve like his Euro-American counterparts, and could change for the better. As far as he was concerned, Choctaws were destined to be a central part of civilization's ultimate triumph. From this perspective, Pitchlynn crafted a Choctaw identity that could accommodate the outside pressures of an imposing White American society while maintaining his own human dignity.

The Diplomat

If Pitchlynn's education offered him an intellectual foundation for his ideas about race, civilization, and savagery, his work as a diplomat provided him with a high-stakes forum for the expression of such ideas. From as early as the 1820s Pitchlynn was engaged in diplomatic affairs. From 1826 to 1828 Pitchlynn acted as secretary of the interdistrict council meetings.[24] In 1828 Pitchlynn was selected to represent the Choctaws during an expedition to survey the western lands ceded to them at Doak's Stand, and he and his father were among the several thousand who met with federal agents at Dancing Rabbit Creek in Noxubee County, Mississippi. Almost immediately after relocating to present-day Oklahoma, Pitchlynn was elected district chief, and after the formation of the Choctaw Constitution, he acted as principal Choctaw commissioner in the 1837 discussions at Doaksville. Pitchlynn would eventually be elected to the position of local councilman in 1842, but throughout the 1840s and 1850s Pitchlynn devoted most of his political energy toward advocating on behalf of the Choctaws in Washington DC. Pitchlynn's political career culminated when he was elected principal chief of the Choctaw Nation in 1864.[25]

It was in the realm of diplomatic relations that Pitchlynn seems to have expressed his shape shifting tendencies most clearly. He rose to prominence at a time when U.S. leaders were moving away from Indian assimilation programs and toward wholesale removal and expulsion; that is, he became a politician in an era when U.S. policymakers were more concerned with the exclusion of (rather than the inclusion of) Native people. Thus, although early nineteenth-century national leaders such as Thomas Jefferson expressed a desire for Native and White American communities to "meet and blend together, to intermix, and become one people," the new generation of policymakers that emerged in the 1830s was more aggressively fatalistic.[26] During treaty talks at Dancing Rabbit Creek in September 1830, for instance, the two U.S. representatives, Colonel John Coffee and Secretary of War John Eaton, warned the Choctaws: "Decide to remove, and liberal provisions will be made to carry you to a country where you can be happy. . . . There your great father can be your friend; there he can keep the white man's laws from interrupting and disturbing you; and there, too, he will guard you against all enemies, whether they be white or red."[27] Pitchlynn's response to such pressures was often an appeal from the position of one civilized man to another, and his frequent appeals echoed the civilization discourse of missionaries and government officials. In a letter written in 1832, Pitchlynn appealed directly to Secretary of War Lewis Cass: "I beg, sir, that for a whole nation to give up their whole country, and remove to a distant, wild, and uncultivated land, more for the benefit of the Government than the Choctaws, is a consideration which, I hope, the Government will always cherish with the liveliest sensibility. The privations of a whole nation before setting out, their turmoil and losses on the road, and settling their homes in a wild world, are all calculated to embitter the human heart."[28]

A wild world was where the federal government had banished his people, Pitchlynn argued, and the relocation was certainly lamentable. What the federal government could do, he claimed, was to make the Choctaws' transition from their tamed homeland to an untamed wilderness seamless. This was necessary because denying assistance was sure to "embitter the human heart." With this emotional claim, Pitchlynn was making a strong point that the new wave of scientific racist thought was trying to dismiss: Choctaws were just as human as the White Americans who were forcing them to leave their ancient homeland.

Taken as a whole, the use of civilization discourse allowed Pitchlynn to posture Choctaws in perceptibly advantageous ways. Pitchlynn's narration of recent occurrences, highlighted by the critical event of removal to a wild land, wove together disparate messages in a way that advanced what he perceived to be Choctaw interests. Not only did this strategy provide a defense for Choctaw claims to their early nineteenth-century homeland, but it also asserted the basic humanity of the Choctaws. As Pitchlynn understood the matter, he and his people could be both civilized *and* Indian. He expressed as much to Osage representatives during a diplomatic expedition in the 1820s: "Though they might throw away their eagle-feathers, and live in permanent cabins, there was no danger of losing their identity or name."[29]

The Slaveholding Patriarch

Pitchlynn's experiences with educational institutions and the federal government were two of the more important sources of his identity, but other facets of his life, particularly his role in the enslavement of African Americans, also presented him with ways of advantageously forging his identity in nineteenth-century North America. Pitchlynn was born to a slave-owning father, so slavery was nothing new to him when he began to amass his own collection of human chattel during his young adulthood. Early in life, Pitchlynn was entrusted with managing plantation affairs while his father was away on diplomatic missions, and the young Pitchlynn always knew he would appropriate some of his father's human property later in life.[30] There are also some indications that John Pitchlynn asked his sons James and Peter to engage in slave trading on his behalf. By the late 1820s Pitchlynn owned at least four of his own slaves, and he would use removal and relocation to Indian Territory as an opportunity to expand his slaveholdings by converting his real estate assets into transportable slave property. By October 1832 Pitchlynn owned or had an interest in forty-five African American slaves out west, and by the end of the Civil War at least 135 slaves were under his ownership.[31]

Pitchlynn's role as a Choctaw slaveholder epitomized his shape shifting attributes. For Pitchlynn, as for other prominent Choctaws, slaveholding allowed him to maintain his responsibilities as a chiefly figure while still actively participating in the greater economic changes of the nineteenth century. As previously mentioned, accumulation of wealth and goods had long been among the most important features of chiefly authority in Choctaw society. Since the start of the eighteenth century, if not earlier, Choctaw leaders had consolidated their authority through their ability to redistribute goods to their followers. When trade accelerated between Choctaws and Europeans during the eighteenth century, Choctaw chiefs continued to pursue their chiefly duties by securing favorable trade relationships and access to goods outside of their communities. Slaveholding was yet another opportunity for Choctaw leaders to amass and control the distribution of wealth throughout Choctaw country. Greenwood LeFlore, for instance, spent his whole life building his fortune upon the backs of slaves, reaping the benefits of participation in the market economy of the Atlantic world. But LeFlore did not hoard his profits; instead, he was always sure to open his home to other Choctaws and share his wealth.[32] At least in this respect, it was not unnatural or improper for an aspiring Choctaw leader to pursue slave-based wealth. Choctaws had long understood that chiefs were authorized to accumulate wealth through slavery as Pitchlynn and LeFlore did.

But slaveholding did not come without its complications for Pitchlynn and the other slaveholding Choctaws in the aftermath of mass removal and relocation. Two issues demanded that Pitchlynn be flexible with his slaveholding identity: the increasing involvement of missionaries in the slavery controversies of the United States (which extended to Indian Territory) and the racial nature of slavery in North America. For most of the first half of Pitchlynn's life, the enslavement of African and African American men, women, and children did not present significant philosophical problems. The ideological frameworks of missionaries, educators, and government agents prior to the 1840s—with their emphasis on Euro-domination and a civilizing mission—were capacious enough to allow for the enslavement of other humans. In fact, nearly all of these messengers actively engaged in slaveholding: the missionaries living among the Choctaws held several slaves in bondage to help maintain their missions; African American slaves built and sustained some of the operations at the Choctaw Academy in Kentucky; and many of the federal Indian agents either owned or traded in slaves. As Israel Folsom reminded Pitchlynn in 1848, even the stories inscribed in scripture provided a defense of slavery: "We have abundant proof from Holy Bible of the right granted to buy bond men and bond women to inherit & possess our children after as forever."[33]

The North-South sectional controversies prevalent in the United States during the mid-nineteenth century, however, found their way to Choctaw country by the late 1840s, and the ABCFM missionaries were pressured to move against slavery.[34] The problem with the ABCFM controversy over slavery as it related to Pitchlynn was that it, along with the broader dissemination of abolitionist literature, represented a firm intellectual assault on the compatibility of racial slavery and Christian-based civilization. Prior to the 1840s Pitchlynn's interests as a slaveholder and his drive for civilization worked hand-in-hand for him; slaveholding allowed him to fulfill his chiefly duties, to avoid the Choctaw shame of working in the fields as a man, to worship a Christian God, and to demonstrate that Choctaws could engage in civilized (i.e., agricultural) economic production. Abolitionists and, to a lesser extent, Christians at large were beginning to challenge the assumptions that enslavement was the natural (and best) condition for African Americans and that slavery and Christianity were compatible. This intellectual assault on slavery could have caused Pitchlynn to rethink his views on racial slavery. But it did not.

As it did on most slaveholders in the United States, abolitionism had the opposite effect on Pitchlynn. Pitchlynn's ideas regarding African American inferiority had the potential to undermine many of Pitchlynn's beliefs regarding the nature of humanity and civilization, but for Pitchlynn this never happened. In fact, he thought rather poorly of African Americans. His correspondence with friends and relatives often revealed his recurring use of the belittling term *boy* to refer to his male slaves, and he sometimes expressed his disgust when encountering supposedly "insolent" African Americans. During the sectional crisis, Pitchlynn was among the most outspoken critics of abolitionism. He would reveal his understanding of the true nature of human differences when he assumed office as principal chief of the Choctaw Nation in 1864. Speaking in defense of the Confederacy, Pitchlynn declared: "There is no other hope left for us; for who would seek conditions of pardon, or except [*sic*] them when offered by the Government of Abraham Lincoln, which has waged the most cruel, relentless and desolating war that ever disgraced any nation that claimed to be civilized and refined. And what confidence can a Choctaw have in that Government whose perverted or unnatural will, reverses the social order, and arrays brother in deadly conflict against brother for negro freedom and equality."[35]

Pitchlynn had long believed that Choctaws were capable of achieving all that Euro-Americans had achieved; they only required the proper circumstances and opportunities. African American capabilities, however, were an entirely different issue, he reasoned. As a civilized slaveholding man, Pitchlynn knew how to reformulate issues of identity to his own interests and expectations. In matters concerning slavery and African American people, Pitchlynn was an unabashed racist.

The Beacon of Civilization

Thus, when Pitchlynn witnessed the White former slaves of Pawnee Indians during his 1837 expedition out west (mentioned at the outset of this chapter), what struck him most forcefully was the horror of their captivity among uncivilized people, not necessarily captivity itself. Upon reflecting on the captivity of the former slaves, Pitchlynn scribbled in his journal: "I am of the opinion that the Taweash or Pawnees as they are some times called are the most Cruel Indians to prisoners than any tribe."[36] Because the former captives originated from a civilized (White) world and because Pitchlynn was also a civilized man, he could not help but share in their suffering. It did not matter that he kept his own slaves in captivity, because his slaves were Black and held captive by a civilized man. But as Pitchlynn would learn quickly in the aftermath of forced relocation to Indian Territory in the 1830s, living a civilized existence was not always easy or attainable. Indeed, life on the Great Plains, where Indian Territory was located, was very different. Nomadic and seminomadic Native plainspeople ruled the region and asserted considerable economic and cultural influence. Markets were not easily regulated by government administrators, and sedentary lifestyles were constantly threatened by attacks and raids. Choctaws were able to carve out their own spaces in Indian Territory, but the larger geopolitical outlook reflected plainspeople's power and dominion.[37]

As for all Choctaws, the move west weighed heavily on Pitchlynn. When Pitchlynn first moved his family west, he had selected a site at New Hope, near the Choctaw Agency at Skullyville. Hopes ran high, but river floods, illnesses, and other maladies pressured Pitchlynn to relocate his family after only a short stay. Over the next few years, he moved his family to various locations: the Red River area (1833), Mountain Fork (1834), and Wheelock Mission (1837). And in addition to the instability of his living situations, the move west tore Pitchlynn from his beloved father and mother. Letters from John to Peter bear testament to the pain and anguish that resulted from relocation: "I am truly sorry we are so fare [sic] a Part and I am so old that there is not much hopes of our ever seeing each other."[38] Leaving his parents only exacerbated the trauma of relocation for Pitchlynn. During this period, spatial shifting was as integral to his identity formation as anything else.

Pitchlynn was terribly disappointed with the wild nature of his new habitat. Nearly everywhere he looked, he witnessed a dearth of civilization. The western lands were abundantly "prairie" and lacked the natural resources required to transplant and rebuild his people's developing civilization. In fact, everything needed to be tamed; even the animals were "exceedingly wild," in Pitchlynn's estimation. It took the efforts of friends and relatives to comfort him. In a letter to Pitchlynn dated November 28, 1833, Samuel Garland encouraged Pitchlynn to embrace his role as a civilizing force in the new Choctaw territory. Garland wrote that Pitchlynn's new land near the Red River was a fitting place for such an esteemed man: "I see no alteration or no difficulty why that a man should not live contented or satisfied in this civilized country as well as in that wild region."[39] Friendly encouragement aside, Pitchlynn and company were still left to wonder: Could the Choctaw people live peacefully in their new homeland? Could they successfully spread civilization?

As the sudden neighbors of autonomous Native peoples, Pitchlynn

and other Choctaws could not escape the turmoil of the western frontier. Reports of Comanche, Pawnee, and Kiowa depredations ran
rampant across Choctaw country. Friends, relatives, and state officials cautioned one another about the dangers of the Plains Indians.
In May 1831, for instance, Colonel Matthew Arbuckle reported: "The
Commanche and Pawnee Indians in the summer resort in great numbers on the boarders [sic] of the Cross Timbers, and within about one
hundred and forty, or fifty miles of this post. In the Fall they generally go further South and West. They will continue to do injury to our
citizens and the Red People on this Frontier, until they are severely
chastised; or they have a permanent interest to induce them to remain
at peace." By removing to the southern portion of the Great Plains,
Choctaw immigrants had encroached upon Comanche, Pawnee, and
Kiowa territory, and this remained apparent to the Choctaws for
decades. In 1846 Pitchlynn's brother Thomas wrote to Peter regarding "Commanches [who] have killed some & a family in Texas." Even
as late as 1858, Pitchlynn was receiving news of "hostile" Indians who
"intend to make war generally on the frontier."[40] In the West, Pitchlynn and his sedentary counterparts were intruders. From the perspective of the local inhabitants, Pitchlynn and his people took on
the shape of agents of Euro-American colonialism rather than that
of fellow plainspeople.

It seems as though Pitchlynn never really felt satisfied with the
life he built in Choctaw country after removal. Although he invested
considerable time and financial resources in his plantations, his slaveholding ventures yielded only moderate financial returns. Even as
Pitchlynn found his calling in diplomatic advocacy, spending year
after year in Washington DC, such activities stole his time and energy
from a life with his family at Wheelock Mission. Moreover, his son
Lycurgus grew as restless with the conditions out west as his father
did. "I want to live in a civilized country," Lycurgus wrote to his
father in 1858. "I want society—Intellectual society. It will be years
before this country will be anything. I want to mingle daily with
smart men. I want to come in contact with mind[,] intellect and talent. A man living in this country his energies are apt to stagnate."

Relocation to a wild world made the story that Pitchlynn told of his people tragic:

> Once our possessions embraced the valuable and fertile territory now included in the States of Mississippi, Alabama, and Louisiana, and over which our sway was undisputed and supreme. There the bones of our ancestors for many generations repose, and there the Choctaws hoped to remain to watch over them, and to be perpetuated as a free and independent nation. But another and stronger race came and swept us away into a distant and wilderness land, where we had to struggle against the depressing effects of sad and painful reflections upon the hard and unyielding policy which deprived us of our father-land and cherished homes.[41]

The Shape Shifter

As unflattering and, in some regards, self-deprecating as Pitchlynn's descriptions of western-dwelling Native people were, it was through the adoption of a civilized persona that Pitchlynn gained comfort in his role as leader of the Choctaw people. As a prominent member of Choctaw society, Pitchlynn saw himself as carrying out a sacred, manly duty, that is, gauging and engaging the outside world beyond his community. The language he used, however, was that of a man who was bearing the torch of civilization. Contact with White traders, federal agents, missionaries, his Choctaw elders, and many others had molded Pitchlynn's understanding of self and purpose in such a way that he could appropriate and deploy seemingly contradictory ideas in unique but successful ways. When Charles Dickens ran into Pitchlynn aboard a steamboat in 1842, Dickens caught a glimpse of the shape shifting Pitchlynn: "He was dressed in our ordinary everyday costume, which hung about his fine figure loosely, and with indifferent grace. On my telling him that I regretted not to see him in his own attire, he threw up his right arm, for a moment, as though he were brandishing some heavy weapon, and answered, as he let it fall again, that his race were losing many things besides their dress; and would soon be seen upon the earth no more: but he wore it at home, he added proudly."[42] Like his clothing, Pitchlynn's identity shifted according to context.

In many respects, Pitchlynn was a man of his times. Born during an era of massive change, he spoke multiple languages, engaged in new and speculative economic endeavors, pushed for political change, advocated for the political autonomy of his people, participated in the sectionalism of the 1840s, 1850s, and 1860s, and loudly proclaimed his love for and amazement with an all-powerful God. But despite such seemingly typical qualities and characteristics, Pitchlynn often articulated ideas that revealed a man who shifted across various, often contradictory identities. Pitchlynn's ideas about race were, after all, out of sync with the prevailing scientific racism of the mid-nineteenth century.[43] While intellectuals, scholars, scientists, and politicians were decrying the impotence of the flailing federal government's Indian civilization programs, Pitchlynn was marching on with the belief that he and his people, as Indians, were on their way to being as civilized as the White Americans to the east. Seeing himself as a civilized man who was shining the light of civilization upon his people, Pitchlynn could walk and talk with an air of confidence that impressed many observers, including the famous author Dickens.

While Pitchlynn's unique embrace of civilization discourse may have comforted and empowered him amid the rapid changes he and his people experienced during the nineteenth century, it was not without its social and political costs. By adopting Euro-and Euro-American ideas about certain inherent differences between humans, Pitchlynn internalized notions of African and African American inferiority. As far as Pitchlynn was concerned, no evidence existed that African Americans deserved the rights and privileges of civilized men and women. Enslavement, rather, was the appropriate condition for Black people, and it was neither his place nor his interest to protest or even suggest otherwise. So Pitchlynn and a significant number of his Choctaw counterparts actively spread anti-Black racial slavery to the West. And in relation to the so-called wild Indians of the Great Plains, Pitchlynn believed he was a civilizer. As such, Pitchlynn often self-consciously alienated himself from the ruling plainspeople of his new homeland. This effectively meant that his people had to put their faith in an untrustworthy White American government, find new (also immigrant) allies, or go it alone in a foreign land. In the end, none of these strategies proved very successful.

But all of this is not to suggest that Pitchlynn suffered from any sort of personal psychological distress from his creative navigation of the many racial and cultural formulations that he encountered throughout his life. Although his ideas contributed to the broader dehumanization of non-White peoples in North America, Pitchlynn thought it personally advantageous to characterize plainspeople as wild and African Americans as inferior. Pitchlynn's recorded lamentations seem to have come from his recognition of the overwhelming nature of White American expansion and not from his own inability to adjust to changing times. Pitchlynn continuously worked to make the most of his circumstances, and his shape shifting positioned him as a unique agent of historical change. Even as Euro-Americans were lumping all Native people together in degrading, racialized terms, Pitchlynn adapted to the ideologies and cultural frameworks that he found valuable while discarding or ignoring those that failed to speak to his distinct historical experiences. Thus, despite appearances to the contrary, it was not difficult for Pitchlynn to be simultaneously Choctaw and White, a slaveholder and a critic of captivity, or even a civilized man with a savage past.

Notes

1. Peter P. Pitchlynn Journal, n.d., folder 3, box 6, Peter Perkins Pitchlynn Papers, Choctaw Nation, Native American Manuscripts, Western History Digital Collections, University of Oklahoma, Norman. This journal has been published as the tail-end portion of Peter Pitchlynn's "diary" in Peter Pitchlynn, "A Man between Nations: The Diary of Peter Pitchlynn," ed. Speer Morgan and Greg Michaelson, *Missouri Review* 14 (1991): 90–92.

2. Pitchlynn, "Man between Nations," 70, 76.

3. Pitchlynn's history seems to support Fredrik Barth's contention that identities tend to gain greater comprehension, articulation, and currency during

historical moments of cross-cultural encounters. Fredrik Barth, *Ethnic Groups and Boundaries: The Social Organization of Culture Difference*, 2nd ed. (Long Grove: Waveland Press, 1998), 9–38.

4. Richard White and Sandra Faiman-Silva have advanced the dependency argument. Richard White, *The Roots of Dependency: Subsistence, Environment, and Social Change among the Choctaws, Pawnees, and Navajos* (Lincoln: University of Nebraska Press, 1983), xiv–xix; Sandra Faiman-Silva, *Choctaws at the Crossroads: The Political Economy of Class and Culture in the Oklahoma Timber Region* (Lincoln: University of Nebraska Press, 1997), 3–6. Also see Clara Sue Kidwell, *Choctaws and Missionaries in Mississippi, 1818–1918* (Norman: University of Oklahoma Press, 1995), 18–23.

5. Donna L. Akers, *Living in the Land of Death: The Choctaw Nation, 1830–1860* (East Lansing: Michigan State University Press, 2004), xix. Although much more considerate of external influences, the works of Barbara Krauthamer and James Carson Taylor make similar arguments regarding the importance of Choctaw cultural conventions, specifically, adherence to matrilineal descent, in determining the identities of multiethnic Choctaw individuals. Barbara Krauthamer, *Black Slaves, Indian Masters: Slavery, Emancipation, and Citizenship in the Native American South* (Chapel Hill: University of North Carolina Press, 2013), 30–31; James Carson Taylor, "Greenwood LeFlore: Southern Creole, Choctaw Chief," in *Pre-Removal Choctaw History: Exploring New Paths*, ed. Greg O'Brien (Norman: University of Oklahoma Press, 2008), 221–22; Taylor, *Searching for the Bright Path: The Mississippi Choctaws from Prehistory to Removal* (Lincoln: University of Nebraska Press, 1999), 5–7.

6. W. David Baird, *Peter Pitchlynn: Chief of the Choctaws* (Norman: University of Oklahoma Press, 1972), 19–22. Also see Henry Benson, *Life among the Choctaw Indians, and Sketches of the South-West* (Cincinnati: L. Swormstedt & A. Poe, 1860), 101–6.

7. Recent scholarship on Native American history has been more nuanced when it comes to analyzing multiethnic identities in Native America. See, for instance, the works of Tiya Miles and Claudio Saunt, which emphasize the multiple sources of Native identity. Tiya Miles, *Ties That Bind: The Story of an Afro-Cherokee Family in Slavery and Freedom* (Berkeley: University of California Press, 2005), 104–5; Claudio Saunt, *A New Order of Things: Property, Power, and the Transformation of the Creek Indians, 1733–1816* (Cambridge: Cambridge University Press, 1999), 67–89. Tensions, nonetheless, remain among those who claim Native ancestry. Anger, bitterness, and frustration erupted, for instance, at a conference on Black Indians at Dartmouth College in April 2000 as participants fought over ownership of Native identity.

See Claudio Saunt, *Black, White, and Indian: Race and the Unmaking of an American Family* (Oxford: Oxford University Press, 2005), 6–9. For a discussion of monoraciality, see G. Reginald Daniel, *More Than Black? Multiracial Identity and the New Racial Order* (Philadelphia: Temple University Press, 2002), 115–16, 178–79.

8. Michael Omi and Howard Winant have offered a useful explanation of *identity formation*, particularly as it relates to the history of the United States. According to Omi and Winant, "The definitions, meanings, and overall coherence of prevailing social categories are always subject to multiple interpretations. No social category rises to the level of being understood as a fixed, objective, social fact" (*Racial Formation in the United States*, 3rd ed. [New York: Routledge, 2015], 105).

9. Peter P. Pitchlynn to Israel Folsom, February 15, 1858, folder 14, box 3, Pitchlynn Papers.

10. Peter P. Pitchlynn to Daniel Folsom, June 15, 1858, folder 27, box 3, Pitchlynn Papers.

11. The four foundational structures of Choctaw culture are outlined in Taylor, *Searching*, 5, 11–25. Choctaw politics and economy are discussed in Arthur H. DeRosier Jr., *The Removal of the Choctaw Indians* (Knoxville: University of Tennessee Press, 1970), 8–12. For discussions of Choctaw factionalism, see Patricia Galloway, "Choctaw Factionalism and Civil War, 1746–1750," in O'Brien, *Pre-Removal Choctaw History*, 74; and Kidwell, *Choctaws and Missionaries*, 3–4, 15–17.

12. Taylor, *Searching*, 25. For a discussion of kinship and gender, see Faiman-Silva, *Choctaws at the Crossroads*, 7–13; and Fred Eggan, "Historical Changes in the Choctaw Kinship System," *American Anthropologist* 39 (January 1937): 34–52. Angie Debo has explained Choctaw agricultural life in *The Rise and Fall of the Choctaw Republic* (Norman: University of Oklahoma Press, 1961), 10–11.

13. Baird, *Peter Pitchlynn*, 6–7, 19.

14. Peter P. Pitchlynn to [unknown], January 12, 1835, folder 8, box 7, Pitchlynn Papers. Clara Sue Kidwell has discussed Pitchlynn's role as a student of written Choctaw in *A Gathering of Statesmen: Records of the Choctaw Council Meetings, 1826–1828*, ed. Marcia Haag, Henry J. Willis, and Clara Sue Kidwell (Norman: University of Oklahoma Press, 2013), 30.

15. Peter P. Pitchlynn to James McDonald, December 13 and 17, 1830, folder 19, box 1, Pitchlynn Papers.

16. By the end of his life, Pitchlynn was even known to be an authority on so-called traditional Choctaw narratives. Charles Lanman, *Recollections of*

Curious Characters and Pleasant Places (Edinburgh: David Douglas, 1881), 93–94.

17. The first report on ABCFM activities among the Choctaws was published in 1820: American Board of Commissioners for Foreign Missions, *Report of the American Board of Commissioners for Foreign Missions; Compiled from Documents Laid before the Board, at the Eleventh Annual Meeting, Which Was Held at Hartford, Con. Sept. 20, & 21, 1820* (Boston: Chocker and Brewster, 1820), 55. For a summary of ABCFM activities, see Joseph Tracy, "History of the American Board of Commissioners for Foreign Missions: Compiled Chiefly from the Published and Unpublished Documents of the Board," in *History of American Missions to the Heathen, from Their Commencement to the Present Time* (Worcester: Spooner & Howland, 1840), 100.

18. Baird discusses Pitchlynn's school years in Baird, *Peter Pitchlynn*, 17, 21. Pitchlynn's memories of the schoolhouse were summarized in Charles Lanman, "Peter Pitchlynn, Chief of the Choctaws," *Atlantic Monthly* 25 (April 1870): 486. Carolyn Thomas Foreman has detailed the work of the Charity Hall school in Carolyn Thomas Foreman, "Charity Hall: An Early Chickasaw School," *Chronicles of Oklahoma* 11 (September 1933): 914, 923. For a report on the school, see Indian Affairs, *American State Papers: Documents, Legislative and Executive, of the Congress of the United States*, 2 vols. (Washington DC: Gales and Seaton, 1832–34), 2:277.

19. For Pitchlynn's involvement with the Choctaw Academy, see Carolyn Thomas Foreman, "The Choctaw Academy," *Chronicles of Oklahoma* 6 (December 1928): 453; Lanman, "Peter Pitchlynn," 486. The quote is from Peter P. Pitchlynn to Jas Barbour, November 5, 1825, folder 7, box 6, Pitchlynn Papers.

20. In 1841 Pitchlynn was made superintendent of the Choctaw Academy by the Choctaw General Council. That same year, Pitchlynn relocated the academy from Kentucky to Choctaw country. Foreman, "Choctaw Academy," 478.

21. The first quote from the 1820 report is in ABCFM, *Eleventh Annual Meeting*, 50. The subsequent quote is in ABCFM, *Report of the ABCFM. . . at the Twelfth Annual Meeting* (Boston: Crocker and Brewster, 1821), 69.

22. The ABCFM Prudential Committee remarks are found in ABCFM, *Twelfth Annual Meeting*, 62. The second quote is in ABCFM, *Report of the ABCFM. . . at the Ninth Annual Meeting* (Boston: Samuel E. Armstrong, 1818), 77.

23. Baird, *Peter Pitchlynn*, 20.

24. It was during these great council meetings that the leaders of the three districts came together to assess the vast changes that had been sweeping across Choctaw territory, and Pitchlynn recorded these talks in the Choctaw

BARBA

language—a remarkable feat, considering the written form of Choctaw was only in its infancy.

25. The original, untranslated manuscript of Pitchlynn's notes from the 1828 council is available in Peter P. Pitchlynn Council Records, folder 4, box 6, Pitchlynn Papers. For Pitchlynn's political service record, see Baird, *Peter Pitchlynn*, 32, 39, 44, 54, 55, 64, 73, 100–101, 136–37. Pitchlynn's comments on Choctaw removal to the West after his election are in *Senate Documents*, 23rd Cong., 1st sess., July 10, 1832, 394.

26. Jefferson quoted in DeRosier, *Removal*, 24. For a discussion of the evolution of Anglo-American national views on Indians, see Reginald Horsman, *Race and Manifest Destiny: The Origins of American Racial Anglo-Saxonism* (Cambridge MA: Harvard University Press, 1981).

27. *Senate Documents*, 23rd Cong., 1st sess., September 18, 1830, 257.

28. Pitchlynn's appeal is in *Senate Documents*, 23rd Cong., 1st sess., July 10, 1832, 396. He is also quoted in Baird, *Peter Pitchlynn*, 44; and in Debo, *Rise and Fall*, 56.

29. Lanman, "Peter Pitchlynn," 489.

30. When John Pitchlynn traveled to Washington DC with Choctaw delegates to negotiate a treaty in 1824, the elder Pitchlynn left the family plantation in Peter's hands. John Pitchlynn to Peter P. Pitchlynn, September 29, 1824, folder 4, box 1, Pitchlynn Papers. In the elder Pitchlynn's will, he bequeathed to Peter five of John's African American slaves. John Pitchlynn will, September 11, 1824, folder 2, box 1, Pitchlynn Papers.

31. Both Taylor and Baird have discussed Pitchlynn's slaveholding past. See Taylor, *Searching*, 80–81; Baird, *Peter Pitchlynn*, 44–45, 84.

32. Taylor, "Greenwood LeFlore," 227.

33. For discussion of missionary slaveholding in Choctaw territory, see Tracy, "History of the ABCFM," 149. Foreman identifies the presence of slaves at the Choctaw Academy in "The Choctaw Academy," 464. For Folsom's defense of slavery, see Israel Folsom to Peter P. Pitchlynn, February 23, 1848, folder 2, box 2, Pitchlynn Papers.

34. For the ABCFM controversy, see Tracy, "History of the ABCFM," 149; *Slavery and the American Board of Commissioners for Foreign Missions* (New York: American Anti-Slavery Society, 1859), 3–4, 7.

35. For disparaging remarks about African Americans, see Edmund Folsom to Peter P. Pitchlynn, August 12, 1832, folder 30, box 1, Pitchlynn Papers; Pitchlynn quoted in Foreman, "Choctaw Academy," 464. A typed version of Pitchlynn's address is available in Peter P. Pitchlynn, "The Inaugural Address of Gov. Pitchlynn," typescript, 1864, folder 6, box 6, Pitchlynn Papers.

36. Pitchlynn Journal, n.d., folder 3, box 6, Pitchlynn Papers.

37. Much has been written on Native geopolitical conflicts on the southern Plains during the mid-nineteenth century. See, for example, Pekka Hämäläinen, *Comanche Empire* (New Haven CT: Yale University Press, 2008), 141–80; and James F. Brooks, *Captives and Cousins: Slavery, Kinship, and Community in the Southwest Borderlands* (Chapel Hill: University of North Carolina Press, 2002), 306–10.

38. For biographical details, see Baird, *Peter Pitchlynn*, 50. For his father's letter to Pitchlynn, see John Pitchlynn to Peter P. Pitchlynn, January 10, 1835, folder 45, box 1, Pitchlynn Papers.

39. Pitchlynn's remarks about the "wild" western land are in Pitchlynn Journal, n.d., folder 3, box 6, Pitchlynn Papers. For his correspondence with Garland, see Samuel Garland to Peter P. Pitchlynn, November 28, 1833, folder 39, box 1, Pitchlynn Papers.

40. Colonel Arbuckle's report is quoted in Grant Foreman, *Advancing the Frontier: 1830–1860* (Norman: University of Oklahoma Press, 1933), 113. Thomas Pitchlynn made his comments about Comanches in Thomas Pitchlynn to Peter P. Pitchlynn, June 9, 1846, folder 105, box 1, Pitchlynn Papers. News of "hostile" Indians was reported in H. M. C. Brown to Peter P. Pitchlynn, August 27, 1858, folder 30, box 3, Pitchlynn Papers.

41. Regarding Pitchlynn's moderate financial successes, see Baird, *Peter Pitchlynn*, 83. Pitchlynn's correspondence with his son can be found in Lycurgus P. Pitchlynn to Peter P. Pitchlynn, January 4, 1858, folder 7, box 3, Pitchlynn Papers. For Pitchlynn's historical narrative of the Choctaw people, see "Colonel Pitchlynn's Address, Delivered to President Pierce, upon Presenting the Appeal of the Choctaw Delegation for a Settlement with the Government," *Papers Relating to the Claims of the Choctaw Nation against the United States, Arising out of the Treaty of 1830* (n.p., n.d.), 4.

42. Charles Dickens, *American Notes for General Circulation*, 2 vols. (London: Chapman and Hall, 1842), 2:95–98.

43. By the 1840s most mainstream intellectuals, politicians, scholars, and scientists were convinced that the races of the earth were inherently different. Most agreed that the White race was superior to all, and many argued in favor of polygenesis. Horsman, *Race and Manifest Destiny*, 116–38.

9

Half-Butterfly, Half-Caste

Sadakichi Hartmann and the Mixed-Japanese Drama "Osadda's Revenge"

Rena M. Heinrich

The confession scene begins with a knife. In the 1890 unpublished play "Osadda's Revenge," the mixed race Japanese protagonist, Hidetada, reveals a dagger hidden beneath his clothing. He discloses to his lover, Clarissa, his plans to find and murder his White father to avenge his mother's death. Hidetada is later confronted by Clarissa, who he discovers is his half sister. Distraught over their forbidden love, she is desperate to save their father from her brother's deep-seated vengeance. For over a century, this symbolist melodrama by Japanese German playwright Sadakichi Hartmann lay in obscurity. After it was first produced in 1890, Hartmann himself lost the manuscript and recovered it again fifteen years later; thereafter it remained among his papers. Until the twenty-first century, many scholars believed that the play had actually never been produced, but reviews of the 1890 production reveal that not only was "Osadda's Revenge" Hartmann's debut as a playwright, but Hartmann himself performed the role of the half-Japanese protagonist out for revenge.[1]

The character Hidetada in "Osadda's Revenge" could easily be interpreted as a reinforcement of the tragic Eurasian trope in which the pathological "half-breed" character engages in deviant criminality, in this case in premeditated murder and an incestuous relationship with his sister. However, a closer look reveals multiple interpretative threads in the dramatic narrative, including the use of shape shifting to navigate the limitations of racial hierarchy, as well as the validity of parentage, and a reconsideration of mixed race not as a modern-day phenomenon but as an experience that existed among communities of color in the nineteenth century. The existence of "Osadda's Revenge" stands as a testament to the visibility of Asian multiracial people onstage in the United States at the fin de siècle. This is significant because other theatrical narratives, such as the seminal *Madama Butterfly* (1904), have dramatized the mixed race subject—a child named Sorrow—as an object rendered invisible.[2]

Furthermore, the Orientalist narrative of *Madama Butterfly* has dominated the performance opportunities of Asians and Asian Americans in the West throughout the twentieth and twenty-first centuries. It is perhaps ironic that "Osadda's Revenge" has languished in obscurity, since the play itself dismantles the romanticization of "East meets West" in *Madama Butterfly*. Never in the Orientalist drama or any of its other iterations, including David Henry Hwang's play *M. Butterfly* (1986) and the musical *Miss Saigon* (1989), does the mixed race child of the interracial union speak.[3] The multiracial child has remained silenced by those who would write about her, monoracial voices with particular political agendas. This has been the erasure of the mixed race Asian voice in theater.

Hartmann is arguably America's first hapa, or mixed-Asian, playwright.[4] The dramatist wrote about mixed race in America as early as 1890, ten years before the multiethnic child in *Madame Butterfly* appeared on American stages in 1900 and five years before T. S. Denison penned his yellow-face comedy, *Patsy O'Wang* (1895).[5] As a mixed race figure, Sadakichi Hartmann moved through many different identities and contexts. Throughout his lifetime he adopted different personae, wrote under a myriad of pen names, and, though culturally German, performed his Japaneseness in elite social circles that were accessible to him because of his Eurasian identity. Like Hartmann, his mixed race protagonist, Hidetada, moves through cultural circles with relative ease, demonstrating a mixed race experience different from that previously seen on American stages.

Few studies have surveyed mixed-Asian characters in nineteenth-century drama. Theater scholar Joyce Flynn has examined multiraciality in the depiction of mixed race Black characters in narratives such as *Uncle Tom's Cabin* (1858), *The Escape* (1858), and *The Octoroon* (1859).[6] While Flynn briefly mentions the play *Patsy O'Wang*, she does not include multiracial Asian roles in her survey but focuses primarily on period narratives that explore Black and White hybridity, American Indian mixed-blood people, and Jewish assimilation. What then of the mixed race Asian figures? Does theater also serve as an archive for the mixed-Asian experience in the nineteenth century?

"Osadda's Revenge" exists as one such example. Hartmann contended with a fraught association with his status as a mixed race person. His experiences and his circumstances as a multiethnic Eurasian shed a special luminosity on the period in which he lived, in which mixed blood was often viewed as producing an impure biology and a wayward mind. "Osadda's Revenge" creates a rupture in the nineteenth-century mixed race discourse perpetuated by White authors of dramas like *Patsy O'Wang* and *Madame Butterfly* who depict mixed race subjects as objects or unnatural "creatures." Hartmann's unpublished play is valuable as a drama that details a mixed-Asian hapa experience in 1890, especially when contrasted with mixed race characters whose depictions, penned from outside of the hapa experience, reify racialized portrayals of otherness. Another famous example is Edward L. Price's melodrama *In the Tenderloin* (1894), which capitalized on the criminality of the infamous half-Chinese, half-Irish thief George Appo. In the 1894 New York production, Appo appeared onstage as himself in a narrative partly based on his real-life experience as a pickpocket and an informant for the Lexow Committee, a New York State Senate empaneled commission investigating police corruption in New York's Tenderloin district.[7] While Appo's mixed race body onstage no doubt afforded him an opportunity to wrest a certain amount of spectatorial control from a stereotypical portrayal, his performance within a theatrical framework controlled by White theater makers reenacted representations of otherness and reinforced society's belief in the mental degeneracy and immoral behavior of the impure, pathological half-breed.[8] Hartmann's play "Osadda's Revenge" intervenes in the-atrical spaces where the depictions of mixedness have been manipu-lated by monoracial playwrights. Historian Jolie A. Sheffer asserts that these interventions are not modern-day occurrences.[9] In many ways, "Osadda's Revenge" parallels dramatizations seen in twentieth- and twenty-first-century theater in which mixed race playwrights disrupt monoracial depictions of mixedness and reconstruct hapa subjectiv-ities in theatrical realms.

Hartmann's ability to permeate different social contexts elucidates the process of shape shifting as a means to navigate the racialized land-scape of daily life. Historian Paul Spickard defines shape shifting as the mixed race person's ability to sidestep predetermined racial cate-gories and slip through the porous boundaries of race because of his or her ethnic ambiguity. While racial expectation assumes that a per-ceived phenotype ensures an assignment to the most superficially cor-rect racial category, ethnically ambiguous mixed race bodies can also shape shift and slip into many different racial designations. This pro-cess is often facilitated by social and historical context, geographical location, the subject's personal genealogical knowledge, and the per-formance of self and its reception.[10] In his life and in the play "Osadda's Revenge," Hartmann demonstrates how he capitalizes on his ambig-uous racial phenotype and "makes do," using the opportunities that materialize to his advantage. Rather than simply "passing," a maneu-ver that articulates singular movement from a subjugated category of color into Whiteness, Hartmann shape shifts and moves ambiguously between multiple racial identities.

Hartmann's thoughts and approaches for engaging with a society that at times both accepted and shunned him closely resemble the same thought processes and challenges undertaken by hapa subjects in the late twentieth and twenty-first centuries. This is significant, as it indicates that the mixed race experience is not just a modern-day phenomenon. Hartmann's work reveals an alternative way of being in monoracial spaces and an ability to navigate the normative nar-ratives that persistently demonized mixed race identity, one that is perhaps fueled by his choice to be Japanese rather than German. In

Hartmann's own voice, in both personal essays and theatrical texts, he writes about an experience where his ethnic backgrounds both arm him with an extraordinary agency and prevent him from being fully accepted in society. Through the play "Osadda's Revenge" Hartmann uses theater to manage with the means available to him. He writes not from the margins but from his own center as a mixed race subject actively participating in a society where his mixedness garners a variety of reactions from the community at large. The voice of his multiethnic character, Hidetada, reflects Hartmann's keen understanding of mixed race subjectivity.

Sheffer's analysis of late nineteenth- and early twentieth-century mixed race fiction reveals a multiethnic America in which race mixing and miscegenation were much more prevalent than contemporary discourse suggests. I focus specifically on Sheffer's consideration of the "multiracial nation-family" trope as explored in mixed race writer Winnifred Eaton's short stories. According to Sheffer, the fictional aesthetics of multiraciality began decades before the advent of the Civil Rights movement of the 1950s and 1960s. Sheffer contends that despite a persistent rhetoric of nativism, mixed race narratives provide us with a "model of a nation as always already multiracial and multicultural."[11] The roots of this idea can be found in the mixed race romances popular at the end of the nineteenth century and into the twentieth century, like those written by Eaton. Of Chinese and British descent, Eaton published under the pen name Onoto Watanna and masqueraded as a Japanese author. She is well known for her collections of short stories and romance novels, which often depicted the mixed race experience at the turn of the century.[12]

Multiracial romances like Eaton's work dramatize mixed race characters who, trapped in liminal space, grapple with finding their place in White society. As Sheffer contends, this need for acceptance and belonging is realized in romantic relationships. The play "Osadda's Revenge" functions as a multiracial romance; like the fictional narratives Sheffer analyzes, the play employs a melodramatic twist that indulges in forbidden interracial and incestuous desires.[13] In Hartmann's play, Hidetada's lust for his sister provides him with an unlikely tactic that acknowledges him as an undeniable member of his family of origin. His sister's full-fledged acceptance of Hidetada as her brother validates him as an equal and reinstates the privileges he lost when his father abandoned him. In the play we also see Hartmann's early explorations with symbolism, which dominate his later dramas and position him as a significant contributor to the genre in theater. Through his craft, Hartmann utilizes various tactics—his European theater training and the themes of his dramatic narratives—both to establish himself in White society and to differentiate himself in the landscape of American drama.

Sadakichi Hartmann (1867–1944) had many names. By 1905 he had published under the names Sidney Allan, A. Chameleon, Caliban, and Chrysanthemum, among half a dozen others. He aligned himself with luminaries, penetrating their social circles while occupying different professions. He was Walt Whitman's secretary and Alfred Stieglitz's lifelong friend. He corresponded regularly with Ezra Pound and Stéphane Mallarmé. He appeared as the Court Magician in Douglas Fairbanks's 1924 silent film *The Thief of Bagdad* and was frequently found drunk with John Barrymore in John Decker's studio in Los Angeles. Hartmann is most famously known as an art critic and a pioneer in the burgeoning field of photography at the beginning of the twentieth century. Historian Jane Calhoun Weaver has noted that "American art and photography in the United States simply could not have become what they are today without his remarkable presence."[14] The prolific Hartmann, however, was also a poet, a novelist, a journalist, and a short story author. When the desire to produce work in all these other genres left him, he inevitably returned to his lifelong passion. His first love was theater.[15] He continued through the end of his life to write plays and perform in staged readings of his own work and those of his beloved authors, such as Henrik Ibsen and Edgar Allan Poe, whose middle name he adopted for one of his personae, Sidney Allan.[16] As mixed race English scholar Linda Trinh Moser notes, "Of all his creative efforts, Hartmann seemed most interested in drama."[17] As a dramatist, Hartmann is most well known for his realist play, *A Tragedy in a New York Flat* (1896), and five symbolist plays about religious figures: *Christ* (1893), *Buddha* (1897), *Mohammed* (1899), *Confucius* (1923), and *Moses* (1934). A careful consideration of his papers at the University of California, Riverside Special Collections, however, reveals the manuscripts of seventeen other plays and the outline for an eighteenth, not including the plays Hartmann recounts writing in his early years in Boston, whose manuscripts appear to be lost to history.[18]

Asian American scholar Esther Kim Lee has argued that Hartmann is perhaps the first Asian American playwright, noting that while "his plays do not address Asian American issues, they are rare symbolist plays with intercultural themes."[19] However, perhaps due to the vast volumes of literary work produced by Hartmann, very little attention has been paid to his life as a theater artist, much less to his work as an Asian American dramatist. Yet his love of theater quietly and persistently dominates the literature on Hartmann's life, his accomplishments, his dark, troubled moments, and his very own words. I suggest that Hartmann is the first Asian American playwright, and in his plays "Osadda's Revenge" (1890) and "Boston Lions" (1890–96) he explores Asian American identity through mixed race hapa characters who are based on his own experiences.[20]

Hartmann's obscurity as a playwright, however, was not a fact lost on him. He lamented his own lack of success as a theater maker and a dramatist. As he dolefully writes in his unpublished essay "Aspirations of a Playwright,"

> The trouble is that a playwright cannot work independently, he has to write a play specially for a specific purpose, for an actress or actor, cater to the box office and the fads of the time. So what's the use.
>
> My real ambition in the dramatic line was so remote from ordinary facts and conditions. If a man writes *Christ* he should not meddle with writing a popular play. So I am really glad that all my attempts are buried in oblivion, and aside from my religious dramas none remain but my *Boston Lions* and *Tragedy in a New York Flat*.[21]

Hartmann may have believed he was a failure, but his early plays stand firmly in the transition from naturalism to symbolism in theater. His later works, such as *Christ* and *Buddha*, reveal a theater artist

who developed and expanded the symbolist movement. The symbol-
ists were not interested in an accurate depiction of the natural world,
which they considered to be an illusion. Instead they sought to uncover
"hidden deeper truths," which they believed were revealed onstage
through symbols and accessed through the senses.[22] Furthermore,
what his plays reveal about the representation of multiracial identity
continues to resonate with us today. It is his plays alone that exist as a
theatrical archive for mixed-Asian subjectivity in the late 1800s. The
actions and choices of both Hartmann and characters like Hidetada
demonstrate the ways in which mixed people have sought to navigate
and interrogate monoraciality since the nineteenth century.

The circumstances surrounding Hartmann's birth and childhood
informed his choices to use shape shifting as a means to traverse the
social systems in place in the nineteenth-century world. The child of
a German father and a Japanese mother, Carl Sadakichi Hartmann
was born on the island of Dejima in Nagasaki Harbor around 1867.[23]
Dejima was a manmade islet well known for having first housed the
interracial, multiethnic families of Portuguese traders and Japanese
women and their mixed race children in 1636. The island was solely
designated as a Dutch trading post in 1641 during Japan's period of
isolationism before the Meji restoration.[24] Though Hartmann's father
is remembered as German, there was no German state in those years,
only an assortment of German-speaking principalities. There was,
however, a powerful Dutch state, which had a diplomatic relationship
with Japan. Many of the so-called Dutch merchants in Dejima were,
in fact, citizens of those other German-speaking entities. Hartmann's
father, Carl Hermann Oskar Hartmann, a multilingual government
official from Hamburg, was among them.[25] Hartmann's mother was
known only as Osada, and her class and her status in society are not
entirely known. Historians disagree over whether she was of the servant or the merchant class and even whether she was Carl Hartmann's
mistress or wife. Osada died when Hartmann was less than a year old.
He and his older brother, Hidetaru Oskar, were taken back to Hamburg to be raised by their paternal grandmother and their uncle Ernst.
There Hartmann was baptized Lutheran and raised in considerable

wealth. Known in his youth as Carl, he was well educated and credited his uncle for instilling in him a lifelong interest in the arts, of which theater was an early interest. Sadakichi Hartmann, however, would reinvent the personae of his parents many times over the course of his entire life. He was especially consumed with the vision of his unknown mother and the circumstances of the early death that robbed him of her guidance and care.[26]

Racial bias was a constant in Hartmann's life. Culturally, he was German. In fact, there is very little evidence that he interacted with the Japanese community in Europe or in the United States. Phenotypically Asian, however, Hartmann was not fully accepted as a member of German society. As Weaver notes, early in his life, despite his luxurious upbringing, he was shunned by his peers for being Japanese.[27] Of mixed marriage, or "intercopulation," Hartmann remarked that it was one of the "best character molders. I do not particularly recommend it from personal experience or the adventures of my children."[28] Not accepted as entirely German and having no connection with his Japanese family, Hartmann often referred to himself later in life as the son of Madama Butterfly, "an innocent haunted by a tragedy he could not set right."[29] This is significant, as Hartmann often identified with the narrative, even though he was born thirty years before John Luther Long's short story "Madame Butterfly" (1898) was published.

His father's marriage set the stage for "Osadda's Revenge." When Hartmann was thirteen, his father married Helena Mayer, an ambitious widow with two daughters of her own. Mayer wanted nothing to do with her new husband's "half-breed" sons. After the nuptials, Hartmann was eventually disinherited and sent to live with a great-uncle and great-aunt in Philadelphia. He arrived in America "on a hot June day" in 1882.[30] As a result of his banishment, his stepmother was able to secure inheritances solely for her daughters, Elsa and Rosa. Hartmann later compared his stepmother to the character Laura in August Strindberg's play *The Father*, musing, "She was willing to wait as long as she was sure to conquer eventually."[31] His uncle's entire fortune ultimately also went to Mayer's daughters.

The acting profession intrigued Hartmann, who perhaps came to view it as an extension of shape shifting. While in Philadelphia, he took a series of odd jobs and voraciously continued his education at public libraries and secondhand book stores. He read on a variety of topics, and though he focused mainly on the fine arts, he recollected that his "greatest urge was for the stage."[32] He took voice lessons to prepare for an acting career and spent precious funds on theater tickets. His favorite playwright was the controversial Norwegian naturalistic writer, Henrik Ibsen, whom Hartmann considered to be "the greatest dramatist of modern times."[33] Hartmann was astounded that Ibsen was virtually unknown in the United States when Hartmann first arrived.[34] Hartmann eventually left his guardians in Philadelphia and moved to Boston.

Hartmann used his racial ambiguity to his advantage and created opportunities he might not otherwise have had. For instance, in 1884 Hartmann knocked on the door of American poet Walt Whitman in Camden, New Jersey, at the suggestion of a friend who disclosed where the writer lived. Hartmann was then just sixteen years old. When the old poet opened the door, Hartmann simply said, "I would like to see Walt Whitman," to which Whitman responded, "And you are a Japanese boy are you not?" Hartmann explained his ethnic background, replying, "My father is German, but my mother was Japanese, and I was born in Japan." He would later remark that Whitman was "the only person I met in those years who recognized my nationality at first glance."[35] Hartmann was, of course, thoroughly German. He had a heavy German accent, and though his phenotypic characteristics marked him as an Asian, he had no cultural connection to Japan. Though he and Whitman talked about Japan and "the beautiful bay of Nagasaki," Hartmann later remarked, "I did not know much about it from personal recollection."[36] While people saw Hartmann as authentically Japanese, and no doubt he was by birth, they read his visage as exotic rather than simply as European. This demonstrated White society's tendency to see race as a determining factor in "othering" certain individuals, but it was a tendency that Hartmann used to his advantage.

Whitman, though intrigued by Hartmann, also expressed confusion over his racial background and his desire to pursue a career in performance. During their first meeting, they spoke not of poetry but of theater. Hartmann introduced Whitman to the work of Ibsen. They spoke earnestly about Shakespeare's fools, and Hartmann asserted that he was "too tall" to play any of them, though he was committed to pursuing an acting career. Whitman discouraged Hartmann from pursuing this passion, citing Hartmann's mixedness as a deterrent to his possible success: "I fear that won't go. There are so many traits, characteristics, Americanisms, inborn with us, which you would never get at. One can do a great deal of propping. After all, one can't grow roses on a peach tree."[37]

Over the course of their relationship, Whitman racialized Hartmann many times, often citing his Japanese heritage as the dominant biological force driving Hartmann's personality. When he was agreeable to Whitman, Hartmann was Whitman's "old friend the German-Japanese." When Whitman was enraged, Hartmann was simply "that damned Japanee."[38] Whitman's struggle in classifying the racially ambiguous Hartmann further emphasizes the monoracial attitudes Hartmann encountered as a mixed race figure in late nineteenth-century America.

Despite Whitman's discouragement, Hartmann's forays into theater continued to pepper his everyday life. In each city where he lived, he engaged in theater. He had trained in technical theater in Germany during the age of *Gesamtkunstwerk,* or the "total work of art."[39] His experimental sensibilities reflected his training in Richard Wagner's total theater, which fused the artistic elements of music, drama, dance, light, and spectacle into a complete artistic vision. Hartmann spent eight months in 1885 as an apprentice in the court theater in Munich, learning set design from Kurt Lautenschläger, who designed the architecture for the innovative "Shakespearean stage."[40] He received acting training in Dresden and studied dance in Paris.[41] He wrote extensively on theater and dance for various arts magazines and gave acting and voice lessons in New York.[42] He turned to journalism as a means to make money, and he considered the myriad of lifestyle essays he wrote to make a living to be menial work. When he was twenty-three, he published four hundred copies of his first symbolist drama, *Christ*, which he dedicated to August Strindberg.[43] In the drama, Hartmann depicted Christ in scandalous scenes of sexual temptation. Of the play, the leading symbolist poet Stéphane Mallarmé, whom Hartmann met in Paris in 1892, said, "You painted . . . a vast fresco as I have dreamed of, decorating the popular palaces of this time and future times. The beauty of it is that its colors are those of the dream, delicate and powerful at the same time so that even a lonely soul amidst the acclaim of the masses has his exquisite share of beauty. In this manner, the book is human because of its expression as well as its artistic value."[44] But in Boston, the play was considered blasphemous. It was immediately banned, and copies of the script were publicly burned. Theater critic James Gibbons Huneker described the play as "absolutely the most daring of all decadent productions."[45] Hartmann was arrested for publishing and selling obscenity on December 21, 1893. He spent the subsequent Christmas Day in jail.

Hartmann, influenced by his European training, persisted in his exploration of symbolism in theater making. This was often misconstrued as eccentric behavior brought about by a weak mind and impure biology. In his next play, *Buddha*, Hartmann included in its stage directions guidelines for the use of colors and various perfumes that would extinguish "the illusion of reality" and ignite the raw emotions and pure imagination of the spectator.[46] In its closing scene, Hartmann scripted an impressive spectacle of pyrotechnics, which "was specifically praised by Mallarmé."[47] In November 1902 he produced a perfume concert at the New York Theatre under the pseudonym Chrysanthemum, a name he wielded when he wanted to assert his Japanese cultural identity.[48] The performance, called "A Trip to Japan in Sixteen Minutes, a Melody of Eight Odors," reflected Hartmann's desire to cultivate a performance for the senses that did not privilege sight. Symbolist theater had begun to employ the use of smells via perfume fountains, incense, and even scented programs to influence the mood of its audiences.[49] Hartmann's creation of symbolist "olfactory art" also mirrored personal experiences. He had worked as a perfume peddler in his early years in Philadelphia and had perhaps been influenced by Whitman, who explored the connection between smell and memory in his poetry.[50] The perfume concert was billed as "the chief attraction" in an evening of vaudevillian performances that included the Rossow Midgets and the cancan-kicking Meredith Sisters, who later assisted Hartmann costumed as "Japanese twin geisha girls."[51] In the concert, Hartmann attempted to create the experience of traveling from New York to Japan by submerging large sheets of cheesecloth in various perfumed scents. Using industrial fans, Hartmann blew the aromas into the audience while delivering a travel monologue of the journey. He called the aromatic contraption the Hartmann Perfumator, and the *New York Times* review provided the following description of his creation: "Two boxes about the size of beehives were placed on the stage. Behind them were powerful electric fans, and the conductor was going to put in the boxes linen saturated with perfumes, the extracts of flowers from different nations. The air currents were to drive the odors into the theatre."[52] An announcement for the much-anticipated affair declared, "The Nose will be guaranteed arrival in Yokohama." The evening's audience was filled with a menagerie of patrons that included those with hay fever, who wanted to enjoy the pollen-free scent of flowers, as well as a group of "deaf-mutes," who were attracted to an event they could experience with their noses.[53]

The early modernist performance of smellscapes, however, was largely a failure. Hartmann's aromas failed to travel farther than the first few rows of the theater, which led to brutal heckling from the balcony. His perfumes also competed with the thick tobacco smoke that had filled the theater during the previous acts. After only two "travel stops" in New York and Germany, Hartmann "could not go on. He bowed and with his face filled with very real pain said in a broken voice that he would have to be excused."[54] The disappointed allergy-ridden spectators trickled out of the theater with the deaf-mutes, whose fingers rapidly proclaimed their horror at the audience's treatment of the artist.

Publicly, Hartmann's failed attempt at creating a concert of scents was largely attributed to his impure ethnic parentage, signaling a popular belief in the mentally weak and unstable psychological state of the mixed race body.[55] As Christina Bradstreet observes, the *New York Times'* announcement of the performance indirectly referred to Hartmann as a "weakling and . . . a degenerate." Bradstreet notes that "his art, it was inferred, was as unhealthy as his exotic mixed race persona . . . since olfactory imagination was linked to mental degeneracy."[56] Hence, Hartmann's impetus for creating a symbolist performance, typical of smaller theaters in Paris at the time, was linked to the inferiority of his mixed race biology.[57] While this kind of exploration of the senses was on the rise in symbolist theaters in Europe, in America Hartmann's cutting-edge aesthetics were racialized. His European influences, together with an ambiguous Asian countenance, made him appear odd to American theater critics and audiences, but his strangeness was attributed not to his Europeanness but to his mixed Asianness.

Similar unfortunate attempts at experimental theater continued throughout Hartmann's life and were attributed to his eccentric character. In March 1917 he produced a controversial performance of Ibsen's *Ghosts* (1881) in the Russian Hill neighborhood of San Francisco. Hartmann rented the old Hanford Mansion and dubbed it "The House of Mystery."[58] The program for "The House of Mystery" performance series featured two performances of *Ghosts* and one presentation of Hartmann's plays *Buddha* and *Confucius* on subsequent nights. The performance of *Buddha* was billed as a "Color Drama of the Future" to be presented "with special color settings," while *Confucius* would be fully realized with Chinese dancing and music.[59] Hartmann played the role of Oswald in *Ghosts*, a performance he considered to be "twenty-eight years late," since he was fifty when he played the young artist character. During the show, he directed that a fire be ignited in the yard to correspond with the burning orphanage in the play's second act. When the fire spread to the house and almost burned the audience inside alive, Hartmann was again arrested and banned from producing the play in San Francisco. In the timeline for his autobiography, Hartmann simply referred to the incident as "'The House of Mystery' episode."[60] More than likely, Hartmann canceled the other two plays on the bill, although an ad for the remaining "House of Mystery" performances ran in the *San Francisco Chronicle* the following week.[61]

However eccentric Hartmann's theatrical experiments were, theater remained central to his artistic aesthetic and seemed to facilitate his personal life as a shape shifter. Hartmann was often found lecturing in Japanese kimono, capitalizing on his Asian visage and educating audiences on "authentic" Japanese perspectives. As he mused, "I personally never think of myself as a German or Asiatic. Others do it for me. I am supposed to be a Eurasian and all my early amazing success and enterprise is due to that fact. The first Eurasian in Boston, lecturing—how interesting! All doors opened!"[62] While he was often racialized for his multiethnic parentage, his Eurasian ancestry also gained him access to opportunities he might not otherwise have had.

Hartmann's shape shifting enabled him to further widen his access to employment on the lecture circuit. By 1902 Hartmann had created an alter ego named Sidney Allan as a pseudonym to write for Alfred Stieglitz's photography magazine, *Camera Notes*.[63] Soon thereafter, Sidney Allan began appearing in public and lecturing throughout New England. The dignified Allan wore a three-piece suit and donned a derby hat and a monocle. He was far more sartorially put together and, as a writer, more controlled and serious than the bombastic bohemian Hartmann.[64] He also physically resembled the German Stieglitz, whom Hartmann considered a kindred spirit. Allan lectured on a variety of topics that seemed beyond Hartmann's personal code of ethics, such as his most famous lecture, titled "Good Taste and Common Sense," and by 1911 Allan's calendar was filled with national lecture tours. Over the years, many newspaper reporters interviewed Sidney Allan, unaware that he was, in fact, Sadakichi Hartmann. George Knox and Harry W. Lawton observed that the "mobility of Hartmann's features lent themselves to almost any treatment," which enabled Hartmann to shape shift into a variety of different personas of his own creation.[65] However, though the versatility and illegibility of Hartmann's visage often served him, in his personal essay "In Search of My Likeness," Hartmann lamented his easily shifting countenance: "Can you imagine anything more embarrassing than offering your portrait to a friend and he answering . . . 'a very nice picture that, but who is it?'" Each attempt to capture his physical likeness on film was, as he put it, "a pictorial transfiguration."[66] Hartmann was a favorite subject of photographers, and his ability to shape shift has been captured numerous times on film. Knox and Lawton have asserted that no other literary figure was photographed as much as Hartmann at the turn of the century.[67]

In "Osadda's Revenge," therefore, Hartmann blended many aspects of his life: the loss of his mother, his anger toward his father, his dismay at being displaced by his stepsisters, and his longing for a family to which he could return. Like Hartmann, Hidetada in "Osadda's Revenge" moves through society as a Eurasian shape shifter and uses his racialized identity to his advantage. With it, he gains access to different social circles as he seeks to murder his father and avenge his mother's death. Hartmann describes his assessment of the play in his essay "Aspirations of a Playwright," reflecting, "A strictly amateurish, but by far, more serious effort than all of them is my Japanese romance, a lurid three act melodrama, one half tragedy, and the other pure caricature and horseplay. The hero was a young half-breed who falls in love with his step-sister. I wrote for my first stage appearance and it was performed with me in the leading part in Patterson [New Jersey]. The serious part of the play contained much fervor and poetic imagery, and as far as plot and actor are concerned, it was well constructed."[68]

In "Osadda's Revenge," Hartmann created a theatrical romance that draws on his many European influences. Hartmann leaned on his European training as a means of making do, since he knew no Japanese dramatists. This is significant, because he was considered Asian, although he was raised as a European, demonstrating society's false belief in biology as the determining factor in shaping an individual's character rather than culture. Employing similar plot points and character relationships, Hartmann alludes to Shakespeare's *Othello* (1604) and Ibsen's *Ghosts*. He produced the latter, a favorite play of his, multiple times in both Boston and San Francisco.[69] These plays, written by two European dramatists whom Hartmann admired and respected, seem to have carried a special meaning for him.

In Winnifred Eaton's short stories, Jolie A. Sheffer analyzes how incest serves to disrupt race and racial hierarchy and put mixed race siblings and White family members on an equal footing. Similarly, Eaton wrote a short story titled "A Father" whose plot closely resembles Hartmann's play.[70] When considering the character Clarissa, Hidetada's love interest, as a possible representation of Hartmann's stepsisters, the analysis of what Sheffer calls an "incest-recognition plot" proves useful here. According to descriptions filed with "Osadda's Revenge" in the archive at the University of California, Riverside, Hartmann was disillusioned by the loss of his inheritance to his stepsisters. In his relationships with a series of mentors who were replacements for his father, he constantly revisited the need for revenge that consumed his thoughts in Philadelphia.[71] Theater scholar Peter B. Hodges notes the "naked way [Hartmann] exposes" his own personal demons within the narrative of the play.[72] Hartmann's Hidetada asserts his desire to belong as he proclaims his Whiteness and strives for equality in the multiracial landscape of the nineteenth century.

Hartmann's first task seems to be to upend the tragic Eurasian trope by displaying an educated superiority over his White counterparts. "Osadda's Revenge" begins at a debutante ball at a hotel in Newport, which was widely regarded as a summer resort town for the New England upper class. Edith Dayton arrives with her merchant father, Mr. Dayton, anxious to see her beau, a medical student named George van Bos. Her sister, Clarissa Fulton, enters carrying a bouquet of chrysanthemums. Though married, she is smitten by a Japanese suitor named Hidetada. Dayton and his daughters are joined by a cast of characters who represent a privileged elite, including an older pretentious socialite named Helena Blueblood and Baron d'Epignol, who repeatedly tells his companions that he is a member of the Académie française and a poet.

Blueblood is the first character to provide a description of Hidetada, the half-Japanese gentleman with whom Clarissa is in love. After detailing his handsome physical aspects, she coos about his literary prowess, saying, "How well he is poised in literature. He made some very sagacious quotations, for instance he allowed himself to say 'She loved me for the danger I had past, and I loved her that she did pity them.' I naturally knew at once that my favorite poet Browning had written those lines."[73] Blueblood, of course, mistakenly attributes these lines to the wrong writer. They are from Shakespeare's *Othello* and not the work of the English poet Robert Browning.

Hartmann's reference to *Othello* in the play enacts what J. Douglas Clayton and Yana Meerzon call a "dramatic palimpsest," which enables an audience to experience two dramatic texts at once.[74] Much like a literal palimpsest, in which the original incompletely erased material bleeds through a new image on reused parchment, the use of Shakespeare's drama becomes a kind of underwriting that evokes Othello and Desdemona, one of the most famous interracial couples in Western classical literature, in "Osadda's Revenge." This double reception brings the memory of the first text to the second and creates a richer, more nuanced experience in which the mood and tone of *Othello* enhance Hartmann's narrative. Blueblood's allusion to Shakespeare allows Hartmann to foreshadow Hidetada's exchange with Clarissa and creates a shorthand through which to experience their relationship. The interraciality of Othello and Desdemona's relationship not only foreshadows the mixedness present in Hidetada's romantic relationship with Clarissa but also conjures and reconstitutes another couple who haunt the text: Hartmann's own interracial biological parents. Lastly, the nod to *Othello* is also meant to foreground the hypocrisy of the privileged American elite, whose ignorance of European writers and culture Hartmann found shocking. Hartmann's frustration here is obvious as the arrogant and pompous Miss Blueblood mistakes William Shakespeare for the more contemporary Robert Browning.[75] Furthermore, Blueblood misquotes Shakespeare, saying "danger" instead of "dangers," as in the original text. In the play, Hartmann thumbs his nose at a high society that could not recognize Shakespeare and knew little of Ibsen. Hartmann claims his intellectual superiority over White mainstream culture to prove that he is far from, as Christina Bradstreet notes, the mentally defective offspring often thought to come from an impure, interracial union.

Hidetada's incestuous advances seems to be a way for Hartmann to attempt to win back his inheritance, even in a fantastical realm like theater. When Hidetada and Clarissa finally meet each other alone, Hartmann directly references *Othello*, establishing Clarissa as Desdemona and Hidetada as Othello. Clarissa says, "Therefore tell me what sorrowful story lies hidden in your heart. Be assured that I would appreciate your trust in me; it is not curiosity which prompts my tongue to speak, but a burning desire with my soul that is akin to yours." Her words mirror Desdemona's show of adoration and her devotion to Othello. Like Desdemona, Clarissa is drawn to her love interest's troubled past. Clarissa continues, imploring Hidetada to "speak to me. Let me be no longer ignorant of the great torturing passions of your existence."[76] As Othello recounts in act 1, scene 3, "she loved me for the dangers I had past, and I loved her that she did pity them."[77] Hidetada similarly loves having Clarissa as a devoted and sympathetic confidante.

Within the dramatization of an incestuous relationship, Hartmann asserts himself as an equal to his own stepsisters. When Clarissa affirms that she and Hidetada are similar, describing her soul as "akin" to his, she foreshadows their blood ties as siblings.[78] Sheffer refers to this as an incest-recognition plot, in which a romantic relationship establishes siblings as equals. The incest taboo cannot ignore that the lovers are related.[79] Later in the play, this prevents Hidetada from consummating his romantic relationship with his sister, but it undeniably positions him as an equal member of the family and his father's son. Clarissa's affection further negates Hidetada's illegitimate status as her mixed race brother. When Hartmann hints that the lovers are "kin" in Clarissa's innocent declaration, he also proclaims himself an equal to his own stepsisters and, therefore, rightfully deserving of his inheritance.[80]

Hartmann further displays his cultural and intellectual prowess through his creation of the character Clarissa. As a composite of many influences in Hartmann's life, she seems to be an amalgamation of Helene Alving and Regina Engstrand from Ibsen's *Ghosts*. Like Helene, Clarissa is married to a philanderer. Clarissa's husband is in prison for fraud during the course of the play, and he eventually dies there, leaving Clarissa a widow like Helene. Yet Clarissa resembles Regina Engstrand as well and enters into a romantic relationship with her brother, unaware that they are related.[81]

Clarissa is also reminiscent of Clara, a young woman whom Hartmann courted in Boston in 1887. Hartmann and Clara shared an admiration of Walt Whitman and spent long hours reading his work together. As they fell in love, Hartmann began taking Clara to visit the poet. Despite their apparent devotion to each other, Hartmann recounted that the affair was "purely osculation," much like the relationship between Hidetada and Clarissa. The relationship ended abruptly and seemingly irreparably later that year after Hartmann returned from another trip to Europe in the fall of 1887. Clara had sent Hartmann a box of roses for his birthday on the same day that Hartmann asked for his letters back. Upon realizing his mistake, Hartmann buried his face in the roses and wept.[82]

It is no coincidence that Hartmann's first love in the United States was named Clara. The character Clarissa may be inspired by her, but the name's meaning also serves another purpose in the text. Clarissa is a related form of Clara or Clare, meaning "clear" and "bright." Later in the narrative, it is Clarissa who tries to talk sense into Hidetada, vehemently denying her approval of their incestuous relationship. However, Hidetada's choice for a romantic partner is clear. She is the only spot of clarity and brightness in his life. As the White legitimate sister, she is guaranteed financial security and belonging. Hidetada finds a way to be equal to his rival heir, however, demanding recognition as the forgotten and abandoned half-breed son. When Clarissa tries to reason with him, she offers her love as a sister. Hidetada counters, "I want a nearer tie!" He knows he will not receive the equality he deserves if he settles for being her sibling. Eventually in this exchange, Clarissa relents, replying, "Take me. I am yours," signaling her acceptance of him as an equal.[83]

In "Osadda's Revenge" the mixed race child, now an adult, speaks, his words penned by an author who lived through an experience not unlike Trouble or Sorrow in *Madame/a Butterfly*.[84] Yet he has remained silenced, a dismissed object, peripheral to a story about Orientalism and essentialism in race, a narrative that the child's very body and subjectivity destroy. In "Osadda's Revenge" Hidetada admonishes the White imperialist entitlement that has led to his abandonment: "The great crime which so many foreigners committed who settled there. Women were good enough for them while staying in Japan, but when they returned, their children were forgotten. How many . . . hearts have been forsaken? How many tears were shed for them? . . . How many a child had to suffer for this—father's wrong?"[85]

In his lifetime, Hartmann was critical of the White imperialist project. He referred to White colonizers as "devils [who] claim that they come as benefactors as they relieve the natives of the tsetse fly, when they themselves are worse than any plague of flies."[86] While both Blueblood and Clarissa identify Hidetada as a "foreigner" earlier in the text, the protagonist also uses the word when referring to his White father and other Europeans like him who refuse to claim their mixed children.[87] Dayton feebly replies that he is not the only one to have ever committed such a crime, but Hidetada refuses to accept this as an excuse:

DAYTON: That is happening every day all over the world.

HIDETADA: Sad if it is true. But no man can defend such villainy.[88]

Hidetada does not speak from a marginalized site, and his use of the word "foreigner" decenters the West's positionality in the text. Through "Osadda's Revenge" and with the aid of the European dramatists who raised him, Sadakichi Hartmann confronts his father's rejection and claims Japan and Europe together as the center from which he speaks.

In the final moments of the play, Hartmann's desires to reconcile his relationships with his father, his stepsisters, and his first love begin to coalesce. At the play's end, it is Clarissa's maid, Cora, whose name invokes the "core," "center," or "heart," who dissuades Hidetada from carrying out his plans for revenge. In her cri de coeur, she reasons that if Hidetada killed his father, he would dishonor the love his mother had for both of them:

CORA: If your mother has ever cherished the memory of your father with all the tenderness a woman has, then she has forgiven him long, long ago.

HIDETADA: It is true, she never blamed him for his crime, she pardoned him and loved him still.

CORA: And then her son will kill that man who she so loved, who was the greatest joy of all her life? That can never be right.[89]

Cora acts as a mother-surrogate and as the final arbiter in Hidetada's quest for revenge. Hidetada's ultimate refusal to destroy the only man his mother loved, along with his father's long-awaited recognition, eventually eases his need for vengeance. He addresses Dayton and Clarissa as his father and sister, having finally gained acceptance into the family that he had lost. Then, perhaps as a final olive branch to Clara, Hartmann speaks through Hidetada in his last lines to his sister: "Clarissa, our love has not been in vain, it taught me some great lesson . . . to find life worth living."[90] This lesson learned is what Hartmann consistently, fearlessly endeavored to do: to pursue a life worth living.

Very little exists of the original production other than the 1890 description in the *New York Clipper Annual*, which reported that the author made "a stellar debut."[91] Peter Hodges notes that Hartmann had assembled a cast of amateur actors in New York for the show and opened the performance at the Apollo Hall in Paterson, New Jersey, a city often remembered as the place where East Coast actors received their first big break.[92] Hartmann's leading ingenue, a night watchman's daughter, was "naivete personified," with an abundance of wavy hair; evidently, Hartmann would tolerate and forgive anything she did.[93] Though according to surviving newspaper accounts the performance was well received, the production seems to have had a predictable outcome, since Hartmann made do with an amateur cast and a leading lady whom he cast for his own self-interest rather than for her acting ability.

Newspaper descriptions of the production illuminate the racialized landscape that perhaps led Hartmann to capitalize on his Japanese

Fig. 9.1. Sadakichi Hartmann. J. C. Strauss, *Sadakichi Hartmann*, 1911, box 49, folder 21, Sadakichi Hartmann Papers, Special Collections and Archives, University of California, Riverside.

phenotype. Hartmann is identified in a review in *America: A Journal for the Americas* as a "gentleman" who is encouraged as a Japanese for-eigner to write in English: "As long as these foreigners do not insist in writing plays in their native lingos they are welcome to scribble as much as they please. After all a play written in English by a Japanese is far better than a paper printed in German in this country." The article further describes Germans, perhaps ironically, as "imported citizens who have wit enough to dispense beer but not enough to learn the language of the country they fatten upon."[94] Hartmann's decision to fully shape shift into a "Japanese gentleman" seems to be a reaction to the American negative sentiment toward Germans and an attempt to capitalize upon the admiration and attention poured upon Japanese people in the late nineteenth century. As Sheffer notes, Japanese success in the Sino-Japanese War (1894–95) spurred a widespread fascination with Japanese culture. The Japanese were embraced as far more appealing and exotic than the sinister and menacing Chinese.[95] No doubt the audience's encounter with the mixed race body of Sadakichi Hartmann onstage aroused a burgeoning attraction to Japanese people and cultural products. Hartmann's Germanness lent itself to the project of making Hartmann seem more exotic and, in a subversive move on Hartmann's part, assisted in making him more Japanese.

Hartmann closed his personal essay "Erbschleicherei" by saying of his stepsisters' inheritance: "Now in 1933 it is all a dead issue—the world's war and the shift of mundane possessions—I do not know what has become of them and do not particularly care. I stop here abruptly as all this really does not belong to the part of my career which I endeavored to describe, only that it played such an important influence and intangible force in the development of my early life."[96] Whether or not Hartmann had truly forgiven them by 1933, perhaps in those early years in Boston and Philadelphia he desired to bury his thoughts of revenge and dreamed of reconciliation. At the end of "Osadda's Revenge," Hidetada relinquishes his dagger to Cora's outstretched hands and pledges to begin a new life.

Notes

1. "Americanisms," *America: A Journal for Americans* 4, no. 8 (1890): 206; and "Theatrical Chronology 1890," *New York Clipper Annual* (1891), 5, http://www .columbia.edu/cu/lweb/digital/collections/cul/texts/ldpd_5655288_003/pages /ldpd_5655288_003_00000014.html?toggle=image&menu=maximize&top= &left=.

2. *Madame Butterfly* (1898) is a short story by John Luther Long, who was inspired by Pierre Loti's novel *Madame Chrysanthème* (1887). Long's short story was adapted into a one-act play, *Madame Butterfly*, by David Belasco in 1900. Puccini saw the play in London in the same year and was inspired to write the 1904 opera. See John Luther Long, *Madame Butterfly* (New York: Century Company, 1917); David Belasco, *Madame Butterfly: A Tragedy of Japan*, in *Representative American Plays* (New York: Century Company, 1917); and Giacomo Puccini and John Luther Long, *Madama Butterfly: Opera in Three Acts: Founded on the Book by John L. Long and the Drama by David Belasco* (New York: G. Ricordi and Company, 1905).

3. See Alain Boublil, *Miss Saigon: A Musical* (Milwaukee: Hal Leonard Corporation, 1990); and David Henry Hwang, *M. Butterfly* (New York: Penguin Group, 1986).

4. The word "hapa" comes from the Hawaiian term *hapa haole* and refers to multiethnic individuals with one native Hawaiian parent and one non-Hawaiian parent. *Haole* originally meant "stranger" or "foreigner" in native Hawaiian, and after contact with the West in 1778, it referred specifically to White Europeans or White Americans. *Hapa* is a Hawaiian pidgin term for "half" or "part." *Hapa haole* identifies a mixed-heritage native Hawaiian who is half White. The Japanese American community—and ultimately the Asian American community—appropriated the term in Hawai'i, extending its definition to mean part Asian descent. Hapa has been popularized as the preferred contemporary term for mixed race Asians and often refers to an individual with one Asian and one non-Asian parent. See Haunani-Kay Trask, *From a Native Daughter: Colonialism and Sovereignty in Hawaii* (Monroe ME: Common Courage Press, 1993), 26; and Antonia N. Glenn, "Racing and E-Racing the Stage: the Politics of Mixed Race Performance" (PhD diss., University of California, San Diego, 2004), 12.

5. The mixed race Asian character more frequently studied from this period is the title character from the 1895 farce *Patsy O'Wang*, by Euro-American playwright T. S. Denison. In Denison's yellow-face comedy, the mixed-Chinese and Irish character Patsy O'Wang transforms from a docile Chinese cook to an ambitious, self-possessed Irishman. The metamorphosis dramatizes the supposed hyperbolic instability of the tragic "half-breed" and exposes the anxiety surrounding the miscegenation of immigrant populations in the United States. For further discussion, see Gregory T. Carter, "'A Shplit Ticket, Half Irish, Half Chinay': Representations of Mixed-Race and Hybridity in Turn-of-the-Century Theater," *Ethnic Studies Review*, no. 31 (2008): 32–54; T. S. Denison, *Patsy O'Wang*, in *The Chinese Other 1850–1925: An Anthology*

of Plays, ed. Dave Williams (Oxford: University Press of America, 1997), 125–48; and Hsin-yun Ou, "Ethnic Presentations and Cultural Constructs: The Chinese/Irish Servant in *Patsy O'Wang*," *Canadian Review of American Studies* 43, no. 3 (2013): 480–501.

6. Joyce Flynn, "Melting Plots: Patterns of Racial and Ethnic Amalgamation in American Drama before Eugene O'Neill," *American Quarterly* 38 (1986): 417–38.

7. Timothy J. Gilfoyle, "In the Tenderloin," in *A Pickpocket's Tale: The Underworld of Nineteenth-Century New York* (New York: W. W. Norton and Company, 2006), 420.

8. Josephine Lee, *Performing Asian America: Race and Ethnicity on the Contemporary Stage* (Philadelphia: Temple University Press, 1997), 97; Celine Parreñas Shimizu, "The Bind of Representation: Performing and Consuming Sexuality in *Miss Saigon*," in *The Hypersexuality of Race: Performing Asian/American Women on Screen and Scene* (Durham NC: Duke University Press, 2007), 30–57. Celine Shimizu discusses a similar phenomenon in the portrayal of Asian American actresses in productions of *Miss Saigon*. Shimuzu contends that although the actors craft performances of female power, the audience continues to witness hypersexualized Asian women in positions of subservience due to what she refers to as the "bind of representation." No doubt George Appo's portrayal of his criminal past served to reinforce the White audience's anxiety about the ills of miscegenation. For a description of the production, see Gilfoyle, "In the Tenderloin," 260–70.

9. Jolie A. Sheffer, *The Romance of Race: Incest, Miscegenation, and Multiculturalism in the United States, 1880–1930* (New Brunswick NJ: Rutgers University Press, 2013).

10. Paul Spickard, "Shape Shifting: Reflections on Racial Plasticity," in this volume.

11. Sheffer, *Romance of Race*, 9, 4. See Onoto Watanna [Winnifred Eaton], *"A Half Caste" and Other Writings*, ed. Linda Trinh Moser and Elizabeth Rooney (Urbana: University of Illinois Press, 2003).

12. Eaton's older sister, Edith Eaton (1865–1914), also wrote fictional accounts about the mixed race experience, often under the "Chinese" pen name Sui Sin Far. The Eaton sisters spent most of their lives in Europe or the United States (like Hartmann) and in Canada.

13. Sheffer, *Romance of Race*, 1, 4.

14. Jane Calhoun Weaver, introduction to *Critical Modernist: Collected Art Writings*, ed. Jane Calhoun Weaver (Berkeley: University of California Press, 1991), 43.

15. In his essay "Three Years in Philadelphia," Hartmann describes falling in love with the theater upon seeing the famous American actor Thomas Wallace Keene onstage: "And when Thomas Keene came, and I saw him in MacBeth and Richard III, it happened that I became despairingly in love with the stage." See Sadakichi Hartmann, "Three Years in Philadelphia: June 1882–February 1885," box 6, Sadakichi Hartmann Papers, Special Collections and University Archives, University of California, Riverside.

16. Weaver, introduction, 30.

17. Linda Trinh Moser, "Sadakichi Hartmann (1867–1944)," in *Asian American Poets: A Bio-bibliography Critical Sourcebook*, ed. Guiyou Huang (Westport CT: Greenwood Press, 2002), 129.

18. Sadakichi Hartmann, "Aspirations of a Playwright," 1920–30, box 5, Sadakichi Hartmann Papers. Hartmann mentions two plays he wrote in Boston, "A Child Actress" and "Abraham Lincoln." I have been unable to locate them. According to Peter Hodges, "A Child Actress" (or "Mademoiselle Bébé") was lost during a trip Hartmann made to Europe in 1891. See Peter B. Hodges, "The Plays of Sadakichi Hartmann" (PhD diss., City University of New York, 1991), 30–31.

19. Esther Kim Lee, *A History of Asian American Theatre* (Cambridge: Cambridge University Press, 2006), 13. Lee quotes Hartmann's biographer Jane Calhoun Weaver.

20. Hartmann, "Aspirations of a Playwright." In this essay Hartmann notes that of all his plays, he had a "special fondness" for "Boston Lions." In the comedy, he writes about his experiences on the lecture circuit in Boston and names the caricature of himself Nichi Swartzman. He wrote the manuscript under the pen name "Caliban."

21. Hartmann, "Aspirations of a Playwright."

22. Daniel Gerould, "The Art of Symbolist Drama: A Re-assessment," in *Doubles, Demons, and Dreamers: An International Collection of Symbolist Drama*, ed. Daniel Gerould (New York: Performing Arts Journal Publications, 1985), 7.

23. Sadakichi Hartmann, *White Chrysanthemums: Literary Fragments and Pronouncements*, ed. George Knox and Harry Lawton (New York: Herder and Herder, 1971), 23. Hartmann never knew the exact year of his birth, an omission that troubled him his entire life.

24. Frits Vos, "Forgotten Foibles: Love and the Dutch at Dejima (1641–1854)," *East Asian History*, no. 39 (2014): 139–52.

25. The city of Hamburg was crucial to German overseas economic prosperity. For further discussion, see Richard J. Evans, *Death in Hamburg: Society and Politics in the Cholera Years 1830–1910* (Oxford: Clarendon Press, 1987), 28–34.

26. Hodges, "The Plays," 9, 60.

27. Weaver, introduction, 39.

28. Hartmann, *White Chrysanthemums*, 119.

29. Michelle Legro, "A Trip to Japan in Sixteen Minutes," *The Believer*, May 2013, http://www.believermag.com/issues/201305/?read=article_legro.

30. Hartmann, *White Chrysanthemums*, 24.

31. George Knox and Harry Lawton, introduction to *The Whitman-Hartmann Controversy: Including Conversations with Walt Whitman and Other Essays*, ed. George Knox and Harry Lawton (Frankfurt: Herbert Lang Bern, 1976), 13; and Sadakichi Hartmann, "Erbschleicherei," 1, box 6, Sadakichi Hartmann Papers. In Strindberg's *The Father*, the character Laura can push her own agenda by convincing authorities that her husband is mad, although the play can also be read as a woman trying to outwit a system that is intrinsically patriarchal. Hartmann translated the play in 1889. See Hartmann, "Aspirations of a Playwright."

32. Hartmann, "Three Years in Philadelphia." This essay includes multiple revisions in the same version. The essay was written in 1891 and revised in 1915 and 1933.

33. Sadakichi Hartmann, "On the Lack of Culture," in Weaver, *Critical Modernist*, 168.

34. Hodges, "The Plays," 27–28. In September 1888 Hartmann proposed a season of plays at Union Hall in Boston featuring *Pillars of Society*, *A Doll House*, and *Ghosts*. Hodges notes that the repertory was to be completed with Hartmann's translations of *The Father* and Heyse's *The Death of Don Juan*.

35. Knox and Lawton, introduction to *The Whitman-Hartmann Controversy*, 15.

36. Sadakichi Hartmann, "My First Visit," in Knox and Lawton, *The Whitman-Hartmann Controversy*, 68.

37. Hartmann, "My First Visit," 68.

38. George Knox and Harry Lawton, "Introduction Notes," in Knox and Lawton, *The Whitman-Hartmann Controversy*, 48n10.

39. Simon Williams, *Wagner and the Romantic Hero* (Cambridge: Cambridge University Press, 2004), 165.

40. Simon Williams, *Shakespeare on the German Stage: Volume 1, 1586–1914* (Cambridge: Cambridge University Press, 1990), 185–86.

41. After moving to the United States, Hartmann returned to Europe four separate times in 1885, 1886, 1888, and 1892. See Knox and Lawton, introduction

to *The Whitman-Hartmann Controversy*, 17–19; and Hartmann, *White Chrysanthemums*, 24.

42. Moser, "Sadakichi Hartmann (1867–1944)," 126. Hartmann published a wealth of articles on acting and European dramatists and even ran advertisements for dance and acting lessons in *The Theatre: An Illustrated Weekly Magazine, Drama, Music, Art*, vol. 6, ed. Deshler Welch (New York: Theatre Publishing Company, 1889–91).

43. Elinor Fuchs, "Strindberg 'Our Contemporary': Constructing and Deconstructing *To Damascus* (I)," in *Strindberg's Dramaturgy*, ed. Göran Stockenström (Minneapolis: University of Minnesota Press, 1988), 77. According to Fuchs, an unmarked copy of *Christ* can be found in Strindberg's library.

44. Stéphane Mallarmé to Sadakichi, 1893, box 30, Sadakichi Hartmann Papers.

45. Knox and Lawton, introduction to Hartmann, *White Chrysanthemums*, xix.

46. Sadakichi Hartmann, *Buddha* (New York: privately printed, 1897), 23. On the back of page 104 in the "Osadda's Revenge" manuscript, Hartmann has similarly listed colors that seem to accompany the drama's three different acts. See C. Sadakichi Hartmann, "Osadda's Revenge," 104, 1890, box 7, Sadakichi Hartmann Papers.

47. Weaver, introduction, 4.

48. Tia Anne Vasiliou, "'The Power of Suggestiveness': Sadakichi Hartmann, Thomas Wilmer Dewing, and American Modernism" (master's thesis, University of California, Riverside, 2011), 76.

49. Christina Bradstreet, "*A Trip to Japan in Sixteen Minutes*: Sadakichi Hartmann's Perfume Concert and the Aesthetics of Scent," in *Art, History and the Senses: 1830 to the Present*, ed. Patricia Di Bello and Gabriel Koureas (Burlington: Ashgate Publishing Company, 2010), 53.

50. Bradstreet, "*A Trip to Japan*," 53.

51. "Perfume Concert Fails," *New York Times*, December 1, 1902, 5; "Program of Rice's Sunday 'Pops,'" 1902, box 28, Sadakichi Hartmann Papers.

52. "Perfume Concert Fails."

53. "Comparisons Most Odorous," *New York Times*, October 6, 1902, 8.

54. "Perfume Concert Fails."

55. Cynthia L. Nakashima, "An Invisible Monster: The Creation and Denial of Mixed-Race People in America," in *Racially Mixed People in America*, ed. Maria P. P. Root (Newbury Park: Sage Publications, 1992), 165–67.

56. Bradstreet, "*A Trip to Japan*," 62.

57. Simon Williams, theater historian, described small Parisian theaters during our discussion in March 2017.

58. Hartmann's financial ability to produce his theater projects is nebulous. To support himself and his family, he sold manuscripts, lectured on various topics, and asked acquaintances and friends for money, often receiving checks from contemporaries like Alfred Stieglitz and Ezra Pound. Hartmann's second wife, Lillian Bonham, wrote about their financial hardships in her diary in 1917: "It is hard for him to make up his mind to taking a steady job." A few months after the House of Mystery production, Hartmann was arrested in Redwood City, California, for failure to adequately support his wife and children. He pleaded guilty and spent three days in jail, after which he returned to the lecture circuit. See "Poet Arrested for Theft of L.A. Taxicab," *Oakland Tribune*, May 23, 1933, C7; Lillian Bonham diary entry, July 24, 1917, box 43, Sadakichi Hartmann Papers; and Hodges, "The Plays," 2–3.

59. Sadakichi Hartmann, "Program: The House of Mystery," 1917, box 30, Sadakichi Hartmann Papers.

60. Hartmann, *White Chrysanthemums*, 27.

61. "Hartmann to Read Own Play Tuesday," *San Francisco Chronicle*, March 11, 1917, 24.

62. Hartmann, *White Chrysanthemums*, 115.

63. Weaver, introduction, 39. Hartmann befriended Alfred Stieglitz in 1898.

64. Hartmann proclaimed himself the "King of Bohemia" when he lived in New York's Greenwich Village. See George Knox and Harry W. Lawton, introduction to *The Valiant Knights of Daguerre*, ed. George Knox and Harry W. Lawton (Berkeley: University of California Press, 1978), 1.

65. Knox and Lawton, *Valiant Knights*, 18, 15.

66. Sadakichi Hartmann, "In Search of My Likeness," box 6, Sadakichi Hartmann Papers.

67. Knox and Lawton, introduction to *White Chrysanthemums*, xxiv.

68. Hartmann, "Aspirations of a Playwright." This seems to be the only time Hartmann refers to the character of Clarissa as Hidetada's stepsister. He may have changed this detail in a revision of the script, although it is my opinion that he may have been indirectly thinking of his own stepsisters here.

69. Hartmann, "Aspirations of a Playwright." Hartmann was well versed in Shakespeare's plays. He also translated Wilhelm Hauff's *Othello*.

70. Sheffer, *Romance of Race*, 56, 61. Eaton's short story was written ten years later, in 1900.

71. Hartmann, "Osadda's Revenge."

72. Hodges, "The Plays," 54–55.

73. Hartmann, "Osadda's Revenge," 5.

74. J. Douglas Clayton and Yana Meerzon, *Adapting Chekhov: The Text and Its Mutations* (New York: Routledge, 2013), 5.

75. Browning died in December 1889, six months before the play was produced.

76. Hartmann, "Osadda's Revenge," 13, 14.

77. William Shakespeare, *Othello*, in *The Complete Works of William Shakespeare*, ed. William Aldis Wright (New York: Doubleday and Company, 1936), 935–79.

78. Hartmann, "Osadda's Revenge," 13.

79. Sheffer, *Romance of Race*, 56.

80. Before Hartmann was sent to Philadelphia, his older brother, Taru, was sent to work as an apprentice on a farm in Holstein, Germany. Taru eventually immigrated to the United States and settled in Denver, Colorado. His life in Denver is largely unknown. See Sadakichi Hartmann, "Kiel," 1915, box 6, Sadakichi Hartmann Papers; and Sadakichi Hartmann, "A Luncheon with Whitman," in Knox and Lawton, *The Whitman-Hartmann Controversy*, 76.

81. Henrik Ibsen, *Ghosts; An Enemy of the People; The Wild Duck*, ed. William Benfield Pressey (New York: Holt, Rinehart and Winston, 1966). The incestuous sibling relationship is found in many European dramatic plots, any of which could have also influenced Hartmann's play. See, most notably, John Ford, *'Tis a Pity She's a Whore* (London: Nick Hern Books, 2002); John Webster, *The Duchess of Malfi* (Mineola NY: Dover Publications, 1999); and Richard Wagner, *Die Walküre*, ed. and trans. Rudolph Sabor (London: Phaidon Press, 1997).

82. Knox and Lawton, introduction to *The Whitman Hartmann Controversy*, 18, 19.

83. Hartmann, "Osadda's Revenge," 94, 101-2.

84. In Belasco's play, the mixed race child is named Trouble. See David Belasco, *Madame Butterfly: A Tragedy of Japan*, in *Representative American Plays* (New York: Century Company, 1917).

85. Hartmann, "Osadda's Revenge," 70.

86. Hartmann, *White Chrysanthemums*, 117.

87. Early in the play, Miss Blueblood enjoins her party "to speak about the foreigner to everyone we meet." Later Clarissa confesses, "I love this foreigner with all my heart and soul." Hartmann, "Osadda's Revenge," 6, 9.

88. Hartmann, "Osadda's Revenge," 70.

89. Hartmann, "Osadda's Revenge," 101–2.

90. Hartmann, "Osadda's Revenge," 104.

91. "Theatrical Chronology 1890."

92. Hodges, "The Plays," 55–56; and Craig Morrison, *Theaters* (New York: Library of Congress, 2006), 130. Built in 1887, Apollo Hall was rebuilt as the Lyceum

Theatre and reopened in 1905. Harry Houdini performed at the same theater in 1926, less than two months before he died in Detroit.

93. Hodges, "The Plays," 55–56. Hodges quotes Hartmann's biographers Harry
Lawton and George Knox.

94. "Americanisms." This is ironic, as Hartmann regularly wrote articles in German for the *New Yorker Staats-Zeitung*, a popular German-language newspaper, from 1898 to 1902 to make money. See Weaver, *Critical Modernist*, 118.

95. Sheffer, *Romance of Race*, 57. This brief period of fascination with the Japanese culture was short-lived. The Japanese military success during the Russo-
Japanese War (1904–5) cultivated anxiety about Japanese expansion and turned
popular opinion against the Japanese.

96. Hartmann, "Erbschleicherei," 3.

10

Shape Shifting in the Transpacific Borderlands

Expressions of Japanese Chicano Culture and Identity

Maria Jose Plascencia and George J. Sánchez

Shape shifting takes on different qualities based on historical periods, shifting national borders and relationships, personal preferences, and societal limitations. In certain contexts, the act of shape shifting can be a form of border crossing and translation and can raise critical questions regarding cultural borrowing and authenticity for all concerned. Indeed, in the postmodern era, we believe, it is possible to shape shift without actual personal contact, drawing on the plethora of media-saturated images and transnational landscapes of news and entertainment.

In some ways, Japanese society has long been home to individuals and communities ripe for shape shifting. Having historically gone through periods of intense interaction with other Asian cultures, followed by relative isolation as an island nation worried about outside influences, Japan entered the twentieth century seeking a modernization that would propel it as a world power. This not only led Japan to a fascination with colonial power over its Asian neighbors but also contributed to experimenting with cultural styles, technology, and architecture from Europe and the Americas. The phrase *wakon yosai* (Japanese spirit, Western technology) has come to represent this dualism in Japan since the nineteenth century, allowing the Japanese "to develop a sense of identity based on the relationship between Western technology and Japanese cultural traditions."[1] At the same time, it also led to a fascination with U.S. and European eugenic science in Japan and the construction of a new national identity that relied on notions of racial purity and cultural homogeneity as core values in imperial Japan. In the early twentieth century, Japan's struggle toward modernization pushed government policies that encouraged working-class laborers to migrate to the Pacific Islands and the Americas, including Hawai'i, the U.S. mainland, Brazil, Peru, Mexico, and, to a lesser extent, the rest of the Western Hemisphere.[2]

The disaster of World War II for imperial Japan restructured this history of cultural exchange and linked Japan solidly to the fortunes of international, particularly American, economic and cultural development. In trying to rebuild its economic fortunes from the ruins of war, Japan moved decidedly to develop a corporate culture that could thrive on product development and cultural exchange, particularly how to develop consumer items—from automobiles, to televisions, to electronics—that met the growing needs of the middle class in the recovering Europe and the expanding United States. This process reasserted a strong national identity of homogeneity among the Japanese population while also encouraging many to engage with outside influences directly for global positioning and cultural experimentation.[3] The context of shape shifting in Japan by the 1970s, in other words, was rooted in Japan's growing confidence in its own expanding economic development without necessarily abandoning strong Japanese sensibilities about the world and the best ways to operate in the increasingly global arena. Not until the twenty-first century did Japan produce "a dramatic shift in its characterization from a unique and homogeneous society to one of domestic diversity, class differentiation, and other multidimensional forms," leaving behind the view that Japan is a monocultural society that it once took for granted.[4]

In the postmodern era, cultural exchange has occurred often and rapidly as transpacific "soft power." Academic discussion of this exchange has usually concentrated on dominant forms of societal culture, focused on the most prevalent corporate forms of cultural transaction. Whether it be the west to east exchange of Disneyland modified by Japanese sensibilities or the east to west exchange of "Hello Kitty" or various forms of anime and manga to the United States, cultural studies has focused on the interaction driven by large corporate forces moving products and icons across the Pacific.[5] This chapter will instead focus on cultural exchange, border crossing, and shape shifting between minority cultures and individuals and communities drawn from racially oppressed populations and economically depressed subcultures.

Shin Miyata as Informant and Shape Shifter

Shin Miyata met us at a coffee shop in downtown Tokyo in May 2014, ready to inform us about his relationship to Chicano culture in Japan. We had traveled together with thirteen other undergraduates and five other staff from the University of Southern California to Japan to participate in an undergraduate course aimed at taking first-generation college students abroad for the first time in their lives. Each student was required to write a research paper as part of the course, and Maria Jose had decided to concentrate on the phenomenon of Japanese citizens taking on the dress, music, and mannerisms of East Los Angeles Chicanos even though they had never traveled to the United States. Shin had agreed to be our informant on this phenomenon.

Before leaving for Japan, Maria Jose was doing research on this topic in Los Angeles, and everyone she interviewed told her that she had to meet Shin. They left a strong impression that her project would be incomplete if she did not interview Shin in Tokyo. What we learned from Miyata-san that afternoon was instructive and revealing. The Japanese Chicano movement, as Shin refers to it, is a subcultural movement that attracts individuals who do not feel like the dominant Japanese life narrative tells their story. Musician, record producer, performance artist, and cultural critic Ruben Guevara explained that the "Japanese have embraced a seemingly 'expressive' Chicano culture to offset their strict and repressive society," which they have grown up in.[6] The Japanese Chicano movement is similar to other Japanese subculture movements, like the Harajuku fashion movement or the hip hop subculture, in that it gives individuals an alternative community to Japan's strong national identity of homogeneity.

But what we learned about Shin's own path to understanding Chicano culture was critical for us to classify him as a cultural shape shifter.[7] Chicano culture traveled to Japan through popular media, especially movies and music. Miyata first learned about Chicano culture through films and television. In the 1970s Shin Miyata was majoring in Spanish as a college student in Japan when he came across the movie *Corvette Summer* and the television show *Chips*. He became fascinated with lowriders and *calo*, Mexican American slang originating in the U.S. Southwest during the Pachuco era of the 1940s. The dominance of American cultural products, such as films and music, in Japan during the 1970s had exposed Shin to Chicano culture inadvertently and indirectly. He was drawn to its appeal as a rebel culture amid a largely White frame of reference from the United States.

As Japan's economy grew strong and its culture became more connected with a global and largely Western media, especially that of the United States, individual Japanese like Shin Miyata became interested in aspects of Latino and Chicano culture in the United States that had previously been ignored in Japanese society. After college, Shin took a job for an international record company, BMG (Bertelsmann Music Group), and part of his responsibility was to bring over popular musical and comedy groups to Japan from the United States. Two of the groups he brought over in the 1970s were Carlos Santana and his band, as well as Cheech and Chong, the Chicano/Asian fusion comedy group. Recordings of both were circulated in Japan by BMG, and Shin began the process of learning about the evolving culture of Chicanos in U.S. popular culture.

Miyata was first specifically exposed to East Los Angeles Chicano music in 1983 when he bought Ruben Guevara's compilation album *Los Angelinos: The Eastside Renaissance*.[8] Chicano music, like Guevara's album, made its way to Japan because Japanese record shop owners stocked their music inventory from Los Angeles, often purchasing Chicano albums. Miyata was inspired to spend a year in East Los Angeles educating himself about what being Chicano really was. In 1984 he settled in City Terrace. He took Chicano studies courses at East Los Angeles College, where he learned the importance of history

and cultural significance in the Chicano identity. A Boyle Heights
Japanese priest introduced him to Mexicanos—especially the growing Mexican immigrant communities of Los Angeles—who further
exposed him to authentic Chicanismo of East Los Angeles at a time
when the ethnic pride in and cultural politics of being of a U.S.-
born Mexican American were exploding. From Mexican Americans
watching over the homes of Japanese Americans from Boyle Heights
sent to internment camps to Ralph Lazo, a teenager of Mexican Irish
descent, actually joining his Japanese American friends in Manzanar
War Relocation Center from May 1942 to 1944, the Boyle Heights
neighborhood of East Los Angeles has had a long tradition of racial
interaction between Japanese and Mexican communities.[9] Miyata was
able to utilize that history to facilitate his foray into an education in
Chicano musical traditions.

Miyata went back to Japan and began writing articles on Chicano
culture and music. He made it his mission to continue importing Chicano culture to Japan but, most importantly, to educate the Japanese
engaging in Chicanismo about the importance of history and the cultural roots of the identity. He opened his own record company, Barrio
Gold Records, and began importing Chicano music to Japanese record
shops, as well as organizing music tours of various bands from East
Los Angeles. Shin Miyata took an important step on the way to shifting shape as a translator in the spread of Chicano culture throughout
Japan. Most importantly, he has made it his mission to educate Japanese Chicanos on the depths and complications that come with that
identity, even when translated from English to Japanese.

The Japanese Chicano Movement

How is there a market for Chicano culture in Japan? Around the
automobile factories on the outskirts of Nagoya and Tokyo in Japan's
industrial center, youth alienation from the corporate culture that
dominates contemporary Japan has led to a search for alternative subcultures, such as the Harajuku and hip hop subcultures. One of the
alternative subcultures, according to Miyata, is the Japanese Chicano
movement. According to Miyata, the Japanese Chicano movement is

divided into three different sections: fashion, cars, and music. Each of these appeals to a slightly different audience, and each draws from different aspects of the original Chicano culture.[10]

Fashion is the most visible of the three. Inspired by movies like *Blood In Blood Out* (1993) and *Mi Vida Loca* (1994), youth are the largest Chicano fashion participants, which usually means dressing in stereotypical "nineties cholo" clothing. As Luis Rodriguez describes, "They wore well pressed Dickies pants, 'locs' (wrap-around shades), extralong flannel shirts or long cotton athletic shirts in black and gray. A few had T-shirts with images of lowrider cars as well as 'cholas' and 'cholos.'"[11] While cholos are not necessarily equivalent to Chicanos, they are a critical part of the Japanese Chicano movement. According to Guevara, a cholo is "a Xikano outsider, with their own codes of honor," who should be considered Chicano if they are respectful of their roots and engaged in making a difference for their community.[12]

Japanese imitating both Chicano and cholo culture are more likely influenced by both U.S. Chicano culture and transnational African American hip hop. In Tokyo there are a few "hip hop" shops where Japanese cholos and cholas can find fashion pieces for their closets. For example, the store NYC Broadway in Harajuku was a small shop stocked with baseball caps reading "L.A." and "Dope" as well as Dickies pants, long plain tees, flannels, and all the items needed to put together a cholo outfit. Miyata explained that most of the people participating in Chicano fashion are young people in their late teens and young adults who do not really know what Chicano culture is.[13] These "wannabes" are not shape shifters like Miyata and other Japanese Chicanos, because they are simply appropriating clothing. However, appropriating clothing can be the first step in shape shifting. Expressing resistance through clothing, such as the cholo style, is crucial in the youth movement against Japan's conservative traditions. It is one of the many styles young people use as they establish their freedom of expression, similar to those using the Harajuku or Gothic fashion styles in contemporary Japan. Yet the true Japanese Chicanos, like Miyata, do not necessarily engage with this fashion. When we met Miyata he was wearing casual jeans and a T-shirt. You would not recognize him as a

key part of the Japanese Chicano movement just by looking at him.
He does not feel the need to dress a certain way in order to be active
in maintaining the Japanese Chicano community.

Lowriders and car shows play an important part in cultivating the
community. Lowriders became popular during the 1980s in Japan
because of *Cheech and Chong* movies and hip hop music videos. Do
not expect to see lowriders roaming the streets of Tokyo, because
you'll only find them in places with more street space. Nagoya, for
example, is a leading city in lowrider culture; it is where the first shop
opened and where the Japanese auto industry is concentrated. Cities
like Nagoya are perfect for this car culture because home garages and
streets are wider and have more room for cars. Lowrider shows are
held across Japan, including in Tokyo. Most of these shows include
about 150 cars.[14]

The importance of lowriders in Japanese Chicano culture also has to
be understood in relation to contemporary Japanese society's emphasis on small, efficient cars and speedy transit in trains and subways.
To go "low and slow" in Japan is to violate a whole host of societal
norms and to map the local streetscapes completely differently from
others in Japanese society. Because of the serious limitations on space
throughout urban Japan, the customization of a large vehicle, especially an American-made one, can be easily portrayed as something
fundamentally against Japanese character and the social ecology of
Japan. To invest in a lowrider and participate in lowrider culture
and car clubs is to distinguish oneself as a rebel in Japanese culture.
A recent minidocumentary, *Chicano*, dives into the investment Japanese Chicanos give to their cars, the shows, and, most importantly,
their community.[15]

The shows are not just about individuals and their cars. These
shows have also become family events, crucial as a space of freedom
of expression and community engagement. Most people bring their
children, dressed in cholo couture, of course. Lowrider culture is probably the most established in Japan out of the three subdivisions of the
Japanese Chicano movement. Media has played a key role in the popularity of lowriders in Japan, as it did in the spread of the Japanese

Chicano movement. A Japanese version of *Lowrider* magazine, *Lowridaz*, was published up until 2015, covering car shows both in Japan and abroad. Miyata wrote for *Lowridaz*, extending his influence on the Japanese Chicano movement beyond music. Although the magazine was eventually discontinued, it inspired Japanese Chicanos to establish their presence in various media outlets. Today, Japanese Chicanos connect to a growing international Chicano network through YouTube and social media sites such as Instagram and Facebook. Roy Chicano, although not Japanese, is a tattoo artist in Thailand who identifies as Chicano. He uses #Chicano and #ChicanoTattoo on his Instagram (@RoyChicano). People searching these tags can find his public Instagram and connect with him. On YouTube, people can also find many videos of Japanese lowrider shows.[16]

Music is the probably the deepest aspect of the Chicano movement in Japan because it more effectively teaches Chicano philosophies and lifestyle. Chicano music made its way to Japan beginning in the early 1980s because record shop owners traveled to Los Angeles to buy music to resell in their Japanese stores. Today, Barrio Gold Records is the biggest importer and distributor of Chicano music. Tower Records is BGR's main customer. Tower Records stores are located all over Japan, with huge stores in vibrant districts like Tokyo's Shibuya. Chicano music is not explicitly labeled Chicano music in the stores, however. You have to go searching for your favorite Chicano artists under different genres. They are organized into whatever they most sound like. For example, if the artist sounds more like rap or hip hop, he or she will be placed in that category, while people like Santana will be found in the "World Music" category. Miyata has organized tours of Chicano musicians to Japan. While their shows are typically sold out in small venues, there are only two to three hundred people at these shows. Though the numbers are relatively small, the aficionados are committed not just to following the music but also to following the lifestyle.

Confronting Appropriation and Authenticity

Indeed, Miyata confessed to us that he has had trouble introducing new Chicano forms of music to the Japanese Chicanos who he felt were committed to a particular form of 1990s cholo culture.[17] He brought over the more Caribbean-influenced group Quetzal, for example, but many of the Japanese Chicanos did not recognize the jarocho beat of Quetzal as particularly Chicano. But Miyata feels it is critical for Japanese Chicanos to be aware of the broader cultural changes in East Los Angeles that bring different rhythms and cultural forms into the picture. More recently, he has experimented with bringing Chicano Batman to Japan and vows to continue the education of Japanese Chicanos in the latest musical innovations in East LA.

Shizu Saldamando described the Chicano movement in Japan as "infatuation with American culture by the Japanese," or a trend that would eventually fade.[18] As many people have stated, the Japanese take ideas/trends from abroad and make them their own. This is not the case with the Japanese Chicano movement. It may have begun as a fascination with what media represented, leading to an imitation of what members of the movement saw on-screen. However, it has become a cultural movement to establish a new identity. Miyata explained that most of the individuals who are committed to the Japanese Chicano movement are from the countryside and connect to the root of what it means to be Chicano.[19] They find comfort in the music that talks about the struggles of being oppressed by American society or the pressure to fit into a category defined by others who do not understand your story. In other words, these Japanese do not feel like they fit into the dominant Japanese narrative of discipline, uniformity, and economic comfort.

Like the children of immigrants in places like East Los Angeles, people growing up in the Japanese countryside or near urban factories are poor or working class. While growing up, they spent very little time with their parents, who were always working in places such as automobile factories, similar to immigrants in the United States. The Japanese youth experiencing this connected with ideas and imagery of urban alienation and gang life. Although they never participated in actual gang life, they found comfort in the idea of a street family. Also, they felt understood by the lyrics of Chicano music; indeed, Miyata says, "They like the 'sad' stories in Chicano music." Contrary to the

young group of Japanese participating in the Chicano fashion movement in the twenty-first century, most of the people dedicated to the
lifestyle and the music are now parents in their thirties and forties.
These are people who were teenagers in the 1980s and 1990s and were
directly exposed to the movies and earlier Chicano music. Today, they
dress their own young children in cholo attire, creating a new generation of Japanese youth exposed to Chicano culture.

Shin Miyata himself does not feel any less Japanese because he considers himself a Japanese Chicano. While he is a cultural translator
and a shape shifter, this does not mean he has abandoned his Japanese
identity. Instead, he has incorporated a Chicano sensibility into his Japanese cultural identity, connecting with another population through
culture and popular forms of entertainment and leisure style. Miyata
himself does not find it necessary to take on Chicano dress, although
others in the movement do. While he may critique some in the Japanese Chicano movement for being wannabes, he has dedicated his
professional and personal life to be a conduit between these two cultures in a postmodern world of exchange.

Of "Blood Ties" and Return Migrations

Cultural brokers like Shin Miyata are not the only entrepreneurs who
are facilitating the new transnational identity formations that are shaping Japanese Latinos in the postmodern era. Katsunori Toda, an official at the Ministry of Foreign Affairs and a major player in reshaping
Japanese policy toward immigration, crafted a racial interpretation
focused on "blood ties" to give priority to Nikkei from Latin America
over non-Japanese Asians in providing opportunities for legal migration of ethnic Japanese to Japan.[20] Although the Revised Immigration
Law of 1990 sought to prioritize the return migration of ethnic Japanese who had been born and grew up in Brazil or Peru, their experiences in Japan often disappointed both the Japanese state officials
and the actual migrants themselves concerning whether acceptance
on the basis of blood ties alone would be sufficient.[21] While Miyata
promoted identification across the transpacific borderlands based on
cultural affinity and connections via similar economic alienation,

Toda encouraged a major change of policy based on blood ties and racialized ethnicity.

With an expanding economy focused on global exports, Japan began experiencing a foreign-worker problem in the 1980s due to labor shortages, especially in service and working-class occupations, which most Japanese avoided. New arrivals from the Philippines, Bangladesh, Pakistan, South Korea, Malaysia, and China responded to the rising demand, even though Japanese law prohibited unskilled foreign laborers. Wanting to maintain ethnic and class homogeneity, the incumbent conservative government decided to create a new long-term resident category that could only be filled legally by Nikkeijin without Japanese citizenship but with documented Japanese ancestry up to the third generation. Given the troubles that many key Latin American economies were in during the 1980s and 1990s, this opened up new economic opportunities for Japanese Latinos, especially from Brazil and Peru, to come work in their ancestral homeland.[22]

This "return migration" became extremely popular as an economic solution to the problems of Japanese Latinos, particularly in Brazil, since wages in a Japanese factory were as much as ten times those paid to Brazilian professionals. As many as 250,000 Japanese Brazilians migrated to Japan for work during the late 1980s and through the 1990s, amounting to as many as one in every five Japanese Brazilians. Most who left Brazil were middle class and had been educated and trained as professionals or white-collar businessmen and businesswomen, but they were willing to do working-class labor because of the extreme pay difference. Most intended initially to only come for a few years, but increasingly they stayed on in Japan for over a decade, with many eventually becoming permanent residents.[23]

Despite the promises of equal treatment due to racial ancestry and similar look, from the start Japanese Brazilians and other Latin American were treated as *gaijin* (foreigners) by the Japanese themselves. Since most who came to Japan were born in Latin America, with Spanish or Portuguese as their native tongue, few came with adequate Japanese-language skills to fit in easily. In Japanese cities, they faced housing discrimination and experienced limited options regarding

factory employment and possibilities of economic advancement. Moreover, Japanese residents could easily see that the Japanese Brazilians
dressed differently, carried their bodies differently, and generally had
a more relaxed approach to daily interaction, often offending the sensibilities of native Japanese. Various studies showed that interethnic
interaction was severely limited between the two groups, even when
they worked together on the assembly line. Faced with both residential segregation and separated leisure activities, Japanese Brazilians
eventually built their own social institutions in Hamamatsu, Toyota
City, Nagoya, Tokyo, and other industrial cities where they lived and
worked, exhibiting what amounted to diasporic behavior from Brazil, even in their supposed "ethnic homeland."[24]

The social alienation experienced by Japanese Brazilians and Latin
Americans in Japan was very similar to the social alienation felt by Japanese Chicanos emerging from working-class families who were also
embedded in similar factory jobs in Japan's industrial cities. Indeed,
Shin Miyata communicated that some of the "Japanese Chicanos" he
encountered worked at the same factories with Japanese Brazilians
and Latin Americans and connected across these lines to discuss similar alienations. They even tried to learn a little Spanish or Portuguese
to become more authentic "Chicanos."[25] Anthropologist Takeyuki
Tsuda describes the type of globalization affecting Japanese Brazilians
as "contiguous" globalization, "involving the actual physical movement of people, goods, and capital across national borders," during
which the migration of peoples creates new global conditions "physically present in the local society." The tensions and social alienation
experienced by Japanese Brazilians in Japan shatter previously positive and idealized perceptions of Japanese culture and replace their
self-consciousness with predominantly *negative* associations with Japaneseness and a resurgence of local consciousness through an assertion of Brazilian identity.[26]

In contrast, the social alienation experienced by Japanese Chicanos
is a result of "noncontiguous" globalization, or "the flow of information and images across national boundaries in which the globalizing
agent influences local societies over a geographic distance without

being physically present." Tsuda compares this type of globalization to what Arjun Appadurai calls "mediascapes," which occur in
what Manuel Castells calls the "space of flows," or "the noncontiguous space of telecommunications and media networks that makes
the exchange and transmission of information and images possible
over long distances."[27] Although Tsuda believes that "noncontiguous globalization is more likely to elicit positive responses from local
societies," the adoption of Chicano culture by Japanese nationals
embodies a nonconformist identity that challenges the hegemony
of the nation-state, specifically challenging "Japan's nationalist project of assimilating culturally incongruous minorities under an ideology of national homogeneity."[28] In this way, the shape shifting of
Japanese Chicanos is connected to and reinforced by the challenge
put forward by the self-consciousness identity formation of a new
minority consciousness by Japanese Brazilians and other Japanese
Latin Americans in Japan.

Producing Japanese Chicano Culture

The Japanese Chicano movement has itself evolved; it is no longer
about simply consuming and interpreting. Japanese Chicanos have
become engaged in producing their own Chicano culture, especially
through the arts. For example, many Japanese Chicanos have begun
making their own music. M.O.N.A. (aka Sad Girl) is a Japanese rapper who has traveled to East LA not only to learn more about Chicano culture but also to shoot her music video for her song "MAP."[29]
There are other musicians like her who have taken Chicano music
and made their own artistic contributions to the genre. Throughout
their work, they often praise or recognize the origins of Chicano culture, just as M.O.N.A. did by shooting her music video throughout
East Los Angeles.

Japanese Chicanos are making their contributions in other ways as
well. Tattoos have become a key part of the movement. Shin Miyata
explains, "They go get a new tattoo every weekend. Many have become
tattoo artists."[30] Tattoos are still a big taboo in Japanese society because
they are associated with Yakuza gangs and, as a result, crime. College

students were amazed to see the tattoos of coauthor Plascencia but were quick to say that Japanese are very anti-ink: "They will not let you into the public baths or hot springs," a student at Kansai University explained. Because Japanese society is so against tattoos, the Japanese Chicano movement has embraced skin ink as a way to challenge dominant society. More than dressing like a cholo or driving around in a lowrider, tattoos are a key personal way to challenge the uniform Japanese culture. Tattoos help the Japanese Chicano movement make a statement and break away from the limitations dominant Japanese culture places on individuality and self-expression.

A small group of Japanese Chicanos has made it a key part of the movement to travel to East Los Angeles, where they pinpoint the birth of Chicano culture. Like Shin Miyata's early trip, many visit East Los Angeles to educate themselves on the roots of the culture they have now embraced as their own. Some of the most talented Japanese Chicano tattoo artists have themselves migrated permanently to East Los Angeles to begin businesses in the "motherland" of Chicano graffiti and visual art through body ink.[31] In Los Angeles they join artist turned tattoo specialist Shizu Saldamando, a Los Angeles–based mixed Japanese and Mexican American who opened a tattoo parlor in Boyle Heights, an area that has openly celebrated the Japanese tattoo tradition, which is often shunned in Japan itself.[32] The peregrination to East Los Angeles of Japanese Chicano artists has become a vital part of understanding and incorporating their own Chicano identity. Indeed, Japanese Chicano tattoo artists are now a key part of the Eastside business and artistic community.

The Japanese Chicano movement is a cultural movement developing an alternative identity for the individuals born in the country who don't identify with the hegemonic. It is a community shape shifter that understands that culture is fluid and constantly mixed, stained, and blended. The first step in shape shifting, as Miyata stated, is that the movement's members "are Japanese but they want to be Chicanos."[33] These people feel more connected to the Chicano experience than they do to the dominant Japanese narrative. Chicanos both here and abroad fall between the cracks, unnoticed by the dominant society. Most of

Fig. 10.1. Shin Miyata in Tokyo with the authors wearing a Barrio Gold Records T-shirt. Courtesy of Maria Jose Plascencia.

the time they are given little attention by society, regardless of the constant economic and discrimination struggles they face. When they are noticed, it is often just to be used as scapegoats and often labeled as "problem people." The Chicano movement in the United States is a fight for equal rights in education and employment, as well as for respect as people of color, because they were and are not respected equally to Whites. As Rodriguez explains, "Most of our fighting here has been against racism, against bad schools, against the lack of decent jobs, and terrible housing."[34] While the Japanese Chicanos face different kinds of issues, they still feel invisible in Japanese society. Engaging in the Japanese Chicano movement is their way of developing their identity and establishing themselves in the Japanese landscape. As Ruben Salazar stated, "A Chicano is a Mexican American with a non-anglo image of himself," which can be translated to "a Japanese Chicano is a Japanese with a non traditional Japanese image of himself" because of the dramatic different experiences they have in comparison to those of the middle class or the city.[35]

Conclusion: Transpacific Shape Shifting

Shin Miyata, with a career in educating and translating Chicano culture to Japan, is a shape shifter. He does not think that Japanese Chicanos are any less real than Chicanos from East Los Angeles, but he does think they should be fully informed about the shifting nature of culture in East Los Angeles. He calls it the Japanese Chicano movement because it is a resistance to the hegemonic culture of Japan. In a way, this is activism for individuality in a postmodern and transnational world. He operates with full knowledge of both communities and does what he can to bring these two communities together through music and cultural exchange. And his perspective on the shifting nature of cultural identity is something that the diverse Chicano, Mexicano, and Latino community of California can learn from also.

Notes

1. Morris Low, "Technological culture," in *The Cambridge Companion to Modern Japanese Culture*, ed. Yoshio Sugimoto (Cambridge: Cambridge University Press, 2009), 130.

2. See Michael Weiner, "'Self' and 'Other' in Imperial Japan," in *Japan's Minorities: The Illusion of Homogeneity*, 2nd ed., ed. Michael Weiner (New York: Routledge, 2009), 1–20, for a discussion of the relationship between ideas of racial homogeneity and national identity in pre-1945 imperial Japan. For a general introduction to immigration between Japan and the United States, see Eichiro Azuma, *Between Two Empires: Race, History, and Transnationalism in Japanese America* (Oxford: Oxford University Press, 2005).

3. Indeed, the period from 1970 to 1995 seems to have produced increased calls for the "uniqueness, exclusiveness, and superiority" of Japanese culture from the highest levels of Japanese society, recalling the 1890 Imperial Rescript on Education. See Gavan McCormack, "Kokusaika: Impediments in Japan Deep Structure," in *Multicultural Japan: Palaeolithic to Postmodern*, 1st paperback ed., ed. Donald Denoon, Mark Hudson, Gavan McCormack, and Tessa Morris-Suzuki (Cambridge: Cambridge University Press, 2001), 274–78; and Kosaku Yoshino, *Cultural Nationalism in Contemporary Japan: A Sociological Enquiry* (London: Routledge, 1992). For an excellent article on how Japan has exported its own culture while balancing a commitment to globalization in the late twentieth century, see Ross Mouer and Craig

Norris, "Exporting Japan's Culture: From Management Style to Manga," in Sugimoto, *The Cambridge Companion*, 352–68.

4. Yoshio Sugimoto, "'Japanese Culture': An Overview," in Sugimoto, *The Cambridge Companion*, 1.

5. For Disney in Japan, see Masako Notoji, "Cultural Transformation of John Philip Sousa and Disneyland in Japan," in *"Here, There, and Everywhere": The Foreign Politics of American Popular Culture*, ed. Reinhold Wagnleitner and Elaine Tyler May (Hanover NH: University Press of New England, 2000). For recent literature on contemporary Japanese culture in the United States, see Casey Breinza, *Manga in America: Transnational Book Publishing and the Domestication of Japanese Comics* (London: Bloomsbury Academic, 2016); and Christine R. Yano, *Pink Globalization: Hello Kitty's Trek across the Pacific* (Durham NC: Duke University Press, 2013).

6. Ruben Guevara, email with Maria Jose Plascencia, April 20, 2014.

7. Shin Miyata, interview with Maria Jose Plascencia and George Sanchez, May 29, 2014.

8. See Jonny Whiteside, "LA People 2009: Renaissance Man—Ruben Guevara," *LA Weekly*, April 20, 2009.

9. See George J. Sanchez, "Disposable People, Expendable Neighborhoods: Repatriation, Internment and Other Population Removals," in *A Companion to the History of Los Angeles*, ed. William Deverell and Greg Hise (Hoboken NJ: Wiley-Blackwell Publishing, 2010). For more information on Ralph Lazo, see Cecilia Rasmussen, "Following His Beliefs Led Him to Manzanar," *Los Angeles Times*, May 27, 2007, B2; and *Stand Up for Justice: The Ralph Lazo Story* (2004), educational narrative short film produced by Nikkei for Civil Rights and Redress (NCRR) and Visual Communications (VC).

10. Miyata, interview.

11. Luis J. Rodriguez, "Tokyo: Living La Vida Lowrider," *Bello*, September 2007, Santa Ana, California.

12. Guevara, interview.

13. Miyata, interview.

14. See, for example, Lowriders in Odaiba, Japan, https://www.youtube.com/watch?v=fp33bpO8xrM.

15. *Chicano*, prod. and dir. Louise Ellison, 8 min., 2017, Vimeo.

16. *Lowriders Invade Japan: Classic Legends Car Show*, YouTube, Driving Line 2015, https://www.youtube.com/watch?v=X4Tz5eD-5BU.

17. Miyata, interview.

18. Shizu Saldamando, interview with Maria Jose Plascencia, May 15, 2014.

19. Miyata, interview.

20. Keiko Yamanaka, "Feminization of Japanese Brazilian Labor Migration to Japan," in *Searching for Home Abroad: Japanese Brazilians and Transnationalism*, ed. Jeffrey Lesser (Durham NC: Duke University Press, 2003), 177; Joshua Hotaka Roth, *Brokered Homeland: Japanese Brazilian Migrants in Japan* (Ithaca NY: Cornell University Press, 2002), 278–79.

21. For accounts that point to the lack of positive reception toward Japanese Brazilians in Japan, see Daniel Touro Linger, *No One Home: Japanese Brazilian Selves Remade in Japan* (Stanford CA: Stanford University Press, 2001); Takeyuki Tsuda, *Strangers in the Ethnic Homeland: Japanese Brazilian Return Migration in Transnational Perspective* (New York: Columbia University Press, 2003); and Hotaka Roth, *Brokered Homeland*.

22. Yamanaka, "Feminization," 175–77.

23. See Takeyuki (Gaku) Tsuda, "Homeland-less Abroad: Transnational Liminality, Social Alienation, and Personal Malaise," in Lesser, *Searching for Home Abroad*; and Tsuda, *Strangers*, 92–93.

24. See Hotaka Roth, *Brokered Homeland*; Linger, *No One Home*; Tsuda, *Strangers*.

25. Miyata, interview.

26. Tsuda, *Strangers*, 356–61.

27. Tsuda, *Strangers*, 357. See Arjun Appadurai, "Disjuncture and Difference in the Global Cultural Economy," in *Global Culture: Nationalism, Globalization and Modernity*, ed. Mike Featherstone (London: Sage Publications, 1990); and Manuel Castells, *The Informational City: Information Technology, Economic Restructuring, and the Urban-Regional Process* (Oxford: B. Blackwell, 1989).

28. Tsuda, *Strangers*, 361, 363.

29. https://www.youtube.com/watch?v=ooYxrVerTJQ.

30. Miyata, interview.

31. Miyata, interview.

32. See Lawrence-Minh Bui Davis, "Arturo, Looking at Art: On Japanese Latino Art and Asian-Latino Intersections," and Kris Kuramitsu, "Capturing a Free Fall: Japanese Latino Artists in Los Angeles," in *Japanese Latino Artist Research Project: A Project of the Japanese American National Museum*, ed. Clement Hanami and Claudia Sobral (Los Angeles: JANM, 2016). For a revealing review of the contrasting feelings toward Japanese tattooing, see Jon Mitchell, "Loved Abroad, Hated at Home: The Art of Japanese Tattooing," *Japan Times*, March 3, 2014.

33. Miyata, interview.

34. Rodriguez, "Tokyo."

35. Ruben Salazar, "Who Is a Chicano? And What Is It the Chicanos Want?," editorial, *Los Angeles Times*, February 6, 1970.

11

Betwixt and Between

A Personal Odyssey through the Twilight Zone

G. Reginald Daniel

Hypodescent and the One-Drop Rule

On December 2, 1955, my first-grade teacher at James M. Bond Elementary School in Louisville, Kentucky, began class by saying, "Yesterday, in Montgomery, Alabama, a colored woman, Mrs. Rosa Parks, was arrested for refusing to let a White passenger have her seat on the bus. It's time we colored people stood up for our rights!" The question of "rights" went over my head, and I was especially confused by the phrase "we colored people." I knew that everyone was "colored." Some people were brown. Others were pink (which I knew to be a blend of red and white) or beige or tan (which were blends of varying degrees of brown and white). I remember how excited I was that year when Crayola came out with a box of crayons that included pink, beige, tan, and so on, although I was somewhat perplexed by the crayon labelled "flesh." It was similar to tan, but I knew that not everyone was flesh colored. Nevertheless, I was happy to see my own tan color among the crayons. Up to that time, crayon boxes had included only the basic colors. Consequently, I could not get pink, beige, or tan, except when I did watercolors and had access to white paint to blend with red or brown, respectively. Just to get a clarification from my teacher, I raised my hand and asked who "colored" people were. "Everyone in this school!" she said, quite startled. "What color are they?" I asked. "We're brown! We're Negroes!" I had seen brown people. (In fact, there were many at my school.) I also knew that my own tan-colored skin tone was part brown. However, I had never heard of the color "negro" before, much less come across it among my crayons or paints. Consequently, this whole discussion left me quite confused.

At the end of class, my teacher gave me a note to take home to my mother instructing her to have a long talk with me about being Negro and about segregation. My mother told me that she had avoided this topic because she did not want me to develop a sense of inferiority because we could not go certain places. She now tried to explain the absurdity of segregated schools, water fountains, public parks, theaters, restaurants, hospitals, funeral homes, cemeteries, and so on. She agreed that our family was "tan" rather than "brown." (There were some pink and beige family members, however, who I later found out were not pink or beige at all but looked "White." I had never seen anyone the color of the white crayon or blackboard chalk.) She went on to explain how we came to be "tan" Negroes, throwing in details about African slavery, about our African, European, Native American, and Asian Indian ancestry. She concluded by saying that although we were a blend of many things and thus only part Negro, we were still members of the Negro race (???!!!), which was another word for colored people. This struck me as being somewhat illogical, so I said, "But, Mommy, when you mix brown and white, you don't get brown or white, you get tan." She told me it was not the same with people. I did not agree, but outwardly I acquiesced. However, I could not understand how I could have Asian Indian and African and Native American and several European backgrounds and be Negro. How can you take one part of my whole background, the African part, and then get rid of all the rest? That's stupid, I thought. That doesn't make any sense. One plus one equals two, not one.

I shelved this issue until the summer of 1965, when I read an article in *Ebony* magazine that discussed race relations in Brazil. As I browsed through the article, my eyes fell upon a passage that spoke of these mysterious creatures called "mulattoes." They were the products of racial blending between Africans, Europeans (primarily Portuguese), and Native Americans and were intermediate to these groups. Just like me! . . . Just Like Tabatha on *Bewitched*; like Mr. Spock on *Star Trek*! . . . Like twilight, that zone between day and night, which we all pass through at dusk and dawn. . . . I knew I existed! There was a word for what I was. "I'm a mulatto!" I also began to think, "I'm going to Brazil, because there I'll get to be who I really am." I imagined that my "problem" lay in the fact that I did not know anyone else who identified as multiracial.

The real turning point came in the fall of 1965, when I entered my sophomore year in high school. By that time, Louisville schools had been integrated. Two White female classmates approached me between classes at my locker and asked to borrow my history book. Right after they departed, the White guy whose locker was to my left said, "You know, we hang niggers for messing with white women?" The Black guy whose locker was on my left said, "Yeah, you might be a half-white nigga', but you're still a nigga'." Both laughed hysterically and went off down the hallway together, looking back at me and pointing their fingers mockingly. After I got my composure, I went on to class. The rest of the day, however, I felt a sense of humiliation and could not get that scene out of my mind.

When I went to sleep that night, I had a dream in which I was an octopus standing at the top of a very steep and lengthy stairway. One half of me was black and the other half was white. I was wearing white tennis shoes on my black tentacles and black tennis shoes on my white tentacles. Just behind me was a large white statue of a blind-folded woman holding a scepter in one hand and a balance scale in the other. Right behind her was an expansive white building with columns that I knew to be the House of Justice. Far below me at the bottom of the stairway there were millions of people pointing their fingers at me and laughing. I knew that they did not believe I could reach the bottom stair without tripping over my tentacles. As I descended the stairs my heart pounded. The tentacles went in all directions, intertwining to the left, then to the right, sometimes forward, sometimes backward. I knew that I would fall at any minute. The crowd's laughter grew louder and louder as I approached the bottom of the stairway, and I felt I could go no farther. When I reached the last stair, there was dead silence. Suddenly, all of the tentacles lunged forward and landed on the ground with absolute precision. I awoke somewhat startled and disoriented but absolutely clear about the dream's significance in terms of that day's events and its even deeper meaning as to how I should live my life. It beckoned me to embrace my various backgrounds as a means of achieving a sense of wholeness and my own humanity even in the face of ridicule. In the long run, I sensed that justice would prevail.

This quest reached a crescendo in the turbulent late 1960s and early 1970s during the height of the Black Power movement when I was an undergraduate at Indiana University. There I was saying to Black activists, "I'm mixed, and I'm your brother." "No, you can't be mixed and be our brother; you gotta be Black." And I responded, "But I am mixed." They said, "No, you're Black." This attitude among African American students was given license by certain White and Black faculty members. Everyone was uncomfortable with me talking about the fact that I was "mixed," particularly given the racially tense and polarized atmosphere.

In this process, the classroom became not merely an academic arena but also a platform for self-discovery, transformation, and personal liberation, albeit most often under the winking or frowning scrutiny of my peers and superiors. I wanted to gain insight into the origin of the social mechanism in the United States that prevented individuals—particularly those of partial African descent—from embracing their other backgrounds. The first thing that became apparent to me, however, was that although we recognize certain physical traits as marking off population aggregates as different from one another, in fact, a "mixed" lineage is the norm rather than the exception, regardless of one's identity.[1]

Moreover, all humans share 99.9 percent of their genes. Consequently, physical (phenotypical) differences among humans reflect only 0.1 percent of some of the differences in genetic information that are transmitted through one's ancestors.[2] So there are populations that, taken as aggregates, exhibit higher incidences of particular genetic and physical traits than do other populations, taken as aggregates. Yet the 0.1 percent of the genetic information that determines phenotypical traits associated with racial differentiation is itself the product of millennia of genetic "mixing."[3] If you trace back twenty generations, each individual has 1,048,576 ancestors.[4] If we trace back farther, the number of ancestors, as well as the myriad possibilities in terms of their "racial" composition, is staggering.[5]

As a graduate student at Indiana University (MA, 1973) and the University of California, Los Angeles (PhD, 1987), I embarked on a more in-depth study of racial formation, particularly in Brazil and the United States. They were the two largest slaveholding nations in the Americas, and both inherited European norms granting Whites privileged status relative to other racial groups. Yet Brazil and the United States defined Black-White relations differently in their respective racial orders. Brazil has displayed widespread miscegenation and cultural blending. It implemented a ternary racial order characterized by fluid racial markers distinguishing individuals as White, multiracial, and Black based on physical appearance rather than ancestry. Moreover, there was no legalized racial discrimination. Social inequality was supposedly based on class and culture. This earned Brazil the reputation of being a "racial democracy." However, during the year I spent studying as a Fulbright scholar at the Federal University of Brazil in Rio de Janeiro (1977–78), Brazil's nascent Black movement began challenging the racial democracy ideology, underscoring the existence of pervasive, if largely informal, racial discrimination, apart from questions of class or culture.[6] These findings, which were confirmed by my firsthand observations and research in Brazil, were very disillusioning. Nevertheless, it was also validating in Brazil to be racially designated in a way that was actually synchronous with my own personal identity.

The United States, by contrast, is a binary racial order that necessitates racial identification as either White or non-White. It has historically been characterized by legalized racial discrimination, most notably with the implementation of Jim Crow segregation in the late nineteenth and early twentieth centuries. This discrimination was reinforced by rules of hypodescent.[7] These social devices, which rely on ancestry rather than physical appearance in arriving at racial categories, designate individuals of multiracial backgrounds based on the background of color.[8] The dominant European Americans began enforcing rules of hypodescent during the late seventeenth and early eighteenth centuries. The objective was to draw social distinctions between the dominant "White" European Americans and the subordinate "non-White" groups of color. Hypodescent was implemented primarily in the areas of interracial intimacy and more specifically interracial marriages in an attempt to preserve so-called White racial "purity" as well as White racial privilege. These restrictions significantly reduced the quantity of miscegenation and fluidity of racial boundaries compared to those in Brazil.[9]

Hypodescent has been applied most stringently to the first-generation offspring of unions between European Americans and people of color. Frequently, these "mixed" individuals, particularly successive generations of individuals whose lineage has included a particular background of color along with European ancestry, have been allowed more flexibility in terms of their self-identifications. This elasticity has not been extended to individuals of African American and European American descent. The first-generation offspring of interracial relationships between African Americans and European Americans, as well as later generations of individuals whose lineage has included African American along with European American ancestry, have experienced the most restrictive rule of hypodescent: the one-drop rule. The one-drop rule of hypodescent designates as Black everyone with any African American ancestry ("one drop of blood").[10]

This mechanism, which is unique to the United States, has historically precluded any choice in self-identification and ensured that all future offspring of African American ancestry have been designated as Black. The one-drop rule gained currency as the informal or "commonsense" definition of Blackness between the seventeenth and nineteenth centuries. It did not become a customary part of the legal apparatus until the early twentieth century (circa 1915). However, its legacy continued to help maintain White racial privilege by supporting legal and informal barriers to racial equality in most aspects of social life. At the turn of the twentieth century, for example, these legal restrictions reached extreme proportions with the institution-alization of Jim Crow segregation.[11]

Multiracial Identity and the Monoracial Imperative

Since the late 1980s, public discussions on race in the United States have increasingly included references to a multiracial identity, which itself is paradoxically an unintended consequence of the one-drop rule. That is to say, the rule not only drew legal boundaries solidifying racial subordination but also legitimated and forged African American iden-tity accordingly. This identity in turn formed the basis for mass mobi-lization in the Civil Rights movement in the 1950s and 1960s that led to the dismantling of Jim Crow segregation—and ultimately to the removal of the last legal prohibitions against intermarriage in 1967 in the landmark *Loving v. Virginia* decision, which overturned statutes in the remaining sixteen states prohibiting racial intermarriage—and the implementation of civil rights legislation.[12]

The *Loving* decision did not, however, derive from the Civil Rights movement itself, although the changing climate engendered by the movement paved the way. It originated in a lawsuit filed by an interra-cial couple, Richard Loving, who was European American, and Mil-dred Jeter, who was an African-descent American. They took their case to the Supreme Court, which ruled antimiscegenation laws uncon-stitutional. The removal of the last legal prohibitions against inter-marriage, along with the implementation of civil rights legislation, dissolved the formal mechanism banning individuals of African descent from having avenues of contact with Whites as equals. This not only has resulted in increased racial intermarriage but also has led many interracial couples to socialize their offspring to identify with their multiracial backgrounds.[13]

Prior to 1980, the growing multiracial population had received limited attention from educators, researchers, social scientists, and mental health professionals. Furthermore, the extant research was outdated, contradictory, or based on small-scale case studies of chil-dren who were experiencing "problems" with identity and were referred for psychological counseling.[14] In the case of children of African American and European American parentage, most professionals stressed the importance for them to cope as African Americans because society would view them as such. Consequently, their mental health was assessed in terms of how successfully or unsuccessfully they achieved an African American identity. These frameworks (particularly misinterpretations of sociologist Robert E. Park's theories) argued that marginality itself was necessarily pathological and the source of lifelong personal conflict characterized by divided loyalties, ambivalence, and hypersensitivity due to the mutually exclusive nature of White and non-White racial identities.[15]

Accordingly, the prevailing ideology focused on the "psychological dysfunctioning" of multiracial offspring as a justification for discouraging miscegenation rather than on the social forces that made psychological functioning problematic for multiracial individuals. Thus, certain theorists (e.g., Everett Stonequist) not only distorted or at least misinterpreted Park's actual theory of marginality but also overshadowed other contemporary theorists who argued that marginality could potentially imbue individuals with a broader vision and wider range of sympathies due to their ability to identify with more than one racial group.[16]

The theories on "negative" marginality have been further refuted by theories formulated since the 1970s and by data collected since the 1980s.[17] In turn, the concept of "positive" marginality (or liminality) has gained greater acceptance among health professionals and in the larger society.[18] There is a growing consensus that multiracial-identified individuals may variously experience some of the ambiguities, strains, and conflicts that come "naturally" with marginality in a society that views racial identities as mutually exclusive (or dichotomous) and hierarchical categories of experience. However, these feelings can be counterbalanced by increased sensitivity to commonalities and an appreciation of the differences in interpersonal and intergroup situations as an extension of their feelings of kinship with their various backgrounds.[19]

Various Shades of Gray

Between 1988 and 1998 I observed multiracial-identified individuals, particularly those of European American and African American backgrounds, who attended various local, regional, and national conferences sponsored by support groups for interracial couples and multiracial-identified individuals. I found that the carriers of this identity included a smaller number of "multigenerational" persons whose experience was similar to mine as compared to the contemporary "first-generation" offspring of interracial unions, who were considerably larger in numbers.

First-generation individuals have one parent who is both socially and self-designated as Black and one who is socially and self-designated as White, regardless of these parents' actual genealogy. This identity encompasses having more than one racial reference group in the more immediate present and can involve intimate contact with both parents' extended families. The experience of Allegra Larsen (this name and the names of other individuals have been changed unless otherwise indicated) is typical of many first-generation individuals. Allegra's mother is European American, and her father is African American. She has intimate contact with aunts, uncles, and cousins on both her mother's and father's sides of the family and has visited both sets of grandparents during summer vacations. Both of her parents' families host holiday and other social gatherings attended by African American and European American relatives.[20]

Multigenerational individuals have resisted identifying solely with the African American community, although they have parents or even generations of ancestors who have been viewed and have identified as Black: their backgrounds include African American, European American, and other ancestries (particularly Native American). Specific backgrounds are not typically delineated in the home or by extended family, however. Consequently, the multigenerational identity is based primarily on having more than one racial reference group in the more distant genealogical past.[21]

Ashley Fisher, a public accountant, is a multigenerational individual in his midforties whose mother is of African American, Native American (Choctaw), and Irish American descent; his father is of African American, Native American, Asian Indian, and German American descent. Yet both parents and several generations of antecedents identified solely as Black. Ashley was socialized in the African American community and identified as African American until he went to college. At that time, he began to explore and embrace an identity that included the other components of his background.

Valery Coleridge, a social worker in her early forties who is of West Indian descent, had a similar experience. Valery was socialized in the African American community. At an early age, she became frustrated at not being able to identify with her Chinese, Asian Indian, and European ancestry, even while she embraced a Black identity. She always felt like an imposter when she denied her other backgrounds. African American children taunted her because of her light skin, and she strongly embraced an African American identity so as to fit in. Her frustration increased when she attended a historically Black college during the height of the Civil Rights and Black Power movements in the late 1960s and early 1970s. Only in the 1990s, when Valery joined a support group for multiracial-identified individuals, did she finally feel she had found a home and begin fully to assert her multiracial identity.[22]

Multiracial-identified individuals of European American and African American backgrounds, whether first generation or multigenerational, display liminal identities that have multiple and shifting points of reference rather than fixed or predictable parameters.[23] These individuals indicate a shift from the "either/or" mentation that underpins U.S. binary racial thinking to a "both/neither" framework that acknowledges shades of gray.[24] Accordingly, multiracial-identified individuals manifest identities that may variously display a differential affinity or resonance with specific components of their backgrounds, as well as the groups that embody them, on an integrative-pluralistic continuum.[25]

Individuals who embrace an integrative (or "both Black and White") identity reference themselves in the African American and European communities. They are comfortable in African American and European

American social settings and can "shuttle" between both groups. That said, some individuals have a stronger orientation toward European Americans; others exhibit a stronger orientation toward African Americans. Individuals who exhibit a pluralistic (or "neither Black nor White") identity feel a stronger resonance with other multiracials as part of an emerging collective subjectivity.[26] These multiracial identity formations should not, however, be viewed as mutually exclusive. Individuals may hold complex views that draw from both configurations simultaneously or sequentially over their life course.[27] Data show that their identities are influenced but not determined by their phenotypical traits; family, peers, and society also have a significant impact.[28]

Rodney Barrett, a college senior who has an African American father and European American mother, displayed an integrative identity. He grew up in integrated neighborhoods and went to integrated public schools but gravitated socially toward African American students and was very much involved in the Black Student Alliance in high school. In college, Rodney joined an African American fraternity and tended to socialize largely with African American students. He listened to various types of music but was particularly committed to rap and reggae because of their politically engaged stance. Rodney felt he was able to "shuttle" between both groups, but he felt greater acceptance from African Americans, was more comfortable in African American social settings, and was more committed to issues concerning the Black community.[29]

Patricia Landry, a college sophomore who has an African American father and European American mother, also displays an integrative identity. Yet her situation was almost the reverse. She spent her formative years in a predominately European American suburb in northern California among affluent Whites. Most of her childhood associates were European American, and her tastes in music, clothing, and so on followed along the lines of her European American friends. It was not until she went to college that she had much contact with African Americans. Because her exposure to Black vernacular culture had been limited, she initially felt awkward in Black social settings and felt some discomfort with the highly politicized nature of Black identity. Yet her interest in Black history grew, and in time she developed close friendships with African Americans. She admitted, however, that she still felt more comfortable in European American social settings similar to those she had experienced growing up.[30]

Meloney Parks, a college senior who has a European American father and an African American mother, exhibited a pluralistic identity. She grew up in a diverse environment on the East Coast. Although she generally felt more accepted by European Americans than by African Americans, she felt a stronger resonance with multiracial individuals. She always sought out other multiracial students in high school and was instrumental in organizing a multiracial student support group on her college campus, as well as several national collegiate multiracial conferences. Meloney also helped publish an anthology of poems and essays written by multiracial college students. Her goal was to pursue graduate study in social welfare in order to work with multiracial youth in juvenile facilities.[31]

Notwithstanding the varied and complex permutations of their identities, some individuals experienced race in a more immediate sense. Everyday encounters were more racialized. Others viewed their racial identity as merely one of the many factors they share with various groups of people. Their primary sense of self is the one they share with the largest number of people. It is grounded in a more inclusive, universal, or human self. The "metaracial" identity that is derived from this self seeks to transcend questions of racial, cultural, or any other specificity without denying their value and significance.[32]

Alexis Reed, who was a college junior, displayed this identity. She was raised in Los Angeles by an African American father and European American mother. She maintained friendships with her African American, European American, Latina/o, and Asian American peers and with a few multiracial-identified peers. She was a freelance flutist and had studied music in the United States, Europe, and Latin America. In high school Alexis developed an interest in chamber music as a means of enhancing intercultural communication. In college she furthered that goal by organizing a woodwind quintet that reflected the campus's racial and cultural diversity both in the makeup of the musicians and in its repertoire. Alexis found support for her identity in Eastern philosophy, particularly in Taoism and in the principles of yin and yang expressed in the *I Ching*. These systems of thought support the belief that opposites are not absolutely different but are relative and complementary categories of experience in which each extreme contains some aspect of the other. The metaphysical world is viewed as the domain of the "real" self, whereas the world of physical matter, of which race is a part, is considered an illusion.[33] Marcus Bradford, a college senior, exhibited a similar identity. His father is an African American serviceman stationed in Germany, and his mother is a German national. Marcus was born in Germany but came to the United States at age three to live with his family in Washington DC. He established close friendships with peers from the different countries and cities in which he lived; he speaks both German and English fluently. In his last two years of high school, he excelled in soccer, was a member of the debate team, and was an active member in the Model United Nations. In college African American and European American peers, as well as those in other racial and ethnic groups, viewed him as a leader. He wanted to pursue a degree in international law and eventually wanted to work at the United Nations or in the diplomatic service. His goal was to see the United Nations (or some other international body) move beyond its limited character and serve as a genuinely "democratic universalist" governing body. This would not only provide a forum where national, regional, and local conflicts and disputes could be negotiated but also serve the interests of the global community rather than the narrow interests of a few powerful nations.[34]

The preceding data indicate that multiracial-identified individuals variously resonate with the specific components of their backgrounds, as well as the groups that embody them. They operationalize their identities without, however, necessarily privileging any one background over the other in terms of intrinsic value and worth.[35] Therefore, it is important to point out the critical distinction between these "new" or contemporary multiracial identities, meaning those formed largely during the post-*Loving* era, as compared to some previous ones.

Previous and contemporary identity formations involve resistance
to normative configurations. However, in previous strategies, multiracials have frequently sought to achieve social advantages closer to
those of Whites in the racial hierarchy. This has been particularly true
of tactics such as passing. The phenomenon of "passing" has typically
occurred when individuals of a more European American phenotype
and cultural orientation have made a covert break with the African
American community, either temporarily or permanently, in order
to enjoy the privileges of the White community. Though commonly
viewed as a form of opportunism, passing can also be considered an
underground tactic, a conspiracy of silence, that seeks to beat racial
discrimination at its own game. Those individuals who were unwilling or unable to pass often distanced themselves from the Black masses
by forming elite groups known as "blue-vein societies." These exclusive groups shaped and perpetuated a pernicious colorism among
African-descent Americans by giving preferential treatment to individuals who more closely resembled European Americans in terms
of consciousness, behavior, and phenotype.[36]

Similar patterns of behavior have been apparent among triracial
isolate communities. Some two hundred or more communities commonly referred to as "triracial isolates" by social scientists, if not by the
communities themselves, emerged in the nineteenth century when
some multiracials formed separate enclaves either on the fringes of
villages and towns or in isolated rural enclaves. These communities
have been scattered throughout the eastern United States, particularly
in the Southeast. They have been known to have European, Native
American, and African ancestry; historically, most have affirmed only
their Native American and European American ancestries; and some,
such as the Lumbee of North Carolina, have fought for federal recognition as Native American groups. Some of these groups, such as
the Melungeons of Appalachian Tennessee, Kentucky, and Virginia,
have begun to affirm their African, along with their Native American and European, ancestry. Since the mid-twentieth century, many
individuals from these communities have migrated to the cities. This
trend, along with increased intermarriage (generally with European

Americans), has led to the extinction of many communities and the loss of collective identity.[37]

Meanwhile, after the U.S. annexation of Louisiana and the Gulf ports of Mobile, Natchez, and Pensacola in the early nineteenth century and the subsequent implementation of the one-drop rule, many multiracial "Creoles of color" fought to maintain the privileges they enjoyed under French and Spanish rule. Their social status had been considerably inferior to that of Whites but somewhat superior to that of Blacks. Others responded by passing for White. Still others joined Blacks in challenging the onslaught of segregationist policies in the Jim Crow era. Indeed, in the 1960s, younger Creoles felt the heightened pride and consciousness that affected all individuals of African descent.[38] Many began to realize, like others before them, that it was advantageous to join forces, at least politically, with Blacks in the fight for civil rights, where unity among all individuals of African descent is essential if gains for Creoles as well are to be made.[39]

Though interrogating racial categories and perhaps subverting the racial hierarchy that buttressed those categories, these strategies have been less a reaction to the forced denial of European American ancestry than to the denial of the privileges that have accrued to such ancestry. Consequently, they were rarely aimed at dismantling the hierarchy.[40] Contemporary multiracial identity formations, unlike these previous ones, contest the mutually exclusive nature of racial boundaries and also challenge the hierarchical valuation of racial differences. This does not dismiss the fact that some contemporary individuals may identify as multiracial out of a desire to enhance their status in the racial hierarchy, as have previous identities, rather than challenge that hierarchy. Those who display *critical* multiracial identities resist pressures to conform to the existing racial order, with its inequitable power relations.

The growing numbers of individuals who identify as multiracial interrogate hypodescent, as well as the monoracial (or singular racial) imperative that buttresses U.S. categories of racial difference. Hypodescent necessitates identification as either White or non-White and designates multiracials descended from European Americans and Americans of color based on the background of color. Monoraciality precludes identification with more than one racial background, whether it is a European American background combined with a background of color or a combination of several backgrounds of color. Both social devices have become a sin qua non in the U.S. binary racial order. This means, for example, that people in the United States are induced to reinforce, even if unintentionally, the notion that European Americans (and Whiteness) and Americans of color, as well as various differences among the latter, are categories of experience that are mutually exclusive, if not hierarchical, and that have an objective and independent existence of their own.[41]

Monoraciality, along with rules of hypodescent, has suppressed multiracial identities through macroaggressions (e.g., larger societal practices that discriminate against, ignore, or erase multiracial individuals from the national imagination) and mesoaggressions involving institutions and organizations, respectively (e.g., not being able to fill out a form that reflects how one identifies), that structure the behavior of actors in the political and cultural economy. The rule has also sustained microaggressions in the sphere of interpersonal relations, where individuals are the perpetrators. These microaggressions can involve brief and commonplace daily verbal, behavioral, or environmental indignities that communicate hostile, derogatory, or negative racial slights and insults toward multiracial individuals. These slights may encompass questioning the legitimacy of and negating an individual's identity through erasure and bullying, often promoting a view that a multiracial individual's identity or experiences are psychologically "abnormal" (e.g., multiracial individuals are often told they have issues because they are mixed). These individuals are often accused of trying to deny their "actual" and appropriate identity (meaning a monoracial identity) as a way of avoiding the racial stigma associated with the less prestigious ancestry in the background (typically the background of color). Marc P. Johnston and Kevin L. Nadal argue that these discriminatory attitudes and practices, whether intentional or unintentional, form part of what they refer to as "monoracism."[42]

Monoraciality and its companion, the rule of hypodescent, form the lynchpin of constructions of Whiteness and its associated privileges and unearned social advantages, including cultural, social, economic, political, and other resources. These privileges and unearned social advantages, in turn, result in grossly inequitable access to education, employment, health care, transportation, and housing, perpetuating significant differences in overall quality of life.[43] These social devices also benefit traditional monoracial groups of color, which have the advantage of large numbers of societal outlets and resources, cultural, social, economic, political, and otherwise, for individuals of their groups. But monoracial people of color are also victims of pervasive and egregious forms of oppression perpetuated by White racism. Consequently, they do not experience anything near the same advantages as Whites. This situation may make it difficult for them to recognize their own monoracial privilege and monoracist biases.[44]

Therefore, monoraciality and hypodescent may go hand in hand, but they are not necessarily synonymous. The impetus behind support of monoraciality and rules of hypodescent, by extension, among European Americans compared to communities of color differs considerably. European Americans historically formulated hypodescent to sustain monoracial imperatives based on the dichotomous and hierarchical ranking of racial and cultural differences in support of White racial exclusivity. George Lipsitz maintains that the resulting "possessive investment" in Whiteness has been critical to maintaining White racism and racial privilege, notwithstanding the increasing repudiation beginning in the 1960s and 1970s of notions of White racial purity that supported the ideology of White supremacy.[45] White racism and racial privilege manifest themselves by means of a matrix of practices that leads to significantly different life chances along racial lines. These outcomes are not merely the by-products of benign neglect. They are also the accumulation of the purposeful designs of Whites that assign people of different racial groups to differential and inequitable social spaces.[46]

The unintended consequences of hypodescent for groups of color, especially African Americans, was that by drawing boundaries that excluded Americans of color from having contact as equals with

European Americans, hypodescent has legitimated and forged monoracial group identities among the former. According to Rhett S. Jones,
Whites' possessive investment in hypodescent and monoraciality is
grounded in the belief that they are necessary for maintaining solidarity, as well as community, in the struggle against the inequities
perpetuated by White racism, oppression, and privilege.[47] Communities of color uphold monoraciality and the accompanying dichotomi-
zation of racial differences by *rearticulating*, rather than *reproducing*,
rules of hypodescent. This process essentially involves repetition of
hypodescent with a difference in support of racial difference without
hierarchy, that is, difference based on equality.

That said, multiracial identity formations interrogate monoracial
norms supporting European Americans' investment in Whiteness and
the associated cultural, social, economic, political, and other advantages. These formations also call into question the equally profound
investment communities of color have in preserving monoracial identities, a mindset that overlooks or outright rejects the possibility of
a multiracial identity formulated on egalitarian or antiracist, that is,
critical, premises. A critique of monoraciality should not be understood, however, as a dismissal of monoracial forms of identification
in and of themselves as illegitimate. The purpose is, rather, to question the external ascription of monoracial categories of identification as the norm against which all other forms of identification are
deemed unacceptable through the various aforementioned discriminatory attitudes and practices.

From Multiracial to Metaracial

By the 1990s the nascent multiracial movement, composed of interracial families and multiracially identified individuals, had lobbied for
and successfully brought about changes in official data collection, as
in the census, that would permit individuals to affirm a "multiracial"
identification by checking more than one box—instead of only one
box, as previously—in answer to the race question.[48] I became part of
this multiracial movement in the spring of 1988 when I joined MASC
(Multiracial Americans of Southern California), which is one of the

fifty or more groups that emerged in the 1980s and 1990s to provide support for interracial couples and multiracially identified individuals. I was the first secretary of the AMEA (Association of MultiEthnic Americans, 1988–89), a national umbrella organization composed of the various local support groups for interracial couples and multiracially identified individuals. Eventually, I became a member of the advisory board of the AMEA (1988–2010) and was a former advisory board member of Project RACE (Reclassify All Children Equally, 1992–97). These two organizations were instrumental in bringing about revisions in the collection of official racial and ethnic data that allowed individuals to check more than one box in answer to the race question beginning with the 2000 census.[49]

In my capacity as an advisor I have been able to observe firsthand the historical development of the multiracial movement. I was called upon by both the AMEA and Project RACE to make recommendations and help formulate strategy. In addition, I was asked to submit written testimony in support of their goals during the congressional hearings (1993–97) that were sponsored by the Office of Management and Budget (OMB), which is the branch of the government responsible for implementing changes in federal statistical surveys, to determine what if any changes would be made in reporting racial and ethnic data on the decennial census. I have also received a great deal of media attention as an expert on the topic of multiracial identity. One of the most memorable moments was my July 10, 1997, appearance on MSNBC evening news the day after OMB officials announced that they were recommending changes that would make it possible to check more than one box on the census and official forms that collect data on race and ethnicity.

During the same time period that I became part of this multiracial movement, I also began teaching as a part-time lecturer in Latin American and African American studies at the University of California, Los Angeles, and eventually secured a position as an assistant professor in the Department of Sociology at the University of California, Santa Barbara. Since the spring of 1989 I have taught a course called Betwixt and Between, which is one of the first and longest-running

university courses to deal specifically with the question of multiracial identity by comparing populations in diverse parts of the world,
beginning with European exploration and colonial expansion in the
sixteenth century. I have also published books, articles, and chapters
that explore this topic. Several of these chapters appeared in the first
comprehensive volumes on the topic of multiracial identity in the
United States.[50]

My research and teaching on the topic of multiracial identity, as
well as my participation in the multiracial movement, have been a
source of tremendous validation for me. I had been alone in my multiracial identity since my childhood. This sense of isolation I had
experienced, given the historical lack of a formally recognized multiracial community in the United States and an accompanying sense
of community identification, had abated. Now there were growing
numbers of similarly identified individuals. I had finally found "my
people," so to speak. I felt a powerful resonance with other multiracials. Indeed, I recall a very emotional experience with a woman I met
at a support group in Los Angeles, Multiracial Americans of Southern
California (MASC). She spoke of the joy she felt being able to use the
word "brother" in reference to me as someone with the same experience and identity. She had used the term in reference to African
Americans but did not feel the same primary sense of racial kinship
that she would have felt with other multiracial-identified individuals, had she known any.

Quite unexpectedly, however, I felt somewhat constrained by being
defined as a member of any racial group, multiracial or otherwise.
More important, the issue was not about race but about categories,
pure and simple. I suspected that all along I had been seeking not only
to affirm a racial identity that reflected the multiplicity of my ancestral backgrounds but also to embrace the metaracial identity that I
previously discussed, which is grounded in a more inclusive, universal, or human self and transcends questions of racial, cultural, or any
other specificity.

Along with the startling revelation about this shift in my own inte-
rior development, I also came to realize that the monoracial imperative,

which underpins categories of racial difference, is itself reflective of an even broader "monological" paradigm. This framework necessitates the study of things in isolation and in parts, which delineates them into mutually exclusive (or dichotomous), oppositional, and hierarchical categories of experience. It emphasizes "the precision of interpretation" and "the reduction of ambiguity," along with complexity and multiplicity, by acknowledging no shades of gray.[51] According to this mindset, singularity is the norm in terms of the construction of all categories of difference encompassing race (White or non-White), gender (masculine or feminine), sexuality (straight or gay/lesbian), and a host of other categories of experience, including one's stance on critical social issues relating to morality and politics (e.g., prolife or prochoice).[52] This cornerstone of Western European materialist rationalism and a defining characteristic of the last several hundred years of human history, which sociologists refer to as modernity, is premised on the almost sacred "law of the excluded middle."[53] The monological paradigm is part of what Pierre Bourdieu defines as the "doxa," that is to say, the sphere of sacred, sacrosanct, or unquestioned social concepts or dogmas that have acquired the status and effect of a force of nature.[54]

It also became clear to me that the counter to this monological mindset has made itself felt in a variety of disparate, yet ultimately related, phenomena, which in current academic parlance are often referred to as the postmodern turn. The date for the emergence of postmodernism proper is generally located in the early 1970s.[55] It figures prominently in the works of twentieth-century Western European (particularly French) thinkers.[56] Yet the term "postmodern" reflects a temporal ambiguity, as well as an elusive, elastic, and equivocal sense of presence that defies any consensual definition. That said, postmodernism jettisons modernity's dichotomous and hierarchical ranking of differences, as well as its totalizing universalism, which leveled these differences.[57] It critiques the resulting "monological" paradigm, that is, the "either/or" mentation that underpins the modern worldview.[58]

In contradistinction to this mentation, postmodernism displays a "both/neither" perspective in which various differences are commingled.[59] Therefore, postmodernists have supported the "law of the included middle." They have frequently sought to deconstruct modernity's dichotomous hierarchy by exhibiting "liminal," "hybrid," or "mixed" phenomena that are undecipherable with reference to modernity's framework. This strategy demonstrates the difficulties of defining one category of experience without including elements of the other.[60] Rather than reverse the dichotomy, however, this strategy questions the hierarchical "grounds on which the dichotomy is erected."[61]

I believe the contemporary articulations of multiracial identity display an affinity with this even more fundamental postmodern turn away from the "either/or" mentation and the accompanying dichotomous and hierarchical ranking of differences associated with modernity. The objective is to shift toward a "both/neither" framework that also deconstructs the dichotomous and hierarchical ranking of differences. Indeed, the concept of multiraciality, when based on egalitarian (e.g., "critical") premises, can serve as what Naomi Zack refers to as an "intellectual weapon" and a "theoretical wedge" in providing a more incisive critique of racial essentialism and racial hierarchy.[62] This critique should include broad programmatic initiatives in the media and educational system that disabuse the nation of the illusions and falsehoods perpetuated by several hundred years of Eurocentric thought. That mindset has ignored, obscured, and erased the genetic comity, as well as shared ancestral and cultural bonds, that compose our greater humanity.

Notes

1. Jack D. Forbes, "The Manipulation of Race, Caste, and Identity: Classifying Afro-Americans," *Journal of Ethnic Studies* 17, no. 4 (1990): 37–38.
2. Michael Banton, *Racial Theories*, 2nd ed. (Cambridge: Cambridge University Press, 1998), 1.
3. Robin Marantz Henig, "The Genome in Black and White (and Gray)," *New York Times Magazine*, October 10, 2004, http://www.nytirnes.com/2004/10/10/rnagazine/10GENETIC.htrnl/; Philip V. Tobias, "The Meaning of Race," in *Race and Social Difference*, ed. Paul Baxter and Basil Sansom, Penguin Modern Sociology Series (London: Penguin Books, 1972), 19–43.

4. "Roots," *60 Minutes*, CBS, October 7, 2007; Steve Olson, *Mapping Human History: Discovering the Past through Our Genes* (New York: Houghton Mifflin Company, 2002), 32–48.

5. Biological and ancestral notions of race overlap but are not synonymous. The former is based on one's genetic inheritance, irrespective of ancestral background. The latter is grounded in the ancestors in one's genealogy, irrespective of genetic concerns. That said, the new autosomal DNA test offered by a growing number of companies has complicated the relationship between biology, ancestry, and identity. The test involves swabbing the mouth and mailing a sample for DNA analysis, which can pinpoint the geographical origins of the various portions of an individual's genetic makeup. This technology may have the unintended consequence of reifying the link between ancestry, biology, and identity. Yet increased awareness of the myriad ancestors in one's genealogy and DNA inherited from them would also call into question any lingering notions of racial purity and may prompt more individuals to display more fluid monoracial, if not actual multiracial, identities.

6. G. Reginald Daniel, *Race and Multiraciality in Brazil and the United States: Converging Paths?* (University Park: Pennsylvania State University Press, 2006), 185–94.

7. The prefix "hypo-" has various but similar meanings. Anatomically, "hypo-" means "below, beneath, or under." Medically, it means "deficient or less than normal." Consequently, when applied to intergroup relations, the concept is used to convey that "mixed" individuals are assigned the status of the stigmatized and subordinate background. See J. Meletis and V. Goratsa, "Derivatives of the Hellenic Word 'Hema' (Haema, Blood) in the English Language," *Archives of Hellenic Medicine* 29, suppl. 1 (2012): 8–36.

8. This is most applicable for individuals who are part African American but less true for people who are part Latina/o. It is less true still for people who are part Asian and even less true for many people who are part Native American, unless they have reservation connections.

9. Daniel, *Race and Multiraciality*, viii–xi.

10. U.S. attitudes toward the "dual minority" offspring of unions between African Americans and other groups of color (e.g., Native Americans, Chinese Americans) have varied. More often than not, these individuals have been subject to the one-drop rule. See Jack D. Forbes, *Black Africans and Native Americans: Color, Race and Caste in the Evolution of Red-Black Peoples* (Oxford: Basil Blackwell, 1988); James W. Loewen, *The Mississippi Chinese: Between Black and White* (Cambridge MA: Harvard University Press, 1971). There has

been greater ambivalence displayed toward offspring whose ancestry has combined other backgrounds of color. These include Asian Indian / Mexican Americans ("Punjabi Mexicans") and Filipino/Mexican Americans ("Mexipinos") in California. See Karen Leonard, *Making Ethnic Choices: California's Punjabi Mexican Americans* (Philadelphia: Temple University Press, 1992); Rudy Guevarra Jr., *Becoming Mexipino: Multiethnic Identities and Communities in San Diego* (New Brunswick NJ: Rutgers University Press, 2012). Some of this ambivalence is due to the fact that these other groups of color occupy a more ambiguous position in the U.S. racial hierarchy compared to that of African Americans. Also, membership in these groups—except perhaps in the case of Native Americans—has been less clearly defined in U.S. law. Consequently, the racial subordination of Americans of color by European Americans, while similarly oppressive, has not been exactly the same. This makes it more difficult to assess intragroup relations among groups of color in terms of the rule of hypodescent. See G. Reginald Daniel, *More Than Black? Multiracial Identity and the New Racial Order* (Philadelphia: Temple University Press, 2001), x.

11. Daniel, *More Than Black?*, ix–xi, 16–17, 37; F. James Davis, *Who Is Black? One Nation's Definition* (University Park: Pennsylvania State University Press, 1991), 9, 11, 118; Winthrop Jordan, "The Historical Origins of the One-Drop Rule in the United States," *Journal of Critical Mixed Race Studies* 1, no. 1 (2014): 99, 103–15.

12. Alex Lubin, *Romance and Rights: The Politics of Interracial Intimacy, 1945–1954* (Jackson: University Press of Mississippi, 2005), ix–xxi, 51–59, 66–95; Rachel Moran, "Loving and the Legacy of Unintended Consequences," *Wisconsin Law Review* 2 (2007): 239, 249–50.

13. Many argue that the statistical significance of *Loving* is limited given that it was most relevant in the southern states and even there did not result in a significant growth in the numbers of Black and White intermarriages, which have been very small compared to those of other groups. In 2008 Black-White marriages were 14.4 percent among Black men and 6.5 percent among Black women. In 2010 8.4 percent of all marriages were interracial, and only about 8.9 percent of all married Blacks were wedded to a non-Black partner. They contend that the Immigration and Nationality Act of 1965, which increased immigration from Asia and Latin America, was much more significant given the substantial growth in outmarriage from these communities, which compose the majority of interracial marriages. In the case of multiracials of Asian / Asian American descent, we would also add that missionary history, commerce, militarization, and U.S. wars in Asia

and the Pacific have played significant roles in the development of multiracial demographics in the United States and abroad.

That said, *Loving* is important because it removed the negative legal sanction and stigma associated with interracial marriage and thus legitimized such marriages, which were previously proscribed. Circumstances would be quite different if those proscriptions had not been removed. Moreover, the power of *Loving* is in its positive affectivity or emotional resonance as a historic landmark in the development of a sense of community, evident in the annual June 12 Lovingday.org celebrations across the United States. See G. Reginald Daniel, Laura Kina, Wei Ming Dariotis, and Camilla Fojas, "Emerging Paradigms in Critical Mixed Race Studies," *Journal of Critical Mixed Race Studies* 1, no. 1 (2014): 16.

14. Christine Ijima Hall, "Please Choose One: Ethnic Identity Choices for Biracial Individuals," in *Racially Mixed People in America*, ed. Maria P. P. Root (Thousand Oaks CA: Sage Publications, 1992), 250–64.

15. Daniel et al., "Emerging Paradigms," 16.

16. Aaron Antonovsky, "Toward a Refinement of the 'Marginal Man' Concept," *Social Forces* 35, no. 1 (1956): 57–67; Milton M. Goldberg, "A Qualification of the Marginal Man Theory," *American Sociological Review* 6, no. 1 (1941): 52–58; Arnold W. Green, "A Re-examination of the Marginal Man Concept," *Social Forces* 26 (December 1947): 167–71; Alan C. Kerckhoff and Thomas C. McCormick, "Marginal Status and Marginal Personality," *Social Forces* 34, no. 1 (1955): 48–55.

17. W. S. Carlos Poston, "The Biracial Identity Development Model: A Needed Addition," *Journal of Counseling and Development* 69, no. 2 (1990): 152–55; Maria P. P. Root, "Within, Between, and Beyond Race," in Root, *Racially Mixed People*, 3–11; Roy Dean Wright and Susan N. Wright, "A Plea for a Further Refinement of the Marginal Man Theory," *Phylon* 33, no. 4 (1972): 361–68.

18. Liminality can also be observed among individuals who are simultaneously members of two or more culturally distinct groups, second-generation immigrants, recent migrants from country to city, and women in nontraditional female roles. These phenomena share a similar process of proceeding from "either/or" to "both/neither."

19. Robert E. Park, "Human Migration and the Marginal Man," *American Journal of Sociology* 33, no. 6 (1928): 881–93; Everett V. Stonequist, *The Marginal Man: A Study in Personality and Culture Conflict* (New York: Russell and Russell, 1937), 10–11, 24–27.

20. G. Reginald Daniel, "Two Parent Ethnicities and Parents of Two Ethnicities: Generational Differences in the Discourse on Multiethnic Identity; A

Preliminary Study," unpublished manuscript (1994, 1998), 7–8. Data were obtained between 1988 and 1998 through observations of the public behavior of students attending the University of California at Los Angeles, Santa Barbara, and Santa Cruz and from individuals participating in California support groups and attending regional and national conferences on multiracial identity.

21. Daniel, *More Than Black?*, 6, 100–106.

22. Daniel, "Two Parent Ethnicities," 10–11.

23. Peter S. Adler, "Beyond Cultural Identity: Reflections on Cultural and Multicultural Man," in *Topics in Cultural Learning*, ed. Robert W. Brislin (Honolulu: East-West Center, 1974), 2:23–40; Philip M. Brown, "Biracial Identity and Social Marginality," *Child Adolescent Social Work* 7 (August 1990): 319–37.

24. Individuals who display monoracial rather than multiracial identities necessarily fall outside the parameters of this framework.

25. G. Reginald Daniel, "Black and White Identity in the New Millennium: Unsevering the Ties That Bind," in *The Multiracial Experience: Racial Borders as the New Frontier*, ed. Maria P. P. Root (Thousand Oaks CA: Sage Publications, 1996), 135–36; Maria P. P. Root, "Resolving 'Other' Status: Identity Development of Biracial Individuals," in *Complexity and Diversity in Feminist Theory and Therapy*, ed. Laura S. Brown and Maria P. P. Root (New York: Haworth Press, 1990), 185–201; Kristen Renn, *Mixed Race Students in College* (Albany: State University of New York Press, 2004), 67–93; Kerry Ann Rockquemore and David L. Brunsma, *Beyond Black: Biracial Identity in America* (Thousand Oaks CA: Sage, 2002), 41–48.

26. Daniel, "Black and White Identity," 136–37; Root, "Resolving 'Other' Status," 185–205; Renn, *Mixed Race Students*, 67–93; Rockquemore and Brunsma, *Beyond Black*, 41–48.

27. Poston, "The Biracial Identity Model," 152–55; Daniel, *More Than Black?*, 106–11.

28. Daniel, *Race and Multiraciality*, 164; Nikki Khanna, "'If You're Half Black, You're Just Black': Reflected Appraisals and the Persistence of the One-Drop Rule," *Sociological Quarterly* 51 (2010): 96–121.

29. Daniel, "Two Parent Ethnicities," 19.

30. Daniel, "Two Parent Ethnicities," 19.

31. Daniel, "Two Parent Ethnicities," 20.

32. Daniel, "Black and White Identity," 136–37; Daniel, *More Than Black?*, 106–11; Rockquemore and Brunsma, *Beyond Black*, 41–48; Renn, *Mixed Race Students*, 67–93; Root, "Resolving 'Other' Status," 185–201; Rockquemore and Brunsma, *Beyond Black*, 71–72.

33. Daniel, "Two Parent Ethnicities," 17–18.

34. Daniel, "Two Parent Ethnicities," 17–18.

35. Daniel, *More Than Black?*, 93–111.

36. Daniel, *More Than Black?*, 48–60.

37. Daniel, *More Than Black?*, 68–75.

38. Virginia R. Domínguez, *White by Definition: Social Classification in Creole Louisiana* (New Brunswick NJ: Rutgers University Press, 1986), 23–50, 113–15, 134–40; James Haskins, *The Creoles of Color of New Orleans* (New York: Thomas Y. Crowell, 1975), 118–28.

39. Daniel, *More Than Black?*, 86–89.

40. Daniel, *More Than Black?*, 6–7, 11.

41. Daniel et al., "Emerging Paradigms," 11.

42. Marc P. Johnston and Kevin L. Nadal, "Multiracial Microaggressions: Exposing Monoracism in Everyday Life and Clinical Practice," in *Microaggressions and Marginality: Manifestation, Dynamics, and Impact*, ed. Derald Wing Sue (Hoboken NJ: Wiley, 2010), 125.

43. George Lipsitz, *How Racism Takes Place* (Philadelphia: Temple University Press, 2011), 6.

44. Kevin L. Nadal, Yinglee Wong, Katie Griffin, Julie Sriken, Vivian Vargas, Michelle Wideman, and Ajayi Kolawole, "Microaggressions and the Multiracial Experience," Special Issue, *International Journal of Humanities and Social Science* 1, no. 7 (2011): 43.

45. George Lipsitz, *The Possessive Investment in Whiteness: How White People Profit from Identity Politics* (Philadelphia: Temple University Press, 1998), 2.

46. Lipsitz, *How Racism Takes Place*, 6.

47. Rhett S. Jones, "The End of Africanity? The Bi-racial Assault on Blackness," *Western Journal of Black Studies* 18 (1994): 201–10.

48. Daniel, *More Than Black?*, 128–51; Kimberly Williams, *Mark One or More: Civil Rights in Multiracial America* (Ann Arbor: University of Michigan Press, 2006), 2, 39–64.

49. Daniel et al., "Emerging Paradigms," 10.

50. These include *Racially Mixed People in America* (1992) and *The Multiracial Experience: Racial Borders as the New Frontier* (1996), which were edited by psychologist Maria P. P. Root. I am a cofounding editor and editor in chief of the *Journal of Critical Mixed Race Studies*.

51. T. Maliqalim Simone, *About Face: Race in Postmodern America* (New York: Autonomedia, 1989), 141.

52. Ken Wilber, *The Marriage of Sense and Soul: Integrating Science and Religion* (New York: Random House, 1998), 141; Ruth Colker, *Hybrid: Bisexuals,*

Multiracials, and Other Misfits under American Law (New York: New York University Press, 1996), 1–10.

53. Sociologists designate modernity as the period beginning between the sixteenth and eighteenth centuries that encompasses the social formations of Western Europe. It was characterized by the ascent of materialist rationalism, secularism, capitalism, and individualism over other kinds of mentation. This led to a shift from traditional or premodern societies based on small, homogeneous, kin-based communities (typically rural), where religious and sacred traditions guided human existence, to more heterogeneous societies, where individualistic and secular concerns increasingly eclipsed communal and sacred ones. For a discussion of the "law of the excluded middle," see Stanley Teitelbaum, "Making Everything Perfectly Fuzzy," *Los Angeles Times Magazine*, April 1, 1990, 24–42.

54. Pierre Bourdieu, *Outline of a Theory of Practice*, trans. Richard Nice (New York: Cambridge University Press, 1970), 159.

55. Hans S. Bertens, "The Postmodern *Weltanschauung* and Its Relation to Modernism: An Introductory Survey," in *A Postmodern Reader*, ed. Joseph P. Natoli and Linda Hutcheon (Albany: State University of New York Press, 1993), 25–71.

56. Notable French postmodernist thinkers include Jean-François Lyotard (1924–98), Michel Foucault (1926–84), Jean Baudrillard (1929–2007), Gilles Deleuze (1925–95), Felix Guattari (1930–92), and Jacques Derrida (1930–2004). Judging from their writings, Lyotard, Foucault, Baudrillard, Deleuze, Guattari, and Derrida are all deconstructive postmodernists. See Huston Smith, *Beyond the Post-modern Mind*, 2nd rev. ed. (Wheaton IL: Theosophical Publishing House, 1989), 241.

57. Jean Baudrillard, *The Mirror of Production* (St. Louis: Telos Press, 1975), 88–89.

58. Wilber, *Marriage of Sense and Soul*, 141.

59. Pitirim Sorokin, *Social and Cultural Dynamics: A Study of Change in Major Systems of Art, Truth, Ethics, Law, and Social Relationships*, revised and abridged (Boston: Porter Sargent, 1957), 28–29, 623–28, 699–704.

60. Jacques Derrida, *Writing and Difference*, trans. Alan Bass (Chicago: University of Chicago Press, 1978), 278–83; Pauline Marie Rosenau, *Postmodernism and the Social Sciences: Insights, Inroads, and Intrusions* (Princeton NJ: Princeton University Press, 1992), 5–7; Steven Seidman, introduction to *The Postmodern Turn: New Perspectives on Social Theory*, ed. Steven Seidman (New York: Cambridge University Press, 1994), 1–23; Simone, *Race in Postmodern America*, 141.

61. Ali Rattansi, "'Western' Racisms, Ethnicities, and Identities in a 'Postmodern' Frame," in *Racism, Modernity, and Identity: On the Western Front*, ed. Ali Rattansi and Sallie Westwood (Cambridge: Polity Press, 1994), 30.

62. Naomi Zack, *Race and Mixed Race* (Philadelphia: Temple University Press, 1993), 99.

12

Shape Shifting into Blackness in the Post–Civil Rights Era

Margaret Hunter

Who is Black? Scholars, politicians, and cultural critics have grappled with this question for centuries. As debates over U.S. census categories raged and U.S. court decisions evolved, racial categories shifted tremendously over time. The "post–civil rights era," typically defined as the time period after the major legal civil rights victories of the 1960s, symbolizes a significant shift in how we think about racial identity and subordination. In our current post–civil rights era, legal definitions of race are less relevant to individual lives, but institutional discrimination remains totalizing. In 2015 people all over the country were discussing the White woman, Rachel Dolezal, who was "passing" as a Black woman and serving as president of the NAACP chapter in Spokane, Washington. After months of revelations, accusations, and exposes, Rachel Dolezal became a household name and a subject of racial anger, curiosity, and ridicule.[1] The national discussions over her identity all grew out of the fundamental question: What does it mean to be Black in the post–civil rights era? The post–civil rights era frames racial discourse through color-blind language. This era contains the paradox of legal rights for all individuals but persistent institutional racial discrimination. How does Dolezal's performance of shape shifting illuminate the contradictions of racial identity in this context?

As a biracial (African American and White) person, I pondered the curious case of Rachel Dolezal, and I could not help but compare her claims to Blackness against those of my newly found cousins. My cousins, whose light-skinned Black parents passed as White for decades, have recently learned that they are Black. My cousins, who were raised as White people, are working through what it means, in their circumstances, to suddenly be Black. They are undergoing their own shape shifting, which is not completely unlike Dolezal's. I wondered to myself, if my cousins, who lived their whole lives as White people surrounded by White people, are in fact Black, and Rachel Dolezal, who lived a large part of her life as a Black person surrounded by Black people, is in fact White, then what does it mean to be Black (or White) in the post–civil rights era? Whose claims to Blackness are valid, and on what basis?

I have spent much of my own life in and out of the center and margins of Blackness as a mixed race person who grew up in an integrated Black and White community in the Midwest. The paradox of race for my cousins and Rachel Dolezal has left me pondering these questions: What is the nature of Black identity, and what is its relationship to Black lived experiences? The recent trend of DNA ancestry tests has only contributed to the growing divergence between identity and lived experience. Although few people actually change their racial identities after learning the results, the popularity of the tests belies a broader sense that race is more complicated and ambivalent than we have previously understood in the United States.

Signifiers of Blackness are everywhere, especially as they refer to the urban street style popularized by mainstream hip-hop. Commercial jingles, celebrity gossip, and the ubiquitous group advertisements that always feature at least one African American body to demonstrate the inclusive nature of the university, hospital, bank, or country club being featured demonstrate the mainstreaming of Blackness today. While institutional racism rages on, African American bodies and cultural symbols are used constantly to communicate that U.S. culture is inclusive and urbane.[2]

This chapter investigates how non-Black people engage with Blackness in the post–civil rights era. As Paul Spickard describes in chapter 1 of this volume, not all shape shifting is passing, and passing is a much more complicated phenomenon than previously acknowledged. Shape shifting better captures the plasticity of race and the impermanence of racial categories. How, then, do non-Blacks shape shift in order to take up political, intellectual, and cultural forms of Blackness that, in the past, have been the exclusive terrain of African Americans? The goal of this chapter is not to question who is really Black or what kinds of Black experiences are "authentic" Black experiences, as much of the previous passing literature has done. These are impossible questions to answer and do not move forward a project of racial justice. Instead, I outline how lived Black experiences of many sorts have become split apart from Black identities and the implications of that split for African American communities. I am not suggesting that all non-Black people who engage in political, intellectual, or cultural Blackness are mimicking Blackness or culturally appropriating Blackness in problematic ways. In fact, there are some ways in which more people taking on aspects of Blackness (like political or intellectual Blackness) might lead to better outcomes for the Black community at large.

The Post–Civil Rights Context

Color blindness remains the dominant discourse on race and racism in the United States in the post–civil rights era. Color blindness, or color-blind racism, is a form of racial discourse that eschews any acknowledgment of racial difference and minimizes the role that institutional racism continues to play after the gains of the Civil Rights movements.[3] Following the overtly racial and often racist dialogues of the Jim Crow era, the 1980s ushered in a new silence around racism where any utterance about race as identity or social structure was viewed as racist. The new cultural silence around racism allowed purportedly race-neutral social structures and policies to operate with highly racialized outcomes. The unequal funding of public education, the increasingly punitive criminal justice system, and the stubborn racial wealth gap all reflected seemingly race-neutral policies with highly racialized outcomes.[4]

Scholars of color-blind racism, also called the "new racism," argue that the new racial discourse has four primary frames: abstract individualism, naturalization, cultural racism, and the minimization of racism.[5] Both abstract individualism and the minimization of racism are central to understanding the new forms of Blackness in the post–civil rights era. Abstract individualism relies on the liberal notion of the individual's ability to make free choices in a social/political/economic system. In the framework of color-blind racism, abstract individualism refers to Whites' understanding that everyone makes free choices to, for example, live in certain neighborhoods and work hard (or not) in school and is rewarded for individual choices and efforts. Whites tend to view themselves as individuals and not members of a racial group per se, and many Whites assume that all people in the United States have an equal opportunity to succeed.[6] In the framework of color-blind racism, differences in outcomes can be attributed to individual choices and efforts.

Abstract individualism also helps explain how Whites may come to take on certain Black identities, like cultural Blackness. If Blackness is simply an individual attribute and disconnected from a collective identity, then anyone can "try on" Blackness for a time. In this perspective, people "happen to be Black" instead of existing as part of Black histories and communities. The framework of abstract individualism helps explain how many people understand race (as individual identity) in the post–civil rights era. The individualistic nature of this definition of race allows race to be reduced to identity and disconnected from collective, historical experience.

The minimization of racism is the second framework of color-blind racism that helps explain the new forms of Blackness today.[7] Racism is frequently minimized in public discussions of race in several ways. Racial inequality may be rearticulated as class-based inequality, which many understand optimistically as "unfortunate but necessary" in a capitalist economy. Conversely, the minimization of racism describes racial inequality as an outcome that reflects African Americans' lack of effort or incompetence in a meritocracy. The minimization of racism is central to this chapter because when racism is minimized, then all that is left in terms of race is identity disassociated from history or social context. Racial shape shifting, as I am describing it, occurs most easily when the racial discourse understands racial difference as primarily about individual identity and not about history or social structure. Individual people, Whites especially, can take on Black identities more easily when those identities are seen as disconnected from larger communities or social histories. They are untethered to systems, genealogies, or racial communities and therefore can be tried on and discarded without repercussions. The minimization of racism creates a context whereby non-Blacks can access aspects of Black identity such as political orientations, intellectual histories, or cultural practices without any actual experiences of Blackness, including cultural practices, history, or discrimination.

It was within this context of color-blind racism that the new and much larger Black middle class began to grow. After Reconstruction the original Black middle class was vertically integrated in segregated neighborhoods where Black doctors, lawyers, and schoolteachers lived with low-income manual laborers. The Black community was more integrated by class, and Black residents of varying class levels shared some social institutions like churches and schools. By the 1980s the new Black middle class was growing at a fast pace, spurred by the significant legal gains of the Civil Rights movement and Black inroads into many professional occupations.[8] Middle-class Black families moved in large numbers from inner-city, racially segregated neighborhoods to first-ring, integrated suburbs outside of many major U.S. cities.[9] While residential segregation continued to be a defining feature of American cities, many African American middle-class families lived in all-Black middle-class suburbs next to traditionally Black neighborhoods, or they lived in moderately integrated first-ring suburbs.[10] This post–civil rights shift in housing options for the middle class left primarily low-income and working-class African American families in increasingly dilapidated and underresourced inner-city neighborhoods that once stood as the core of Black communities across the nation.

Movement from vertically segregated Black neighborhoods left the Black middle class increasingly alienated from traditional Black institutions such as churches, schools, and local political organizations that remained in many city centers.[11] Although many African American residents of the suburbs maintained some contact with organizations in their old neighborhoods, their social ties were weakened, and the network was less embedded.[12] The movement of the African American middle class to the suburbs and the consequential weakening of social ties between the Black middle class and traditionally Black neighborhoods and social institutions led to the relative divergence of middle-class Black experiences from the Black experiences of low-income and working-class families.[13] This has contributed to a situation where Black identities are increasingly bifurcated and, in some cases, disconnected from traditional Black lived experiences in Black communities. Consequently, new Black identities have emerged for many African Americans that are not entirely framed by a Black bourgeoisie (as in the past) or by an economically integrated African American community. The fracturing of African American identities from traditionally segregated Black communities marks a new era in Blackness and Black identity.

The second major factor in creating new forms of Blackness in the post–civil rights era is the explosion of hip-hop as a cultural form and economic force. Hip-hop began in the South Bronx in the 1970s but quickly became a global cultural and arts movement with a multi-billion-dollar footprint. Although hip-hop was multiracial in its origins, rap music was branded as a Black cultural product when it was mass-marketed in the late 1980s and early 1990s.[14] In its "golden era," hip-hop offered a cornucopia of voices and stories that represented a broad swath of African American lives and experiences. By the late 1980s gangsta rap was proving to be extremely commercially lucrative, especially among White consumers, which led to a narrowing of the images projected by rap artists who were signed for music contracts with major labels.[15]

Artists who performed gangsta characters were most popular with White audiences and therefore dominated the rap genre. Gangsta rap became a mainstream phenomenon, and a narrow set of Black identities, such as the Black criminal, the Black pimp, and the Black mogul / organized criminal became dominant icons in popular culture. Hip-hop capitalism packaged, mass-marketed, and sold these identities for high profits for decades. The shift of hip-hop into mainstream popular culture helped create a key set of Black identities that already had a long history in the White imaginary. Connecting to historical controlling images of African American men as violent and sexually predatory, these identities were marketed by African American and White music executives as a part of "Black cool." Narratives of danger, strength, power, and dominant sexuality helped construct the new Black rap identities as desirable costumes for Whites and others to try on, masquerade in, or experiment with. Hip-hop's ability to raise these cultural images to iconic status helped construct a context where Black identities were products for sale, to be consumed and then discarded when the fun was over.

I argue that the post–civil rights context has created a unique moment when Blackness has been decoupled from lived Black experiences. As the African American middle class grew substantially and then moved out of segregated African American neighborhoods Blackness began to shift, and Black experiences were no longer necessarily deeply connected to substantial Black communities. This phenomenon need not be evaluated as either good or bad; it is simply the result of changes in legal-political-economic structures as they relate to racism in the United States. The changes for the Black middle class, coupled with the mainstream popularity of hip-hop and its marketing of a narrow set of Black identities, opened up access to understanding Blackness and Black identities from new social positions. The disconnection between "being Black" and "performing Blackness" is highlighted in the post–civil rights era, and temporary shape shifting into Black identities by people who are not Black is increasingly common.

There is now a marked increase in the number of non-Blacks who inhabit a kind of post–civil rights "Black" identity. In the following sections, I outline the emergence of three forms of Blackness in the post–civil rights era: cultural Blackness, political Blackness, and intellectual Blackness. Each of these kinds of Blackness may be performed by non-Blacks and tried on or discarded at will. As Spickard describes in chapter 1, this chapter investigates individually initiated changes to racial identity for a specific purpose or gain, although not necessarily a cynical one. This form of shape shifting is not a change in an individual's actual racial identity, as Rachel Dolezal tried to do, but instead is an aspect of one's racial performance.

Cultural Blackness

Cultural Blackness may be the form of Blackness with the longest genealogy in the United States. "Black cool" dates back to at least the 1920s.[16] Black cool describes the phenomenon of Whites (among others) imbuing a form of outsider status or "cool" to aspects of African American culture such as music, dance, and the visual arts.[17] Jazz clubs, the Lindy hop, and art galleries featuring graffiti art are all examples of Black cultural products that increased in status because Whites viewed them as exotic, sexual, or rebellious and associated them with Blackness in ways they viewed as focused on the body and/or the primitive. White views of these Black cultural products aligned with White views of African Americans in general: they were focused on the body rather than the mind, and they were barbaric/primitive and childlike. African American cultural forms are most popular with Whites when they can be interpreted in existing frameworks for understanding Blackness as bodily, savage, sexual, and childlike.[18]

Even when interracial contact in social venues was relatively rare and its consequences were high, some Whites attended music and dance clubs featuring African American artists to demonstrate that they were urbane and sophisticated or to show rebelliousness. Greg Tate describes this phenomenon as "everything but the burden": the practice of Whites consuming Black culture while never understanding or taking on any of the burden of Blackness in a racist society.[19]

In the post–civil rights era, the consumption of Black cultural products has reached an all-time high. Hip-hop music, dance, and visual arts have achieved unprecedented popularity across a racially diverse global audience. U.S. Whites in particular consume mainstream hip-hop in huge numbers. The popularity of mainstream hip-hop with White Americans may be directly related to the way that Blackness is represented in it: as criminal, poor, dangerous, and out of control.

This image of African Americans fits squarely into the White imaginary and therefore makes hip-hop an exceptionally popular cultural product for sale.

Recently, Black cultural products have shifted from being primarily *consumed* by Whites to also being *produced* by Whites. The massively successful rapper Iggy Azalea, a White woman born and raised in Australia, is a prime example of this shift. Azalea, who set records as the first female rapper to have a single at number one on the Billboard charts for seven consecutive weeks, dominated the pop music and hip-hop scenes in 2014 and 2015.[20] Although her music has received mixed reviews among critics, she is hugely popular among fans, especially U.S. Whites.

In the post–civil rights era, when the cultural production of Blackness can be separated from Black lived experiences, White artists like Iggy Azalea can shape shift and create Black cultural products with huge success.[21] Azalea's rap success is built in part on her mastery of the linguistic conventions of African American–style rap music. In fact, her so-called blaccent is at the center of a media firestorm around race, authenticity, and cultural appropriation.[22] Her lyrics and style mimic those of African American rappers, a skill that she cultivated while living in the southern United States for several years after growing up in rural Australia.

Unlike other successful White rappers such as Eminem and Macklemore, Azalea avoids acknowledging her Whiteness. Her "rap standpoint," or social position in the rap landscape, assumes an African American centrality. Her language, dress, and topics all center African American aesthetics. In this way she performs a "cultural Blackness" disconnected from actual racial structures, people, or histories.[23] Minstrelsy, or the performance of blackface, is not a new cultural construction, but Azalea's performance exists in a post–civil rights context where it is increasingly common for people to inhabit Black cultural identities as a part of their entire persona, not just as a concert performance.[24]

Some critics have argued that what Azalea is doing is not new at all but yet another iteration of Whites performing in blackface for a White audience.[25] They suggest that Azalea is not doing anything "post–civil rights" at all and that her production of cultural Blackness (and her massive success doing it) is simply a reprise of earlier artists' actions, such as those of Elvis Presley. In fact, what Azalea is doing is actually unlike Elvis Presley. Elvis Presley used African American music and dance styles and made them palatable to White audiences by performing Whiter versions of them as a White person. Presley was popular because he was selling his Whiteness. Iggy Azalea is doing the exact opposite; she is selling her Blackness. Azalea's rap appeal is in her performance of Blackness, her ability to inhabit a Black identity that she suggests is an authentic performance.[26] Even linguists Maeve Eberhardt and Kara Freeman suggest that Azalea's mastery of Black English is impressive for someone who lived in the southern United States for only a few years. White audiences love Black hip-hop performers who perform aspects of Black identity and experience that are intelligible through dominant narratives of Black criminality, but they like White performers who are Black even better.[27] The best evidence for this is the massive album sales for White rappers relative to Black rappers.[28]

Cultural Blackness in the post–civil rights era is a form of shape shifting that allows individual non-Blacks to inhabit or clothe themselves in Blackness through the production of Black cultural products. These products, often found in mainstream hip-hop, are also highly valuable to White audiences who are anxious to consume images of Blackness rendered from the White imagination. For example, liquors, clothing lines, and headphones are all merchandising lines branded by high-profile African American rappers with broad, multiracial consumer bases.

Political Blackness

The idea of political Blackness in the post–civil rights era first gained traction with President Bill Clinton's 1992 election campaign. Clinton was a White southerner but was perceived as a moderate on racial issues. In fact, he downplayed racial issues during his 1992 campaign in order to court the so-called Reagan Democrats of the South.[29] After his election many African Americans viewed him as an ally, although ultimately that would be challenged after the three strikes law and welfare reform legislation passed during his presidency.

In a 1998 *New Yorker* article, Toni Morrison referred to Clinton as "America's first Black president":

> African-American men seemed to understand it right away. Years ago, in the middle of the Whitewater investigation, one heard the first murmurs: white skin notwithstanding, this is our first black President. Blacker than any actual black person who could ever be elected in our children's lifetime. After all, Clinton displays almost every trope of blackness: single-parent household, born poor, working-class, saxophone-playing, McDonald's-and-junk-food-loving boy from Arkansas. And when virtually all the African-American Clinton appointees began, one by one, to disappear, when the President's body, his privacy, his unpoliced sexuality became the focus of the persecution, when he was metaphorically seized and body-searched, who could gainsay these black men who knew whereof they spoke? The message was clear: "No matter how smart you are, how hard you work, how much coin you earn for us, we will put you in your place or put you out of the place you have somehow, albeit with our permission, achieved. You will be fired from your job, sent away in disgrace, and—who knows?—maybe sentenced and jailed to boot. In short, unless you do as we say (i.e., assimilate at once), your expletives belong to us."[30]

Morrison's much-misunderstood quotation described President Bill Clinton as Black not because of his ease in Black communities or his humble origins. She described him as Black because he was assumed to be guilty, violating sexual norms, and scapegoated for the nation's problems. She viewed the impeachment hearings as evidence he was treated unfairly and with bias, guilty before the trial.[31]

Regardless of Morrison's original intent of the "first Black president" moniker, Bill and Hillary Clinton (and most of the American public) understood it as an affectionate compliment, the "you're one of us" stamp of approval so many Whites long for from African

Americans. Clinton was at ease in Black communities, and he cultivated his status as a White person who had an affinity with African
Americans, allowing him to maintain his White privilege while also
currying favor among politically well-connected African American
politicians and leaders. "The Clintons' relationship with the African-
American community has been deep and mutually beneficial," wrote
Gil Troy for *Politico* magazine.[32]

Bill Clinton's deep connection with Black political leaders and the
Black electorate persevered throughout his presidency and into the
many political campaigns of his wife, senator, and then Secretary of
State Hillary Clinton, despite major missteps such as crime and welfare policies that deeply hurt Black communities.[33] Both Clintons had
access to extraordinary amounts of racial political capital, even when
Hillary Clinton ran against Barack Obama in 2008. In fact, several
notable African American political elites backed Hillary Clinton in
the early days of the 2008 Democratic primary race. The Clintons are
"politically Black" in that their political power is deeply connected
to Black political power, and their orientation to many major political issues is aligned with African American mainstream political
leaders.[34] They perform a political Blackness through alliances, positions, and orientations to political issues. Much like cultural Blackness, political Blackness is only possible in the post–civil rights era
when multiracial political coalitions are increasingly common and
there exists a critical mass of powerful African American politicians.
In fact, it is the "New American Majority" that writer Jonathan Capehart argues is central to Hillary Clinton's success.[35] Composed primarily of African American and Latino voters, as well as progressive
Whites, this new majority, argues Capehart, is central to any politician's success. Hillary Clinton's political shape shifting is not necessarily a bad thing. Her ability to leverage political Blackness to build
a multiracial and progressive political base very nearly propelled her
into the White House.

Hillary Clinton has embraced the Black Lives Matter movement in a
way that has differentiated her from many other politicians. Although
Black Lives Matter has more resonance with younger African American

voters than older African American voters, Clinton's connection to the movement and her willingness to share the stage with its leaders reinforced for the Black community at large her political Blackness.

In Hillary Clinton's bid for the U.S. presidency, her status as the first female candidate of a major American political party was central to her campaign. But equally important was her ability to lead a multiracial coalition of progressive voters. Her open and frank dialogues about racism and immigrant rights led to her leadership of leftist Whites, African Americans, Latinos, Asian Americans, and others in a coalition only strengthened by Donald Trump's Far Right, European-style racism and xenophobia. She was the first White candidate of a major party to lead an overtly multiracial coalition with several key racial issues as central to her campaign. Her performance of political Blackness benefited her campaign but came up short against the growing White working-class racial resentment in the United States.

Another example of political Blackness has come from the Black Lives Matter movement. Created from the outrage over the dozens of high-profile police shootings of African American men and boys, Black Lives Matter is a grassroots movement against the police violence and legal corruption that hold no one accountable for the deaths of African Americans by the state. Police violence is a multiracial problem, and Black Lives Matter is actually a multiracial movement, even though the focus has been on African Americans. Many in the movement see the voices of African American and Latino leaders as central to decision making and interaction with the press, largely because those communities have been most impacted by police violence. Interestingly, in some cities in particular, White participants in Black Lives Matter have begun to take on larger and larger roles in the movement, to the chagrin of many of the Black and Latino participants. In Oakland, California, for example, people of color in the movement began to encourage White participants to walk behind the people of color in the marches as a way to rein in what felt like White power encroaching on Black and Latino leadership. In this way, Whites are shape shifting into political Blackness, where they attempt to lead social movements at the center of African American civil rights struggles today. Both for better and for worse, non-Blacks continue to shape shift into political Blackness and take on the issues and orientations central to African American lives in the United States. For some shape shifters, politics is an end in itself, but for others, political Blackness is built on a Black intellectual foundation.

Intellectual Blackness

Intellectual Blackness may be the most recent development of postracial Blackness. Intellectual Blackness describes an intellectual orientation to ideas, theories, and social problem solving that stems from a Black intellectual tradition. Many African American scholars, especially in the humanities and social sciences, have long been deeply influenced by a canon of key Black thinkers from the United States and Africa and across the African diaspora, such as W. E. B. Du Bois, Harold Cruse, Angela Davis, Frantz Fanon, and Patricia Hill Collins.[36] People who take on an identity of intellectual Blackness center their intellectual inquiry in the ideas of these canonical thinkers and make intellectual and academic arguments based in this Black-centered body of work.

For generations, intellectual Blackness in the United States has primarily been inhabited by African American scholars. African American scholars have been influenced by thinkers of all backgrounds, but many have dedicated their work to improving the condition of Blacks in the United States and therefore lean heavily on the work of Black scholars before them. In many disciplines, African American and other Black thinkers are ignored, disparaged, or characterized as narrow thinkers for their focus on Black liberation. Aldon Morris's recent book, *The Scholar Denied: W. E. B. Du Bois and the Birth of Modern Sociology*, outlines the many ways that Du Bois's work was marginalized and ignored in the social sciences despite the fact that his work was at the forefront of American sociology.[37] While marginalization of scholars of color still happens today, these dynamics have shifted somewhat given the institutionalization of the discipline of ethnic studies in the United States.[38] As ethnic studies courses have become increasingly common on college campuses, large numbers of non-Black college students have been exposed to the ideas of scholars of color, especially African American writers.

It is now common to read non-Black authors, especially White authors, who write about racism from an intellectual perspective grounded in a Black intellectual tradition. There already exists a long history of White authors writing about the African American experience from a White perspective, sometimes constructing Black communities in pathological ways.[39] But more recently, it is White authors employing the discourse and theoretical framework of Black scholars that is growing in frequency. This intellectual shape shifting has allowed some Whites to write very influential books on the African American experience and maintain a significant grounding in Black intellectual thought.[40]

Intellectual Blackness has created a perplexing phenomenon where non-Black actors can create knowledge about the Black experience by drawing on influential Black authors but without traversing a lived Black experience of any kind. It is important to acknowledge that there is a multiplicity of Black experiences in the United States today from which a scholar may draw. Most Black scholars will live out multiple Black experiences in their lifetimes that differ by class, sexuality, race, nationality, region, religion, and language. These Black experiences typically happen in relation to some sort of Black community. For example, in his film *Black Is . . . Black Ain't*, Marlon Riggs highlights the tensions within the African American community around various forms of the Black experience.[41] His work clarifies that there is no unitary Black experience; instead, there is a series of contested and conflicting Black experiences, all of which are connected to the history of African Americans and various kinds of Black diasporic communities.

What are the disadvantages and advantages of the open access to intellectual Blackness in the post–civil rights era? If more people are reading and thinking about racism from the perspective of African Americans (and of other communities of color), knowledge production about racism will increase and improve. Certainly, more people should read Du Bois, Fanon, and Collins as they grapple with ideas about racism. When non-Blacks take up these perspectives they may bring new insights, new applications, and new challenges to the paradigms of the canonical Black thinkers. However, it is also possible that Whites in particular may use the authority of their Whiteness, coupled with an identity of intellectual Blackness, to make powerful arguments about Black lives.

One example of this phenomenon is the recent publication of Alice Goffman's ethnographic study *On the Run: Fugitive Life in an American City*.[42] Goffman's book, which has generated more publicity for the discipline of sociology than anything in recent memory, has been widely criticized for, among other things, caricaturing low-income African American communities and the people who live in them.[43] While she writes from the purported position of intellectual Blackness, which gives her work more racial authority, she offers ethnographic stories of African American men without a larger context of social institutions.[44] Goffman takes strident positions against the prison-industrial complex but offers little analysis of the social institutions in which the subjects are embedded. In his well-documented criticisms of the book, Victor Rios argues that Goffman's focus on sensational stories and her unusually close relationships with the people she is studying undermine the overall argument.[45] He suggests that she has "gone rogue" as an ethnographer and has written a book using a "jungle trope" on the Black community. Moreover, her own position in the field as a young White woman from a wealthy family is largely uninterrogated in her work.[46] Her Whiteness gives her claims about Black life a racial authority they might not otherwise have. Intellectual Blackness can have clear benefits to the African American public, but it can also mask long-standing scholarly interpretations of Black community life rooted in White racism.

Another example of intellectual Blackness can be found in the work of Tim Wise. Wise, who is also White, is best known for his critiques of Whiteness in his recent books *Dear White America: Letter to a New Minority* and *White Like Me: Reflections on Race from a Privileged Son*.[47] Wise's intellectual project is rooted in African American intellectual history, but his topic is White experience rather than

Black. His published work and public talks focus on understanding White privilege and the unspoken habitus of Whiteness that undergird much of the nation's racism. Through a combination of personal reflection, cultural analysis, and polemics, Wise unpacks White racism for a general audience.

Unlike in Alice Goffman's work, Wise's own White identity is central to his essays and public speeches. In fact, he uses his own Whiteness to gain access to and legitimacy with his often primarily White audiences. And unlike Iggy Azalea, Wise is not selling his own Blackness. In fact, Wise is selling his Whiteness, his White allyship, and his status in the field of antiracism as a White advocate. Although he is "intellectually Black," his social identity remains White. It is this paradox that led to a series of social media dustups on Facebook and Twitter that revolved around the issue of White privilege in the field of antiracist work. Many fans of Wise felt betrayed or disappointed by his words, but I argue that those exchanges reveal the nature of shape shifting in the post–civil rights era. It is very challenging for Whites to shed their White orientations, regardless of how many Black theorists they read. And that does not diminish the important work that White antiracists do, but it does place them in a broader racial context that constrains all of our work.

In an ironic conclusion to this essay, when Tim Wise was invited to give a talk at Eastern Washington University, he was informed that a faculty person in the Africana Studies Department objected to the invitation because she felt he had no authority to speak on the subject of racism as a White person. It was later revealed that the objecting faculty person was Rachel Dolezal.[48] This revelation brings the discussion back to its original question. How do Whites shape shift into Blackness in the post–civil rights era? Who has claims to Blackness now, and on what basis do people make those claims?

I have argued that cultural Blackness, political Blackness, and intellectual Blackness are phenomena of the post–civil rights era, during which Black lived experiences have become separated from Black identities. This split is neither good nor bad, but it is inevitable. Shape shifting complicates the previous discourse of passing and makes room for more nuanced and ambivalent understandings of movement across racial identities. Given the realities of an increasingly class-divided African American community in the postindustrial era and the massive mainstream popularity of Black images through hip-hop, Blackness has become separated from traditional Black experiences in the United States. This fracturing of identity from experience has allowed many people across racial groups to shape shift into various kinds of Black identities. When non-Blacks, especially Whites, take on Black identities and make claims about the African American community, that practice can be harmful. On the other hand, it can also be beneficial to have a wider audience connected to Black political, intellectual, and cultural contributions than in the past. Non-Blacks may bring innovations, new perspectives, and ideas to understanding Black experiences, or racism more generally, by immersing themselves in Black cultural production, Black political action, or Black intellectual thought. As identities become increasingly divorced from experiences, shape shifting will continue to raise important questions about the meaning of Blackness in the new millennium.

Notes

1. Allison Samuels, "Rachel Dolezal's True Lies," *Vanity Fair: Hive*, July 19, 2015.
2. Zeus Leonardo and Margaret Hunter, "Imagining the Urban: The Politics of Race, Class, and Schooling," in *The International Handbook of Urban Education*, ed. M. Foster (Dordrecht, the Netherlands: Springer, 2007), 779–801; Brian Behnken and Gregory Smithers, *Racism in American Popular Media: From Aunt Jemima to the Frito Bandito* (Santa Barbara CA: Praeger, 2015).
3. Eduardo Bonilla-Silva, *Racism without Racists: Color-Blind Racism and the Persistence of Racial Inequality in America* (Lanham MD: Rowman & Littlefield, 2009); Patricia Hill Collins, *Black Sexual Politics: African Americans, Gender, and the New Racism* (New York: Routledge, 2005).
4. Michael Brown, Martin Carnoy, Elliott Currie, Troy Duster, David Oppenheimer, Marjorie Schultz, and David Wellman, *White-Washing Race: The Myth of a Colorblind Society* (Berkeley: University of California Press, 2003).
5. Bonilla-Silva, *Racism without Racists*.
6. Brown et al., *White-Washing Race*.

7. Bonilla-Silva, *Racism without Racists*.

8. Bart Landry, *The New Black Middle Class* (Berkeley: University of California Press, 1988); Paul Attewell, David Lavin, Thurston Domina, and Tania Levey, "The Black Middle Class: Progress, Prospects, and Puzzles," *Journal of African American Studies* 8, no. 1–2 (2004): 6–19.

9. Douglas Massey and Nancy Denton, *American Apartheid* (Cambridge MA: Harvard University Press, 1998); Mary Pattillo-McCoy, *Black Picket Fences: Privilege and Peril among the Black Middle Class* (Chicago: University of Chicago Press, 1999).

10. Cherise Harris, *The Cosby Cohort: Blessings and Burdens of Growing Up Black Middle Class* (Lanham MA: Rowman & Littlefield, 2013).

11. Elizabeth R. Cole and Safiya R. Omari, "Race, Class, and the Dilemmas of Upward Mobility for African Americans," *Journal of Social Issues* 59, no. 4 (2003): 785–802.

12. Nikki Khanna, "Country Clubs and Hip-Hop Thugs: Examining the Role of Social Class and Culture in Shaping Racial Identity," in *Multiracial Americans and Social Class: The Influence of Social Class on Racial Identity*, ed. K. O. Korgen (New York: Routledge, 2010), 53–71.

13. Karyn Lacy, *Blue-Chip Black: Race, Class, and Status in the New Black Middle Class* (Berkeley: University of California Press, 2007); Keesha Moore, "What's Class Got to Do with It? Community Development and Racial Identity," *Journal of Urban Affairs* 27, no. 4 (2005): 437–51.

14. Jeff Chang, *Can't Stop Won't Stop: A History of the Hip-Hop Generation* (New York: Picador, 2005).

15. Tricia Rose, *The Hip Hop Wars: What We Talk About When We Talk About Hip Hop—and Why It Matters* (New York: Basic Civitas Books, 2008).

16. David Levering Lewis, *When Harlem Was in Vogue* (New York: Knopf, 1981).

17. Rebecca Walker, introduction to *Black Cool: One Thousand Streams of Blackness*, ed. R. Walker (Berkeley: Soft Skull Press, 2012).

18. bell hooks, *We Real Cool: Black Men and Masculinity* (New York: Routledge, 2003).

19. Greg Tate, "Nigs R Us, or How Blackfolk Became Fetish Objects," in *Everything but the Burden: What White People Are Taking from Black Culture*, ed. Greg Tate (New York: Broadway Books, 2003), 1–14.

20. Jeff Guo, "How Iggy Azalea Mastered Her Blaccent," *Washington Post*, January 4, 2016.

21. Brittney Cooper, "Iggy Azalea's Post-racial Mess: America's Oldest Race Tale, Remixed," *Salon*, 2014, http://www.salon.com/2014/07/15/iggy_azaleas_post_racial_mess_americas_oldest_race_tale_remixed/.

22. Maeve Eberhardt and Kara Freeman, "'First Things First, I'm the Realest': Linguistic Appropriation, White Privilege, and the Hip-Hop Persona of Iggy Azalea," *Journal of Sociolinguistics* 19, no. 3 (2015): 303–27.

23. Jelani Cobb, "Black Like Her?," *New Yorker,* June 15, 2015.

24. Cecelia Cutler, *White Hip-Hoppers, Language, and Identity in Post-modern America* (New York: Routledge, 2014).

25. Bethonie Butler, "Is Iggy Azalea 'the Realest' or Is Her Authenticity up for Interpretation?," *Washington Post,* May 29, 2014.

26. Cobb, "Black Like Her?"

27. Mickey Hess, "Hip-Hop Realness and the White Performer," *Critical Studies in Media Communication* 22 (2005): 372–89.

28. Cutler, *White Hip-Hoppers.*

29. Paul Frymer, *Uneasy Alliances: Race and Party Competition in America* (Princeton NJ: Princeton University Press, 2010).

30. Toni Morrison, "Talk of the Town: Comment," *New Yorker,* October 5, 1998.

31. Ta-Nehisi Coates, "It Was No Compliment to Call Bill Clinton 'The First Black President,'" *Atlantic,* August 27, 2015.

32. Gil Troy, "Why Black Voters Don't Feel the Bern," *Politico,* March 7, 2016, http://www.politico.com/magazine/story/2016/03/why-black-voters-dont-feel -the-bern-213707.

33. Danielle Kurtzleben, "Understanding the Clintons' Popularity with Black Voters," National Public Radio, March 1, 2016, http://www.npr.org/2016/03 /01/468185698/understanding-the-clintons-popularity-with-black-voters.

34. Laura Meckler, "Black Women Rally behind Hillary Clinton," *Wall Street Journal,* April 28, 2016, http://www.wsj.com/articles/black-women-rally-behind -hillary-clinton-1461866619.

35. Jonathan Capehart, "Why Black Voters Remain in Hillary Clinton's Corner," *Washington Post,* February 25, 2016.

36. W. E. B. Du Bois, *The Souls of Black Folk* (New York: Penguin Books, 1903); Harold Cruse, *The Crisis of the Negro Intellectual: A Historical Analysis of the Failure of Black Leadership* (New York: New York Review of Books, 1967); Angela Davis, *Women, Race, and Class* (New York: Vintage, 1983); Patricia Hill Collins, *Black Feminist Thought* (New York: Routledge, 1990); Frantz Fanon, *Black Skin, White Masks,* trans. R. Philcox (New York: Grove Press, 1952).

37. Aldon Morris, *The Scholar Denied: W. E. B. Du Bois and the Birth of Modern Sociology* (Berkeley: University of California Press, 2015).

38. Philip Q. Yang, *Ethnic Studies: Issues and Approaches* (Albany: State University of New York Press, 2000).

39. Robin D. G. Kelley, "Lookin' for the 'Real' Nigga: Social Scientists Construct the Ghetto," in *That's the Joint! The Hip-Hop Studies Reader*, ed. M. Forman and M. A. Neal (New York: Routledge, 2011), 134–52.

40. For example, Mitch Duneier, *Sidewalk* (New York: Farrar, Straus and Giroux, 2000); Jennifer Tilton, *Dangerous or Endangered? Race and the Politics of Youth in Urban America* (New York: NYU Press, 2010).

41. Marlon Riggs, *Black Is . . . Black Ain't*, DVD, Docurama Studio, New York, 1994.

42. Alice Goffman, *On the Run: Fugitive Life in an American City* (Chicago: University of Chicago Press, 2014).

43. James Forman Jr., "The Society of Fugitives," *Atlantic*, October 2014.

44. C. J. Pascoe, "Racism, Punishment, and the Lives of Young Men of Color," *Society Pages*, December 3, 2014, https://thesocietypages.org/girlwpen/2014/12/03/racism-punishment-and-the-lives-of-young-men-of-color/.

45. Victor Rios, "Book Review: *On the Run: Fugitive Life in an American City*," *American Journal of Sociology* 121, no. 1 (2015): 306–8.

46. Gideon Lewis-Kraus, "The Trials of Alice Goffman," *New York Times*, January 12, 2016.

47. Tim Wise, *White Like Me: Reflections on Race from a Privileged Son* (Berkeley CA: Soft Skull Press, 2005); Wise, *Dear White America: Letter to a New Minority* (San Francisco: City Lights Publishers, 2012).

48. Katherine Timpf, "Author: Dolezal Said I Had 'No Authority' to Speak about Racism at University Because I'm White," *National Review*, June 18, 2015, http://www.nationalreview.com/article/419992/author-dolezal-said-i-had-no-authority-speak-about-racism-university-because-im-white.

PART 3

Compelled Identity

13

Mudrooroo

Aboriginal No More?

Paul Spickard

Mudrooroo was an Australian who once was known as Colin Johnson and also went by other names. He occupied many identities: Indigenous Australian, Buddhist priest, beatnik, famous writer, Aboriginal activist, former Aboriginal, and, lately, Aboriginal once again. It is a complicated tale of repeated identity shifting, sometimes by Mudrooroo's own choice and sometimes by the force of others.

Adam Shoemaker, an eminent scholar of Aboriginal literature, wrote of Mudrooroo in 2011: "I believe that—had Mudrooroo died in 1994 or 1995—his reputation as a literary pioneer would live on today untarnished. His works would be extensively taught, anthologised and discussed. . . . Mudrooroo played a central role in [a vital] transformation—a cogent increase in mainstream recognition of the merit of Indigenous writers and their work. . . . [T]he strong, written Indigeneity he had passionately advocated [for so long just then was coming] into stronger focus."[1]

In order to understand the fluctuating identity journey of Mudrooroo, it will be helpful to understand a few things about the history of racial hierarchy and racial mixing in Australia.[2] Racialized relationships have been complex throughout Australia's history. Prior to British intervention, the Indigenous population was fairly thinly spread across an immense landscape, with concentrations in river valleys and in some coastal areas. There were many different Native peoples in Australia with distinct names, territories, languages, and lifeways. Outsiders—mostly British in origin—insisted on lumping them all together as "Aboriginal." That has never been an accurate designation; nonetheless, it has been a persistent one.

In addition to Europeans and Aboriginal Australians, some outside peoples were brought in systematically, including Afghan camel drivers in central and Western Australia and Pacific Islander contract laborers in Queensland. In the early generations of British conquest and settlement, there was a lot of racial mixing, largely White men and Aboriginal women, but also Aboriginal men and White women, White women and Chinese men, and other combinations galore.[3] This meant that huge numbers of people whose families were multigenerational in Australia had complicated racial ancestries. There was also a lot of racial violence. Some was associated with conquest (and extermination campaigns) and some with practices that approached racialized enslavement. In social relationships, White supremacy (and among Whites, British supremacy) was the rule of the day. It remains an active force in Australian society, barely disguised, to this day.

In the late nineteenth century and throughout much of the twentieth, Whites tried to get a handle on Australia's racial pluralism. One mechanism was the White Australia policy. That was not one law but a series of governmental and social actions, commencing with the Immigration Restriction Act of 1901, that sought to bar non-White immigrants (especially Asians and Melanesians) from coming into Australia. Their vision was enunciated near midcentury by Prime Minister John Curtin: "This country shall remain forever the home of the descendants of those people who came here in peace in order to establish in the South Seas an outpost of the British race."[4] Another method to bring about White supremacy was the Aboriginal assimilation policy. The idea was to segregate people who were deemed fully, biologically unmixed Aborigines, punish them, and prevent them from flourishing. The next step was to take mixed race children (especially girls) and turn them into White people.[5]

Both the White Australia policy and the assimilation policy were intended to make and keep Australia White. They imagined that

Aboriginal people would wither and disappear and that Australia would become a White republic. The former didn't happen, but not for lack of effort on the part of White Australians. The latter has been the political reality in Australia throughout the twentieth and twenty-first centuries.

In recent decades, racialized relationships in Australia have taken on two dominant shapes. In eastern cities with international outlooks (Sydney, Canberra, Melbourne, Brisbane, Adelaide, etc.), cosmopolitanism is the order of the day. It is mostly a matter of mixing between White and Asian Australians in those places. In the Northern Territory, in northern Queensland, in the western part of South Australia, and in the vast stretches of Western Australia, there exist relatively small numbers of White people (except in a few cities like Perth and Fremantle). In those regions, one feels the presence of somewhat larger numbers of Aboriginally descended people, including people of mixed Aboriginal and White ancestry. In these areas, relationships between White Australians and Indigenous Australians are frequently fraught. It is in Western Australia that we encounter Mudrooroo.

Colin Johnson / Mudrooroo

The story of Colin Johnson, a man of several names and many identities, is a cautionary tale about shape shifting.[6] One may have a complicated family history that presents one with multiple ethnic options, and one may wish to inhabit a particular identity that connects with part of that history, but one's identity is not necessarily purely a matter of one's own choice. One's options may be constrained, whether by the dominant discourse of the majority group in society or by the subdominant discourse of a minority group with whom one might be associated. And both dominant and subdominant groups can change their minds.[7] Colin Johnson took on several identities over a long career. He was rather a famous poet, novelist, playwright, essayist, and academic and a leader in the cultural politics of Aboriginal Australia for several decades. And then, quite suddenly, he was forced to stop being all of those things. He was accused of being a racial fraud, and then he was forced to give up his lifelong identity against his will.

Fig. 13.1. Colin Johnson / Mudrooroo, from Aboriginal to not and back again.
Courtesy of Tom Thompson, ETT Imprint.

Johnson's early life was difficult and not unlike the lives of many other poor children in mixed race families. He was born in 1938, the youngest and perhaps the darkest in color of many children, in East Cuballing, a tiny hamlet in southwestern Australia.[8] His father died while Colin was in the womb, whereupon eight of the older siblings were taken into care by the state. The home seems to have been a tumultuous one, with not much money or parental supervision. As he described it later, "For the first nine years of my life we lived in the small town of Beverley where no one would talk to us, because we were poor and black. . . . When we went to school, we were segregated with the other Aboriginal children. . . . [My mother] was treated as an Aborigine and we were treated as Aborigines, too."[9] When Colin was nearly nine he and an older sister Shirley—"the terrors of the town," in his words—were charged with theft and removed from their mother's care.[10] Colin was placed at Clontarf Boys' Town, a Christian Brothers home near Perth, where he remained for seven years.[11] He left at sixteen, then lived on his own for two years, pursuing the profession of burglar, before returning to an institutional setting: a couple of stretches in Fremantle Prison.

While he was there, he met Dame Mary Durack, a wealthy novelist, poet, and do-gooder. She noticed that he liked to read, to talk about ideas, and to write; she became his mentor. He read Allen Ginsberg and Jack Kerouac and imagined himself a Dharma Bum. He traveled on the cheap across Southeast Asia to India, on to London to see the Beat scene there, and back to Australia, where he took a job in Melbourne. With encouragement from Durack, Johnson wrote a Kerouacesque novel, *Wild Cat Falling*, about Aboriginal life in Western Australia; it was published in 1965.[12] Two years later, with the proceeds from selling the paperback rights to Penguin and in the company of his new wife, Jennie Katinas (a migrant from Lithuania), he headed for India again. They became disciples of a Tibetan Buddhist teacher named Kalu Rinpoche. Jennie soon returned to Melbourne, but Johnson stayed on for six years, eventually becoming a Buddhist monk himself. He found his way back to Melbourne in 1974, but soon he was off again, this time following an American woman, Elena

Castaneda, to San Francisco. There he sampled the remains of the Beat scene, met Lawrence Ferlinghetti, lived with the Moonies and the Salvation Army, then hitchhiked up the West Coast. He was thrown out of British Columbia for reasons that remain obscure. In California he finished his second novel, *Long Live Sandawara* (about a late nineteenth-century hero of Aboriginal resistance); then he returned to Melbourne.[13]

Patsy Millett, a friend from those years, described Johnson's wanderings this way:

> Over a relatively short period, he declared himself in turn a bohemian beatnik, an existentialist, a vegetarian and a Buddhist. . . . The one facet of his ever-changing identity that was taken as read—beyond query—was his Aboriginal ancestry. . . . [T]here is no doubt that from his earliest awareness, this nomad from the south-west of Western Australia identified himself with the indigenous people of that area. . . . Johnson came out of a time when no one would make a claim to Aboriginality if it were not true, since there was scarcely any advantage in doing so. . . . Moreover, along with many other part-Aboriginals, he had shared an initiation of abandonment, alienation and discrimination—and thus, as a youth, it was to these people that he turned for companionship.[14]

On his return to Australia, Johnson took up his Aboriginal heritage in earnest. He met the Aboriginal activist Harry Penrith (later Burnum Burnum), and together they worked at the Monash University Aboriginal Research Centre. Johnson also began to study for an undergraduate degree at Melbourne University. Along with historical and political writings, out came a third novel, *Dr. Wooreddy's Prescription for Enduring the Ending of the World*.[15] That same year (1983) he married again, to an academic named Julie Whiting. He and Jack Davis also founded the National Aboriginal and Islander Writers, Oral Literature and Dramatists Association.

Not just Colin Johnson but a lot of other Aboriginal and mixed race people were mounting a movement for recognition and redress in Australian society in those years. In 1988 many thousands of Aboriginal and

Torres Straits Islander people marched through the streets of Sydney celebrating their survival despite the dominating presence of White Australians for two centuries. At the height of this movement, Johnson decided to change his name to Mudrooroo (a Nyoongah word for the paper bark tree). When he sought to make the change legally, he learned that he needed a second name to complete the switch, so he added Nyoongah (meaning "person" but also a generic name for several Indigenous peoples of extreme southwest Australia) as a surname. As he said, "I've always been a Nyoongah and I'll be a Nyoongah till the day I die."[16] Several more books appeared—novels, volumes of poetry, and, increasingly, literary criticism. Sometimes he wrote as Mudrooroo Nyoongah, sometimes Mudrooroo Narogin, and increasingly just as Mudrooroo.

His crowning critical achievement was *Writing from the Fringe: A Study of Modern Aboriginal Literature in Australia* (1990, expanded from his honors BA thesis, which he completed at Murdoch University in Perth). In that book, Mudrooroo attempted to delineate a shape for what Aboriginal literature ought to be.[17] In teaching, writing, and criticism, Mudrooroo had risen to the status of an icon. Even a critic of Mudrooroo such as Maureen Clark had to admit that, "acknowledged for over two decades as the arbitrator in matters of authentic Aboriginal writing, his was the voice of Indigenous Australia."[18] He was head of Aboriginal studies at Murdoch. *Wild Cat Falling* was taught in schools across the country. But he who rises high sometimes falls far. Mudrooroo was given over to making authoritative, sometimes injudicious statements. Although he wrote of Aboriginality as primarily a matter of culture and experience, he sometimes also claimed that in order to be authentically Aboriginal, you also had to have a blood connection. Aboriginality, he wrote in *Us Mob*, rests on descent but also "includes a learnt portion, and to stress degrees of 'blood' is in effect playing the Master's game, which is always one of dealing with possession, legality, paternity and caste." In that book, he was trying to connect ideas about Aboriginal identity and peoplehood in Australia with discussions of such matters in other places by people like Frantz Fanon, Albert Memmi, and Trinh Minh-ha.[19]

It may have been a matter of professional jealousy that tipped things against Mudrooroo. Sally Morgan had written a huge best seller, *My Place*, that Mudrooroo criticized severely. Morgan had only discovered her Aboriginal ancestry as a teenager, and her memoir charted her experience of discovery and subsequent identity change. The book was immensely popular (and also heavily criticized by several Aboriginal writers) because it seemed to allow White people an easy way to believe they had understood Aboriginal experience.[20] Mudrooroo was especially scathing among these critics: "New writers such as Sally Morgan . . . do not see themselves as part of an active ongoing movement, but as individuals either searching for their roots or seeking equal opportunity in a multicultural Australia." Mudrooroo was trapped in Black Power, while Sally Morgan had moved on to multiculturalism and self-actualization, which proved to be more durable impulses.[21] *My Place*, said Mudrooroo, is "not really an Aboriginal book—it's coming from outside and exploring our Aboriginality. . . . [It is] a sanitised version of Aboriginality." Morgan, he said, was successful because "the time has arrived when you can be young, gifted and not very black, and end up selling 400,000 copies. . . . Just because something is written by a person who identifies as an Aborigine doesn't make it an Aboriginal work."[22]

At this point Mudrooroo's career had reached its apogee. In 1996 *Us Mob* won the Kate Challis RAKA Award for Indigenous creative art, the twelfth and final book or career prize Mudrooroo would win.

And then the roof fell in. An Indigenous writers' conference voted to censure Mudrooroo for his comments about Sally Morgan (he later apologized and retracted them). Betty Polgaze (née Johnson), Mudrooroo's oldest sister, then in her seventies, had been doing amateur genealogy for some years, and she chose this time to go public with what she had found. She was living as a White woman and was married to a White man; had she been known to be Aboriginal at the time that she married, she would have been required to seek official permission to marry her husband, and she did not have that permission. It is not clear whether Betty had ever known her youngest brother, as she was a teenager and out of the house before he was born, but it

is certain that she had not seen or known of him in more than half a
century. When finally they met, Mudrooroo recalled:

> The first thing she said to me was: "Why do you want to be an Aborig-
> ine, they're dirty." I was actually startled and stared at this old brown
> woman who looked like a Noongar woman. . . . I . . . didn't know
> what to make of [my sister] and felt insulted and hurt. . . . They weren't
> my kind of folks and there was nothing in their looks to even sug-
> gest that they were descended from Afro-Americans and not Noon-
> gars. Betty reminded me of those sad dark women who when girls
> had spent hours scrubbing their faces in order to rub off the black.[23]

Betty Polgaze's research showed that her mother was descended five
generations back from one of the first Irish families in Western Australia and that her father's father was a Black American, the descen-
dant of enslaved people, who had emigrated from North Carolina.
Apparently, for Betty Polgaze, being descended from a Black American was less of a threat to her Whiteness than being descended from
an Aboriginal Australian. What her research did not show was the
many other branches of her family tree; five generations back there
should have been thirty-two in all, and Betty reported only on these
two. Given the amount of informal mixing that occurred in the early
generations of the encounter between Aboriginal Australians, Europeans, and others, it would not be surprising at all if Betty and Colin's
mother had Aboriginal ancestry.[24] Betty chose to focus on the pioneer Irish White family; to explain her own olive complexion, dark
eyes, and dark hair as products of her grandfather's American Blackness; and to ignore the other branches of her ancestry. (My friends in
African American studies circles find it comical that, apparently in
Betty Polgaze's mind, descent from an African American slave made
her White in the Australian context.) But her younger brother Colin,
now famous author Mudrooroo, cast a threat upon the Whiteness to
which she seems clearly to have aspired.[25]

Betty Polgaze made contact with Robert Eggington, a man of part
Aboriginal ancestry and an official with the Dumbartung Aboriginal
Corporation in Western Australia. Eggington pronounced himself

shocked by what he regarded as an imposture and went to the press.[26] A well-known journalist, Victoria Laurie, investigated and wrote at least two pieces for the *Australian* questioning Mudrooroo's Aboriginal authenticity, and frenzied, gossipy discussion was on.[27] Several newspapers and magazines ran features.[28] Within a couple of years there was a huge, purportedly scholarly literature about what many eager critics framed as the Mudrooroo hoax; they were barely able to conceal their gloating tone.[29] Only a few people spoke up on Mudrooroo's behalf, among them the acclaimed Aboriginal writer Ruby Langford Ginibi: "Who are these people who are bent on pulling him down? He has not got to prove himself to anyone. . . . I say this, that he couldn't write the way he does if he is not Aboriginal. . . . If these people are gonna hold Mudrooroo up to scrutiny, they better question every one of us claiming Aboriginality to be fair and they better also stop non-Aboriginals having a field day with all our Koori resources at that Institute of Aboriginal Studies in Canberra."[30] Such protestations were drowned out in a cacophony of gossipy condemnation. Adam Shoemaker summed up the outcome: "The 1996 denunciation of Mudrooroo was so powerful, so complete and so all-encompassing that his creative persona literally disappeared from view. His works were all-but-effaced and his memory all-but-erased."[31] Immediately, *Wild Cat Falling* was removed from the compulsory reading lists for A-levels across the country.

Mudrooroo's response was bewilderment, followed by pain. He apparently had not been expecting any of this, and he was left reeling. He had been hoist by his own petard, accused of Aboriginal inauthenticity even as he had accused Sally Morgan of the same. When another much-older half-sister, Joyreen, demanded he take a DNA test to determine (a) if he had Aboriginal ancestry and (b) if she was really his birth mother, as he suspected, he agreed to the test, but the results were not published. He did not bother to contest the accuracy of Betty Polgaze's genealogy. A Nyoongah organization challenged him to come before them and prove his Aboriginality. In shock, and apparently unable to imagine how to prove that, he did not respond. As he reflected a year later:

When, in 1996, it was declared that Mudrooroo was of Negro ancestry, thus negating thirty years of being an Aborigine, it necessitated
some identity searching: what did this mean to me? I had discovered
that identity is a fragile thing and can be taken away, just as it can
be given. As I had not confronted such a crisis before, did it mean
that through some genetic oversight I had lost my culture and had
become authentic? Though with a little diligent research I might reestablish my racial credentials; but then for what? . . . Whatever my
identity is, it rests on my history of over fifty years and that is that. . . .
I have done my part in the Aboriginal struggle and, now . . . I do not
intend to pursue an Aboriginal identity merely for the sake of claiming a piece of land.[32]

In the end, Mudrooroo kept his Aboriginal name, but he decided to
go back to concentrating on his Buddhist identity. As he wrote later:

It is my religion and my work that gives me a sense of identity and
worth. . . . I realized the depth of the antagonism and hostility there
was against me. This affected me deeply. I doubted that I had any
talent to write and stopped. It was then that His Holiness the Dalai
Lama appeared to me in a dream, laughed, and told me to come to
India. I woke up and, old as I was, took to the road again. Away from
Australia life turned sweet as the 21st century dawned. I ended up in
Nepal under the smile of a Buddhist monastery housing the relics
of the famous Lama Zopa who had spread Buddhism in the West. I
married Sangya Magar, an Indigenous Nepali, on 22 May 2002, and
I have a son, Saman, a bright kid who wishes to be a space engineer
and terraform Mars.[33]

There in India, Mudrooroo professed to be happy—still Aboriginal,
but no longer an activist, and more given to his Buddhism than to
his Aboriginality.

When one talks about Mudrooroo, because of this history, the question of authenticity inevitably comes up. A lot of people are obsessed
by it.[34] Authenticity policing of this sort is common in ethnic studies.
Especially among Native American scholars, there is always somebody

who is ready to say that so-and-so isn't really an Indian. Native American novelist Michael Dorris was frequently dogged by rumors that he was simply a White man pretending to be an Indian, and the regents of the University of Colorado found a couple of people who were willing to question professor and activist Ward Churchill's Indigenous credentials in an attempt to discredit his political critique and remove him from a faculty position.[35]

For a very long time, Mudrooroo / Colin Johnson was an Aboriginal person in his own mind and in the minds of everybody else. And then almost everybody else changed their minds. Manifestly, this guy was an authoritative Aboriginal voice for more than three decades. He was widely accepted as such by both Aboriginal Australians and others. Given where and how he came up, he had every reason to think himself an Aboriginal person of mixed ancestry. Lots and lots of people who were part Aboriginal had stories like his. There is no hard evidence that Mudrooroo was *pretending* to be Aboriginal.

There is reason to doubt both the motivation and the accuracy of the genealogical work done by Betty Polgaze, his sort-of sister. It seems clear that she had lived her life as a White person and wanted to remain White. Mudrooroo's very public Aboriginality was inconvenient toward that end. Polgaze's genealogical work, as it has been reported, is incomplete. She made much of one Irish immigrant family five generations back and of a Black American ancestor three generations back. But there are thirty other ancestral lines in which there plausibly could have been an Aboriginal ancestor, and Polgaze paid no attention to them.

Then there was the matter of the DNA test. We don't know for sure if it actually took place or what its findings may have been. Let us disregard whether or not Joyreen was found to be related to him in the manner of mother and son. And let us assume that the test came back with a determination that Mudrooroo's DNA showed no evidence of Aboriginal ancestry. That tells us nothing about Mudrooroo. In 1998, when he is reported to have agreed to take the test, a lot of people believed that DNA was a kind of magical template that could tell all manner of hidden things about a person. These days we are a bit more skeptical. DNA is good for many things, and it could indeed demonstrate that

Joyreen and Colin were close relatives (but that was clear anyway). DNA testing can tell a person a lot about the percentage likelihood of contracting certain diseases. But it has been demonstrated conclusively that DNA ancestry testing for racial or ethnic ancestry is junk science. There are no markers (nor groups of markers) for Aboriginality, or Germanity, or Finlandity. Whatever group you choose, and whatever marker you choose, there are people inside the group who lack the marker and people outside the group who possess the marker, so the markers cannot tell you if a particular person is a member of a racial or ethnic group. The markers of many people, taken together, can tell something about the frequency of specific markers within particular racial populations, but DNA cannot tell you anything at all about an individual person's racial identity.[36]

In the end, the authenticity question is less important than the shifting of this man's shape. That is quite a remarkable story. Colin Johnson / Mudrooroo was a part-Aboriginal person (and episodically some other things, like a beatnik and a Buddhist monk) for more than half a century. He grew famous and influential in that identity. And then, in the blink of an eye, he was thrown out of that fraternity because pretty much everybody decided, against most of the evidence, that he was a fraud. It is a cautionary tale for those who like to think about shape shifting.

And Then . . .

There is a coda to this story. In 2011 Mudrooroo, his wife, and their teenaged son quietly moved to Brisbane. He took up writing again but stayed out of public view. He remained attached to both his Buddhist identity and his Aboriginality, and he had achieved a certain peace. As he wrote in an autobiographical sketch dated 2015: "For this old fellow it really doesn't matter. . . . His life is all but over and eventually all that will remain will be his books such as *Wild Cat Falling*. People have read and enjoyed my work and that is enough for me."[37]

ETT Imprints published a new autobiographical novel, *Balga Boy Jackson*, in 2017. After a generation away, Mudrooroo came back into print and proclaimed that he was, in fact, Aboriginal after all. In *Wild Cat*

Falling, Mudrooroo's first book, the author was young and brash and full of himself, pissed off at the world and trying to be artful and cool (with great success, one must say). Now, in *Balga Boy Jackson* almost half a century later, Mudrooroo goes over much of the same territory—his boyhood to young adult years—but he is calmer, more linear and detailed, not wanting so much to make a splash as to be understood. *Wild Cat Falling* made a huge impact, but *Balga Boy Jackson* is deeper and truer. While the tone of *Wild Cat Falling* was pulsing and spiritually empty, *Balga Boy Jackson* is contemplative, elegiac. It has less heat and light but more strength.[38] At this writing, Mudrooroo's publisher promises that a multivolume memoir will soon be completed, and he is bringing Mudrooroo's earlier works back into print.[39] A new French-language edition of *Wild Cat Falling* came out in Paris in 2017.[40]

In 2017, a man in his late seventies looking back at the identity controversy of twenty years before, Mudrooroo reflected, "It appears that many persons are out to grab some sort of identity even though they have never lived it" (this seems to be a reference to Sally Morgan) "or if living it disavowing it" (probably a reference to his sisters Betty and Joyreen). "And so it goes on until you grow tired of disputation and become a refugee going off to explore your religion where difference is not so important and liberation is. . . . Except I still know that I am a Noongar, no matter what my sister says. Let any person believe and prove what they want to be; but Mudrooroo declares himself to be an Aborigine, his existential being a Noongar."[41]

Mudrooroo died in hospice in Brisbane on January 20, 2019. He is survived by his wife and son and by his many books.

Notes

I discovered many shape shifters in Australian history during an extended research visit to Australian National University, the University of Western Australia, and Griffith University in 2016. I thought seriously of writing about Gordon Matthews, Sally Morgan, Bobbi Sykes, Mary Terszak, or Burnum Burnum. See Gordon Matthews, *An Australian Son* (Port Melbourne: Heinemann Australia, 1996); Laksiri Fernando, "'An Australian Son' Of Sri Lankan Descent?," *Colombo Telegraph*, September 17, 2013; Sally Morgan, *My Place* (Fremantle: Fremantle Press, 1987); Roberta Sykes, *Snake Dreaming*, 3

vols. (Sydney: Allen and Unwin, 1997–2000); Gerry Carman, "'Black Power'
Activist Had ASIO Spooked," *Sydney Morning Herald*, November 19, 2010;
Mary Terszak, *Orphaned by the Colour of My Skin: A Stolen Generation Story*
(New York: Routledge, 2015); Marlene J. Norst, *Burnum Burnum: A War-
rior for Peace* (East Roseville NSW: Kangaroo Press, 1999); Burnum Burnum,
Burnum Burnum's Aboriginal Australia: A Traveller's Guide, ed. David Stewart (North Ride NSW: Angus and Robertson, 1988); Jerry Schwab, "Ambiguity, Style and Kinship in Adelaide Aboriginal Identity," in *Being Black:
Aboriginal Cultures in "Settled" Australia*, ed. Ian Keen (Canberra: Aboriginal Studies Press, 1988), 77–95; Ian Anderson, "I, the 'Hybrid' Aborigine:
Film and Representation," *Australian Aboriginal Studies* 1 (1997): 4–14; Dennis Foley, "Too White to Be Black, Too Black to Be White," *Social Alterna-
tives* 19, no. 4 (December 2000): 44–49. I am grateful to many people for
their ideas and encouragement during that visit, including at ANU, my host,
Ann McGrath, Peter Read, Cressida Fforde, Maria Haenga-Collins, Carolyn Strange, Malcolm Allbrook, Carroll Pursell, and Angela Woollacott; at
UWA, Farida Fozdar and Shino Konishi; and at Griffith University, Juliette
Milner-Thornton. More recently, I am especially grateful to Tom Thompson of ETT Imprint, Mudrooroo's publisher, and to Mudrooroo himself for
guidance and information. Also thanks to Roxanne Houman for her helpful ideas regarding this chapter.

1. Adam Shoemaker, "Mudrooroo: 'Waiting to Be Surprised,'" *JASAL* 11, no. 2
(2011).
2. Places to begin on race in Australia include, on the Aboriginal population
and its history, Peter Read, *The Stolen Generations: The Removal of Aboriginal Children in New South Wales, 1883 to 1969* (Surry Hills NSW: New South
Wales Department of Aboriginal Affairs, 2006; reprint of 1981); Peter Read,
A Rape of the Soul So Profound: The Return of the Stolen Generations (St. Leonards NSW: Allen and Unwin, 1999); Margaret D. Jacobs, *White Mother to a
Dark Race: Settler Colonialism, Maternalism, and the Removal of Indigenous
Children in the American West and Australia, 1880–1940* (Lincoln: University of Nebraska Press, 2009); Bronwyn Carlson, *The Politics of Identity: Who
Counts as Aboriginal Today?* (Canberra: Aboriginal Studies Press, 2016); Gillian Cowlishaw, *Blackfellas, Whitefellas, and the Hidden Injuries of Race* (London: Blackwell, 2004); Cowlishaw, *Rednecks, Eggheads, and Blackfellas: A Study
of Racial Power and Intimacy in Australia* (Ann Arbor: University of Michigan Press, 1999); Cowlishaw, *Black, White, or Brindle: Race in Rural Australia*
(Cambridge: Cambridge University Press, 1988); Gregory D. Smithers, *Science, Sexuality, and Race in the United States and Australia, 1780–1940*, rev. ed.

(New York: Routledge, 2017); Stan Grant, *Talking to My Country* (Moss Vale NSW: HarperCollins Australia, 2016); Doris Pilkington, *Follow the Rabbit-Proof Fence* (New York: Hyperion, 2002); Lawrence Bamblett, *Our Stories Are Our Survival: Cultural Continuity at Erambie Mission* (Canberra: Aboriginal Studies Press, 2013). On White people, their issues, and policy, see James Jupp, *From White Australia to Woomera: The Story of Australian Immigration*, 2nd ed. (Port Melbourne VIC: Cambridge University Press, 2007); Laksiri Jayasuriya, David Walker, and Jan Gothard, eds., *Legacies of White Australia: Race, Culture and Nation* (Crawley: University of Western Australia Press, 2003); Ghassan Hage, *White Nation: Fantasies of White Supremacy in a Multicultural Society* (New York: Routledge, 1998). On recent immigration and multiculturalism, see Yin C. Paradies, "Beyond Black and White: Essentialism, Hybridity and Indigeneity," *Journal of Sociology* 42, no. 4 (2006): 355–67; Elli Vasta and Stephen Castles, eds., *The Teeth Are Smiling: The Persistence of Racism in Multicultural Australia* (St. Leonards NSW: Allen and Unwin, 1996); Alice Pung, ed., *Growing Up Asian in Australia* (Carleton VIC: Black, 2008); Cat Thao Nguyen, *We Are Here: My Family's Courageous Journey to Survive* (Sydney: Allen and Unwin, 2015); Brian Murphy, *The Other Australia: Experiences of Migration* (Melbourne: Cambridge University Press, 1993); Marie M. de Lepervanche, *Indians in a White Australia* (Sydney: Allen and Unwin, 1984); Ghassan Hage, *Arab-Australians: Citizenship and Belonging Today* (Carlton South VIC: Melbourne University Press, 2002).

3. Ann McGrath, *Illicit Love: Interracial Sex and Marriage in the United States and Australia* (Lincoln: University of Nebraska Press, 2015).

4. "Fact Sheet—Abolition of the 'White Australia' Policy," http://www.europarl.europa.eu/meetdocs/2009_2014/documents/danz/dv/0220_13_1/0220_13_1en.pdf, retrieved January 14, 2018.

5. Read, *Stolen Generations*; Read, *Rape of the Soul*; Jacobs, *White Mother to a Dark Race*; Pilkington, *Follow the Rabbit-Proof Fence*.

6. Among the sources for this section are these primary sources: Victoria Laurie, "Blacks Question 'Aboriginal Writer,'" *Weekend Australian* (Sydney), July 20–21, 1996, 3, 12; Victoria Lurie, "Identity Crisis," *Weekend Australian*, July 20–21, 1996, 28–32; Roger Martin and Shaun Anthony, "Author's Identity Crucial: Academic," *West Australian* (Perth), July 24, 1996, 3; Roger Matin and Shaun Anthony, "Family Adds Fuel to Literary Fire," *West Australian*, July 27, 1996, 15; Ruby Langford Ginibi, "The Right to Be a Koori Writer" (letter), *Australian* (Sydney), August 7, 1996, 12; Patsy Millett, "Identity Parade," *Bulletin*, August 27, 1996, 74–75; Tom Morton, "Mudrooroo's 'Career'" (letter), *Australian*, August 7, 1996, 12; Terry O'Connor, "A Question of Race,"

Courier-Mail (Brisbane), March 28, 1998, 24; Andrew Williams, "Mudrooroo to Undergo DNA Test," *Courier-Mail*, March 30, 1998, 4.

Other scholars' evaluations include Adam Shoemaker, *Mudrooroo: A Critical Study* (Sydney: Angus and Robertson, 1993); Graeme Dixon, "The Mudrooroo Dilemma," *Westerly* 41, no. 3 (Spring 1996): 5–6; Tom Little and Lorna Little, "The Mudrooroo Dilemma," *Westerly* 41, no. 3 (Spring 1996): 7–8; Lucy Frost, "Fear of Passing," *Australian Humanities Review*, March 1997; Sue Hosking, "The Wanda Koolmatrie Hoax: Who Cares? Does It Matter? Of Course It Does!," *Adelaidean* (University of Adelaide student newspaper), April 21, 1997, 2, 6; Mary Ann Hughes, "The Complexity of Aboriginal Identity: Mudrooroo and Sally Morgan," *Westerly* 43, no. 1 (Autumn 1998): 21–27; Hughes, "An Issue of Authenticity: Editing Texts by Aboriginal Writers," *Southerly* 58, no. 2 (1998): 48–58; Suvendrini Perera and Joseph Pugliese, "Wogface, Anglo-Drag, Contested Aboriginalities . . . Making and Unmaking Identities in Australia," *Social Identities* 4, no. 1 (1998): 39–72; John Barnes, "Questions of Identity in Contemporary Australia," in *Australian Nationalism Reconsidered*, ed. Adi Wimmer (Tübingen: Stauffenberg, 1999); Carolyn D'Cruz, "'What Matter Who's Speaking?': Authenticity and Identity in Discourses of Aboriginality in Australia," *Jouvert* 5, no. 3 (2001); Maureen Clark, "Unmasking Mudrooroo," *Kunapipi: Journal of Post-colonial Writing* 23, no. 2 (2001): 48–63; Clark, "Mudrooroo: Crafty Impostor or Rebel with a Cause?," *Australian Literary Studies* 21, no. 4 (October 2004): 101–10; Vin C. Paradies, "Beyond Black and White: Essentialism, Hybridity, and Indigeneity," *Journal of Sociology* 42, no. 4 (2006): 355–67; Debasish Lafiri, "Beyond the Pleasures of Otherness: Mudrooroo Narogin's Politics of Aboriginality," in *Australian Literature: Identity, Representation and Belonging*, ed. Jaydeep Sarangi (New Delhi: Sarup, 2007), 66–79; Maureen Clark, *Mudrooroo: A Likely Story: Identity and Belonging in Postcolonial Australia* (Brussels: Peter Lang, 2007); Shoemaker, "Mudrooroo: 'Waiting to Be Surprised'"; Eva Rask Knudsen, "Aboriginal Affair(s): Reflections on Mudrooroo's Life and Work," *LINQ* 39 (2012): 105–16.

Mudrooroo's own direct writings on identity include Mudrooroo Narogin, *Writing from the Fringe: A Study of Modern Aboriginal Literature in Australia* (Melbourne: Hyland House, 1990); Mudrooroo Nyoongah, "Passing for White Passing for Black: An Ideological Con-pro-testation," *Continuum: The Australian Journal of Media and Culture* 8, no. 2 (1994); Mudrooroo, *Us Mob: History, Culture, Struggle: Introduction to Indigenous Australia* (Sydney: Angus and Robertson, 1995); Mudrooroo, "Tell Them You're Indian," in *Race Matters: Indigenous Australians and "Our" Society*, ed. Gillian Cowlishaw and

Barry Morris (Canterbury: Aboriginal Studies Press, 1997): 259–68; Mudro-oroo, "Portrait of the Artist as a Sick Old Villain 'Me Yes I Am He the Villain': Reflections of a Bloke from Outside," *JASAL* 11, no. 2 (2011); Mudrooroo, "Me—I Am Me!" (typescript courtesy of Tom Thompson, Sydney, dated 2015); Mudrooroo, *Balga Boy Jackson* (Exile Bay: ETT Imprint, 2017). See also an old website, http://mudrooroo.com/, retrieved July 17, 2016.

7. On the concepts of dominant versus subdominant discourses, see Paul Spickard, "What Must I Be? Asian Americans and the Question of Multiethnic Identity," *Amerasia Journal* 23, no. 1 (Spring 1997): 43–60.

8. There is at least some doubt as to whether the woman listed as his mother on his birth certificate was in fact his mother. At points later in life, Johnson suggested that his much older half-sister Joyreen, who signed the birth certificate, may actually have been his biological mother (O'Connor, "Question of Race"). Accounts differ as to whether there were eight, nine, or twelve children.

9. Mudrooroo, "Portrait of the Artist"; O'Connor, "Question of Race."

10. Mudrooroo, "Portrait of the Artist."

11. The Clontarf Boys' Town came under much-belated scrutiny and condemnation for physical and sexual abuse of the boys in its care during the era that Colin Johnson was confined there. See Joseph Cantanzaro, "Secret Report Exposes 'Horrifying' Child Abuse," *West Australian*, May 30, 2012; Emily Moulton, "Royal Commission Told of Torture, Rape and Beatings by Christian Brothers in WA," *Perth Today—The Sunday Times*, April 28, 2014; Royal Commission into Institutional Responses to Child Sexual Abuse, *Report of Case No. 11: Congregation of Christian Brothers of Western Australia* (Sydney, December 2014).

12. Colin Johnson, *Wild Cat Falling* (Sydney: Angus and Robertson, 1965).

13. Colin Johnson, *Long Live Sandawara* (Melbourne: Quartet Books, 1979).

14. Millett, "Identity Parade," 75.

15. Colin Johnson, *Doctor Wooreddy's Prescription for Enduring the Ending of the World* (Melbourne: Hyland House, 1983).

16. O'Connor, "Question of Race."

17. Mudrooroo Narogin, *Writing from the Fringe: A Study of Modern Aboriginal Literature in Australia* (South Yarra VIC: Hyland House, 1990).

18. Clark, "Unmasking Mudrooroo," 48.

19. Laurie, "Identity Crisis," 32; Mudrooroo, *Us Mob*, 1–17. Cf. Frantz Fanon, *The Wretched of the Earth* (New York: Grove, 1965); Albert Memmi, *The Colonizer and the Colonized* (New York: Orion, 1965); Trinh T. Minh-ha, *Woman, Native, Other: Writing, Postcoloniality and Feminism* (Bloomington: Indiana University Press, 1989).

20. Sally Morgan, *My Place* (New York: Seaver, 1988).

21. Mudrooroo Narogin, *Writing from the Fringe*, 14, cf. 149, 162.

22. Laurie, "Blacks Question," 12; Clark, "Unmasking Mudrooroo," 52–54.

23. Mudrooroo, "Me—I Am Me!"; see also Mudrooroo, "Portrait of the Artist."

24. Mudrooroo's mother had another daughter, Margaret, by another father in 1940, two years after Mudrooroo was born. She stayed in close contact with the mother throughout that woman's long life. Mudrooroo later wrote that "Margaret . . . had always thought that Mum was aborigine" (Mudrooroo, "Me—I Am Me!").

25. We only know about the adult racial identities of three of Mudrooroo's many (at least seven, perhaps as many as eleven) siblings. Two who joined Betty Polgaze in asserting White identities and criticizing Mudrooroo's Aboriginality were also much older siblings, Joyreen Stamsfield and Frank Johnson. Whether any of the others identified as Aboriginal is not known.

26. Amanda Meade, "Novelist Defends His Black Identity," *Australian*, April 6, 1997.

27. Laurie, "Blacks Question"; Laurie, "Identity Crisis."

28. See note 6, first paragraph.

29. See note 6, second paragraph.

30. Ginibi, "Right to Be a Koori Writer."

31. Shoemaker, "Waiting to Be Surprised."

32. Mudrooroo, "Tell Them You're Indian," 263–64.

33. Mudrooroo, "Me—I Am Me!"

34. See note 6, second paragraph.

35. Michael Dorris, *A Yellow Raft in Blue Water* (New York: Holt, 1987); Dorris, *The Broken Cord* (New York: Harper and Row, 1989); Dorris, *Cloud Chamber* (New York: Simon and Schuster, 1997); Ann Weil, *Michael Dorris* (Austin TX: Raintree Steck-Vaughn, 1997); Ward Churchill, *Indians Are Us: Selected Essays on Indigenism, 1985–1995* (Boston: South End Press, 1996); Churchill, *A Little Matter of Genocide: Holocaust and Denial in the Americas, 1492 to the Present* (San Francisco: City Lights Books, 2001); Churchill, *Acts of Rebellion* (New York: Routledge, 2003); Churchill, *On the Justice of Roosting Chickens: Reflections on the Consequences of U.S. Imperial Arrogance and Criminality* (Oakland CA: AK Press, 2003); Churchill, *Kill the Indian, Save the Man: The Genocidal Impact of American Indian Residential Schools* (San Francisco: City Lights Books, 2004); Churchill, *Wielding Words Like Weapons: Selected Essays in Indigenism, 1995–2005* (Oakland CA: PM Press, 2016); Mark Edwin Miller, *Claiming Tribal Identity: The Five Tribes and the Politics of Federal Acknowledgment* (Norman: University of Oklahoma Press, 2013).

36. Paul Spickard, "The Return of Scientific Racism? DNA Ancestry Testing, Race, and the New Eugenics Movement," in *Race in Mind: Critical Essays* (Notre Dame IN: University of Notre Dame Press, 2015), 142–73; Deborah A. Bolnick, Duana Fullwiley, Troy Duster, Richard S. Cooper, Joan H. Fujimura, Jonathan Kahn, Jay S. Kaufman, Jonathan Marks, Ann Morning, Alondra Nelson, Pilar Ossorio, Jenny Reardon, Susan M. Reverby, and Kimberly Tall-Bear, "The Science and Business of Genetic Testing," *Science*, October 19, 2007, 399–400; Kimberly TallBear, "DNA, Blood, and Racializing the Tribe," *Wicazo Sa Review* 81, no. 1 (Spring 2003): 81–107; Patricia Mccann-Mortimer et al., "'Race' and the Human Genome Project: Constructions of Scientific Legitimacy," *Discourse and Society* 15 (2004): 409–32; Dorothy Roberts, *Fatal Invention: How Science, Politics, and Big Business Re-create Race in the Twenty-First Century* (New York: New Press, 2011); Richard C. Lewontin, *Biology as Ideology: The Doctrine of DNA* (New York: Harper Collins, 1991); Lewontin, *It Ain't Necessarily So: The Dream of the Human Genome and Other Illusions*, 2nd ed. (New York: New York Review Books, 2001); Sheldon Krimsky and Kathleen Sloan, eds., *Race and the Genetic Revolution: Science, Myth, and Culture* (New York: Columbia University Press, 2011); Keith Wailoo, Alondra Nelson, and Catherine Lee, eds., *Genetics and the Unsettled Past: The Collision of DNA, Race, and History* (New Brunswick NJ: Rutgers University Press, 2012); Peter Wade, ed., *Race, Ethnicity, and Nation: Perspectives from Kinship and Genetics* (New York: Berghahn Books, 2007); Barbara A. Koenig, Sandra Soo-Jin Lee, and Sarah S. Richardson, eds., *Revisiting Race in a Genomic Age* (New Brunswick NJ: Rutgers University Press, 2008).

37. Mudrooroo, "Me—I Am Me!"

38. Mudrooroo, *Balga Boy Jackson*. Mudrooroo's relationship to narrow facticity was always a complicated one. He wrote, "I use Henry Miller's idea of *fictional autobiography*, believing that the truth lies in discourse, rather than in the content" (Mudrooroo, "Me—I Am Me!").

39. Tom Thompson, ETT Imprint, emails to the author, December 24 and 27, 2017.

40. Mudrooroo, *Chat sauvage en chute libre* (Paris: Babelio, 2017).

41. Mudrooroo, email to the author, December 30, 2017.

Contributors

RYAN R. ABRECHT is assistant professor of history at the University of San Diego, where he teaches a range of classes in ancient Greek, Roman, and world history. A specialist in Roman history, his research focuses on the ancient Mediterranean but also endeavors to put European and Mediterranean history into dialogue with the histories of other regions, such as Central and East Asia. He is particularly interested in understanding the forces that drive immigration and how migrants are received and *perceived* when they arrive in new places. To that end, he analyzes interactions among diverse groups both in borderlands and frontier regions and in the urban neighborhoods of ancient capital cities like Athens, Rome, Constantinople, and Chang'an. He is also currently working on a project that investigates the relationship between climate change and migration in the premodern world, with a special focus on the late antique period in Europe and Asia.

PAUL BARBA is an assistant professor of history and a C. Graydon and Mary E. Rogers Faculty Fellow at Bucknell University. With the assistance of a generous UC MEXUS research grant, he completed his dissertation, "Enslaved in Texas: Slavery, Migration, and Identity Formation in Native Country," and received his PhD from the University of California, Santa Barbara, in June 2016. Paul has presented papers on Blackness in Spanish colonial Texas, narrative identity in Choctaw society, memory and slavery in Indian Territory, and kin making and slavery in the Texas borderlands. He is currently completing his first book project on Hispanic, Comanche, and Anglo-American slavery in Texas, which is under contract with the University of Nebraska Press.

G. REGINALD DANIEL is professor of sociology at the University of California, Santa Barbara. Since 1989 he has taught Betwixt and Between, which is one of the first and longest-standing university courses to deal specifically with the question of multiracial identity, comparing the United States with various parts of the world. He has published numerous articles and chapters that cover this topic. His chapters "Passers and Pluralists: Subverting the Racial Divide" and "Beyond Black and White: The New Multiracial Consciousness" appeared in *Racially Mixed People in America* (1992), edited by Maria P. P. Root, which was the first comprehensive examination of multiracial identity in the United States. Daniel's books, titled *More Than Black? Multiracial Identity and the New Racial Order* (2002), *Race and Multiraciality in Brazil and the United States: Converging Paths?* (2006), and *Machado de Assis: Multiracial Identity and the Brazilian Novelist* (2012), examine the relationship between social structure and racial formation, especially multiracial identities. Daniel is also coeditor of *Race and the Obama Phenomenon: The Vision of a More Perfect Multiracial Union* (2014), to which he contributed a chapter titled "Race and Multiraciality: From Barack Obama to Trayvon Martin." In addition, Daniel is a cofounding editor and editor in chief of the *Journal of Critical Mixed Race Studies*.

RENA M. HEINRICH received a PhD in theater studies from the University of California, Santa Barbara. Her dissertation, "Race and Role: The Mixed-Race Asian Experience in American Drama," explores the shifting identities and cultural commodification of multiracial Asian figures in theater. She is a lecturer in theater at the University of Southern California and California State University, Los Angeles, and her teaching and research range from race and gender in performance to postcolonial theater, from interculturalism to Asian American drama to Chekhov. She is a professional theater director and actor and a contributor to the anthology *The Beiging of America: Personal Narratives about Being Mixed Race in the 21st Century* (2017).

COLLEEN C. HO is a senior lecturer in the History Department at the University of Maryland, College Park. Her research interests include medieval Eurasian travelers, material and artistic transmission in

Mongol-ruled lands, and medievalism studies. A Fulbright scholar and NEH fellow, she has published on Marco Polo, the legend of Prester John, and the Mongol impact on the Crusades. At UMD Dr. Ho's courses include the medieval world from Jesus to the plague, the Mongol Empire, and religious practices in the Middle Ages. She received her PhD in history from the University of California, Santa Barbara.

MARGARET HUNTER is the associate provost for recruitment and student success and holds the Fletcher Jones Chair for Race and Sociology at Mills College. Her research areas include skin-tone stratification in the African American and Latinx communities, education and urban inequality, and media representations of women of color. She has published widely in her fields, including her book *Race, Gender, and the Politics of Skin Tone* (Routledge) and her articles "Buying Racial Capital: Skin-Bleaching and Cosmetic Surgery in a Globalized World" in the *Journal of Pan African Studies* and "Colorism in the Classroom: How Skin Color Stratifies African-American and Latina/o Students" in *Theory into Practice*, which won the article of the year award for that journal. She also teaches a variety of courses on race and gender, including Sociology of Hip-Hop, Sociology of Immigration, and the Sociology of Oakland.

LAURA MOORE teaches U.S. and world history at Cate School. Her research and writing focus on African American and U.S. women's history in the nineteenth and early twentieth centuries. She is currently working on publishing her dissertation, which explores southern enslaved people's material culture and the rise of a politicized consumerism among freedpeople in the Reconstruction era, as a book. Additionally, she has published an article on Helen Noble Curtis, one of only three African American women to serve in World War I France, in the *Journal of Women's History*.

ALYSSA M. NEWMAN is the Hixon-Riggs Early Career Fellow in Science and Technology Studies at Harvey Mudd College. She received her PhD in sociology with an emphasis in Black studies from the University of California, Santa Barbara. Her research interests center around multiraciality and the production of racial meaning through collective identity formation, biology, and genetics, as well as family relationships and reproduction. In addition to a project on multiracial collective identity, she is currently conducting research on the racial logics that inform gamete donor selection. Her article "Desiring the Standard Light Skin: Black Multiracial Boys, Masculinity, and Exotification" has received awards from the Critical Mixed Race Studies Association and American Men's Studies Association.

ANGELICA PESARINI was awarded a PhD in sociology and gender studies at the University of Leeds and received a master's degree in gender, development, and globalization at the London School of Economics. She is a lecturer in social and cultural analysis at NYU-Florence, where she teaches Black Italia, a course that she designed and that is entirely dedicated to the investigation of race, identity, and citizenship in colonial and postcolonial Italy. She previously worked as a lecturer in race, gender, and sexuality at Lancaster University, UK. Angelica conducted research on gender, identity, and the development of economic activities within some Roma communities in Italy, and she has analyzed strategies of survival, risks, and opportunities associated with male prostitution in Rome. Her current work investigates visual racializing practices located at the intersection of "race," gender, and identity in colonial and postcolonial times, with a specific focus on Italy. Her latest publication deals with the materialization of the racial body in Fascist East Africa and the use of blood (Ius Sanguinis) in the current Italian citizenship law.

MARIA JOSE PLASCENCIA was born and raised in Chula Vista, California. Growing up, her life was split across the transborder region of Chula Vista and Tijuana. After graduating from Chula Vista High School, MJ attended the University of Southern California, where she majored in American studies. During her undergraduate years she was a captain of the Trojan Dance Force and participated in other dance projects. MJ danced for two seasons for the NBA Boston Celtics and is now studying toward a PhD in American studies at Yale University. She hopes to become a university professor in border studies and coach her own college dance team in the near future.

GEORGE J. SÁNCHEZ is professor of American studies and ethnicity and history at the University of Southern California. He is the author of *Becoming Mexican American: Ethnicity, Culture and Identity in Chicano Los Angeles, 1900–1945* (Oxford University Press, 1993) and the coeditor of three other books. Professor Sánchez served as president of the American Studies Association in 2001–2, chair of the National Advisory Board of "Imagining America: Artists and Scholars in Public Life" from 2007 to 2011, and president of the Pacific Coast Branch of the American Historical Association in 2015–16. He received the inaugural Equity Award from the American Historical Association in 2011 and was nominated by President Barack Obama to the National Council for the Humanities in 2016. Sánchez received his BA in history and sociology from Harvard University and his PhD in history in 1989 from Stanford University. He was born to immigrant parents from Mexico and was a first-generation college student.

PAUL SPICKARD has taught at fifteen universities in the United States and abroad. He is distinguished professor of history and affiliate professor of Asian American studies, Black studies, Chicana/o studies, East Asian studies, Middle Eastern studies, and religious studies at the University of California, Santa Barbara. He is author or editor of nineteen other books on race, migration, and related topics in the United States, the Pacific, Northeast Asia, and Europe, including *Red and Yellow, Black and Brown: Decentering Whiteness in Mixed Race Studies* (2017), *Race in Mind* (2015), *Global Mixed Race* (2014), *Almost All Aliens: Immigration, Race and Colonialism in American History and Identity* (2007), *Race and Nation: Ethnic Systems in the Modern World* (2005), *Racial Thinking in the United States* (2004), and *Mixed Blood: Intermarriage and Ethnic Identity in 20th-Century America* (1989). His current project is *Growing Up Ethnic in Germany.*

DAVID TORRES-ROUFF is associate professor of history and critical race and ethnic studies at the University of California, Merced. His work addresses the connections between people, place, and public power in the Southwest of North America during the eighteenth and nineteenth centuries. He is the author of *Before L.A.: Race, Space, and Municipal*

Power in Los Angeles 1781–1894 and several articles. His current project addresses the ways Chinese immigrants to California during the nineteenth century understood themselves and others in terms of social and spatial identity. Another book project explores the connections between southwestern systems of peonage, segregation, and extralegal violence and the origins of southern Jim Crow.

Index

In the Borderlands and Transcultural Studies series

To order or obtain more information on these or other University of Nebraska Press titles, visit nebraskapress.unl.edu.

CPSIA information can be obtained
at www.ICGtesting.com
Printed in the USA
LVHW092100191119
637877LV00008B/190/P

9 781496 206633